The Lake Pocket
BOOK

By

*Nancy Phillips, Martin Kelly,
Judith Taggart and Rachel Reeder*

Produced by

*Terrene Institute in cooperation with
U.S. Environmental Protection Agency Region 5*

Artist: Patricia Perry Burgess

Designer: Lura T. Svestka

Reviewers

Dennis Bokemeier, Lake Carroll Association

Tom Davenport, Region 5, U.S. Environmental Protection Agency

Bill Jones, Indiana University

Lowell Klessig, University of Wisconsin

Steve McComas, Blue Water Science

ISBN # 1-880686-08-3

For copies of this book, contact:

TERRENE
INSTITUTE

4 Herbert Street
Alexandria, VA 22305
(800) 726-4853
fax: (703) 548-6299
email: terrinst@aol.com
web: www.terrene.org

Foreword

Recent national, state and tribal surveys indicate our lakes are in trouble. We need your support, involvement and leadership in protecting the lake you cherish.

Ever wonder how that funny-looking long-legged bug can skip across the surface of your lake? Or even what kind of lake it is? Could it be a graben or a caldera, a pan or an oxbow?

Answering correctly may not win you the quiz show jackpot — but it will help you understand how to protect the lake you treasure.

This pocket book distills the science of lakes into a guide for the lake dweller and user. And it recognizes that people, not science alone, determine the ultimate fate of your lake.

So take it with you, tuck it in your pocket — and use it to understand your lake and learn how to manage it wisely.

William H. Funk
President
Terrene Institute
Alexandria, Virginia

Jo Lynn Traub
Director, Water Division
U.S. Environmental Protection
Agency, Region 5
Chicago, Illinois

Contents

CHAPTER 1
Where's Your Lake
COMING FROM?

*N*early everyone loves lakes. We boast about their aesthetic and calming qualities, their recreational or scenic values. But the person is rare, indeed, who pays any attention to subtle changes in a lake's appearance or notices if one of its tiny inhabitants disappears. Yet the water in our lakes is constantly changing: this natural vitality demands our attention and sometimes our help.

But to understand how to treat our lakes — how to protect their natural beauty and usefulness — we must know what happens when water gathers in a pond or lake: where the water comes from and what it brings with it. We must also know how we're going to use the lake and what the lake needs from us.

This knowledge lays the foundation for managing a lake wisely. Whether you own a home or business along the shore, live in a nearby town or just enjoy fishing in its waters, you can use *The Lake Pocket Book* — a guide to lake management — to protect and maintain your lake, or restore it if something goes wrong.

And if you're responsible for making government decisions that affect a lake, this guide will help you deal with the diverse interests that underlie the wise management of this resource.

Use the pocket book to

- recognize the history and condition of your lake by observing its general features;

- identify and define lake problems;

- consider various lake and watershed management techniques to maintain your lake and correct its problems; and finally,

- use practical and site-specific information to help organize lake management projects, encourage community participation and develop support throughout the watershed.

BEGIN WITH
THE BASICS

Most of us are not — and probably don't want to be — scientists. We do not need to learn the complex equations used to measure a lake's depth and volume, or develop models to predict how land-use changes can affect water quality. But, we are curious. We want to know how the lake was formed and how its shoreline contours, surface area, volume and depth interact with soil, wind,

Bathymetry

Bathymetry measures the depths of the oceans or other large bodies of water. *Bathy* means depths; metrics refers to specific measures so the information gleaned establishes the bathymetric conditions of the lake or other water body. Lake managers can usually get this information from state or local environmental agencies.

climate and other conditions in the watershed to affect its quality. And we want this knowledge for practical reasons.

We want to know how to identify potential problems, how to approach treatment and where to go for technical assistance. We begin, therefore, with the simple things that define a lake's natural condition: soil, water, light, heat, wind, rain and their interactions.

A BIRD'S EYE VIEW

Lakes — and their smaller versions, ponds — may be viewed as holes or basins that collect and contain water.

Phytoplankton (free-floating, microscopic algae) will quickly develop in even the smallest ponds if frequent storms do not continually flush the water out. If the water persists even a short while, it collects nutrients from natural sources such as bird and animal droppings. The droppings combine with organically rich sediment and provide a breeding ground for midge fly larvae. In some areas, ponds that form during seasonally heavy rains also host tadpoles whose droppings in turn stimulate the growth of algae and flies. If the tadpoles die, their decay also contributes to the water's nutrient supply.

Thus, even very shallow ponds exemplify the basic interactions between water, nutrients and sediments that characterize larger lakes. Note especially, the importance of nutrients from the watershed, the role of flushing in the lake's life cycle and the impact that species from the upper levels of the food web can have on lower levels (e.g., tadpoles on midge fly larvae, algae and zooplankton).

THE LARGER PICTURE

Lakes and ponds also collect water from groundwater, creeks and rivers; larger ponds and lakes are likely to support a diversity of plants and animals, because they drain a bigger land area and receive more nutrients.

Like bathtubs, larger lakes take time to fill, but once filled, the water "stands" in the basin for a time — it doesn't dry up as quickly as it does in small ponds. Nevertheless, depending on how fast the water comes in and how large the basin is, a lake eventually flushes. Although incoming water may force standing water out, not all lakes drain the same way: some overflow, some lose water through seepage out the bottom, and still others lose water both ways. Lakes that lose water only by evaporation concentrate substances such as salts in their basins; the Great Salt Lake is an example.

A lake's water level can rise during a storm, fall between rains, and may dry out entirely during a drought. The time it takes for the water to come into a lake, seep into the ground or flow out again and be completely replaced is called the *hydraulic residence time*. Hydraulic refers to liquid in motion, the fluid pressure that forces water through an opening such as a pipe or porous rock. The hydraulic or water residence time can be calculated by dividing the volume of the lake by the volume of water that flows into it. A lake containing 200 million gallons of water with an average incoming flow rate of 3.33 million gallons/day, for example, has a water residence time of 60 days.

This helps explain why some lakes have more fish, plants and animals than others: the longer the residence time, the greater the lake's ability to support life. Standing water is similar to a nutrient-rich soup that is constantly being stirred. Algae thrive in the lighted waters near the surface of the lake, while dead or dying algae, sediment and other undissolved substances settle to the bottom of the lake to become food for other forms of life. (This movement of "detritus" to the bottom of the lake is sometimes called "detrial rain.")

Water in lakes with shorter residence times (they're usually smaller) tends to be clearer and have fewer nutrients, precisely because the water is in and out so quickly — long before too much life can develop. Thus, they have less detrial rain and fewer life forms.

Residence time, however, may be less important than the size of the drainage basin. California's Lake Tahoe, for example, has an extremely long residence time and yet is one of the clearest lakes, because its watershed is so small relative to its size. Much of the water entering this lake comes as precipitation falling directly onto its surface.

THE
HYDROLOGIC CYCLE

The water in a lake depends on the hydrologic cycle — the constant circulation of water molecules between the atmosphere and earth driven by the energy derived from sunlight. Globally, the amount of water is a constant; it does not vary in amount, only in form and availability. Solar heating causes the water to evaporate from the earth's surface and rise into the atmosphere, where it may be carried long distances by the wind before it eventually cools, condenses and falls back to earth. Water is also transpired; that is, plants eventually expel some of the moisture they absorb from soil and through their leaves.

The hydrologic cycle

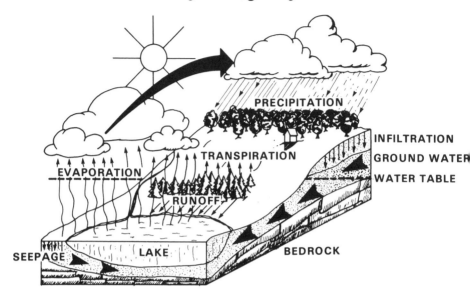

"Evapotranspiration" refers to both ways of returning water to the atmosphere: evaporation from oceans and other open water, and transpiration from plants.

Although the fact that water vaporizes drives the hydrologic cycle, very little water remains as vapor. Wind and temperature currents in the atmosphere cause the water vapor to condense back to the liquid state. This condensed water collects in clouds and eventually falls back to earth as precipitation: dew, rain, sleet, hail or snow. Some precipitation will fall on lakes, rivers or seas; some will infiltrate the earth's surface to replenish groundwater or nourish plants and soils; and some will drain across land to the nearest body of water. This drainage water is called "runoff," because it flows — down hill and over land — to the lowest point in the watershed.

This never-ending hydrologic cycle interacts with other cyclical processes in the lake and watershed. It plays an important role, for example, in the weathering of rocks, the cycling of carbon and other nutrients and the fertility of lake sediments. It is the key component that relates everything in the watershed to everything else. Without the hydrologic cycle, a lake would disappear.

Water Facts

- 97% of all the earth's water is found in the oceans in the form of salt water.

- The remaining 3% is found as fresh water in glaciers, ice sheets, groundwater, surface water and the atmosphere.

- Of all the fresh water, approximately 75% is in glaciers and icesheets, a little more than 24% is in groundwater, 0.33% is in surface waters as rivers and lakes, and .035% is in the atmosphere.

OTHER PROPERTIES
OF WATER

Six physical and chemical properties make water unique and biologically important:

■ **First, water is the universal solvent.** Although not everything dissolves in water, at least half of all natural elements have been found dissolved in water. Indeed, most of the substances needed for life are delivered to the living organism dissolved in water. What's more, water is pretty much an inert solvent: neither the water itself nor the substances it dissolves are changed in, or by, their passage through the water.

What Water (H₂O) is Made of

Hydrogen

- Hydrogen is the simplest and lightest chemical element.

- Hydrogen is the most abundant element, accounting for 75% of the mass of the universe.

- Approximately 90% of all atoms in the universe are hydrogen.

- On earth, hydrogen is usually combined with other elements, most commonly oxygen, carbon or nitrogen.

- Melting point= –434°F (–259°C). Boiling point = –423°F (–253°C).

Oxygen

- An atom of oxygen weighs 16 times as much as an atom of hydrogen.

- Oxygen makes up half of all terrestrial matter on the earth.

- It composes 21% by volume of dry air and 89% by weight of the world's water.

- On earth, oxygen is found as a gas.

- Melting point = –360°F (–218°C). Boiling point = –297°F (–183°C).

■ **Second, water is the only commonly occurring substance on earth that naturally exists in all three physical states.** Depending on temperature, water can be a gas, a liquid or a solid. Water can be melted (converted from a solid to a liquid) by applying heat – the same process that vaporizes it (converts it from a liquid to a gas). Water freezes at 32°F (0°C) and boils at 212°F (100°C).

■ **Third, water exhibits unique properties relative to heat.** A calorie is the unit of heat required to raise the temperature of one gram of water one degree Centigrade (°C); a British thermal unit (BTU) is the heat required to raise a pound of water one degree Fahrenheit (°F). Thus, using either nomenclature, the specific heat of water is, by definition, one; and the specific heat of all other substances is measured relative to water. For example, the specific heat of iron is 0.107 or roughly one-tenth that of water.

■ **Fourth, water can absorb a great amount of heat with only a small increase in temperature.** The converse is also true; as water condenses from a vapor to a liquid and from a liquid to a solid, a substantial amount of heat is released before its state changes. In fact, at 32°F (0°C), it takes 80 additional calories to convert a gram of water from a solid to a liquid; at 212°F (100°C), it takes 539 additional calories to convert a gram of water from a liquid to a gas. The former is the *latent heat of fusion*, the latter, the *latent heat of evaporation*. Although heat and temperature usually are considered the same, they are obviously distinct, and this property affects fish and other aquatic life.

■ **Fifth, water, like most solids and liquids, contracts as it cools —but only to a point.** It becomes denser until it reaches about 39°F (4°C), then its density begins to decrease. When water freezes at 32°F (0°C), about 9 percent is added to its volume; bottles break and water pipes burst, but the ice on your lake floats. This property has an important effect on aquatic life. The denser, warmer water below the ice shields fish and other aquatic life from extreme temperatures.

■ **Sixth, and finally, water has a very high surface tension — except for mercury, one of the highest known.** The surface of the water is the point at which the liquid form meets the vapor form.

Here individual water molecules form an "attraction" to one another, and the liquid attractions are so strong that some things that are actually heavier than water cannot break through the water membrane caused by molecular attraction. This unique property allows water striders to run across the surface of a lake or pond; they're using the water's surface tension for support.

ZONING
FOR LIFE

Another key to understanding your lake is its biological structure, which is closely related to its physical structure. Different areas across the length and width — and depth — of a lake can be recognized by the biological communities that thrive there.

Think about the play of sunlight on the water near the shore; this nearshore area where sunlight penetrates the water to the lake bottom is called the littoral zone. Here, sediments at the bottom receive enough light that rooted plants can grow. Called macrophytes, some of these plants, like cattails, emerge from the water; some grow just tall enough for their leaves to float on the surface of the water; others are completely submerged. Fish and other organisms will find more habitat variety and structure here than in the open water.

As we move from the littoral zone into the limnetic (or pelagic) zone, we enter open water, and observe yet another difference in the lake's biological structure. The open water includes the deeper portion of the lake where light usually cannot penetrate completely. At the point where we can no longer see the bottom of the lake, the limnetic zone divides. The upper portion, where the light enters, is the euphotic zone. Characterized by the presence of light, the water in this zone is frequently mixed by the wind, and free-floating microscopic plants and animals are suspended in the water.

The layer beneath the euphotic zone, reaching from its lower limits to the lake bottom, is the profundal zone. Very little sunlight penetrates this zone, which, of course, does not exist in very shallow lakes.

Sun Facts

The sun is a cloud of hydrogen gas, with its core under high pressure and a temperature of 27 million degrees.

- Diameter: 1.4 million kilometers or 860,000 miles

- Distance from the earth: 150 million kilometers or 93 million miles

- Light spectrum emitted: ultraviolet, visible and infrared

- Life expectancy: approximately 5 billion years

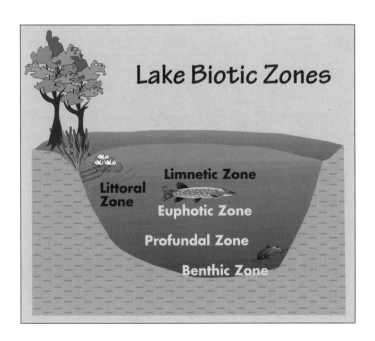

Lake Biotic Zones

Littoral Zone

Limnetic Zone

Euphotic Zone

Profundal Zone

Benthic Zone

The boundary between the water and sediments is the benthic zone. Many benthic organisms grow on the lake bottom; for example, clams, worms, crawfish and bacteria in the profundal benthic zone (and the littoral zone) and rooted plants, among other things, in the littoral benthic zone.

FOOD AND
ENERGY WEBS

The lake's life support system relies on photosynthesis and respiration. In *photosynthesis*, producer organisms (e.g., plants, algae and cyanobacteria [blue-green algae]), convert radiant (from the sun) energy and nutrients into sugars and other organic compounds. This process is called *primary production*, and it supplies most of the dissolved oxygen in the water, an essential source of life for fish and animals there.

Oxygen is also needed to break down organic molecules and release their chemical energy. Plants and animals use this energy and release carbon dioxide through *respiration*, a process that is absolutely essential for your lake; because, while green plants harness the sun's energy and make their own food, other life forms must consume organic matter to obtain their energy.

Ecologists call the process that begins with photosynthesis (the producers) a *food* or *energy web*. The consumers that eat the organic material produced by photosynthesis are classified as *herbivores* (plant-eaters, including tiny zooplankton, snails and some fish); *carnivores* (meat-eating animals); *omnivores* (animals that eat both plants and meat); and finally, the scavengers, known as *detritivores*.

This pyramid builds to higher *trophic* or feeding levels, that is, from such tiny animals as plankton to fish to birds and on up the food chain to ourselves. Only about 10 percent of the energy received at one level transfers to the next higher level; thus, the pyramid shape actually represents where the bulk of the energy resides.

Food Pyramid

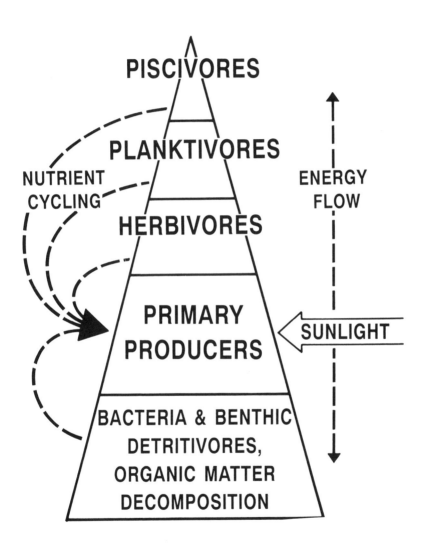

MIXING THE
WATERS

In lakes with sufficient depth, the water column can actually stratify into distinct layers, because of vertical differences in water temperature. Cold water is generally denser than warm water and will collect near the bottom of a lake.

Photosynthesis generally occurs in the lighter, warmer water of the top layer, called the *epilimnion*. This layer rests on the *metalimnion*, a transition zone between the upper, warmer layer and the cooler, heavier waters of the deep stratum, the *hypolimnion*. As the seasons change, the warmer, oxygenated water (epilimnion) cools and sinks to the bottom, carrying much needed oxygen into the depths. When the temperature change brings the epilimnion and hypolimnion to equal density, the waters mix.

This process is called *lake turnover*. In some lakes the water will "turn over" completely on a seasonal cycle — twice a year in temperate zones, once a year elsewhere. And because of this turnover, the lake will be slow to warm in the springtime and slow to cool and freeze in the fall.

THE LAKE
WATERSHED

A lake reflects its watershed. Water and everything it can carry – from soil to oil to animal waste — drain into your lake from its watershed. We all live in a watershed: a land area from which water drains (and carries runoff) to a nearby body of water.

The primary physical features in a watershed vary from deserts to prairies to forests to mountain ranges. And in nearly every watershed, human beings build cities, houses, roads and factories or use the land to farm, mine or log. An aerial view of a watershed resembles a patchwork of such land uses and natural areas (e.g., farms, forests, cities, lakes, roads, airports, wetlands, rivers and streams).

A watershed's landscape can be characterized on a continuum beginning with undisturbed prairies and other untouched natural areas and gradually extending to places modified by humans, such as cities. At the far end of the continuum, the watershed may be seriously disturbed by human activity: overpopulation, for example, or deforestation, intensive agriculture, urbanization or industrialization beyond the sustainable capacities of the land and water.

When the land is used deliberately and carefully, the watershed and, consequently, the lake, should remain healthy. Extreme land uses and human activity, on the other hand, threaten the health and integrity of the watershed and those who live there.

RECOGNIZING
LAKE PROBLEMS

Although your watershed (and your lake) changes naturally over time, responding to storms, floods and droughts, the actions of those who live in the watershed can greatly speed up the rate of change and may pose serious problems to its integrity.

Conditions often mirror such problems. Indeed, if there's a problem in your lake, more than likely it comes from somewhere in the watershed and probably has to do with an increase of nutrients and sediments in the water. The list of common lake quality problems is relatively short and includes

- algal blooms,
- nuisance aquatic plants,
- poor drinking water,
- disappearing fisheries,
- low dissolved oxygen, and
- shoaling (sedimentation).

Watershed runoff – which may include urban stormwater and substances from rural areas — is usually the major source of the water, sediments, nutrients and other materials that nourish the plants and animals that live in your lake; these also come from the atmosphere (dry or wet deposition), groundwater and wastewater discharged through pipes by city and industrial treatment plants and others. The mix of water runoff sources differs for every lake, but the type and amount of contributions from each source are important for developing what ecologists call water budgets.

A lake's budget works just like your household budget. You need to know what and how much is coming into the lake, and how much (and what) is going out. Any type of budget can be developed for the lake, but most often water, sediment and nutrient budgets will be prepared. A budget analysis then helps you determine how to manage your lake. Chapter 4 will go into more detail on developing water and nutrient budgets.

HOW LONG WILL
YOUR LAKE LAST?

Lakes appear as though they will last forever, but they are, in fact, temporary. A lake is only as young as its trophic (amount of nutrients) state. An *oligotrophic* lake is nutrient poor; a *eutrophic* lake is nutrient-enriched; and a *mesotrophic* lake is somewhere in between.

In very eutrophic lakes, where many aquatic organisms compete for dissolved oxygen, suspended particles may cloud the water and the vegetation may make the lake more like a marsh. Excessive nutrients can lead to very productive systems that result in too many producers, large swings in oxygen levels, fish kills and other problems.

A lake may age naturally over thousands of years, but the way people use the land can accelerate a lake's aging process so that it changes rapidly, over dozens of years instead of thousands. This human (anthropogenic) impact is known as *cultural eutrophication*.

DIFFERENT LAKES,
DIFFERENT GOALS

Essentially, lakes depend on their watersheds. If left undisturbed, they will age naturally, but what happens on the land surrounding them can speed up their aging process. Moreover, some actions in the watershed that contribute to a lake's productivity do not help its water quality; and some steps we take to keep a lake pure may threaten a thriving fish population.

We have to know what kind of a lake it is — and what we want to do with it — before we can determine what kind of management is most likely to prevent lake problems or restore the lake to some desired use.

Depending on how you want to use the lake, you will set management objectives to keep its water clear, control algal blooms, manage its biological productivity or ensure a strong fish community. Clearly, these goals are not all mutually exclusive; some will be interactive but others will even be contradictory.

NOTES

CHAPTER 2 Understanding Aquatic CHEMISTRY

*O*n a day when the sun is shining and we are near the water, we do not have to ask if people and lakes belong together: we know they do. The sense of well-being we get from being near the water is one of the reasons developers design shopping malls and other public spaces to include fountains and ponds; and why so many successful hotels and restaurants overlook lakes or rivers.

This chapter examines the chemical properties of water outlined in Chapter 1 — to find out what exists in the water and life of our lakes that makes them so important. We begin by looking more closely at their natural history.

THE LAKE
AS SUBJECT

Lakes usually have definite physical boundaries: namely, the sides and bottom of the basin in which the water collects. This characteristic alone makes a lake relatively easy to observe.

A lake is, in fact, made up of unequal parts of interacting light, energy, sediments, water and life; and how each of these components contributes to the lake is further influenced by altitude, climate and the regional geology — the total history of the lake and its origins.

Standing waters

In simple terms, this *lentic* or standing water habitat is classified as either a lake, pond, swamp or marsh, depending on its size and relationships to soil and vegetation. Swamps are wet lowlands that support mosses, shrubs and relatively large trees (e.g., cypress and gum trees); marshes are broad, treeless wetlands characterized by abundant grasses, rushes and sedges.

Large expanses of water are lakes; smaller expanses of water, particularly if they are quite shallow and thickly vegetated, are ponds. But often this distinction between lakes and ponds is arbitrary. (It is certainly more difficult to distinguish lakes from ponds than to distinguish swamps from marshes.) Not all lakes have the same physical and chemical characteristics, but some lakes that are continents apart have similar features because they had similar origins.

How lakes are formed

Each lake has a unique personal history that helps shape its outward expression. Location, climate and latitude significantly influence a lake, but the way it was originally formed — its geologic history — determines its basic makeup.

In his classic treatise on lakes, G. Evelyn Hutchinson lists 76 types of lakes, formed either by natural geologic processes, humans or animals, such as beavers. Geologic causes are the most common, and include major upheavals — or collapses — in the earth's surface (tectonic lakes) and the impact of volcanoes, meteors, glaciers and other natural forces, including wind and water.

■ **Tectonic lakes.** The oldest lakes are tectonic, those formed by upheavals or subsidence of land along fault lines in the earth's crust. Some lakes in Arkansas and Missouri, for example, were formed by earthquakes attributable to the New Madrid fault.

When land drops between two parallel faults, the resulting basin is called a **graben** because it has steep sides and a flat bottom (like a grave). Lake Tahoe and Pyramid Lake, both in the western United States, are graben lakes. An upward thrust of land created the closed basin that once was Utah's Lake Bonneville (and the Great Salt Lake); and sea level changes helped form Florida's Lake Okeechobee.

■ **Volcanoes.** Active volcanoes produce two kinds of lake basins: **coulee lakes**, the basins formed when lava flows dam valleys; and **crater lakes**, the nearly circular basins created when the lava cools into a hard surface and eventually collapses, leaving an open space in the void beneath the surface. Craters that form when the cone of the volcano collapses are called **calderas**. Oregon's Crater Lake is a classic example in North America.

■ **Meteors.** The impact of a meteor can instantaneously create a lake. The Great Arizona Crater was formed in such a manner; sediments in the bottom of the now dry crater indicate that a lake once existed there. A meteorite shower may also have produced the Carolina Bays, though their exact origins are unknown.

■ **Glacier lakes.** A large number of lakes in the North Temperate zone, including the Great Lakes in North America, were formed by ice sheets or glaciers during the Pleistocene Ice Age that ended only about 10,000 years ago. As the glaciers moved, they deepened and widened the valleys, depressing the land by sheer weight or gouging the earth's surface as they shifted. The depressions then filled with water.

The glaciers also pushed along or left behind large mounds of rock, gravel and other debris, called **moraines**. The moraines (at the side or in front of the ice) dammed streams and rivers, thereby creating still more standing lakes (many of these are found in the Midwest). Sometimes a block of ice remained in the moraine when the rest of the glacier retreated. Eventually this ice melted and formed a lake within the moraine. Such lakes are called **kettle lakes**.

The Pleistocene epoch also produced many **pluvial lakes**. These lakes developed in drier climates (most notably the western United States) during wet periods. Such lakes have no outlets and many disappeared entirely following significant increases in aridity and evaporation. Lake Bonneville, for example, although tectonic in origin, was much larger during the Pleistocene epoch and greatly affected by pluvial (rainy) periods. Today, after repeated episodes of rising and falling waters, only three saline lakes remain in this great basin: the most notable example being the Great Salt Lake.

■ **Dissolution.** Some lakes are formed by dissolution, yet another kind of change in — or under — the surface of the earth. The weathering or sheer wearing away of soluble rock (especially limestone, but also rock salt [sodium chloride] and calcium sulfate) forms fissures, sinkholes, caverns and underground conduits in the earth, which fill with water. Many lakes in central Florida and Mexico's Yucatan Peninsula began as solution basins.

■ **Other natural forces.** Other natural forces that help form lakes include landslides, wind and waves, and river flow. Landslides — mud flows, rock and even peat slides — often create lakes by forming dams. Many of these lakes are short-lived, however, because lake waters may eventually flow across the dam, eroding it and releasing the water.

Wind-formed lakes, commonly called **pans**, are often found in arid regions. These lakes result from wind erosion, which piles sand in a curved mound at the downwind end of a depression. Pans occur on the eastern side of the Rocky Mountains between Texas and Nebraska. Many of them hold water only seasonally.

Shoreline lakes form when waves deposit sand along the water's edge. When the water recedes, the sand eventually forms barriers that cut new bays off from the sea and larger lakes. A shoreline lake is usually dubbed a secondary lake because it originates from a parent lake or waterbody, which in most cases, was formed by other processes. Michigan, for example, has a number of shoreline lakes.

Changes along rivers also create lakes; eroding banks can dam a river's flow, or banks that develop too quickly can block the junction between a tributary and a river's main stem. **Oxbow lakes** (billabongs, if you live in Australia) form when the loop of a meandering stream is cut off from the river. Eroding banks along the Chippewa and Mississippi Rivers formed Lake Pepin on the Minnesota-Wisconsin border; many **lateral** (another name for oxbow) **lakes** are found on the Sacramento and Red rivers in California and Texas; Mississippi and Louisiana boast hundreds of them.

■ **Constructed lakes.** People and beavers — *Homo sapiens* and *Castor* spp. — also build lakes. Beaver-made lakes are usually small, though they can be quite plentiful depending on beaver populations. Beaver dams have played an important role in providing habitat for fish and wildlife. Humans, on the other hand, impound water for many purposes, including hydroelectric power, municipal water supply, agriculture, flood control and recreation. Reservoirs built by the Tennessee Valley Authority and the Bonneville Power Administration in the 1930s, for example, continue to fulfill all these functions.

THE WATER
ENVIRONMENT

The hydrologic cycle (see Chapter 1, page 6) — how water evaporates into the atmosphere, condenses and falls headlong back to earth to nourish life and replenish rivers, lakes and seas — ultimately affects the physical and chemical properties of the water.

In the atmosphere

When vaporized water passes over cities, it picks up acidic components; when it passes over deserts or semiarid lands, it collects dust. By the time it reaches your lake, it will include a mixture of water vapor, several atmospheric gases and other chemicals and dust — including in some cases, sulfur and nitrogen oxides and heavy metals associated with forest fires, factories or incinerators.

If the lake is also fed by runoff from the watershed, its water chemistry will be even more enriched with sediments, nutrients and other chemical and biological substances found there. Look at rock, for example: water that falls on hard rock will move so quickly that it will neither soak into the ground or collect many substances; whereas, water that falls on softer rock will erode some of the rock and carry off many other substances as well.

Forest litter, vegetation and thick soils also contribute organic matter to runoff, but they slow its flow, filtering out some of the biological and chemical substances before it reaches the lake. In sum, rocks and soils, grasses, shrubs and trees — or their absence — greatly affect the water in our lakes. But remember, even precipitation that falls directly on the lake has already been affected by elements cycling in the atmosphere.

In the lake

Even after a good rain, the lake water is not really pure. It is, rather, a dilute aqueous solution in which many chemical reactions take place, ranging from simple physical and chemical reactions (e.g., the dissolving of limestone by acidic water) to complex biochemical reactions (e.g., the uptake of inorganic nitrogen by algal cells and its subsequent conversion to amino acids and eventually proteins).

Aquatic organisms use the chemical and biological properties of water to find food and shelter and to reproduce and care for their young, many without ever leaving the water. Aquatic chemistry, then, and simple physical factors such as light, wind and temperature, help determine what habitats are available in the lake. To help you understand how chemical processes affect a lake ecosystem, we will consider (1) some general chemical processes involving the minerals in water, (2) some important atmospheric gases found in water, and (3) some of the macro- and micronutrients in the water.

AQUATIC
CHEMISTRY

A lake basin contains more than water molecules; otherwise, it would be a pretty sterile environment. All natural waters, including rainwater, contain chemicals of various kinds. In a constantly changing condition, the watershed, the atmosphere, aquatic organisms and processes in the lake all contribute chemicals to the water.

Total dissolved solids

If you were to take a given volume of lake water and filter it to remove all the particulate matter, then evaporate away all the water by heating it to a temperature just above boiling, a residue would remain. This residue is referred to as total dissolved solids (TDS). You can weigh the residue to determine the mass dissolved in a given volume of water. TDS is usually expressed as milligrams per liter (mg/L); however, since 1 liter of water weighs approximately 1 million milligrams, the term parts per million (ppm) is often substituted for mg/L. A mg/liter equals about 1 ppm.

The residue contains organic matter and salts. Heating this residue to a high temperature (typically 932°F [500°C]), would burn off the organic matter and leave only inorganic ash. The amount lost at that temperature tells us how much organic material was in the residue. The amount of ash left tells you the amount of inorganic material in the water.

In marine waters, the TDS is about 35,000 mg/L or 35,000 ppm, most of which is sodium chloride; therefore, the sea is approximately 3.5 percent salt. Fresh water typically has considerably less salt, although the cutoff between fresh and salt (i.e., sea) water is simply one of convenience. Some inland waterbodies are much saltier than sea water. The Great Salt Lake, for example, contains roughly six times more salt than the sea.

Salts and water conductivity

The generic name for many inorganic chemicals in solution is salt, the most common of which is sodium chloride, the chemical we normally think of when we use the word **salt**. There are, however, many salts in fresh water, and in solution, some of them will separate into positively charged (cations) or negatively charged (anions) particles or ions.

The positive and negative ions of one salt can combine with the positive or negative ions of another to form additional chemicals — all of which affect the functioning of the lake.

Many ions are important to the health of living organisms in the lake. Calcium, for example, is needed to form bones and shells and for certain cell processes; magnesium, for photosynthesis; iron, for blood and cell processes; and silica for the hard outer casing of diatom cells.

Because ions have an electrical charge, they conduct electricity, and the conductivity of the water is a measure of the total amount of ions in the water.

The amount and kinds of substances in solution in a lake determine to a large extent the biota (living substances) within it. Most people realize that the biota of a typical freshwater body differ greatly from those of the ocean, and that saltwater fish usually cannot survive in fresh water and vice versa. These differences relate largely to the organism's ability to retain water but rid itself of unwanted salts.

Atmospheric gases

Oxygen and carbon dioxide are the most important atmospheric gases in water. Oxygen is supplied by surface contact, through mixing (wind action) and by photosynthesis. Photosynthesis takes up carbon dioxide and releases oxygen, while respiration consumes oxygen and releases carbon dioxide.

■ **Oxygen.** Since photosynthesis occurs only in the light while respiration is ongoing, oxygen levels ebb and flow on a daily (and seasonal) basis. That is, oxygen levels may fall during the night but increase during daylight. Atmospheric pressure and changes in temperature also affect the amount of oxygen in lakes.

Most aquatic organisms need oxygen to survive. Some insects carry a bubble of oxygen with them when they dive from the surface; some, such as benthic "blood worms" (actually, a group of midge larvae), have adapted to near anaerobic (no oxygen) conditions, but most aquatic organisms, such as lake trout, for example, depend on the oxygen in water. In fact, the kinds of organisms you find in your lake can be a fairly good indicator of the long-term range of the water's oxygen concentrations. Fish kills are frequently the result of too little oxygen — concentrations below the absolute minimum the species needs to survive.

■ **Carbon dioxide.** Although carbon dioxide (CO_2) occurs in small amounts in the atmosphere (particularly in comparison to nitrogen and oxygen), it is highly soluble in water, and seldom lacking in the aquatic environment. Much of the CO_2 found in a lake is generated internally through respiration of biota and decomposition of organic matter, or from rainwater, which absorbs a small amount of carbon dioxide from the air (about 0.8 milligrams per Liter).

At a pH (measurement of acidity/alkalinity) of 7, about 20 percent of the carbon dioxide is carbonic acid, which combines with calcium carbonate to form calcium bicarbonate, a relatively stable, less soluble compound that comes out of solution as solid crystals. The stalactites and stalagmites in caves are formed from calcium bicarbonate; these crystals also collect on mosses and plants around seepage areas where groundwater emerges. The coating of crystalline deposits on leaves and lake bottoms is known as marl. The process ends when enough carbon dioxide has been released to stabilize the solution.

If calcium carbonate and calcium bicarbonate concentrations are high, the water is highly **alkaline**. You probably call it hard water because it takes more soap to make a lather.

A solution is said to be buffered when it contains both an acid and a base in equilibrium and is thus resistant to change in pH. When extra acid is added to a buffered solution, the solution resists a lowering of the pH because the hydronium ions of the base form a salt with the hydrogen ions from the acid. The reverse is true when extra base is added to a buffered solution.

Calcium bicarbonate is an important buffering mechanism. Since only small changes in pH can occur until the bicarbonate is used up, the lake cannot fluctuate too wildly between acidic and alkaline states. In lakes, the major buffering agents are the different forms of carbon that result from an equilibrium between carbon dioxide and water.

Macronutrients

Besides hydrogen, carbon and oxygen, two other macronutrients (elements needed in relatively great supply) — nitrogen and phosphorus — are present in fresh water. One of them, usually phosphorus, sets the maximum limit for plant production, although other factors (e.g., temperature and light) can prevent plants, algae and cyanobacteria from reaching peak production. Nitrogen, however, has been identified as the limiting nutrient in some cases; for example, in certain Florida lakes where the watersheds are naturally high in phosphorus (phosphorus is mined extensively where large marine deposits accumulated millions of years ago).

■ **Phosphorus.** Of all the elements likely to occur in fresh water, phosphorus has probably received more attention than any other because of its effect on primary production. It is generally the macronutrient in shortest supply relative to the nutritional requirements of living creatures (biota).

Typically, phosphorus concentrations in fresh water are reported as either "total phosphorus" (TP) or "orthophosphate" (soluble inorganic phosphorus). Total phosphorus is a measure of all the phosphorus forms (particulate and dissolved) found in an unfiltered water sample. Orthophosphate is the form used by photosynthesizing organisms.

Phosphorus can be present as organic matter (the tissue of living and dead organisms and excreted organic molecules) either dissolved in water or suspended in it as particulate matter. Phosphorus may also occur as inorganic compounds released from various minerals, fertilizers or detergents; again, inorganic forms may occur in solution or as particles suspended in the water column. Generally speaking, only a small percentage of the "total phosphorus" found in water exists as orthophosphate.

Because lake sediments contain much higher concentrations of phosphorus than the overlying water, under certain conditions the sediments can be important sources of phosphorus. In general, however, sediments are a sink (collector) for phosphorus. Phosphorus binds readily to clays and organic material in suspension and settles to the lake bottom. Left undisturbed, phosphorus can become buried and thus removed from the system. Under some conditions, such as high acidity or low oxygen, phosphorus can be released from the sediments back into the water.

■ **Nitrogen.** Nitrogen occurs in many forms in lakes. An equilibrium between the atmosphere and water means that a certain amount of molecular nitrogen (N_2) will be found in solution. In aerobic (oxygenated) waters, nitrate will likely be the dominant dissolved inorganic form, although nitrite and ammonia will also be present. Under anaerobic (without oxygen) conditions, ammonia may be the dominant inorganic form. Most nitrogen, however, will probably be found as an organic compound (e.g., amino acids and proteins).

Although the inorganic forms of nitrogen are those most readily available to plants, most of the nitrogen found in lakes is organic. In overly productive lakes much of the organic nitrogen is phytoplankton biomass or organic detrital material, but in less productive lakes most organic nitrogen is likely to be dissolved.

Nutrient cycles and nutrient budgets as they pertain to lake management will be more fully covered in later chapters.

Heavy metals, trace elements and micronutrients

In large enough quantities, virtually all metals are toxic, even those known to be essential in minute quantities. Fortunately, metals are not particularly soluble in water; most metals are absorbed by clays and fine-grained organic matter. Thus, they are more often found in lake sediments than in water; it is not unusual to find metal concentrations below detection limits in water even when relatively substantial concentrations are found in sediments. Still, all heavy metals (cadmium, copper, manganese, iron, lead and zinc) found in sediments can be transported through the food web (e.g., passing from bacteria to worms to fish). Therefore, metals in sediments remain an environmental concern.

All algae require the micronutrients chloride, copper, iron, manganese, molybdenum and zinc. Some algae also need boron, cobalt, silicon, sodium and vanadium. Following is a sampling of some of the substances found in water.

■ **Arsenic** appears in trace amounts throughout the biosphere, and small quantities occur naturally in water, with concentrations as high as 40 mg/L in some thermal springs.

Natural weathering processes and the combustion of fossil fuels release arsenic; it is also used in medical treatments, in pesticides and herbicides, in metal smelting and in the manufacture of glass and paints.

■ **Boron** plays an important role in the calcium cycle of plants and is often applied as a fertilizer in the form of boric acid.

It is a buffering agent in sea water and in some lakes. Relatively rare in the earth's crust (about 3 ppm), most of the world's borate minerals (borax, kernite and colemanite) are mined from a few closed lake basins in California. Borax (sodium tetraborate) is used for glazes in the ceramic industry, in the manufacture of borosilicate glass (lenses) and as a cleaning agent.

■ **Cadmium**, a soft, blue-white metallic element, is relatively rare in water where it occurs chiefly as a sulfide salt in association with zinc and lead. Cadmium accumulates in soil and water near mines and smelters, while cadmium salts are found in manufacturing wastes from chemical, paint, electroplating and textile plants. The combustion of fossil fuels also releases cadmium to the atmosphere.

Cadmium is nonessential, cumulative and highly toxic to most organisms, including humans, who cannot maintain cadmium at safe levels.

Once absorbed, cadmium is stored largely in liver and kidney tissues and excreted at very low rates.

■ **Chlorine.** A chlorine atom can gain an electron to form chloride, a negatively charged ion (anion). It is one of the most abundant ions in water; approximately 75 percent of all chloride in the earth's outer crust is in solution in the oceans. Because chlorine gas is highly soluble in water and is a strong oxidizer, it is routinely used as a disinfectant in water purification plants.

Chlorine is used in making chlorinated hydrocarbons such as polyvinyl chloride plastics and various pesticides such as DDT. Hydrogen chloride (HCl), also known as hydrochloric acid, is a byproduct of the production of chlorinated hydrocarbons.

■ **Chromium** is a lustrous metal with many industrial uses and several common oxidation states. Trivalent chromium is an essential metal for mammals: without it, the body may not be able to use insulin or glucose. Hexavalent chromium is toxic to humans, irritating and corrosive to the mucous membranes and a known carcinogen. The hexavalent form is used in metal plating, anodizing of aluminum and manufacturing stainless steel and ceramics. Chromium is also added to cooling tower waters to inhibit corrosion.

■ **Cobalt** is a metal ion that functions as a coenzyme in some organisms. For example, cyanocobalamin, the vitamin B_{12} that cyanobacteria require and synthesize, contains cobalt. Cobalt concentrations in uncontaminated water are generally a few parts per billion (micrograms per liter) or less. Interestingly, B_{12} is the only vitamin that is partly a metal.

■ **Copper** is generally present only in trace amounts but is a common heavy metal constituent of most natural waters. High concentrations of copper may occur in mine drainage and in some industrial effluent. Mined and used extensively since prehistoric times, copper is used in electrical products and processes, often alloyed with other metals to form bronzes and brasses. Copper sulfate has been routinely applied to surface waters to control blue-green algae blooms, though this can raise levels of copper in water.

Copper is an essential micronutrient for plants and animals. In plants, it plays a vital role in chlorophyll synthesis and is a constituent of several enzymes; in animals, copper is an important element in invertebrate blood chemistry and hemoglobin synthesis. Like most metallic micronutrients, copper is toxic at relatively high concentrations, but its toxicity varies with its oxidation state and other parameters (e.g., water's temperature, hardness, alkalinity and turbidity).

■ **Iron and manganese.** Iron, the most abundant heavy metal in the earth's crust, is an essential component of several enzymes and a constituent of hemoglobin found in the blood of vertebrates and some invertebrates. Iron is a necessary component of two plant pigments required for photosynthesis. Both iron and manganese are essential micronutrients, but under certain conditions, they can limit photosynthetic productivity, and both are toxic at high concentrations.

Although their aqueous chemistries differ in some ways, manganese and iron are closely related in behavior. Both ions, for example, tend to increase in concentration under low oxygen conditions.

■ **Lead** is not an essential biologic element; it is toxic and accumulates in animal tissues. Lead concentrations in water are generally low and their toxic effect on aquatic organisms is highly variable and species dependent. The extent and effect of lead toxicity in humans is age dependent. Young children, in particular, are susceptible to neurological damage.

Lead enters the aquatic environment through natural sources. The soils in rural areas of North America constitute a significant source of lead, with a background concentration similar to the average lead content of the earth's crust (10 to 15 ppm).

Input from human uses, however, clearly exceeds natural sources. Ore smelting and refining, storage battery production and municipal waste discharges contribute major quantities.

■ **Mercury** is a biologically nonessential trace metal; most waters in the United States contain less than 0.1 microgram per liter. Historically, mercury was used as a pesticide; however, because of its toxicity, this use has been restricted. The major human inputs now result from various commercial and industrial processes (for example, manufacture of paints and mercury switches, dental work and chlorine gas production). Safe substitutes for mercury should always be preferred to the use of this metal.

Mercury compounds that are highly toxic to animals can be produced by microorganisms from its less toxic inorganic form (elemental mercury). Aquatic organisms can take mercury directly from water as well as from food. Because of its low elimination rate, mercury concentrates in body tissues, e.g., concentrations in fish can be 10,000 times greater than in water. That's often the reason "fish advisories" warn that fish and shellfish in specific areas are unsafe to eat.

■ **Molybdenum**, which is released to the environment by the burning of fossil fuels, is used as an alloy in steel, in welding rods and as a lubricant. In humans, molybdenum is used in protein synthesis. It is an essential micronutrient for plants and nitrogen-fixing bacteria, including blue-green algae.

■ **Silicon** generally occurs in moderate concentrations in fresh water in the form of silica (silicon dioxide; SiO_2) and is particularly important to the group of algae known as diatoms, whose "glass" shells are composed almost exclusively of silica. Diatom shells do not decompose easily, and their remains comprise substantial deposits of diatomaeous earth.

In many temperate lakes, the phytoplankton community experiences a spring diatom increase. When this increase is limited by the availability of silica, green algae will begin to dominate.

■ **Vanadium** can be used by certain nitrogen-fixing bacteria (Azotobacter) in place of molybdenum. It is used commercially as an alloying agent in steel.

■ **Zinc** is a biologically essential trace metal, a necessary component of certain plant and animal enzymes. It is generally found in nature as a sulfide associated with other metals such as lead, copper, cadmium and iron. Industrially, zinc is important in galvanizing, in the preparation of alloys for die casting, in brass and bronze alloys and in certain chemical products (paints, fertilizers and pesticides).

Although its taste is unpleasant, zinc is nontoxic to people, but acutely and chronically toxic to aquatic organisms, especially fish. The degree of toxicity is determined by a number of parameters (pH, dissolved oxygen, hardness, temperature and alkalinity). The zinc content of soil typically ranges between 10 and 300 parts per million.

CHAPTER 3

Lake Ecology
AND BIOLOGY

Picture yourself wading in your lake. Right in front of you is a school of minnows. They are a population, a group of individuals of one kind. You look closer at the sandy bottom, and notice a second population, dozens of water snails feeding on the leaves of submerged plants — and then a third one comprised of numerous mussels. Now you are looking at a "community" comprised of minnows, snails and mussels (three populations of species related to one another through their location).

35

As you look up, you become aware of birds flying overhead, of trees surrounding the lake and squirrels chattering. The birds, trees and squirrels belong to different populations but are members of the same community. Beyond them, off in the distance, you see the hilly ridge that forms the outermost edge of the watershed. Now step back, lift and turn your head, noting as you do the whole panorama from water's edge to distant hills. There's nothing static about the vista; it teems with energy and life. It is, in short, a view of the watershed as an ecosystem.

In Chapters 1 and 2, we introduced you to the formation and history of lakes, the influence of geologic processes, and the hydrologic cycle and water chemistry. In Chapter 3, we will revisit some of these concepts, but this time from an ecological perspective.

In this chapter we will introduce the living creatures (the biota) that inhabit the lake and watershed. Then we will discuss their interactions with nonliving (abiotic) factors in the environment. We will recognize how practical methods and tools can be used to manage our lake once we understand the flow of energy through the ecosystem: the interdependencies that link all living things.

ACHIEVING AN
ECOLOGICAL POINT OF VIEW

An ecosystem is basically an assemblage of producer and consumer communities interacting with one another and with their physical environment. It includes physical and chemical elements, such as soil, water, nutrients and salts; large and small living organisms, from microbes to humans; and the myriad of interactions that link them all.

Lakes offer a parade of life forms, sound and color. The birds are probably individuals from various populations, so also the trees and other animals — and these populations clearly interact with one another. Some of the birds may depend on fish for food and trees for shelter, as fish, in turn, depend on plants for food and trees for shading.

But how can we get a perspective on the watershed and the lake that includes us and our needs in the assemblage of populations?

Let's look at how scientists and taxonomists have classified living organisms, using only a few ecological principles, primarily structure and feeding system.

THE FIVE
KINGDOMS

Originally, scientists grouped all living species into two kingdoms; everything was either a plant or an animal, even though bacteria, algae, protozoans and other primitive organisms are neither. Now most scientists prefer a classification system based on five kingdoms.

Kingdoms enfold an even more fundamental order based on cell structure: every living thing is either a prokaryote or a eukaryote. The cells of prokaryotes have no distinct nuclei; the cells of eukaryotes do. All prokaryotes are placed in one kingdom; the eukaryotes make up the other four.

Prokaryotes

■ **1 —** *Monera:* Bacteria and bacteria-like organisms, that is, all the prokaryotic species, make up a separate kingdom at the base, the Monera. This kingdom includes aquatic bacteria and blue-green algae (i.e., cyanobacteria). Monerans, though microscopic, are the most dominant organisms on earth. They have been around for about 3.5 billion years, preceding the other kingdoms by about 2 billion years.

Eukaryotes

■ **2** — *Protista:* Similar, but slightly more structured organisms — those that have a distinct nuclei but are *not* fungi, plants or animals — are classified in the second kingdom, the Protista. Protist species include organisms *like* plants and animals (i.e., algae and protozoa) and some fewer species (e.g., slimemolds, water molds, white rusts and downy mildew) that are similar to fungi.

Next in order after the Protista are the third, fourth and fifth kingdoms: the Fungi, Plants and Animals. All species categorized in these kingdoms are multicellular but differ from each other based on what they eat:

■ **3** — *Fungi* are decomposers that typically secrete digestive enzymes and absorb molecules released by the digestive process that then occurs outside their bodies.

■ **4** — *Plants* make their food by the process of photosynthesis.

■ **5** — *Animals* ingest their food and digest it internally in specialized body cavities.

All five kingdoms are intermingled in lake communities depending on where they can best live (see Chapter 1 for lake zones).

- The littoral zone, where land meets the water, will be colonized by large emergent plants and various animals. Some tiny animals and small fish will flourish in the littoral zone's quiet waters — different ones, however, if the littoral zone is rocky and often hit by waves.

- Different species will live in the open water of the pelagic zone or the dark murky environment of the benthic zone, and a few specialized species will even live at the water's surface.

Monera and Protista

Bacteria and the blue-green algae (cyanobacteria) are the most important monerans in aquatic communities; algae and the protozoa are the most important protists.

■ Although many people assume that **bacteria** are synonymous with "germs," not all bacteria cause disease; in fact, most do not. The most abundant organisms on earth, they are responsible for most of the decomposition and remineralization (conversion of organic forms to inorganic so they can be used by other organisms) processes without which the biosphere would cease to exist. They are an essential component of every ecosystem, and survive under the harshest environmental conditions, deriving carbon and sulfur from complex organic substances. Like members of the fungi kingdom, bacteria are recyclers in the web of life, vital for releasing nutrients from organic matter.

■ The term **algae** refers to a group of eukaryotic organisms (protists) most of which are aquatic, relatively simple in structure (i.e., having no true roots, stems or leaves) and plant-like in that they possess photosynthetic pigments. All algae (even cyanobacteria) and plants possess chlorophyll *a*, but different divisions (or phyla) of freshwater algae are distinguishable by their pigments. Chlorophyta, or "green algae" possess chlorophyll *a*, chlorophyll *b* and carotenoid pigments. The name, Chlorophyta, literally means green plants, and these algae species are believed to be the ancestors of the plant kingdom. Many species of filamentous algae labeled "pond scum" or seaweed come from this phyla (each kingdom is subdivided into phyla), and certain species live symbiotically with a fungus in a mutually beneficial arrangement known as a lichen.

Dinoflagellates (Pyrrophyta or "fire algae"), "golden algae" (Chrysophyta), diatoms (Bacillariophyta) and some species (Euglenophyta) that are more like animals than plants are other important algae groups. Golden algae usually grow in colonies, and diatoms are composed of two glasslike shells that fit together like a pill box.

■ The name **protozoa** literally means "first animals," and these mostly unicellular Protista are precursors of the animal kingdom. Like animals, protozoa ingest their food; they feed on detritus, bacteria, microscopic algae or other protozoans. Some protozoa found in fresh water have tiny whiplike structures called flagella for locomotion (as do some algae). Another group of protozoa (Ciliophora) use short flagella-like structures called cilia to eat and move. Ciliates have two types of nuclei, a larger macronucleus and one or more smaller micronuclei. Paramecium is probably the most familiar ciliate.

Plants

Plants developed about 425 million years ago, making them young in comparison to bacteria and algae. Most are terrestrial and have (in common with green algae) chloroplasts containing chlorophyll *a* and *b* and the carotenoids.

Primitive plants made a number of changes to adapt and expand within the terrestrial environment. The first changes that marked their evolution were the development of a cuticle (a waxy covering on stems and leaves to help prevent water loss) and a covered embryo. The next major advance was the development of vascular tissue — cells that form tubes for moving water and nutrients through the multicellular plant body. Ferns and horsetails are representative of this group of plants.

Plants next developed true seeds, which, in addition to a protective coat, also store food. The first seed plants were the Gymnosperms, which include the conifers found in swamps and bogs (e.g., cypress trees and tamaracks).

Finally — so far, this is their crowning achievement — plants developed flowers, a complex reproductive structure that bears seeds in a protective chamber called the ovary. Flowering plants are called angiosperms from the Greek words for "vessel" and "seeds." With few exceptions, most truly aquatic plants are flowering plants.

Animals

Most people think of an animal as a vertebrate, usually a mammal. However, most animals are invertebrates — in fact, over 95 percent of them — and most animals are aquatic, restricted entirely to marine or freshwater habitats.

The first major distinction that separates animal phyla is the presence of true tissues. The Parazoa, which have only one phylum, have poorly defined tissues and no organs. Sponges (Porifera) are the only Parazoa, and only a few of the 10,000 species of sponges are found in fresh water, where they are typically small and of no commercial value.

All other animal phyla (the Eumetazoa) have organs, a mouth and a digestive cavity. They can be separated into two major groups, phyla that exhibit radial symmetry and phyla that exhibit bilateral symmetry.

- An animal with radial symmetry has a top and a bottom but no front and back and no right and left. Examples include the hydras, jellyfishes, sea anemones, corals, sea walnuts and starfish.

- Animals exhibiting bilateral symmetry are separated on the basis of how their different body layers develop from the embryo.

The following discussion should help you recognize the important animal communities in your lake — especially the ones you cannot see or that you may think are merely pests.

■ Among the simplest freshwater animals are **flatworms** (Platyhelminthes), **rotifers** and **roundworms**. Flatworms are known for their regenerative ability, rotifers as microconsumers, and roundworms as important decomposers.

■ Two classes of **mollusks** occur in fresh water: gastropoda (snails and limpets) and pelecypoda (clams and mussels). As a group, mollusks are soft-body animals usually enclosed in a shell of calcium carbonate that they secrete. The muscular part of **gastropods** extends outside the shell, like a foot; and they commonly have radula, a straplike rasping tongue (some with several hundred teeth as well). Mostly vegetarian, gastropods eat microscopic algae attached to underwater structures.

- Freshwater *clams and mussels*, which are usually found in flowing water rather than lakes, are not very mobile and feed by straining zooplankton, phytoplankton and detritus from the water column. They draw water into their shells and across their

41

mucous-covered gills where cilia help remove food particles. Their larvae, called glochidium, become temporary parasites on fish where they either attach to the gills or become embedded and encysted on the body or fins. The parasitic stage generally lasts no longer than 30 days and usually doesn't harm the fish.

■ **Aquatic earthworms** (Oligochaeta) and **leeches** (Hirudinea) have numerous freshwater species. Similar to terrestrial earthworms, the typical freshwater oligochaeta eats its way through the organic muck that accumulates in the bottom of lakes and slow-moving streams. Another family of worms, the Tubificidae, adapt particularly well to low oxygen and anaerobic conditions, their presence usually indicating organic pollution. Leeches (which are about as popular as snakes) live on invertebrates and fish.

■ **Crustaceans, spiders and insects** are among the million-plus species of arthropods (derived from the Greek words for "joint" and "foot"). Arthropods use their appendages for swimming, paddling, walking, feeding, copulation and defense. The most common and familiar arthropods are insects, but this group also includes water flies (Cladocera represented by the species Daphnia), various other zooplankton (i.e., free-floating microscopic animals) and crayfish, lobster and shrimp.

An entire branch of biology, entomology, is devoted to the study of insects, but less than 5 percent of the 800,000 known species inhabit water some time during their life cycle, and only two orders, the Hemiptera (true bugs) and the Coleoptera (beetles), have aquatic adults.

Insects have an air-filled tracheal system that functions only when its spiracles (breathing holes) are in contact with air. Aquatic beetles and bugs that live beneath the water must surface at regular intervals to renew their air supply. Others manage to take their air supply with them by trapping air bubbles beneath their wings or by using dense growths of fine short body hairs called "pile" to maintain a film of air around their body.

Insect larvae have generally developed specialized body surfaces (e.g., gills) to breathe underwater.

Insects may or may not have wings, but only the winged insects are important in aquatic environments. These insects are further classified as having old wings (Paleoptera) or new wings (Neoptera). Mayflies, damsel flies and dragonflies are old winged; true bugs and stoneflies are new winged (the new wings can be folded back over the body).

- *Mayfly nymphs* (Ephemeoptera), whose primary adult function is to reproduce, are a preferred food of most trout. Dragonflies (Anisoptera) hold their wings horizontally when not in flight, while damselflies (Zygoptera) hold their wings together above their bodies. The adults have large compound eyes and are highly predaceous; they feed on other invertebrates, including gnats, midges and mosquitoes.

- To many people, the word "bug" is synonymous with insect; however, the term "bug" should only be applied to the order hemiptera. *True bugs* are characterized by their piercing, sucking mouthparts — generally a slender segmented beak. The aquatic hemiptera can be found running on the surface of the water held up by surface tension (e.g., water striders, pond skaters, wherrymen); in aquatic vegetation (e.g., marsh treaders); near the water's edge in the sand and mud (e.g., toad bugs); or swimming beneath the surface of the water (e.g., water boatman and backswimmers).

- Trichoptera, or *caddisflies*, are rather nondescript as adults and are frequently described as moth-like and small. A few of the larvae are "free-living forms," but most caddisfly species use sand, small rocks or vegetative matter to build cases, then rely on water currents to funnel food into them.

- *Beetles*, the Coleoptera, are the largest group of aquatic insects, though they usually live in calm, sheltered areas along the shoreline, mostly in association with algal mats or aquatic vegetation. All adults breathe air; beetle larvae acquire oxygen by diffusion across their skin or return to the surface to breathe. Some beetles carry their air supply under their front wing;

others use their wing and hold an air bubble in the short hairs on the underside of their bodies (in somewhat the same way that scuba divers carry an air tank).

Whirligig beetles (of the family Gyrinidae) may be the best known aquatic beetle. They can whirl across the water's surface, dive beneath it or fly above it once they crawl out onto aquatic vegetation. The adult has a divided eye; the upper half for viewing above the water's surface and the lower half for examining its watery habitat.

- Diptera (*flies, gnats, midges and mosquitoes*) are a large group of winged insects. From a human perspective this group contains many pests known for their biting and bloodsucking habits and as disease carriers (e.g., malaria, encephalitis, yellow fever). Many of the adults, as their name implies, have two pairs of wings, but flies have only one pair and a remnant second pair that functions as a pair of "halters," or short balancing organs.

  Mosquitoes (Culicidae), are well known to lake users, but many find other fly species just as troublesome. The Ceratopogonidae, better known as *no-see-ums* or *biting midges*, can be particularly irritating — their small size enabling them to get through screening, under clothing and in the hair. The Chironomidae, midges or *midge flies*, often emerge in great swarms. Although they do not bite, they can get in the eyes, nose and throat. The Tipulidae (*crane flies*) don't bite; they resemble long-legged giant mosquitoes.

■ **Fish** are the most common vertebrates (large, multi-celled organisms with a backbone) in a lake. Most fish eat plankton at least during the early stages of their life, while others feed on other fish (piscivores); some, such as grass carp, consume plants (herbivores); others (carnivores) eat a variety of other animals, e.g., fish and macroinvertebrates; and still others are bottom feeders (detrivores).

While water quality can influence the fish in a lake (see Chapter 4), the type and distribution of fish can also influence a lake's water quality. For example, when large numbers of planktivorus fish are present, zooplankton disappear. When this happens, the phytoplankton community will begin to thrive, and this may cause unpleasant algal blooms. When large numbers of piscivores are present, they reduce the number of planktivorus fish. With these fish absent, the larger zooplankton feed on phytoplankton, thus making the water clearer.

Six major families of fish commonly make their homes in freshwater lakes.

- The **Ictaluridae** family includes the channel catfish (*Ictalurus punctatus*) and the black bullhead (*Ameiurus melas*). These fish can be found in a wide variety of habitats and can tolerate quite stressful conditions, including low dissolved oxygen and high temperatures. Black bullhead, for example, occur mostly in warmwater lakes and reservoirs, and like warm, turbid, eutrophic waters where they may contribute to the internal nutrient recycling and increase algal productivity by stirring up the bottom muds.

- The **Salmonidae** family includes the brook trout (*Salvelinus fontinalis*), rainbow trout (*Oncorhynchus mykiss*), brown trout (*Salmo trutta*), cutthroat trout (*Oncorhynchus clark*) and lake trout (*Salvelinus namaycush*). All of the salmonids prefer clear, cool, well-oxygenated waters. Brook and cutthroat trout are most often found in small headwater lakes, often at elevations above 8,000 feet. They like colder temperatures (68°F or less). Rainbow trout like deep lakes with a good littoral zone and adequate food supply and temperatures around 70°F. Brown trout prefer cooler temperatures, while lake trout like even colder (50°F) areas. Aside from the fact that they enjoy colder temperatures, salmonids also like clean substrate for spawning, and as a group generally do not tolerate pollution well.

- The **Esocidae** family includes muskellunge (*Esox masquinongy*), northern pike (*Esox lucius*) and chain pickerel (*Esox niger*). These fish can tolerate a wide range of water quality and habitat conditions, but prefer shallow, warm bodies of water or coves with lots of aquatic vegetation. Muskellunge like water temperatures between 78 and 90°F, while pickerel like temperatures between 70 and 86°F. These fish feed by sighting their prey, so do not frequent turbid areas. They like to spawn in the marshes adjacent to lakes.

- The **Clupidae** family includes the alewife (*Alosa pseudoharengus*), gizzard shad (*Dorosoma cepedianum*) and threadfin shad (*Dorosoma petenense*). These fish are mostly forage fish for larger fish. All three species feed on plankton. Alewifes basically feed upon zooplankton, while the shads feed upon the phytoplankton and zooplankton.

- **Centrarchidae** is the largest family, and includes the largemouth bass (*Micropterus salmoides*), smallmouth bass (*Micropterus dolomieu*), spotted bass (*Micropterus punctulatus*), black crappie (*Pomoxis nigromaculatus*), white crappie (*Pomoxis annularis*), pumpkinseed sunfish (*Lepomis gibbosus*) and redear sunfish (*Lepomis microlophus*).

  Largemouth bass can adapt to a wide range of conditions although they tend to live in warmer waters (upper 70s°F) near the lake surface, along the soft bottoms and among emergent vegetation. Smallmouth bass prefer cooler water (lower 70s°F) and a harder substrate with rocks or gravel.

  The crappies and sunfish are usually found in quiet, warm waters in small lakes or in the shallows of large lakes. Most crappies and sunfish use aquatic vegetation for shelter from predators, although the white crappie also lives in other areas.

- **Percidae** includes the walleye (*Stizostedion vitreum*) and yellow perch (*Perca flavescens*). Walleye can survive at temperature extremes, but prefer waters with a maximum temperature of 77°F. They generally will be found in large lakes with moderate turbidity. Perch are also very adaptable fish, liking temperatures between 66 and 70°F in lakes with some vegetation, clear water and lake bottoms of muck, sand or gravel.

PRODUCERS,
CONSUMERS AND DECOMPOSERS

The food web — the need all living things have for energy — links the five kingdoms (see page 13). Regardless of their taxonomic status,

- blue-greens, algae and plants are the producers in aquatic systems;
- some of the Protista and members of the animal kingdom are consumers, getting their energy from the food they ingest; and
- bacteria and fungi are decomposers.

Organisms that produce their own food are called "autotrophs" while those that depend on already stored energy in the form of organic matter are called "heterotrophs." A few autotrophic organisms (certain bacteria) are chemoautotrophs; they get energy for making food from chemical reactions rather than directly from light. Most autotrophs, however, get their energy directly from the sun, capturing it through chlorophyll. These organisms are referred to as photoautotrophs or phototrophs.

ENERGY
LINKS

Energy moves through an ecosystem from one organism to another as one organism consumes another. In fact, the reason organisms consume other organisms is not because something tastes good, but to gain energy and thus, survive. Energy transfers from one organism to another through a series of feedings called a food chain.

Cyanobacteria, algae and plants capture energy from the sun via photosynthesis and put it into energy-rich compounds. These producer organisms are the base of the food web, the first trophic level. (Trophic comes from the Greek *trophe* which means food.)

Lakes can be classified by their "trophic state" – the amount of food present in them (see Chapter 4 for a discussion of trophic state).

Organisms that are not producers are heterotrophs, or "other feeding" animals: animals who must get their energy from eating other organisms or their remains. Those animals that feed only on producers are labeled herbivores: "plant eaters" (anything that photosynthesizes). The chief herbivores in terrestrial habitats tend to be insects, rodents and hoofed animals; the microcrustaceans (e.g., Daphnia and other zooplankters) are the primary herbivores in fresh and marine waters.

Carnivore means "flesh eater"; a carnivore eats either herbivores or other carnivores. A carnivore that eats a herbivore is termed a first-level carnivore; whereas, a carnivore that eats a first-level carnivore is termed a second-level carnivore. A top-level carnivore may be an animal such as an osprey or eagle that feeds on a carnivorous fish (e.g., an adult largemouth bass [a second level carnivore] that feeds on a shad [a carnivore] that feeds on zooplankton [a herbivore or primary consumer] that feeds on phytoplankton [producers]). Some animals feed on both plants and animals and, as such, are referred to as *omnivores* (*omni* means all).

Decomposers are heterotrophs, but they do not consume their food by ingestion as do herbivores and carnivores. Decomposers absorb their food. Some release enzymes produced in their bodies into dead organic material; then they digest and degrade this material, and absorb some of it. Other bacteria, the transformers, convert some of this decomposed material into inorganic forms (carbon, nitrogen and other elements) for reuse by photosynthetic organisms (plants and algae). Thus, important nutrients are recycled back into the environment that would otherwise remain locked in dead plant and animal material.

Food chains interconnect to form a food web. At each step (or trophic level) up the chain, roughly 90 percent of energy is lost as heat according to the Second Law of Thermodynamics. This is often referred to as the "10 percent rule," meaning that only about 10 percent of the energy at one trophic level can be captured by the next higher level. As a consequence, less and less useful energy is available at higher levels of the food chain. That's why there are fewer carnivores than herbivores and even fewer top-level carnivores.

NUTRIENT
CYCLING

In contrast to the unidirectional flow of energy (always up), a second essential ecosystem function operates in cycles. And life depends on both: energy and some 30 to 40 chemical elements (see Chapter 2). A few of them, the macronutrients, must be available in relatively large supply; they include carbon, hydrogen, oxygen, nitrogen and phosphorus. Others, although essential, are required in relatively small amounts. These micronutrients include, for example, sodium, molybdenum and zinc.

Although nutrient cycling is not 100 percent efficient, without it life would cease to exist because the supply of essential nutrients would be exhausted. Many lake concerns are actually nutrient cycling concerns, and it is this cycling that makes some lake problems so difficult to control.

Nutrient cycles resemble the hydrologic cycle, and they interact in important ways with that cycle. Nutrient biogeochemical cycles move and chemically transform elements from a geologic reservoir (water, soil, rock and air) into biological organisms and back into the geologic reservoir. In gaseous biogeochemical cycles, the atmosphere is the major reservoir of the element; in sedimentary cycles, rocks are the major reservoir.

Gaseous biogeochemical cycles are typified by carbon and nitrogen. The dominant source of carbon for most organisms is carbon dioxide found in the atmosphere; even the carbon dioxide used by totally submersed aquatic plants and algae results from carbon dioxide gas dissolved in water. In the case of nitrogen, though nearly 80 percent of the earth's atmosphere is nitrogen gas, it is not readily available as a nutrient without the work of microorganisms.

In sedimentary biogeochemical cycles, rocks are the major reservoir of the nutrients, and biologically, phosphorus is the most important example of these cycles. Thus, phosphorus becomes available to the environment and living organisms through the weathering of sedimentary rock. The lack of a significant gaseous phase in sedimentary biogeochemical cycles means that these nutrients usually work their way downhill to the sediments in the bottom of a lake, reservoir or ocean.

Carbon cycle

As noted previously, the source of carbon in nearly all organisms is carbon dioxide occurring either as free (unbound) molecules in the atmosphere or dissolved in fresh or marine waters. For discussion purposes, a good entry point into the carbon cycle is the use of carbon dioxide in photosynthesis. This process, which is made possible with energy from sunlight, leads to the synthesis of organic compounds (first as simple carbohydrates then as complex fats and polysaccharides). When these organic compounds are synthesized by plants, they become the organic matter of the plant (here, the word plant applies collectively to all photosynthesizers). Animals acquire their carbon, and thus, their organic compounds by eating plants.

A certain amount of carbon is released as carbon dioxide into water and air by photosynthetic organisms and animals as they burn their stored organic compounds to get energy to do work. Decomposers release carbon locked up in animal wastes and organisms' biomass (the bodies of living and dead plants, animals and other organisms).

Some carbon is not released and accumulates as stored organic matter in the form of coal, peat, wood or oil. Carbon dioxide can be released from these sources, however, through purposeful or accidental combustion (e.g., in industrial production or forest fires). In the last few hundred years, people have released huge amounts of carbon (as carbon dioxide) to the atmosphere by burning fossil fuels that had accumulated over millions of years. Carbon dioxide is one of the "greenhouse" gases believed to contribute to global warming.

Animal remains such as mollusk shells deposit carbon that will eventually form sedimentary rock (calcium carbonate or limestone). In addition, considerable amounts of carbon can be tied up in the remains of coral and other animals. Photosynthesis in aquatic plants can also cause calcium carbonate to precipitate, with some of it eventually compacted into limestone.

Nitrogen cycle

Simple molecules of nitrogen (i.e., composed of two atoms of nitrogen $-N_2$), make up about 80 percent of the earth's atmosphere. Although this would seem ample, most photosynthesizing organisms cannot use atmospheric nitrogen but require organic forms (urea, protein, nucleic acids) or inorganic compounds (ammonia, nitrite and nitrate). Fortunately for the bulk of photosynthesizers, some bacteria and cyanobacteria can "fix" atmospheric nitrogen into the more usable inorganic forms.

Nitrogen fixation in the terrestrial environment is performed largely by Rhizobium, a bacterium found in the root nodules of leguminous plants (e.g., peanuts, clover and beans). In the aquatic environment, nitrogen is fixed by bacteria and a few species of cyanobacteria. The nitrogen-fixing aerobic bacteria, Azotobacter, is widely distributed in soil and in fresh and salt water.

Lightning also fixes nitrogen by creating nitric acid, which dissolves in rain and becomes nitrate. Until recently, the two natural processes, biological nitrogen fixation (by bacteria and cyanobacteria) and fixation by lightning had been the major sources of nitrogen for plants; however, industrial fixation has now become a major source of nitrogen.

Inorganic nitrogen created by fixation is taken up by photosynthetic organisms and converted into organic nitrogen, which passes through the food web and becomes waste.

Certain organisms (bacteria, actinomycetes and fungi) can metabolize this organic nitrogen into ammonia (an inorganic form of nitrogen) in a process referred to as ammonification. Ammonia is then converted to nitrite nitrogen by a bacteria called Nitrosomonas; other bacteria convert the nitrite nitrogen to nitrate.

The process of converting ammonia — first to nitrite and then to nitrate — is referred to a nitrification. The resulting nitrate can be used by photosynthesizing organisms, or reduced and released as gaseous nitrogen by bacteria. This process is called denitrification.

Phosphorus cycle

Phosphorus, a macronutrient required by all organisms, is an essential element of DNA (deoxyribonucleic acid), the genetic code of cells. It is also the major component of a cell's energy-storing compound (i.e., adenosine triphosphate or ATP for short). In freshwater systems, phosphorus is frequently the nutrient of greatest concern; that is, the supply of phosphorus often determines the overall productivity of the system.

The major supply source of phosphorus is sedimentary rock and natural phosphate deposits. Weathering and mining release inorganic phosphates into the environment. As inorganic orthophosphate, phosphorus is readily taken up by plants and other photosynthesizing organisms and incorporated into their DNA and ATP.

Heterotrophs such as zooplankton acquire phosphorus by filtering and ingesting algae and thus pass organic phosphorus through the food web. Zooplankton excrete a fair amount of phosphorus that can be reused by the producers and redeposited as sediment. Eventually, organic phosphorus, if it is not buried in sediments, will be converted to inorganic phosphorus by bacteria.

Much of the phosphorus entering the cycle is eventually buried in the oceans. Although fish-eating birds carry some phosphorus from the oceans back to land, much is lost to the deep sediments until it is returned to the earth's surface by major geological processes such as uplifts. Companies continue to mine phosphate deposits and import phosphorus via the mining/harvesting of rich guano deposits (sea bird droppings) off the coast of Peru.

Many lake problems result from using nutrients to promote plant growth in a watershed or directly (or indirectly) releasing wastewater containing nutrients into the lake. Note that in relatively undisturbed ecosystems, nutrient releases tightly recycle, balancing supply and demand; problems arise when excess nutrients are added to the system.

HABITAT AND NICHE:
THE PHYSICAL ENVIRONMENT

An organism's physical environment is its habitat. What it does is its niche. For example, a particular species of fish occurs only where the proper gradient of temperature exists in combination with the proper range of dissolved oxygen, where there is an adequate area for spawning and where certain prey species are found, and so on.

Although similar species may inhabit the same space, their niches can overlap but cannot be identical. For example, two species of birds may have almost identical habitat requirements, but one must nest in the upper canopy while the other nests lower to the ground.

It would be unusual, for example, to find thriving populations of gizzard and threadfin shad in the same lake. Presumably their habitat requirements and their niches overlap too much. Because of competition for the same or similar resources, one species either dramatically declines or is eliminated.

Limiting factors: Liebig's Law of the Minimum

In 1840, a German chemist, Baron Justus von Liebig, recognized that plant growth is controlled by the nutrient in smallest supply relative to the needs of the plant. Assume, for example, that a plant requires six times more nitrogen than phosphorus, but nitrogen is only three times more available in the environment. Then, although there is three times more nitrogen than phosphorus, nitrogen is the limiting nutrient since the plant's supply of nitrogen will be exhausted first.

In a lake, the limiting nutrient is generally phosphorus or nitrogen (usually phosphorus for freshwater lakes), although nutrient supplies may vary seasonally.

Ecologists now recognize that plant and animal growth can be limited by environmental conditions other than nutrient supply. For example, temperature may affect the seasonal abundance of phytoplankton: colder temperatures limiting phytoplankton growth and reproduction. And in extremely eutrophic waters, light may control the amount of phytoplankton that develops, since dense phytoplankton populations decrease light penetration.

Range of tolerance

Most organisms have a range of tolerance for most environmental conditions. The species' optimum pH is somewhere in between the lowest and highest pH values that it can tolerate, and those outer limits define its range of tolerance. Certain species of algae, particularly green algae known as desmids, are often abundant in acidic bogs; other species of algae, especially certain species of Eunotia (a diatom), can occur in very acidic water where few other species of algae will survive. Fish differ in their oxygen and temperature preferences; trout, for example, clearly prefer cool oxygenated waters, which naturally limits them to higher latitudes.

An organism's ability to adapt to various environmental factors determines its distribution both temporally and spatially. For example, certain species of midge flies (chironomids) have hemoglobin that allows them to survive in the near oxygenless environment of some lake sediments. Other insects, for example, the mayflies, require relatively "clean" water to survive. As a result of these species' preferences or ranges of tolerance for certain environmental factors, they are often used as indicators of water quality. Insects, in particular, because of their relative immobility and dependence on particular ranges in water quality, are especially good indicators.

Indicator species give a more complete picture of water quality over time than a single set of water quality samples. Because it takes many aquatic insects a year or more to complete the aquatic phase of their life cycle, the dominance of good water quality indicator species would indicate that good water quality has existed for some time. On the other hand, the occurrence of rat-tailed maggots and sludge worms (*Tubifex tubifex*) — species especially adapted to survive in low oxygen concentrations — is a sure sign of chronic pollution by organic (oxygen-demanding) wastes.

Generalists and specialists

Because they can adapt to a wide range of environmental factors, some organisms are referred to as "generalists." Often labeled "weedy species," they thrive under what would be fairly inhospitable circumstances for most. Other species occur only over a relatively small range of a given environmental gradient; hence, they are called "specialists." They are at a disadvantage when conditions widely fluctuate, but they can out-compete a generalist under stable conditions.

The relative abundance of generalists to specialists is a measure of the environmental stability of a system. For example, predominantly rough fish species (e.g., bullhead catfish, gar, bowfin) probably indicate poor water quality in a lake. However, a high diversity of species indicates a healthy system.

NOTES

CHAPTER 4
Collecting Information &
HOW TO USE IT

Do you remember the last time you went down to the lakeshore, experienced something you didn't like, and asked the question "What's wrong with the lake?" Maybe you saw dead fish or plants floating on the water's surface, or smelled something unusual. Perhaps for the first time, you couldn't see the lake bottom.

Once you took the next logical step and began to seek answers to these lake problems, you were (maybe unconsciously) thinking about lake ecology: you were studying the interactions of organisms and their environment. Why does the water look so brown? Why did we have a fish kill? What caused this algae mat? What can we do to prevent another bloom? How can we get rid of these weeds? How come the fishing isn't as good as it used to be? These are difficult questions and require a great deal of thought and investigation to answer.

A fish kill, for example, may be caused by inadequate levels of oxygen in the water column (which in turn may have several causes); but it is also possible that the fish kill was caused by a disease or some other factor. Interactions between organisms and their environment are complex, and often, answers are elusive.

Yet asking these additional questions and searching for answers is the first step toward applying ecological principles to lake management. And we're not alone in asking these questions. They're the same ones that engineers, scientists, park managers, county planners and most other lake users ask. Everyone wants to know how aquatic communities respond to their environment. To find the answers, we must begin — as we began this book — by deciding what we want to accomplish. Clear objectives clarify the information collection process.

SETTING
OBJECTIVES

Recall that in Chapter 1, we made a short list of problems that good lake management can remedy. Observable conditions in your lake are often the first sign of these problems. Observations must, therefore, be properly recorded, classified and analyzed before objectives can be set. This emphasis on problems may be disconcerting at first, but the spur to action is often the need to contain a threat or to remedy an imbalance in some otherwise natural state of affairs.

In all these cases, we begin with an observation — we see "something" in the lake and begin to turn over in our minds all its aspects: Is the condition we are observing good or bad, better or worse than we've noticed before, better or worse than we see at other lakes in this region, normal or below the norm? Does this condition stem from other problems in the lake or is it causing other problems? Will it respond to management initiatives (i.e., changes), and if so, how much improvement can we expect? Will the neighbors and nearby towns support these changes?

Table 1 illustrates how questions such as these can be reshaped as management objectives — and how, when they are, they also turn into categories of information to be collected. Table 1 looks at the relatively simple problem of "cloudiness"; similar tables could be made to deal with other observations, such as too much vegetation or sediment, odors or fish kills.

Data collection

It is important to be clear about what you want to know; when you change a question even slightly, you may also have to change the kind of information you need. Sometimes your question will have many different answers; if so, you may have to gather a great deal of information over a long period of time.

Certain pieces of information can be helpful at various times, and some observations made at the beginning of the process may be relevant again in later stages. You may want to separate the information into different types, to focus on the problem from quantitative, descriptive, subjective and institutional points of view. Each perspective can be useful at different times during the lake management process; one type of information is not necessarily more important than another. Thus, you may want to consider how to collect as much information as possible, for your benefit and that of the lake.

Volunteer monitoring groups may already be collecting quantitative information about your lake, and your state water quality agency may also survey your lake occasionally. Water and sewage treatment plant data may also be pertinent.

Table 1.—Managing by objectives.

MANAGEMENT OBJECTIVE	INFORMATION REQUIRED	INFORMATION CATEGORY
How "cloudy" is the lake water today?	Secchi disk, color and chlorophyll a	Quantitative: Short term, one to several locations
Is this condition better or worse than it was last year?	Multi-year Secchi disk reading, color, chlorophyll a data	Quantitative: Long-term ambient monitoring, one to several locations
How does this compare to other lakes in the area?	Lake survey data from neighboring lakes for Secchi disk, color, chlorophyll a	Quantitative: Short- or long-term monitoring, need several comparative lakes
What makes the lake water "cloudy"?	Color, chlorophyll a, fluorometry data, phosphorus	Quantitative: Short term, one to several locations
Is this condition "normal"?	Lake depth, volume, phosphorus	Quantitative: Short term, one to several locations
Will the "cloudiness" go away if we change something in the lake and/or in the watershed?	Phosphorus, chlorophyll a, phytoplankton, zooplankton, fish surveys, local land use, inflow/outflow nutrient concentrations, inflow/outflow water volumes	Quantitative: Long-term monitoring to establish baseline levels. Descriptive: types of land use
After making changes to the lake and/or watershed, how much improvement will we see?	Multi-year phosphorus, chlorophyll a, Secchi disk, color data	Quantitative: Long-term monitoring, several locations
Will neighbors support these changes?	User surveys	Subjective: Survey of lakefront owners and recreational users
Can the town enforce these changes?	Community ordinance survey	Institutional: Review of lake management efforts
Are there any other problems with the lake in addition to "cloudiness"?	Phosphorus, chlorophyll a, phytoplankton, zooplankton, fish surveys, color, alkalinity, dissolved oxygen, pH, temperature, user surveys	Quantitative: Short- and/or long-term monitoring. Subjective: Survey of lakefront owners and recreational users

Data can be used in a wide variety of ways: to provide a simple snapshot of the lake at a particular instant, to conduct a trend analysis, to make comparisons or to estimate or confirm the influence of change.

Sampling type and frequency

To ascertain the quality of the water in your lake, you need to collect data by taking samples of the water. A *grab sample* is a single sample taken at a certain point in the lake, perhaps at the surface, the bottom or some other discrete point. An *integrated sample* represents various times and areas of the water. Integrated samples can be taken over time (during daylight hours at certain intervals) or over a certain distance (at intervals through the entire water column or the epilimnion). The choice between these two sampling methods depends on the question you are trying to answer.

The frequency of sampling is also determined by the answer you're seeking. Short-term sampling ranges from a single day to perhaps a week and answers the question: "What is the concentration or value of X at this particular time?" Long-term sampling is conducted at regular intervals (such as biweekly or monthly) over a much longer period of time, often years, sometimes indefinitely. Long-term sampling can determine and measure changes against previously established baseline conditions, thus giving you trends.

SAMPLE PARAMETERS

The first step in preparing to collect water quality information is to make a list of everything you want to collect. You'll often hear this referred to as the *parameters* to be covered. Such parameters fall into four groups: physical, biological, chemical and social.

Physical parameters

■ **Light (clarity).** The Secchi disk allows one to make a simple but fairly accurate measurement of the transparency (how deep light penetrates) of the water. Transparency (clarity) can be influenced by the concentration of phytoplankton, detrius (disintegrated material) or dissolved organic substances (e.g., color). When phytoplankton is the chief component of the suspended matter, Secchi disk depth can be used as a surrogate measure of the productivity of a lake. Secchi depth can also be used to estimate the depth to which photosynthesis can take place (the euphotic zone), which is roughly three times the Secchi disk depth.

■ **Temperature.** Temperature readings taken vertically in the water column of a lake can help determine if the lake is stratified, i.e., if different lake layers (epilimnion, metalimnion and hypolimnion) exist.

■ **Precipitation.** The volume and types of precipitation, including runoff, are important in understanding the quality of lake water.

■ **Lake levels.** Establishing the lake's depth and measuring changes in the elevation of the water must be included.

Biological parameters

■ **Plankton (phytoplankton and zooplankton).**
Determining the different types and amounts of plankton in a lake yields information on biomass, productivity, water quality and possible biotic interactions. As the base of the food web, phytoplankton (algae) are an important indicator of the biological structure of the lake. Chorophyll *a* is often used as a surrogate for phytoplankton; in contrast, zooplankton are rarely used as an indicator.

■ **Macrophytes (plants).** Knowing the types and amount of plants present in the lake can help establish a basis for your lake management plan.

■ **Macroinvertebrates.** These little critters contribute to the biomass of a lake, and can be an important part of the biotic interactions. They are often used as indicators of water quality over time.

■ **Fish.** Fish may or may not be important to your lake — yours may be used principally for swimming and boating, and historically, fish may never have thrived there. If you want to use your lake for fishing, however, you need to know what kind of fish (if any) populate your lake, if the type of fish has changed — and, of course, what kind of fish should live in your lake, e.g., those adapted to warm or cold water.

Chemical parameters

■ **Nutrients.** The macronutrients nitrogen and phosphorus are the most frequently measured nutrients, with the resulting data used to predict the potential for algal growth in a lake. There is often a strong correlation between phosphorus, chlorophyll *a* and Secchi disk depth. In some instances, the micronutrients (most often iron) can be very influential in lake productivity.

■ **Chlorophyll *a*.** These values can be used to estimate the amount of algae (phytoplankton) in a lake, because chlorophyll *a* is the photosynthetic pigment found in all algae and most other photosynthetic organisms.

■ **Color.** A lake's apparent color can be attributed to both suspended particles (silt, algae) and dissolved matter.

■ **Turbidity.** This condition is caused by suspended materials (silt, algae) in the water.

■ **Specific conductivity.** Conductivity is a measure of the electrical current that can pass through the lake water. Lakes with lots of dissolved materials that act as charged particles (ions) will have a high conductivity.

■ **Alkalinity and pH.** Alkalinity is a measure of the ability of the lake water to buffer changes in acidity; pH values tell you the relative acidity of the lake water. This parameter directly influences the types of plants and animals that can live in a lake.

■ **Dissolved oxygen.** The amount of oxygen dissolved in the water is influenced by temperature; the amount of dissolved oxygen determines where in the lake various plants and animals can survive.

Social parameters

Why do you and your neighbors enjoy your lake? Is it the thrill of raising your sail at sunrise on Saturday morning? Or watching for nibbles on your fishing line? Maybe you love to swim in the cove – or just snooze in your hammock.

But do some folks grumble about the weeds (that fishers love) impeding swimming and boating? And is your community growing – perhaps more rapidly than you like?

As more and more people build homes around lakes, many of them living there year 'round, you can expect growing disagreement over how your lake is best used.

Remember – lake management will work well only if it reflects a total assessment of the problems and needs and desires of the lake community; science must interact closely with society to establish and achieve those objectives. Begin with a needs assessment.

■ **Uses.** Survey your community to determine how they think the lake should be used. Good surveys don't just happen; you'll need professional help in preparing and asking the questions, and tabulating the results. Maybe you'll find that expertise in your lake community or at a nearby college, extension agent or conservation district.

■ **Development.** Check your homeowners' covenants and local regulations to ensure that new homes and businesses are being sited and constructed in an environmentally sound manner. These documents may need updating.

■ **Values.** Pitched battles between swimmers and fishers may indicate more than a conflict over use of the lake – they may be symptomatic of a perception of loss, a feeling that the "special place" that renewed their energies and their spirits may have vanished.

This makes it even more important to concentrate on collecting all the information possible to ensure that your lake is managed to meet the needs of those who enjoy it — and care for it.

UNDERSTANDING
CAUSE AND EFFECT

Most people can spot the symptoms of their lake problems. They may even equate the symptoms with the problems. For example, they may identify periodic fish kills as the problems; but the real problem may be periodic low levels of dissolved oxygen resulting from algal blooms caused by too many nutrients. Perhaps the fish kills coincide with lake turnover, when bottom water low in dissolved oxygen mixes with overlying water.

While dead fish are a problem, they are really the manifestation of low dissolved oxygen. The low dissolved oxygen could be caused by a number of things that may require more investigation.

No doubt you will also want to know — like many lakefront owners — more about the relationship between cause and effect. The following discussion explains water and nutrient budgets, major factors in the cause and effect equation. Your professional lake manager or water quality specialist will know how to calculate and use these budgets.

Water budgets

Water budgets are used to calculate nutrient budgets. A water budget is simply an accounting of all the water coming into and going out of a lake. Water enters a lake through precipitation (rain, sleet or snow), direct surface runoff, stream flow, point source discharges (industries, cities) and groundwater flow. It leaves as stream flow, evapotranspiration, withdrawals and groundwater seepage. The methods for gathering these data include the following:

■ **Precipitation.** A rain gauge on site will directly measure precipitation; nearby rain gauge stations can give you an estimate. Use this information to determine the amount of water that falls directly onto the surface of your lake. It may take a number of rain gauges to adequately record the precipitation in your watershed.

■ **Point sources.** Flow rates can generally be obtained from the discharger or the regulatory agency responsible for the discharge permit. The agency can also tell you who holds the permit. It's important to note that permitted discharge rates are considered maximums; actual discharge rates are usually lower than the permitted level.

■ **Stream flows.** Stream flows can be measured directly by using a flow meter and knowing the cross-sectional area of the stream at the point being measured. Typically, a discharge rating curve is developed from a series of direct measurements at various flow velocities. With enough information, the discharge can be estimated rather accurately simply by knowing the water level.

■ **Direct surface runoff.** When runoff cannot be measured in a well-defined channel such as a ditch or stream, it can be estimated by knowing the area of land contributing the runoff and multiplying by a number (i.e., runoff coefficient) representative of the land use of the area. For example, 100 acres of forested land contributes

Problems that affect the use of statistical procedures

1. Water quality data records are often short.

2. Techniques and sensitivities of analytical methods have changed over the years.

3. Sampling location and frequency have changed in many instances.

4. Correlations that relate specific variables to limnological and hydrologic behavior are rarely available, so that it is difficult to partition variance.

5. Natural background variability often hides water quality trends.

6. Causal explanation of trends requires a knowledge of human activities, hydrologic processes and land use in the area.

(Source: Techniques for Detecting Trends in Lake Water Quality, Water Resources Bulletin Vol. 20, No. 1).

much less runoff than 100 acres of urban land with many paved (impervious) surfaces.

■ **Groundwater flow**(or seepage) can be measured using a seepage meter: that is, a device installed in the lake sediment to directly meter the amount of water entering or leaving the lake via groundwater flow. Installing seepage meters can be costly, so many times, the budget is simply "balanced" by determining all the inflow and outflow except for groundwater.

■ **Evapotranspiration.** Local weather and agricultural experiment stations can usually supply information on the rate of evapotranspiration.

■ **Withdrawals.** Withdrawal volumes can be obtained from the entity (e.g., a municipal water supply agency or an industry) making the withdrawal. Most withdrawals are regulated by a permitting agency, so the maximum amount permitted to be withdrawn can be obtained from the permit itself. This, however, may not be the actual amount withdrawn. If no permit is required, estimates can be made based on pumping rates (gallons pumped per minute).

Nutrient budgets

Nutrient budgets estimate the amount of nutrients (in pounds or kilograms) that enter and exit a lake. The pounds per year of a nutrient entering a lake are commonly referred to as the total annual nutrient load. Nutrient budgets are derived from water budgets, on the assumption that concentration times flow equals the load from that particular source. Usually, the nutrient budget calculation is made for an entire year and reported as annual load.

Nutrient budgets, like water budgets, help us balance what comes into a lake with what goes out of it. Nutrients enter a lake via stream inflows, groundwater, atmospheric deposition (both wet and dry), point source discharges, internal nutrient recycling and nitrogen fixation. Nutrients can exit a lake via stream outflows, withdrawals or groundwater. Only water leaves a lake through evapotranspiration; nutrients do not.

■ **Stream flows.** The concentration of nutrients in a stream is measured directly by taking a sample of the water to a laboratory for analysis to determine the nutrient concentration in mg/L. The concentration is measured at different times to account for both dry and wet weather (storm) conditions. Wet weather values are usually represented as an "event mean concentration," which is an average of values obtained throughout a storm.

■ **Groundwater.** The concentration of nutrients in groundwater can be estimated using concentrations from well samples. State or local water quality and health agencies sometimes collect well samples, and if you have private wells around the lake, property owners may also have their wells tested. If neither of these resources is available, your lake manager may recommend installing several groundwater wells to obtain the samples. But think twice about this decision; installing wells is not a cheap undertaking.

■ **Atmospheric deposition.** The concentration of nutrients in rainfall (wet fall) is obtained by collecting and analyzing rainwater samples. Nutrients that come from the atmosphere as dry fall need to be estimated from samples taken with special collecting devices. Since these devices are costly, your lake manager may want to contact state or local air and water quality agencies to obtain dry fall values.

■ **Point source discharges.** Pollutant concentrations from point sources are usually monitored. This information can be obtained from the discharger or the agency that issued the permit.

■ **Nutrient recycling.** The nutrient flux from the sediments may need to be estimated, using the scientific literature, or measured *in situ* (in place). The difficulty of determining nutrient flux makes it an unknown (or an estimate) in many nutrient budgets.

■ **Nitrogen fixation.** Depending on the type of organisms in a particular lake, nitrogen fixation may be a significant source of this nutrient. Nitrogen fixation rates can be obtained directly or estimates made from the literature.

■ **Withdrawals.** The concentration of nutrients in a water withdrawal can be obtained from monitoring records of the entity doing the withdrawal or the agency responsible for the permit, assuming the withdrawal is significant enough to require a permit.

LOOKING AT
TRENDS

One of the basic reasons for gathering data is to determine if a parameter is changing over time, or if the value simply varies naturally and cyclically. The answer to this question is not always simple or obvious. Many approaches have been developed to determine trends in a parameter, ranging from simple plots of data over time to complex statistical analysis. Statistical techniques properly applied can extract meaningful information by separating true trends from "noise." You should be aware, however, that statistical procedures have some drawbacks, among which is the need for additional details.

MAKING
COMPARISONS

An indexing system can often help you compare your lake with other lakes. Two common indices are the Trophic State Index and the Shannon Biodiversity Index.

Trophic State Index

The trophic state of a lake refers to the degree to which nutrient enrichment affects the overall productivity of the system. Developed in 1977 by Dr. Robert Carlson of Kent State University, the Trophic State Index (TSI) is predicated on a strong correlation between phosphorus, chlorophyll *a* and Secchi disk transparency. Phosphorus levels as a cause influence the levels of chlorophyll *a* and Secchi depth.

Dr. Carlson developed basic equations (that others have modified for specific areas) based on three assumptions:

- Secchi transparency is a function of phytoplankton biomass;
- Phosphorus is the factor limiting algal growth; and
- Total phosphorus concentration is directly correlated with algal biomass.

◆ **Oligotrophy:** Lack of plant nutrients keeps growth low, lake contains oxygen at all depths, clear water, deeper lakes can support trout.

◆ **Mesotrophy:** moderate plant growth, hypolimnion may lack oxygen in summer, moderately clear water, warmwater fisheries only — bass and perch may dominate.

◆ **Eutrophy:** contains excess nutrients, blue-green algae dominate during summer, algae scums probable at times, hypolimnion lacks oxygen in summer, cloudy water, rooted macrophyte problems may be evident.

◆ **Hypereutrophy:** algae scums dominate in summer, few macrophytes, no oxygen in hypolimnion, fish kills possible in summer and under winter ice.

Definitions from *Water Column* 10:4, Office of Water Management, Indiana Dept. Environ. Management.

The amount of either phosphorus or chlorophyll *a* or the Secchi depth reading can be used to classify the lake in terms of its trophic state. (See the discussion of eutrophication in Chapter 1.)

The easiest and least expensive parameter to use is the Secchi disk depth, while chlorophyll *a* and phosphorus values require more expertise and expense. Volunteer monitors routinely use the Secchi disk; check with your state water quality agency to see if your lake is covered through its volunteer monitoring program.

When using the TSI, remember that your lake may not fit exactly with the equations. For example, your Secchi disk transparency can be influenced by color. The index also does not account for the influence of macrophytes. Because of these limitations, always use the trophic state index along with other information.

Shannon Biodiversity Index

The Shannon Biodiversity Index is probably the most widely used biotic index for describing the state of a lake's biotic community. This index takes into account the number of species and the distribution of individuals among species. The more species and the more evenly distributed they are, the higher the value of the index.

As an ecologist, you would assume that the highest diversity represents a healthy lake system, with good stability and resilience.

If your lake manager chooses to use this index, he or she must be aware that for it to be of value, it must compare to indexes of systems of known good quality.

HOW TO ESTIMATE AND CONFIRM **THE INFLUENCE OF CHANGE**

Your biggest question about your lake may be "If my neighbors and I go ahead and reduce our use of fertilizer, will the lake get better?" A lake model can help you answer this question before you and your neighbors stop using fertilizer.

Lake models are mathematical representations that attempt to describe what is happening in a lake. As you may have guessed, the representation can range from being very simple to being very complex. Some of the simple models are called empirical models; they are based on observed relationships between one variable and another. For example, the amount of phosphorus in a lake can be used to estimate its phytoplankton biomass.

More complex models are called mechanistic models. These attempt to describe what will happen based on the interaction between a number of variables. For example, to determine the phytoplankton biomass, the model may consider phytoplankton doubling rates, zooplankton grazing rates, temperature's effects on respiration and sediment release rates.

You're concerned about using fertilizer so you will use a model that tells you the amount of nutrients your lake needs to meet its management goals. You can then tie your lake model to a nutrient loading model to determine how land-use changes may affect your lake's water quality. Then you can use modeling to figure out how to reduce nutrient loading or develop restoration strategies. That's where you'll find the answer to your question about fertilizer.

But modeling is not a simple process. Like using the indexes, modeling usually requires professional expertise. Just selecting the right model itself can be a confusing task. Modeling doesn't focus on nutrients alone; you'll find models for dissolved oxygen, toxins and many other parameters. So leave the modeling job to your lake manager or consultant.

NOTES

CHAPTER 5

Get it Together–
THEN GET GOING

*T*he expression,"There's no easy way to get there from here," could have been coined especially for those responsible for managing community property — like a lake. Such a job has never been a simple undertaking, partly because so many people are involved — each with a different concern. Of course, that's the good part, too. Getting things done generally requires many individuals with specific skills and talents.

Varying agendas create a diverse community bound by common interest and responsibility for the lake. It's hardly a mission impossible, but it does involve working as a group.

You may already have a lake or homeowners' association. If so, you may also have a lake management committee; if not, forming one within the association will be a relatively easy and logical move. But if you don't have an umbrella organization, how do you form such a committee? If you've read this far, you're concerned about your lake, and you've probably already visited with your neighbors about the need to understand how your lake functions so you can protect this resource — the reason why you all live here in the first place!

So take the next step. And this works whether you're forming a committee within an association or "starting from scratch" (see Chapter 7, "How to Organize Your Lake Organization"). Simply invite the neighbors who share your concerns to sit down and seriously discuss creating a lake management committee for your lake. At this initial stage, the group will probably come up with a list of people they think should serve on the committee. Be sure it's more than just your group; include representatives of all those who are involved with your lake (see the discussion of Public Involvement that follows).

When the lake management committee meets for the first time, the core group should present in writing suggested goals and operating bylaws. Just getting these organizational necessities approved will take more than one meeting, but if the committee is to succeed, it's essential that all members buy in fully to what it intends to do.

Lake management committees have two major responsibilities: to help encourage and manage public involvement and to plan for lake management. A lake management committee must work closely with the lake manager (assuming you have one), who will guide the committee in using professionals who understand the science of lakes and how they function.

If you do not have a lake manager, then you must decide where you will find technical guidance. If you employ a consultant, or actually hire a lake manager, you would be wise to check with the North American Lake Management Society to ascertain that the individual or company is certified for lake management (see Chapter 8).

PUBLIC
INVOLVEMENT

Think of the players in your lake and watershed. Who is your "public"?

- Year 'round residents, those with summer homes — others who rent cabins or camping space by the week or overnight.

- Businesses that depend on the lake: realtors, property managers, marinas, gas stations, rental equipment, restaurants, souvenir and t-shirt shops — you know the list.

- Nearby towns who offer services to those who enjoy your lake: theatres, radio and TV stations, repair shops, grocery and drug stores.

- Local and state government officials who set policies that affect your lake.

And, of course, everyone who lives in the lake's watershed, because their actions directly contribute to the "state of the lake," be it polluted or pristine.

But not everyone needs to be involved in every decision that a lake management committee makes. The level, frequency and purpose of public involvement can change depending on the public's needs and interests. The lake management committee determines when the public should be involved in the decisionmaking process and to what extent.

What does it really mean to be involved in lake management? Public involvement means an exchange of information, ideas and concerns related to community decisions. One's involvement can vary as greatly as the people themselves. Strategists will be needed, but also storytellers, technical experts and teachers, worker bees and resource managers. You must make the community aware of the need to manage the lake you all treasure, and ensure their full participation: their right to discuss problems and help develop actions to solve them, and to share in achieving the lake community's common goals. Each of these activities is critical to a committee's success:

- *Awareness* — lake management issues and decisions should not come as a surprise or shock to people unprepared to deal with lake problems.

- *Discussion* — everyone must be given the opportunity to contribute ideas about what the problems are and what needs to be done. Rejection can often be avoided if the public has been given information on the issues and the opportunity to help develop options. They must know their suggestions are considered.

- *Participation* — creating proposals, analyzing information, suggesting alternative courses of action are most effectively pursued by interested, involved individuals acting together.

- *Action* — in environmental matters as in economic ones, everyone must have the opportunity to contribute his or her own activity to the achievement of the common goal.

Involving the public in decisions promotes better decisions, lasting commitment, greater support and more action.

PLANNING

Some people feel that planning takes too much time — resulting in tomes that do nothing more than gather dust on a shelf somewhere. In fact, some associations will even show you these musty old plans. Other people may be so busy planning the plan that they never complete the first scheduled project.

But planning, and the documents it produces, can be very helpful. Planning forces people to think clearly about what they want while at the same time resolving differences among people with disparate ideas. It also charts a course to follow, a series of steps to ensure that "you can get there from here."

And when the going gets tough and hard decisions need to be made, planning reminds people why they came together in the first place: to manage the lake. These cardinal rules for planning will always serve you well:

1. Keep the planning process as simple as possible. It makes no sense to undertake a large task when all you need is sound professional judgment with a dash of common sense.

2. If activities have already begun, don't try to stop them. Instead, let the momentum continue. You can always bring them into the planning process later.

3. If you know something needs to be done, no matter what, then do it.

WHAT'S A
LAKE FOR?

The foundation for building a lake management plan must be laid on two critical cornerstones: how the lake is used and the status of that use.

Uses

Who decides how the lake is to be used? Basically, each state designates uses for all waterbodies within its boundaries, under the authority of the Clean Water Act. The Act decrees that all waters should be "fishable and swimmable," and in Section 305[b] says their quality should "provide for the protection and propagation of a balanced population of shellfish, fish, and wildlife and allow recreational activities in and on the water."

The Act also charges states or tribes with determining to what extent each lake meets its designated uses. Thus, you can get the list of designated uses for your lake from your state or tribal

Table 2.—Environmental conditions for desired uses.

DESIRED USE	CONDITIONS TO MEET		PROBLEMS AND SOURCES
	FEDERAL REQUIREMENTS	LOCAL REQUIREMENTS	
Drinking water/food processing	Drinking water standards, including ▸ nitrates (< 10 mg/L) ▸ fecal coliform ▸ atrazine (.003 mg/L) ▸ lead (.05 mg/L) ▸ iron (.3 mg/L)		▸ nitrates: fertilizer, domestic sewage, animal waste ▸ fecal coliform: domestic sewage, animal waste, wildlife ▸ turbidity: sediment, plankton ▸ atrazine: agricultural runoff ▸ lead: stormwater runoff from commercial and industrial areas ▸ iron: stormwater runoff
Primary contact recreation (swimming, diving, water skiing, skin diving, surfing)	▸ fecal coliform (200 colonies/100 ml)	Public access, visibility at 30 feet, diverse plant and animal communities, free of excessive weed growth	▸ fecal coliform: domestic sewage, animal waste, wildlife ▸ lack of public access: no accessways or open space ▸ lack of visibility: high turbidity from sediment and plankton abundance ▸ decreased diversity: habitat destruction, reduced water quality ▸ excessive weed growth: nutrient enrichment (phosphorus and nitrogen), nuisance species (transport from other areas)
Secondary contact recreation (fishing, boating)		Public access, free of excessive weed growth	▸ lack of public access: no accessways or open space ▸ excessive weed growth: nutrient enrichment (phosphorus and nitrogen), nuisance species (transport from other areas)

DESIRED USE	CONDITIONS TO MEET		PROBLEMS AND SOURCES
	FEDERAL REQUIREMENTS	LOCAL REQUIREMENTS	
Fish propagation and survival	Water quality criteria (including dissolved oxygen at 6 mg/L cold water, 5 mg/L warm water), habitat for spawning and survival, food supply, temperature requirements		‣ phosphorus: fertilizers, plant materials, detergents ‣ nitrogen: fertilizers, domestic sewage, atmospheric deposition ‣ oxygen-demanding substances: plant material, domestic sewage, carbonaceous substances ‣ lack of habitat: sedimentation from upland areas, streambanks and lakeshore areas, minimal woody vegetation, removal of substrate ‣ minimal food supply: inadequate plankton levels to support fishery ‣ temperature fluctuations: increased temperature of streams entering lake, shallower lake depths
Flood protection	Adequate flood storage volume in the lake, adjacent wetlands, streams and flood plains		‣ storage volume deficit: sedimentation from upland areas, streambanks and lakeshore areas, filling in of wetlands and floodplains
Wildlife habitat	Adequate upland area, adequate near-shore riparian zones		‣ lack of upland areas: conversion of open space to more intense uses such as agriculture or residential development, timber harvesting ‣ lack of riparian zone: disturbance of area for other uses
Irrigation water	Fecal coliform		
Power generation	Water supply		‣ reduced water supply: interbasin transfers
A site for tourism		Open space, aesthetically pleasing	‣ lack of upland areas: conversion of open space to more intense uses such as agriculture or residential development, timber harvesting

81

environmental or water quality agency; and, you might also want to ask for a copy of the last 305[b] report they filed with EPA. If your lake was surveyed for the report, it will tell you how your lake is meeting its designated uses. You can also find this information on EPA's web site.

But this state or tribal list of uses is but a starting point. In developing a lake management plan, you can develop your own list of uses that you think are important for your lake, or that it is being used for, and include on that list the uses designated by the state or tribe.

The lake management committee's decision on lake use must be based on the deliberations of public meetings that include everyone in your community who uses and is interested in the lake. The final list of uses forms the first cornerstone of the foundation for your lake management plan.

Capability

If the first cornerstone tells you what you want to use the lake for, the second tells you whether it's possible; it's known as the status of the use(s). If you are able to use the lake for everything on your list, then the lake is fully meeting the ways your lake management committee — with full participation of the lake community — decreed it should be used.

Familiar lake uses

- Drinking water/food processing
- Primary contact recreation (swimming, diving, water skiing, skin diving, surfing)
- Secondary contact recreation (fishing, boating)
- Fish propagation and survival
- Flood protection
- Wildlife habitat
- Irrigation water
- Power generation
- A site for tourism
- Aesthetics

But something may stop you from enjoying all those uses. In that case, the lake is only partially meeting its designated uses. And in some really severe cases, you may not be able to use the lake at all for some uses: then the lake has failed to meet those designated uses. In these extreme cases, recall — *before* your lake deteriorates from meeting to partially meeting its designated uses — the methods for quantifying lake status that you learned in Chapter 4. You can use this information to move the planning process along. Note, however, that lakes can deteriorate and still meet all their designated uses.

DEFINE
YOUR GOALS

The next phase in the development of a lake management plan is to articulate your goals: broadly state all that your community needs, hopes for or expects to receive from or give back to your lake.

The lake management committee has, no doubt, been thinking about goals from the very beginning of the planning process. One of the easiest ways to begin putting management goals together is group them under three general categories: protection, prevention and restoration.

- Protection goals for uses that are being fully met.

- Prevention goals to ensure that uses — particularly those being partially met – are not degraded.

- Restoration goals for uses not being met.

Next, place the different uses into the broad management categories. For example, the lake management committee may decide that the best approach for Lake Ozawkie would be to protect the picnic and play areas, prevent degradation of the fishery and restore the swimming area. Clearly, lake management planning can be oriented either toward a single goal or several overlapping goals that reflect different aspects of the lake.

Within these general categories, it then becomes important to be more specific about lake management goals.

For example, specific goals for Lake Ozawkie may include the following:

- improve picnic and play facilities by protecting the forests and fields along the lakeshore,

- protect habitat for fish by preventing the invasion of nuisance aquatic plants and managing sediment runoff into the lake, and

- return swimming to the lake by restoring its water quality and depth.

Now that you have some good management goals, think again about how you can actually "get there from here." Use the information in Chapter 4 on determining the status of your lake and using models to develop management objectives. The status of use gives you an idea of what needs to be done, and models can tell you how much needs to be done to get there.

Then, spell it out. The more specific the management objective, the easier it is to get people involved and to keep track of the progress you are making. Look at how Lake Ozawkie residents married their goals with management objectives:

- Preserve open space: purchase 15 acres of land.

- Prevent invasion of nuisance species: inspect all boats launched into the lake.

- Restore swimming as a designated use: reduce fecal coliform counts to less than 200 colonies per 100 mL.

FINDING
PROBLEMS

Now that you have some really clear management objectives, it's time to identify the source(s) of current and potential problems. Although "source/cause identification" has traditionally dealt with water quality, it can also be used to address issues related to other ecosystem values: for example, water quantity, habitat, open space requirements, user conflicts or other aspects of the lake.

Take another look at Lake Ozawkie. So far, we have determined the following management objectives: (1) protecting the picnic and play areas by purchasing open space, (2) preventing nuisance aquatic plants by inspecting boats, and (3) restoring swimming by reducing fecal coliform levels.

The next task for the management committee is to remove any obstacles that might prevent the community from fulfilling these objectives.

As you might imagine, not only does the lake have many uses, and conditions that must be met to provide for those uses, but the lake may also have many problems.

Some of these problems originate in places close to the lake; others may come from miles away. And the location may change over time. The best way to deal with this aspect of management is to embrace the watershed in your plan. This will give you a much better shot at successfully meeting your management goals.

However, in so large an area, where does management begin? You can answer that question only by ranking your lake's problems by priority. Look again at the list of concerns facing Lake Ozawkie's lake management committee:

- Possible conversions of open space to other land uses (e.g., agriculture, residential, timber harvesting)
- Invasive or exotic (non-native) plants transported from other lakes or mistakenly released by homeowners
- Sediment deposition — from upland areas, lakeshore erosion, streambank erosion
- Coliform contamination — from nearby farms, wildlife, residential uses.

Let's rank these problems one by one. Note that invasive plants, sediment and coliform problems have multiple sources; we may have to rank each source as a separate problem for purposes of assigning priority. Quantifying the problems will show us which ones are bigger than the others.

■ **Possible conversions.** Perhaps the easiest way to address conversion of open space is to look at existing and future land-use trends. Are some areas near the lake changing faster than others? If so, are the areas contiguous to the picnic and play areas you want to protect? Perhaps this is the biggest problem area.

■ **Invasive/exotic plants.** Although it is difficult to determine exactly where these plants originate, do your homework. First, find out what other lakes have reported invasions by such plants. Are they close or far away? Then survey boaters to find out which of these lakes they use.

Putting this information together with reported plant sightings can help you locate "plant hot spots." Maybe your boat inspections need to start with the boats coming and going from these "hot spots." Dealing with the source of the problem in this way may help prevent these plants from invading your lake.

Again, if homeowners are the source of invasive plants, do your homework. Are these plants sold at a nursery or aquarium pet store? Educating consumers and the people who sell them may help solve this problem.

■ **Sediments.** Wind erosion generally occurs on large, open uplands. Water erosion happens any place precipitation lands or runs off, usually uplands, streambanks and the lakeshore. Several different models can estimate how much sediment (in tons/year) comes from each of these areas and specific land uses. Then you can determine where the biggest problem areas are.

■ **Fecal coliform.** This common bacteria is found in animal and human waste. As fecal coliform is most commonly transported in runoff, its sources may be almost anywhere within the watershed. The type of land uses in upland areas may indicate how much fecal coliform may be available from wildlife, sewage, farm animals or homes. Again, use models to determine where the biggest problems are.

Although still in the early stages, DNA is now being successfully used to track fecal coliform sources. In many of these cases, failing septic systems were assumed to be the culprit; instead, DNA identified deer and raccoon as the source in rural areas, dogs in cities.

Now that you're organized, the next step is to figure out what needs to be done first. Chapter 6 will help you make this leap from planning to practice. Go on, try your hand at it; you can always come back to earlier chapters to hone your planning skills.

NOTES

_____

_____

_____

_____

_____

_____

_____

_____

_____

_____

_____

_____

_____

_____

_____

_____

_____

_____

CHAPTER 6

Developing A PLAN

*T*omorrow when you wake up, tuck this book under your arm and go back down to the lake. Take another, more comprehensive view of its condition. Your vantage point, like the lake itself, has changed, has it not? Now, when you look into the water, you see more than its beauty and productivity.

Now you can see the *symptoms* of change that we discussed in Chapters 4 and 5: changes reflected in the cloudiness of the water, fewer game fish swimming near shore, occasional oily spots from boats. Changes in the watershed may also be reflected in the water: more buildings and camping grounds on the water's edge, "exotic" (not native) plants proliferating in the littoral zone.

These symptoms concern us — we even complain about them. But we know they are warning signs that we must do something if we expect the lake to be here in years to come, unspoiled and fully functioning for our children.

How we turn our complaints into a framework for solution and action — knowing what's really going on in the lake and what we can do on its behalf — is this chapter's focus.

This chapter will help you develop a management plan for your lake. In Chapter 4, we learned something of the qualitative status of our lakes; in Chapter 5, we learned how we can work together — how a lake management committee might determine what actions to take to maintain the use and status of a lake. Now, in Chapter 6, we will learn the concrete steps we can take to protect or restore our lake.

DON'T EXPECT
THE MOON

Of course, some lakes and reservoirs cannot be restored or even managed so they will support desired uses. Either their physical limitations cannot be overcome, or lake users expect to make the impossible happen. So forget the magic wand and develop a realistic plan.

By correctly identifying causes and sources of lake problems, you can build a solid foundation for sound lake management.

That's why the emphasis here is on actions that use what's wrong with the lake to help us achieve what is feasible. It may be that making a lake fishable and swimmable or bringing summertime phosphorus levels down to no greater that 10 µg/L is the best we can do — that may be the *achievable condition* against which we measure our success.

A common mistake to avoid is focusing on actions that address only the symptoms of lake problems rather than their actual causes. We can avoid this mistake by applying careful, long-range planning. Committees that develop comprehensive management plans keep their project focused on causes and long-term effects (i.e., measurable results), while still addressing the immediate symptoms of the problem. In short, they consider both scenarios in light of what lake users want — and what's actually achievable.

This process is based on a "diagnostic/feasibility study," the precursor to setting realistic lake management goals. Originally Phase I of EPA's Clean Lakes Program for publicly owned lakes, the diagnostic/feasibility study determines what's wrong with your lake and what you can do about it. This approach works on both public and privately owned lakes. You should seek the help of a professional lake consultant in conducting such a study.

WATERSHED MANAGEMENT AND IN-LAKE TECHNIQUES

Management goals and objectives, the basic components of a comprehensive lake management plan, develop rather quickly once lake problems and their causes are identified. A plan consists of one or more management techniques to address a specific problem (symptom) or to deal more radically with its cause (i.e., its source). Only target symptoms if the cause has been addressed. But whether you target the distress signal or the stressor, each technique will address either the lake and/or its watershed.

The challenge is to strike a balance between in-lake and watershed management methods. Because the condition of a lake is dictated primarily by the quality and quantity of water entering the lake, the source of most in-lake problems will be located in the watershed. Therefore, most lake management plans need to emphasize watershed management techniques and controls, while using in-lake techniques to treat symptoms.

Keep in mind that in-lake techniques are mostly rehabilitative; although techniques like aeration and alum treatment produce immediate results, the effects of many techniques may not be apparent for years. Thus, protection must be a priority, using preventive techniques in the watershed and along the shoreline. Always remember, your overall objective is to determine and embrace only those management techniques that will help you meet your lake use goals.

You'll usually find, however, not just one but several different kinds of techniques can be used — either alone or in combination — for each kind of problem or its source. For example, to address excessive nutrients in your lake: if you've already controlled the source, then you can use one or more of at least a dozen in-lake techniques (see Table 3).

To determine the level of action needed, you will want to consider the source, location and severity of the problem as well as any social, economic or technical constraints that may encumber a specific practice. For example, one treatment may get the job done but have unintended negative consequences; another may work, but only in combination with other methods; still others can be used to treat multiple causes. Based on your own situation, use the following questions to help you select a technique:

- What is the problem that this technique can address?
- What side effects does it have?
- How much does it cost (for installation and maintenance)?
- Will this method be acceptable to the public?
- Is it compatible with landowner needs?
- How effective is this treatment?
- Will it have long-lasting results (longevity)?

Table 3.—In-lake restoration and management techniques, by problem and type.

IN-LAKE TECHNIQUE	PROBLEM	TYPE OF TECHNIQUE
Dredging	nuisance algae; nuisance weeds; toxins; excessive shallowness; oxygen demand	Physical
Phosphorus precipitation/inactivation	nuisance algae; toxic	Chemical
Mechanical harvesting	nuisance weeds	Physical
Algaecides	nuisance algae; bacteriological	Chemical
Herbicides	nuisance weeds	Chemical
Biomanipulation	nuisance algae; nuisance weeds	Biological
Dilution/flushing	nuisance algae	Physical
Aeration/destratification	nuisance algae; nuisance weeds; bacteriological; fish kills	Physical
Sediment exposure/water level drawdown	nuisance weeds; excessive shallowness	Physical
Shading	nuisance weeds; bacteriological	Physical
Lake bottom sealing	nuisance weeds	Physical
Hypolimnetic withdrawal	nuisance algae; bacteriological	Physical

- How reliable has this method been in other circumstances?
- Will use of this technique fit your time frame?
- Will government authorities approve this strategy?

■ **Problem.** Does the technique address the problems and causes that you identified in the diagnostic phase of your project? If it's targeted for a particular symptom, has the cause already been addressed?

■ **Side effects.** What are the positive and negative effects associated with this method? Note: some side effects are direct; some are indirect. Some are associated with a specific treatment; others result from an incompatibility among techniques. If you decide to use techniques, with negative side effects, you must either minimize or mitigate these effects.

■ **Cost.** Two types of costs apply to management methods: actual and replacement:

Actual costs include capital, opportunity and operating and maintenance costs; all three must be included in evaluating techniques. Capital costs include the material, equipment, land and labor required to implement the technique. Opportunity costs are associated with removing land from the tax roles, and limiting its type or intensity of use. Operating costs are expenses related to the continued operation and maintenance of a technique; for example, the annual cost of energy (gas, electricity) required to operate an aerator. To estimate the actual cost associated with a technique, compare all three costs on an annual basis over the time frame of the lake management plan.

Replacement costs must also be included in your long-range planning. Equipment or structures eventually may have to be replaced; the costs associated with the full replacement of a technique should be reflected as a contingency in your total budget.

■ **Public/landowner acceptance and compatibility.** Are the proposed watershed and institutional methods socially feasible? Are they suitable for implementation under present land management and use? Will the community's farmers, business people and citizens like these new ways of protecting the lake? Remember, just as everybody causes pollution, so everybody must be responsible for preventing it. You must have buy-in from people living in your watershed.

■ **Effectiveness.** The effectiveness of a management strategy depends entirely on how well it meets the management need. Will it eliminate the water's cloudiness? Or prevent as much erosion as you planned? Remember, the effectiveness of one method may depend on how another works. And a technique's overall effectiveness may be limited by how completely it is implemented. For example, conservation tillage may be proposed to reduce phosphorus and sediment. However, if the entire watershed must convert to conservation tillage to achieve this reduction, it may not be very practical as proposed.

■ **Longevity.** How long a technique remains effective measures its longevity; your lake management plan time frame will determine its desired longevity. Will the technique be effective as long as your plan expects it to? Your plan may have decided to use algaecide, which must be reapplied frequently, to control recurring algal blooms. Although most lake restoration planning will not focus on treating symptoms because this doesn't address the cause of the problem, symptomatic treatments, such as algaecides, can be an important component of a comprehensive lake management plan that addresses causes as well as symptoms.

■ **Reliability.** A technique is reliable if it consistently achieves the expected benefits. Has it been extensively studied under a variety of conditions? Has it been used in your area — and on your type of lake?

■ **Time.** Two aspects of time should be considered: the time it takes to install and operate a treatment and the time that elapses before any benefits become apparent. Maximum benefits may not be seen for several years — some source reduction techniques take that long to be fully implemented. Other techniques operate seasonally and take at least a year to yield any noticeable results.

The next three sections contain information on in-lake and watershed management techniques and institutional controls; apply this information to your own lake and its situation in its watershed.

IN-LAKE
MANAGEMENT
TECHNIQUES

Three general categories of in-lake techniques exist. They either

- control plant growth by using either physical or chemical means;

- improve or modify in-lake conditions for certain organisms that control excessive vegetation biologically (by either physical, chemical or biological means); or

- remove or treat nuisance sediments or organisms by either physical, chemical or biological means. These techniques may remove sediment or reduce its contamination; they treat organisms primarily with bacteria.

The following paragraphs briefly describe the most commonly used in-lake techniques. You will find more information – and other techniques – in the list of suggested readings in Chapter 8. Always, however, use a lake management professional (public or private) in making decisions about how to treat your lake. As mentioned earlier, the North American Lake Management Society certifies such consultants (see Chapter 8).

■ **Dredging** is the process of removing sediment from the lake bottom. It increases water depth and, in some cases, may also remove nutrients, plants and contaminants from the lake. Although in the short term, dredging may increase turbidity, decrease dissolved oxygen and encourage algal blooms, dredging can be a long-term treatment if sources of sediment within the watershed are controlled.

Among the many types of dredging, hydraulic dredging is the most common. Dredging costs vary but are generally high, depending on site access and conditions, nature of the material to be removed and other factors. The costs should be amortized over the longevity of the project.

To consider dredging realistically, include the cost of monitoring, dredging equipment, labor, and transportation and disposal of the dredged materials. Depending on the nature of the dredged material, finding a disposal site for it may be a problem, because disposal of contaminated sediments must meet requirements governing toxic and hazardous waste.

Monitoring costs include (1) pre-dredge screening of the sediment to determine sediment quality, (2) post-dredge monitoring of the lake and the sediment disposal site and (3) in-lake monitoring during dredging to fulfill permit conditions.

■ **Phosphorus precipitation/inactivation.** This remedial method removes (precipitates) phosphorus from the water column and binds phosphorus in the bottom sediment to keep it from entering the overlying water — thus, preventing phosphorus from supplying nutrients for algal growth. Various studies have documented the success of this technique in deep, stratified lakes. Phosphorus must be diverted away from the lake or its source controlled to an acceptable level for this approach to be effective on a long-term basis.

Alum (aluminum sulfate), which can be applied in either granule or liquid form, is the most commonly used binding agent. Possible side effects of alum treatments: increased toxicity, lower pH, increased macrophyte (weed) growth.

■ **Biocontrol.** The objective of in-lake biological control is to control plants naturally over the long term without using expensive machinery or chemicals. Maintaining nutrients at a desirable level is, of course, a major factor, and can often be accomplished by community actions: maintaining septic systems; using pump-out facilities at marinas; using appropriate amounts of lawn care and household chemicals.

Exotic fish and insects are also being used to control aquatic vegetation. At present one fish species and at least seven insect species have been approved by the U.S. Department of Agriculture for release into U.S. waters. Some lakes have introduced triploid grass carp, a genetically sterile form of an Asian fish, to control nuisance plants such as hydrilla. Southern states are using insects to control alligator weed and water hyacinth. One northern insect (*Euhrychiopsis lecontei*) is being used to attack Eurasian watermilfoil.

■ **Dilution/Flushing** is the addition to lake water of water containing fewer nutrients. The purpose is to lower nutrient concentrations and increase the rate at which nutrients are flushed from the lake — resulting in an algae "washout" and lower nutrient concentrations in the water column.

This technique requires large volumes of water and does not remove nutrients from lake bottom sediments. While this approach may succeed in a lake, it may increase eutrophication in slow-flowing waterbodies downstream because it moves nutrients that way. Flushing has to be continuously repeated if the source of nutrients in the lake watershed is not curtailed, or if nutrient levels in the lake bottom sediment are high.

■ **Aeration/Destratification.** These companion techniques increase the oxygen content of the water: aeration creates bubbles to completely mix the lake to a constant temperature throughout the water column; and destratification pumps lake bottom water to the surface to induce mixing with presumably better-oxygenated overlying water. Although commonly practiced together, these techniques can work independently.

In addition to increasing dissolved oxygen, this combination of techniques reduces internal recycling of nutrients and taste and odor problems and promotes the transition of algae species from blue-green to green. If your goal is to support a coldwater fishery, then you may be able to use aeration as a stand-alone technique. Destratification can increase turbidity, and thereby increase particulate nutrients and raise the temperature in the hypolimnion.

■ **Sediment exposure.** This technique is also known as water level drawdown. Sediment exposure manipulates a lake's water levels to expose sediments and rooted aquatic vegetation to drying and freezing conditions. Side effects include (1) possible algal blooms and sediment resuspension, (2) fewer benthic invertebrates because of drying and freezing the lake bottom, and (3) fish kills caused by lower dissolved oxygen resulting from more fish occupying less space because of the lower water level. You may also encounter problems refilling the lake after sediment exposure.

The effectiveness of this technique is limited for seepage lakes. Historic applications have illustrated three important facts:

- Sediment exposure is species specific (see drawdown box).

- Freezing and drying are required.

- It is not suited for annual application since resistant species may become dominant.

■ **Shading** uses chemical dyes to inhibit light penetration to the lake bottom, thus limiting light available for plant growth. The most common dye for this purpose is Aquashade, an inert blue liquid made up primarily of food colors. This treatment's longevity is a function of the lake's water retention time. Please note that the use of chemical dyes in drinking water supplies is usually banned or extremely limited, so be sure to consult local, state and/or tribal authorities before using this technique.

Rooted plants cannot grow through physical barriers, so shading is frequently combined with physical bottom barriers to increase its effectiveness. Because of cost constraints this technique (especially in combination with bottom barriers), is limited to small areas.

■ **Lake Bottom Sealing** uses sediment covers or bottom barriers to prevent rooting and limit light to plants. Barriers, which must be permeable to gases produced by plant decomposition, are made of polypropylene, polyethylene, fiberglass, nylon or other nontoxic material. In the past, burlap, sand, gravel and other similar materials have been used, but eventually plants will root through them. The application of bottom barriers is costly and usually limited to docking areas and swimming beaches. The practice can harm the resident benthic population.

■ **Hypolimnetic Withdrawal** takes water from the lake bottom (where the nutrient concentration is higher and the oxygen lower than in surface water) and discharges it downstream. Removing the nutrient supply decreases the potential for algal blooms.

Responses of common aquatic plants to drawdown

Decrease

- Bladderwort (*Utricularia* spp.)
- Coontail (*Ceratophyllum demersum*)
- Brazilian Elodea (*Egeria densa*)
- Milfoil (*Myriophyllum* spp.)
- Southern Naiad (*Najas guadalupensis*)
- Yellow Water Lily (*Nuphar* spp.)
- Water Lily (*Nymphaea odorata*)
- Robbin's Pondweed (*Potamogeton robbinsii*)
- Fanwort (*Cabomba caroliniana*)

Increase

- Alligator Weed (*Altemanthera philoxeroides*)
- Hydrilla (*Hydrilla verticillata*)
- Bushy Pondweed (*Najas flexilis*)
- Pondweed (*Potamogeton* spp.)

Variable

- Muskgrass (*Chara* spp.)
- Tapegrass (*Valisneria americana*)
- Water Hyacinth (*Eichhomia crassipes*)
- Common Elodea (*Elodea canadensis*)
- Cattail (*Typha latifolia*)

Hypolimnetic withdrawal is appropriate for stratified lakes and small reservoirs with oxygen-poor or nutrient-enriched bottom water. Hypolimnetic withdrawal is usually accomplished through a gravity-fed deep outlet in the dam or by a pipe (siphon) along the bottom. Where gravity doesn't work, an auxiliary pump may be required, which increases the cost of the system and its annual operation. If your lake is nutrient-rich, it's important to control the external nutrient sources.

This technique can have severe downstream side effects. Depending on your state or tribal regulatory standards, discharge water from the lake may require treatment prior to discharge into the receiving water (the stream). This fairly common regulation points to the advisability of involving regulatory people in your planning process from the beginning.

The last three in-lake techniques described here — harvesting, algaecides and herbicides — are true in-lake management techniques that primarily address symptoms. In some situations, they may be the only cost-effective alternatives.

■ **Mechanical Harvesting.** Physically removes macrophytes (plants) from the lake, using a machine to cut and transport the vegetation to a disposal site and thus remove the nutrients stored in the plant. Harvesting eliminates a symptom associated with excessive nutrients, so to be effective, harvesting must be implemented in conjunction with other techniques that reduce the sources of nutrients to a lake.

Mechanical harvesting is time-consuming, labor and energy intensive. Nor are all areas within a lake suitable for harvesting. For example, wetlands and fishery-sensitive areas should be avoided.

Mechanical harvesting may simply trade one problem for another. Once removed, native vegetation may be replaced by exotic nuisance species. The most significant side effect of harvesting is fragmentation of the plant itself, which, without proper care, can actually spread the infestation rather than eliminate it.

Conditions not suitable for in-lake herbicide treatments

♦ High water temperature

♦ Large quantity of plants controlled or destroyed

♦ Nutrient-rich shallow waters

♦ Closed or non-flowing habitats

♦ Large area treated

(Source: modified from EPA, 1993.)

■ **Algaecides.** This in-lake technique uses chemicals — often copper sulfate or another copper compound — to kill excessive algae. The technique works immediately, but usually needs to be repeated several times a year. Side effects include toxicity to other plants and decreased dissolved oxygen, which can result in fish kills.

■ **Herbicides** are chemical agents that attack nuisance weeds. Herbicides' primary side effects stem from the decomposing plant material they create: nutrients can increase in the water column and dissolved oxygen may decline, eventually killing fish. In many cases, however, using herbicides may be the only viable option.

If you're treating a shallow lake with a high surface area, when the water temperature is high, you can expect your lake's water quality to change following a herbicide treatment.

WATERSHED
MANAGEMENT
TECHNIQUES

Recall how watershed was defined in Chapter 1: the watershed is the land area from which water drains into a lake or reservoir. Recall, too, our insistence in Chapter 3 on the interrelationships among communities and abiotic factors in every ecosystem.

Four primary factors affect the quality and function of resources in the watershed: water quality, how it flows, habitat structure and function and energy source. Changes in any or all of these factors can also change the watershed and your lake. Managing the watershed is managing this myriad of factors to secure the integrity and balance of the whole system and the highest quality water resources.

Basically, two types of pollution originate in lake watersheds: point and nonpoint source pollution.

■ **Point source pollution** generally comes from wastewater treatment plants and industrial wastes discharged through pipes or other conveyances. State, tribal or federal permits set limits on these discharges; a regulatory compliance procedure ensures that these limits are maintained. Usually, point source discharges must be treated prior to release.

■ **Nonpoint source pollution** is carried to the lake by runoff from land in the watershed during and following precipitation. Nonpoint sources of pollution depend on the land use and its intensity. Controlling nonpoint source pollution typically relies on a series of management techniques commonly referred to as best management practices or BMPs. Setting up a good BMP plan for your lake's watershed can be simple if you remember some basic principles:

1. Nonpoint source pollution is the result of a process that involves pollutant generation, transport and delivery.

2. BMPs are designed to address pollutants at a particular point in this process. They act as *source reduction* practices (e.g., by

Components of successful watershed nonpoint source projects

1. **Involved all stakeholders.** Local, state, tribal and federal agencies, bankers, machinery dealers and, most importantly, lake users and landowners (or operators) helped design and implement the project.

2. **Identified a common purpose.** Every group and individual involved in the project shared a common commitment to the goal.

3. **Established clear and attainable objectives.** Everyone had clearly defined roles and responsibilities.

4. **Shared leadership.** No one entity "owned" the project.

5. **Achieved flexibility.** The project avoided a rigid structure for decisionmaking and allowed exceptions in particular cases.

6. **Recognized local ownership.** Community-based, local agencies and stakeholders designed the project and spearheaded its implementation.

preventing runoff); or as *management* practices (e.g., using gutters to bypass a specific area); or as *treatment* techniques (e.g., filtering runoff before it reaches the lake).

Sometimes a practice can serve a dual purpose, such as preventing runoff and managing it at the same time. Numerous documents about BMPs are available, some listed among the sources in this handbook. The USDA Natural Resources Conservation Service and state and local water quality agencies can tell you more about BMPs.

Since the quality of your lake depends on the condition of your watershed, you need to establish a partnership between the lake users and watershed residents (many may be the same people). This group can work together to develop a nonpoint source management plan for your lake's watershed. In fact, such partnerships are vital wherever lake projects are contemplated, but the nature of nonpoint source pollution — its diffuse origins and everyone's involvement in it — makes this cooperation a necessity for protecting your lake.

Although there will be many issues to discuss, protection and prevention should be the starting point for any watershed management program; and for many watersheds, restoration must also be considered.

- *Protection* focuses on source controls that are generally nonstructural in nature;

- *Prevention* requires more intense management, including structural controls and treatment practices. Eliminating the generation of point or nonpoint source pollution is the most effective process for preventing water quality problems.

- *Restoration*, probably the most focused of the three approaches, uses both treatment and structural measures to accomplish its objectives.

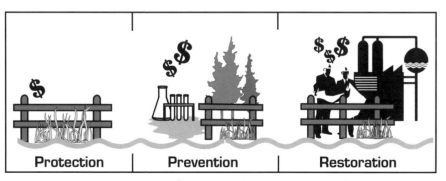

| Protection | Prevention | Restoration |

Management approaches vary in intensity and cost.

Table 4.— A continuum of specific management techniques.

MANAGEMENT TECHNIQUE	FACTOR	OBJECTIVE	DESIGN TECHNOLOGY
Site fingerprinting	Water quality	Protection	Nonstructural source control
Erosion control blanket	Water quality	Prevention	Nonstructural source control/structural treatment
Sediment basin	Water quality	Restoration	Structural treatment
Impervious restrictions	Flow regime	Protection	Nonstructural source control
Disconnected impervious sites	Flow regime	Prevention	Nonstructural source control/structural treatment
Infiltration	Flow regime	Restoration	Structural treatment
Wetlands protection	Habitat structure	Protection	Nonstructural source control
Limited fill with mitigation	Habitat structure	Prevention	Nonstructural source control/structural treatment
Wetlands creation	Habitat structure	Restoration	Structural treatment
Permanent riparian zones	Energy source	Protection	Nonstructural source control
Riparian enhancements	Energy source	Prevention	Nonstructural source control/structural treatment
Organic enrichments	Energy source	Restoration	Structural treatment

When selecting BMPs to address a specific problem, document the primary sources (e.g., urban runoff, animal or crop agriculture, construction, logging or other land use) that you are seeking to control — and the watershed factors, objectives and design technology that you will use. Table 4 provides an example of this.

Always remember that nonpoint source pollution is a "people" problem. Ultimately, every person who lives and works in your watershed must take responsibility for preventing nonpoint pollution: picking up pet waste; depositing used car oil, paint and other common household toxic items in proper disposal facilities; applying appropriate amounts of fertilizer — and on down the list. Protection, prevention and restoration work only if everybody makes them work.

INSTITUTIONAL MANAGEMENT TECHNIQUES

Round out your lake management plan with institutional controls. This category of techniques is based on and defined by local ordinances — rules that reflect community attitudes and help provide a comprehensive approach for managing and protecting local resources. Here, for example, are six potential lake problems that some local communities have managed through community ordinances.

■ **Marina ordinances** ensure proper siting and operation of the facility, proper solid waste disposal, fish and fish-water waste disposal, and facilities for boat cleaning, petroleum management and pump-out services. Proper siting of a facility is extremely important, because incorrectly sited facilities become a chronic problem that is difficult to remediate. Marinas should provide "good housekeeping" facilities for recreational boaters.

■ **Dock/mooring regulations** restrict the number, size, location, building and use of lakeshore structures. Limiting the type of material used in dock construction can prevent the release of

Table 5.—Institutional controls for lake management.

MARINA MANAGEMENT TECHNIQUES	COMMENT
Marina ordinances/dock/moorings regulations	Opponents contend that marina ordinances violate property rights when they restrict type, size and composition.
Fisheries regulations	Limits apply to fish size, quantity of catch and access
Time and space	Reduces lake use conflicts
Boating rules	Limit size and speed of boats and sometimes access and hours of operation; may not be popular with all residents
Access regulations	Confine access and use by nonriparian users

toxic chemicals or other hazardous materials to your lake. Some regulations limit the time periods that docks can be out. The latter, combined with access regulations, deal with overcrowding and thus protect the quality of your lake experience by preventing litter and pollution associated with improper boating.

■ **Fisheries ordinances** regulate the number and size of fish that can be taken and promote specific species survival. Improperly focused fishing regulations can have a tremendous effect on the lake's ecosystem. For more information on fishing regulations related to sizes, species and seasons, consult your state's fish and game authorities.

■ **Time and space zoning** is used to avoid conflicts among user groups by limiting the pursuit of competing activities (such as swimming and boating) to certain times and places. Zoning ordinances are generally accepted and supported by the public only after intensive public information and education campaigns.

■ While many **boating or navigation rules** are enacted for public safety reasons, they provide other benefits as well. Waves caused by excessive speeding erode shorelines and disrupt the tranquility of other lake users. Motor boat access and speeds should be limited in shallow areas, since propellers resuspend bottom sediments, thereby creating turbidity problems and fragmenting weeds — and sometimes releasing nutrients and chemicals trapped in the sediment.

■ **Access regulations** limit the overall number of people in sensitive nearshore areas and can restrict the types of activities allowed. Access regulations may be intended to cover public boat launching facilities, beaches and lakeshore recreational activities, such as hiking and camping.

You may find that your county planning office already has ordinances governing lake management in place (or proposed). Information about such ordinances is also available from the Terrene Institute, local councils of government and state agencies.

ACTING ON YOUR
OWN — NOW!

If we look around us, at home and on our lakeshore, we'll find several things that we can do differently — or do without — to help protect our lakes. Consider, for example, how you handle and store chemicals, care for your lawn and garden, take care of your septic system, your pets and other livestock. Watch yourself consume water!

■ **Chemical Use.** The improper storage, use and disposal of household hazardous chemicals, including automobile fluids, solvents, pesticides and paints can cause water quality problems in your lake.

- Store chemicals in safe containers protected from accidental release or disposal.

- Never dump unused chemicals in your yard or put household hazardous chemicals down your sink. The former might reach the lake through groundwater; the latter can disrupt the chemical and physical breakdown of waste in your septic system or sewage treatment plant.

- Always dispose of unused chemicals and containers in accordance with the label, and always use the least harmful products.

- Recycle used motor oil and antifreeze.

- Consider using natural or biological controls as needed for pest control, and do not routinely use problem or species-specific products.

■ **Lawn Care/Landscaping.** Lakeside landscaping involves planting or preserving a zone of native vegetation around your lake's edge. Lakefront landscaping should allow for full recreational use of the lake and still protect water quality by acting as a buffer to trap runoff and absorb nutrients before they enter your lake. Lawns alone do not make good greenbelts; in fact, you might consider xeriscaping — the use of native plants suitable for your climate (they need little, if any, watering). Select native plant varieties that are attractive, easily maintained and effective buffers. (And cut down on your lawn mowing at the same time!) You can minimize the amount of leaves falling into the lake by planting deciduous trees as far from the water's edge as practical.

- Fertilize lawns and shrubs only when necessary, based on soil fertility test results;

- Reduce the amount of undissolved fertilizer washing into your lake by applying lawn fertilizers only in the spring or early summer growing season.

Lakefront lawn care practices

1. Use the appropriate grass for your climate.
2. Use a fertilizer mix containing potash and a slow release nitrogen.
3. Use the smallest amount of fertilizer necessary to maintain a good grass cover.
4. Avoid washing or leaching nutrients into your lake.
5. Rake and dispose of leaves away from the lake.
6. Do not burn leaves near the lake shore; nutrients concentrate in the ash and are easily washed into your lake.
7. Don't cut grass too close to the ground.
8. You might consider xeriscaping; replace grass with native shrubs, plants and trees.

- Do not remove the thatch on minimally fertilized lawns, but allow it to decompose naturally.

- Do not feed ducks and geese near your lake as bird droppings are high in nutrients and bacteria. Feeding these fowl can change their overwintering patterns and increase summer populations.

Septic system management

♦ Use nonphosphate detergents.

♦ Do not use a garbage disposal.

♦ Keep solvents, plastics and paper diapers out of system.

♦ Conserve water to avoid stressing the septic system; for example, space out wash loads and use water-saving devices.

(Source: modified from EPA, 1993.)

■ **Septic System Care and Maintenance.** Improperly sited or malfunctioning lakeshore septic systems can be a significant source of nutrients to lakes. Ensure your septic system is properly installed and maintained.

Conventional systems consist of a septic tank and an absorption system. The septic tank serves as a settling device for solids, holding them while they break down chemically and physically. The absorption system receives the fluid portion of the wastewater from the septic tank, and then distributes it over a suitable area for infiltration.

Several states have established minimum conditions for locating septic systems, depending on local soil conditions and aquifers. As a precaution, try to keep trees and brush away from the drain field to avoid roots clogging the drains. Inspect your septic system annually to ensure it is in proper working order. Pump regularly, annually for older systems.

IT'S UP TO
US ALL

This brief analysis of lake watershed management has brought us from learning about our lake to knowing how to use lake and watershed management objectives and techniques to keep the lake healthy.

Clearly we cannot do it alone: if we have learned nothing else from living on the lake, we have surely learned that in a watershed, everything is connected to everything else.

Can we change how we act? Probably. And in fact, most changes would actually be quite easy. A few might require some research, and some fewer still might even cost us something in convenience. But citizens who want to protect and manage their lake will learn about its ecology and the threats to its long-term health — and then, exercise their best collective judgment in caring for their lake.

NOTES

CHAPTER 7
How To Organize YOUR LAKE ASSOCIATION

*T*his guide was originally published in 1991 by Terrene Institute in cooperation with the Tennessee Valley Authority and the U.S. Environmental Protection Agency. Although it is now out of print, the basic information remains useful. Please ignore references to the Appendices; they have been deleted because they contained outdated information.

ORGANIZING LAKE USERS: A PRACTICAL GUIDE

Prepared by

The Terrene Institute

In cooperation with

Tennessee Valley Authority
U.S. Environmental Protection Agency

June 1991

Written by Gretchen Flock, Judith Taggart, and Harvey Olem.

Illustrations by Patricia Perry; typography and design by Lura T. Svestka, JT&A, inc.

Photo credits (by page):

(2) Harvey Olem
(7) file photo, Lake Waccabuc
(25) file photo
(28) Judy Mace
(36) file photo
(38) Harvey Olem
(43) Howard Wandell (his father)
(49) Charles Dvorsky
(51) Seattle – King County Convention & Visitors Bureau

For additional copies, contact the

TERRENE
INSTITUTE

1000 Connecticut Avenue, NW, Suite 802
Washington, DC 20036
(202) 833-8317
Fax: (202) 466-8554

Preface

When do you most enjoy your lake? When you push your boat quietly into the water at dawn (and bring home a cooler of fish by noon) or when you plunge in for a quick swim before dinner? Or maybe it's when you stretch out in the hammock to read — and watch the sun play on the water, listen to the birds visit in the woods.

No matter how you enjoy your lake — fishing, swimming, boating, relaxing — that use is, as some put it, "water quality dependent." Swimming is no fun when weeds wrap around your legs; yet a lake without vegetation loses its fish.

Weeds, sediment, and algae can all point to deteriorating water quality. And that translates to restrictions on the way you use your lake; for example, an invasion of nuisance weeds may destroy both swimming and boating. In turn, this loss becomes economic: swimmers and boaters spend their recreational dollars elsewhere, and ultimately, your property values decline.

The answer? Prevention. Don't wait until your boat keel drags on the bottom or algal blooms begin to cover the surface. You are responsible for your lake, not only for what happens along its shores but also for knowing what drains into it from the watershed.

So take ownership now. Use this guide to organize your lake community to protect your lake. Lake associations are vital to lake management, because protection and management must be a group effort. Pollution begins — and ends — with each one of us. One boat leaking oil or a single malfunctioning septic system contribute to a lake's decline.

The following pages take you from developing an organization to making it work, even to dealing with problems your lake may experience. Use the information applicable to your own situation; sources for additional information and assistance are listed in the book's appendices.

Not all is serious business — lake associations can be fun, too, and they can bond those who share the lake. So use this guide in good spirits. May it empower you to continue to enjoy your lake and all it offers you.

Contents

ACKNOWLEDGMENTS

We wish to thank the following individuals who reviewed this guide:

Mike Bira, *U.S. EPA Region VI, Dallas*

Franck Boynton, *Lake Salisbury Association, Va.*

Larry Butler, *Reston Association, Va.*

Richard Dameron, *Virginia Division of Soil and Water Conservation*

Tom Davenport, *U.S. EPA Region V, Chicago*

Joseph Eilers, *E&S Environmental Chemistry, Inc.*

Theresa A. Faber, *U.S. EPA Region II, New York*

Terri Hollingsworth, *U.S. EPA, Washington, DC*

Harry Judd, *Utah State Department of Health*

Lowell Klessig, *University of Wisconsin Extension-Stevens Point*

Anne E. Lyon, *Tennessee Valley Authority*

Barry Moore, *State of Washington Water Research Center*

David Rathke, *U.S. EPA Region VIII, Denver*

Donna Sefton, *U.S. EPA Region VII, Kansas City*

Jonathan Simpson, *North American Lake Management Society*

CHAPTER 1

Who Owns Your Lake?

There are lakes — and then there are lakes. In fact, some are reservoirs; others, ponds. Reservoirs and some ponds were built by damming rivers or streams. Do you live on a manmade or a natural lake? Who built it? Do you and your neighbors own it, or does it belong to the government? The answers to those questions determine the basic structure of your lake association — its powers, its funding, its functions.

Private lakes

Sometimes developments and subdivisions are built around lakes, either natural or constructed as part of the development. Once the development is completed, the builder usually turns over responsibility for management of all common areas to the property owners' organization set up by

covenants attached to the deed. In older developments, the lake may simply "exist," with no provisions for its management. So even if your homeowners' association bylaws don't mention your lake, be aware that you — not the township or county or some other governmental unit — are responsible for most lake management activities in your subdivision.

Public lakes

Your tax dollars manage these lakes and may have built them. But since you live close to the lake, you have a more personal concern for maintaining its integrity.

■ **Federal reservoirs:** Four major agencies build reservoirs, primarily to control flooding and generate power. Although the agencies manage the reservoirs, they work closely with citizens in encouraging public use and care of these waters and shores.

  ✔ Tennessee Valley Authority built reservoirs in the Southeast beginning in the 1930s, principally to generate power and control flooding.

  ✔ Bureau of Reclamation built reservoirs in the West to regulate water and generate power.

✔ U.S. Army Corps of Engineers built reservoirs throughout the country, primarily to prevent flooding.

✔ Soil Conservation Service built flood control and water supply structures throughout rural America.

■ **State lakes:** States own and manage many natural and manmade lakes. State laws and regulations apply to the use of these waters, and citizen participation in their management is vital.

■ **County/city lakes:** Often a lake is a major feature of a community park, and in some areas municipal reservoirs that supply city water also may be recreational centers. Many communities have millponds that originally generated power to saw logs or grind grain.

Your responsibility for your lake differs in a fundamental way, depending on whether you live on a private or public lake.

Private lake: You and your neighbors are <u>directly</u> responsible for maintaining a private lake: you make management decisions and contribute financially to its upkeep.

Public lake: Your responsibility is indirect — a tax-supported public agency makes management and financial decisions. Your responsibility for participating in management decisions for the resource is just as great, however, because you are a member of the public! Since a public agency cannot always specifically manage every lake in its jurisdiction, local initiative is crucial to protecting public lakes.

CHAPTER 2

Organizing to Protect Your Lake

Assuming responsibility for your lake is the first step; the next is to multiply your efforts by those of your neighbors. Lake associations formed by lakeside homeowners and other residents offer a cooperative way to significantly protect your lake. A formally organized group, bound by mutual goals, can be a strong representative voice for your lake within your community and state.

To truly make a difference in the quality of your lake, everyone in the lake community should participate — including the marina operator and the owners of the bait shop and other businesses that depend on the lake. Even nearby towns may have sufficient stake in the lake that their Chambers of Commerce might support your lake association.

An informal gathering of neighbors is often the first step in organizing an association. Focus on the nature of the lake's present or potential problems: select the issue that will be the most pertinent to the greatest number of residents, and discuss the resources that are available to address it. The meeting should end with a consensus on the pertinent issue and the need for an association, along with a timetable and plan for organization.

Before adjourning, select a chair and secretary and ask for volunteers to serve on a steering committee to draft bylaws and nominate officers and directors. Sample bylaws are included in Appendix A.

The charter meeting

The charter meeting brings together the steering committee and the lake community to decide if they want to form a lake association.

To organize this first general meeting, the steering committee should:

- Schedule it at a time convenient for most people in the lake community.

- Select a central meeting place with adequate seating and parking; if possible, tentatively reserve it for a subsequent meeting. VFW halls, hotels, local restaurants, church halls, and public buildings are possible meeting sites.

- Compile a mailing list of all property owners, using municipal maps and tax rolls.

- Put together a real campaign, focusing on your pertinent issue:
  - ✔ Announce the meeting and notify residents by mail, telephone, and newspaper articles;
  - ✔ Follow up this publicity with door-to-door visits to encourage a good turnout; and

✔ Distribute copies of the proposed bylaws before the meeting, so that the community will be fully informed.

• Check to see if you need microphones or audiovisual equipment such as videoplayers and slide or overhead projectors. The size of the meeting facility and the number of people you expect determine audiovisual needs.

• Arrange for a welcome table with a sign-up sheet (see the next section) and name badges.

• Arrange to serve simple refreshments after the meeting. Members of the steering committee might agree to contribute chips and punch or split the expense (perhaps the marina owner could get you a good deal on soft drinks).

Your general meeting could proceed in the following way:

• Call to order by temporary chair of meeting.

• Present purpose of meeting and introduce steering committee.

• Present report of organizing group's initial meeting(s).

• Discuss/vote to adopt bylaws based on steering committee's recommendations.

- Elect officers according to bylaws. President-elect chairs the meeting after the election.

- Discuss association activities (keep brief).

- Appoint committees and plan membership drive.

- Establish a mailing address for the association. This could be the president's or secretary's home or office or a post office box.

- Set a date and place for the next meeting and adjourn.

■ **Parliamentary procedures:** A set of rules to run meetings can allow everyone to be heard and make decisions with a minimum of confusion. Robert's Rules of Order are the basic guidelines used by most organizations. This book is available in most bookstores and your library (see Appendix C).

■ **Guest speaker:** Although not essential at the charter meeting, the right speaker may be a draw. Choose your speaker carefully; a representative from another lake association or a technical expert who could speak briefly and answer questions about your pertinent issue might be helpful. Local consultants, college professors and other teachers, and representatives of state and federal agencies may be well qualified as well as interested in speaking to your group.

　　Contact your speaker well in advance of the meeting so that the publicity can describe the program. Above all, your speaker must understand the importance of tailoring his/her presentation to the introductory nature of the meeting.

■ **Sign-up sheet:** You need to know who's interested in the association. Have a sign-up sheet at the welcome table (where people will fill out name badges). Ask for the following information: name, address, telephone number, family composition, principal occupation(s), and specific interests in the association or project. Encourage people to check off or write in lake issues they consider important and committees they would be interested in joining.

Legal and tax issues

Once you have decided to formally organize, you need to decide how to set up the association according to local and federal law. The following discussion is intended as a general overview of legal and tax issues for organizing and operating a lake association, not as a complete description of legal and tax regulations. Consult a tax accountant or attorney about how to organize with the proper authorities. You may want to seek out lake property owners who have this expertise or who could recommend legal and tax professionals.

Stewardship versus profitability

Lake associations are typically organized as either not-for-profit or profit-making corporations. By far the majority of them are nonprofit. One of the principal differences between the two organizations is their reasons for existence. In simple terms, the ultimate objective of a for-profit organization is to realize a net profit for its stockholders; whereas, the objective for a nonprofit organization is to meet some socially desirable need of its community or its members.

As long as a nonprofit group has sufficient resources to accomplish its objectives, the only justification for having excess income over expenses is to provide for its programs when revenues can't meet those needs. In contrast, if commercial organizations are profitable, they will probably be able to finance their cash needs through loans or from investors.

There are many benefits to organizing as a nonprofit organization. Nonprofit status means an organization is exempt from income tax, although even "exempt" organizations can be subject to tax on certain portions of their income. Nonprofits also qualify for lower bulk mailing rates.

Most nonprofit organizations fall under the Internal Revenue Service "501(c)3" exemption. This refers to the section of the internal revenue code dealing with tax exempt corporations. Organizations exempt under section 501(c)3 can have four basic purposes:

- religious,
- charitable,

- scientific, and

- educational.

Lake organizations are normally considered scientific and educational organizations.

Initial incorporation

You first need to prepare articles of incorporation and bylaws and submit them to the proper authorities. These are legal documents and should be tailored to the specific requirements of the governing authority (see Appendix A for a sample).

The association typically incorporates in the state where its members reside.

IRS registration

Once you have incorporated, you should apply to the IRS for a tax identification number. This is a very simple form that registers the organization with the federal government in much the same way as an individual is registered with a social security number.

At the same time, if you plan to be nonprofit, you may also apply to the IRS for tax exempt status. This is a more difficult process that often requires the help of an attorney or tax accountant. After reviewing the materials submitted, the IRS normally sends a provisional "exemption" letter confirming tax exempt status. The exemption is usually good for five years, during which you are normally required to file annual information returns. This is usually Form 990 and includes information on income, receipts, contributions, disbursements, assets, liabilities, and names and addresses of substantial contributors. Organizations normally having gross receipts of $25,000 or less are exempt from filing Form 990.

The state may also have similar, if often simpler, application and reporting requirements. Washington, for example, has none because it has no income tax. In most states, however, you must file with the Secretary of State.

Contact your state department of revenue for specific
information.

Accounting

Maintaining adequate financial records is essential for
assuring the success of your association. Remember — whether
for-profit or nonprofit, your organization is a business and
should be run as such. Except for a large association that
employs a full-time bookkeeper, an organization's treasurer
normally "keeps the books." This entails keeping a checkbook,
recording all disbursements, receipts, and miscellaneous
transactions in a ledger, and maintaining savings accounts or
other investments.

Most nonprofit lake organizations follow five accounting
principles that differ from those used by most businesses:

■ **Cash instead of accrual accounting:** The association
   must decide which accounting method to select. The simplest
   method — cash accounting — records only cash transactions
   (just like a checkbook). Unpaid bills are not recorded. In
   contrast, the accrual basis takes non-cash factors (such as
   unpaid bills) into account and usually gives a more accurate
   picture of an organization's financial condition. Because of
   its complexity, it is often used only by medium and large
   organizations.

■ **Fund accounting:** This accounting concept separates cash
   and other assets into categories according to the restrictions
   placed on their use. For example, a lake organization may
   set up a fund to be used only for periodic dredging of the
   lake sediments or emergency repair of the dam. Commercial
   operations do not normally use this method, but it is
   essential to the operation of most associations.

■ **Treatment of fixed assets:** This is how an organization
   records its assets. For example, an asset can be depreciated
   over its useful life or written off and then capitalized on the
   balance sheet. Each situation must be examined and treated
   according to the method that makes the most sense.

■ **Transfers and appropriations:** Transfers are frequently made between funds, and appropriations are made from a fund for specific uses. It is important that these transfers and appropriations are properly treated and accurately recorded on financial statements.

■ **Contributions and pledges:** Rarely received by commercial operations, this type of transaction is more common to lake associations. How it is treated is often confusing, particularly for non-cash contributions.

The treasurer familiar with commercial financial accounting and reporting should have no difficulty keeping the books of a lake association once these five accounting principles are understood. See Appendix C for helpful references.

At the end of the association's fiscal year, the treasurer should compile an annual financial report to be distributed to all members — ideally, it should be part of an overall annual report of the association's activities.

Lake districts

Some states, including Wisconsin, Minnesota, Virginia, Washington, and New York, have passed legislation to allow the formation of lake improvement or management districts. This is a joint state-local partnership that gives local lake property owners a strong organization with legal authority to assume more comprehensive management of the lake and powers to assess costs for projects that benefit the lake community.

In general, lake districts have the power to

- Make contracts,
- Hold real estate,
- Disburse monies,
- Tax property within the district, and
- Perform lake management activities, including studying and treating lake problems, diverting or removing nutrients, dam maintenance, and dredging.

Some states allow lake districts to seek sanitary powers from town boards to provide such services as public sewers and water, garbage removal, regulation of septic tanks, and storm water drainage. In Washington, sewer districts (whether or not they actually construct sewers) provide more flexibility for lake management than actual lake management districts, which are difficult to establish.

Residents and property owners within a lake district vote on major decisions, including the budget, at the district's annual meeting. Between meetings, the district is governed by a board whose members are determined by the original legislation. A lake district usually operates under a set of bylaws that establishes procedures for the annual meeting and duties of the board.

Districts may or may not have regulatory powers over the land or water; if not, members can work with local authorities to enact ordinances.

If your state has enacted such legislation and you want to form a lake district, put together a group to investigate the benefits and responsibilities of such an organization and the actual steps in activating a district. The next step is usually to draw up a map of the proposed lake district and hold a meeting of the lake community and county and state agencies. At this point, your group may be able to form a lake district by voting to do so, or you may have to apply to a county or state board.

Other public/private partnerships

■ **Commissions or agencies:** When a need obviously exists, many cities and counties permit formation of commissions or agencies to manage a lake. For example, a group of lake property owners in Connecticut petitioned their city to become a city commission that would be an advisory board to the city council concerning the lake. This commission has no taxing or police powers — but it does have legal standing, local press coverage, city insurance, and access to the city's copy machines, mailing services, and meeting rooms. Plus a line item appropriation in the city budget to conduct lake management activities.

- **Multi-town lake authority:** Some states allow two (or more) towns that border the same lake to form a lake authority that acts as an agent for the towns on lake management issues and projects. The member towns contribute to the authority's budget and interested lake residents volunteer to serve on the authority's board.

  Based on the same concept under which communities cooperate to maintain fire departments and ambulance services, the lake authority could also be applied to lakes that cut across state borders.

- **Informal partnerships:** The many lake associations with no taxing or regulatory authority usually work with their city/county governments on an ad hoc basis to secure grants and other funds to solve lake problems.

  Forming a partnership with your local government — even becoming a quasi-governmental unit — can significantly strengthen your association. It may also mean a trade-off between subjecting your organization to governmental restrictions and retaining your freedom and flexibility as an independent group.

Funding

How you pay your bills depends largely on what bills you decide to incur. In other words, your association's goals and objectives will drive the budget — which, in turn, will drive your funding structure.

If yours is a publicly-owned lake, the budget and financing for maintaining the lake itself have been set by a government unit. But if you live on a private lake, your property owners association is responsible for maintaining your lake.

Beyond this basic responsibility, however, your association — no matter whether your lake is private or public — may choose to support many community activities, some related to protecting the lake (such as monitoring) and others purely social.

Lake associations use various funding mechanisms (limited only by members' creativity and legal restrictions):

- **Dues:** set at a reasonable level — either flat rate or prorated — and usually paid annually.

- **Property owner assessments:** prorated shares for major work, such as repairing a dam.

- **Taxes:** some states permit local lake districts to levy up to a certain rate to manage their lake.

- **Government grants:** Over the past decade, more than 400 publicly-owned lakes have used state grants from EPA's Clean Lakes Program to restore their lakes (for a fuller description, see Chapter 5. Similar funds are available through other federal agencies (the Corps of Engineers, for example) and from state natural resource departments.

- **Foundations:** Private foundations, particularly those focused on environmental issues, often will assist financially with a specific lake project.

- **Industry/corporations:** The dominant business in your nearby community may be interested in helping preserve the recreational opportunities your lake offers, particularly if the corporation sees the lake as beneficial to its employees.

- **Fundraisers:** annual festivals, contests, boat races, gigantic collective garage sales, formal benefits — your association's treasury is limited only by your imagination.

Insurance

Lake associations usually try to carry two types of insurance: directors' and officers' (commonly referred to as D&O) and liability. Some states, such as Wisconsin, provide legal protection for directors and officers of nonprofit organizations. Before completely relying on state protection, find out exactly what it covers; you may want supplemental policies.

The Community Association Institute (1423 Powhatan St., Alexandria, VA 22314; (703) 548-8600) has outlined several provisions to look for when you're considering a D&O policy:

- **Coverage of the volunteer:** committee members, review boards, etc.

- **Policy limit:** do you or the company dictate the limit?

- **Defense and settlement:** can you choose your own defense counsel in the event of a claim?

- **Employee suits:** are suits such as discrimination and wrongful termination covered?

- **Libel and slander:** does the policy cover association publications and presentations by board members?

- **Nonmonetary defense:** does the policy cover costs associated with defending nonmonetary claims?

- **Warranty and severability:** will misrepresentations by previous board members void the policy?

Both because of the trend toward litigation today and the nature of activities around a lake, insurance can be expensive and difficult to obtain. For example, because the cost is so high, lake associations generally do not carry insurance on dam breaks. State laws control insurance carriers so you should contact your local insurance agents — perhaps one belongs to your association — for information on all aspects of insurance for your association and its directors.

CHAPTER 3

Building Membership

A lake association needs a broad membership base to operate successfully. Ideally, membership would include 100 percent of eligible residents; practically, you should strive for a majority of lakeshore property owners and those with direct lake interests, such as marina owners and operators. Moreover, larger memberships give lake associations credibility and a stronger voice when dealing with municipal, county, and state agencies.

Although the membership message is clear and strong — we all have a personal stake in protecting this lake — only a few people will join the association on their own. Therefore, to build membership, a lake association needs one or more designated, active membership recruiters, reinforced by every member spreading the word among their neighbors.

Suggestions for recruiting members follow.

Direct mail solicitations

Use the list you compiled before the charter meeting and recheck it annually with the county recorder of deeds to identify new property owners (including those with undeveloped lots). Mail only to those who have not yet joined (or, in future years, who have not renewed).

If your mailing list exceeds 200, you will want to apply to your local office for a nonprofit bulk mailing permit (to qualify, you must be a nonprofit 301(c)(3) organization). You can use this permit for all association mailings, including newsletters. Nonprofit bulk rate is approximately one third standard first class rate, but you must mail at least 200 pieces presorted (and rubber-banded) by zip code at any one time. The post office will give you complete instructions for using this permit as well as mail bags and rubber bands.

Your membership solicitation should include:

- A flyer, letter, or brochure that succinctly explains the benefits of joining the lake association.

- A membership form to be completed by the addressee and returned to the association. This form should include space for name, address, amount of dues, and other information the association would like, such as how much time members spend at the lake, whether homes are rented during the season, what committee (or other chore) members are interested in. Specify how the form should be returned.

- Options for membership forms (as your financial base grows): (1) a tear-off membership card that can be filled out and retained by the member; (2) a preprinted, postage paid, business reply envelope in which the member returns forms and dues.

Welcome packages

To take advantage of new property owners' enthusiasm about the lake, put together a package to welcome them to the area with a map and description of the lake, a sample lake association newsletter (when you have one), a fact sheet on lake water quality and pollution threats, and a personally signed invitation to join the association (together with membership forms).

House-to-house membership drives

Canvass house-to-house during summer weekends and holidays when most property owners are at home. Canvassers should be armed with membership forms (and a pen), newsletters, an envelope to store dues payments, and enthusiasm. Divide the area into sections, with teams assigned to each. Canvassing may have to be repeated periodically until each property owner has been contacted.

Articles in local press

Photos of the 9-year-old fishing derby winner (with his fish, of course) or of the biggest bass caught on the lake that summer, announcements of new association officers and special events — newsworthy stories make good press and reinforce interest in your association. And they're one of the best ways to communicate with your own members: everybody loves seeing stories about their community and friends in print or on the tube.

Lake activities

Distribute membership forms at special fun days your association organizes — and use this opportunity to educate people about taking care of their lake and how both they and their association figure in the scenario.

CHAPTER 4

Making Your Association Work

Volunteers make a lake association work. They keep the records and perform other administrative duties, assist with managing the lake, and basically energize the association.

To break the workload into manageable tasks, associations usually form specific committees. For instance, committees on membership, publicity, protecting water quality, property use, and weed control. All committees report to the lake association's officers and are governed by the organization's bylaws.

Communicating with members

■ **Newsletters.** This is the primary way to keep members aware of and interested in the lake. Newsletters should be produced at least twice a year — larger organizations put one out quarterly and sometimes monthly during the summer. Newsletters can range from simple, two-page photocopies to more sophisticated material produced on a computer. You will need a dedicated editor (or two) who is an enthusiastic lake supporter and other members who will keep an eye open for pertinent articles that can be excerpted. Don't overlook another association's newsletters and be sure to credit any news source or ask for reprint permission. A winter update on lake issues, especially for members who are summer residents, can keep interest alive and build a feeling of community.

Associations with tax-exempt status can mail materials at low, nonprofit bulk rates (see the earlier discussion of direct mail solicitations for more details). Since newsletters are dues-financed, they should be carefully budgeted for cost per issue and per member.

■ **Local media.** Notify the local paper/radio/tv of association events and people news. Seeing "their lake" on the tube or the front page stimulates pride of ownership among your members and reinforces the credibility of the association.

■ **Questionnaires.** These can be a useful way to get readings on all sorts of association issues, from meeting times to pollution problems. And, to stress the fact that members' opinions are important, report their responses (but no names) in the newsletter. Feedback is essential if a lake association is to respond to the needs and interests of its membership.

■ **Membership records.** Good recordkeeping is essential to an association. Members can be lost by not checking addresses yearly or by using an outdated newsletter mailing list. Records of dues payments should be kept accurately, with reminders sent out promptly.

Personal computers with their simple database programs are an essential tool for any organization today. They expedite mailings, membership tracking and record-keeping, and budgeting. Scan your membership: surely someone with access to a PC will be willing to help the association establish its own computerized base.

■ **Meetings.** Most lake associations have one or more meetings during the summer that combine both business and social functions. To make an annual meeting both interesting and productive, be sure to

✔ **Give members plenty of notice**. If you can, hold the annual meeting the same day in the same month each year, but send notices at least a month ahead as reminders.

✔ **Put together an agenda to keep things moving.** (This is usually done by the board of directors and officers beforehand.) Key agenda items are usually listed on the notice; however, many meeting chairs ask if there are additional topics at the outset, so members with special concerns can make sure these issues are covered.

✔ **Keep the meeting between one to two hours long.**
If the agenda is short, put together a complementary
educational program that speaks to your association's
particular interests. If the agenda is long, have
committees report with various recommendations to
clarify and resolve the issues.

✔ **Be fair.** The chair should make sure that everyone has
adequate time to voice opinions while not allowing the
meeting to degenerate into pointless discussion. The
chair should understand and observe the bylaws, allow
equal time for all points of view, and vote only to break
ties.

✔ **Lead the discussion.** The board of directors should
have budget recommendations ready and be prepared to
offer motions, stimulate discussion, and develop
consensus.

Many meetings end with a social get-together, such as
refreshments, which reinforces the community aspect of the
association and gives everyone a chance to renew
acquaintances.

■ **Board Meetings.** Have regular and frequent board
meetings. Publicize them and invite other members,
including board member spouses, to attend. Encourage
involvement by everyone. And recognize members'
contributions with special awards. Make sure that meetings
are reported in the newsletter.

Typical lake association activities

- Monitoring water quality,

- Stocking fish and surveying populations,

- Removing weeds and algae,

- Operating and maintaining dams,

- Developing and maintaining boat landings and picnic sites,

- Putting up boating and other advisory signs,

- Picking up litter and debris,

- Protecting shorelines,

- Dealing with conflict between uses of the lake, and

- Speaking for members before town, school, and county boards and planning and zoning committees.

Special celebrations are part of living by a lake, be they individual families gathering on Memorial Day and the Fourth of July or lakewide boat races and fairs. The ideas for such special events are limited only by members' imagination (and energy!) and can be used to encourage awareness of the lake resource:

- **Boat parades or races:** build them on themes such as boating safety or lake ecology and distribute pertinent materials.

- **Fishing derbies for children 15 or under:** distribute materials describing the local fish populations.

- **Ice fishing contests in winter (on northern lakes):** include information about local fish on registration forms.

- **Trash pickup day:** ask a hauler to donate a bin. And give out information on recycling.

- **Aquatic weed harvest day:** residents can help harvest weeds and haul them to a predetermined site where they can also add leaves to the mix. If the pile is large enough, bring in a backhoe to turn the mulch for composting. In the spring, residents can take composted material for their gardens.

Obviously, this lake in Washington state has a weed problem.

Yes, preparing and distributing materials takes time — but it will pay off in more educated use of your lake resources. Sources of many of these materials are listed at the end of this guide; you will also find locally oriented information from your county Extension Service and state fish and wildlife agency.

Another factor to consider is publicity. Yours may be a subdivision lake community that doesn't want outside interest. On the other hand, if your public lake needs funding for a project, special events can help build the public support you seek.

Lake Managers

Lake associations don't just happen — and neither do all the activities described. Welding a group of lake property owners into a cohesive group requires management: specifically, one person assuming the management role.

Many lake associations have volunteer lake managers who may not have credentials in aquatic sciences but are willing to spend time administering necessary tasks involved with the lake and the association. Larger lakes that have a strong financial base and multiple problems hire professional lake managers and, often, a staff. In still other situations, particularly planned communities with several small lakes and other common areas, a professional manages the entire community.

Whether your manager is volunteer or paid, every day he/she can expect to deal with a wide variety of challenges, among them:

- revenue and budgets,

- insurance,

- bidding and contractors,

- volunteers (and personnel when the association is large),

- consultants,

- liaison with the county, city, and state,

- maintenance — of the lake, equipment, docks, and so forth,

- safety,

- dam condition and safety,

- watershed management, including erosion,

- floating debris,

- monitoring,

- lake problems: weeds and their harvesting, fish stocking, nutrients, gypsy moths.

If your lake association reaches the point where it needs a professional manager, you should look for individuals who meet the following basic criteria:

- Either a bachelor's or higher degree with lake management course work, plus full-time experience in lake management following attainment of that degree (preferably a minimum of two years); or

- Demonstrated experience in lake management of five or more years.

The North American Lake Management Society is issuing professional certifications to lake managers who meet basically the same criteria and renew their certification regularly through continuing education.

Contact your state university for a list of acceptable lake management courses.

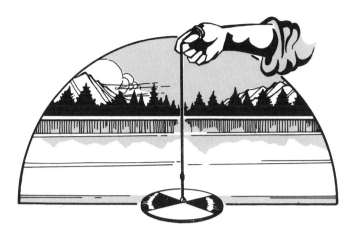

CHAPTER 5

Managing Your Lake

As lake association members, you must educate yourselves — and the rest of the lake community — about the natural processes that affect your lake. To do this, start with the watershed, the drainage area or basin from which all land and water areas flow toward a central collector at a lower elevation — which, in this case, is your lake.

Understanding Natural Lake Processes

The quality of your lake's water is directly affected by drainage from the watershed. If the area around the watershed is farmed, agricultural fertilizers, pesticides, and manure can wash into the lake, raising the nutrient and sediment levels and stimulating weed and algae growth. Severe erosion can result from logging or land development, producing inflows of sediment that can affect water depth and color. And runoff from cities in your watershed brings everything from pet wastes to pesticides, atmospheric pollutants to zinc.

To protect your lake you need to know how the land is used in your watershed and what activities may be generating pollution.

Your first step — and an excellent initial project for the association — is to map your watershed. Start with a map from the U.S. Geological Survey (see Appendix C for ordering instructions). Take it to your local Soil Conservation Service office or soil conservation district and ask them to help you locate current land uses on the map. Then create a transparent map overlay showing farms and industry, towns and parks — everything that's happening in the watershed. Include wetlands and other sensitive areas as well as city and industrial wastewater discharge points.

Look at how your watershed is zoned and the potential for zoning changes. Determine soil type, the amount of paved land. Contact your state Clean Lakes coordinator (see Appendix B) for information about the potential for lake problems in your area. The coordinator is an excellent source for materials and suggestions on managing your lake: that's the nature of the job!

Once you have located your lake in its watershed, look at the lake itself:

- Where does the water come from? Inventory its inlets and outlets.

- How big is your lake?

- How deep is it? How old?

- What kind of shoreline does it have (steep, eroding, vegetated)?

- What plants and animals live in and around it?

- What is its basic water quality?

- How many people live on the lake and nearby?

- Are they year-round residents?

- Are septic systems the principal waste disposal facility? How old are they? How well maintained?

- How is the lake currently used? Are these uses affected in any way?

- Is the watershed under development? Or are other land use changes anticipated?

The more you know about your lake, the better equipped you will be to keep it healthy or take measures to restore it.

Assessing the community's goals

At the first general meeting, discuss how the community views and intends to use the lake. Follow this with a questionnaire to each household. Will recreation be the primary use? If so, define what you mean by "recreation": swimming, powerboating, fishing—or a combination of activities? Or do most of you view this lake as an aesthetic resource, to be enjoyed as a scenic addition to your property?

Select goals for using the lake that are consistent with the lake's capabilities and the community's preferences. You may need some professional guidance here, particularly if you have conflicting goals: a perfectly clear lake is a swimmer's paradise, a fisherman's nightmare.

Planning the use of a lake is a vital management step. Planning can actually improve uses by considering how people and animals consume the space in and around the lake. Three basic phases are involved: (1) developing a plan, (2) putting the plan into effect, and (3) measuring progress.

The following steps (see article by Engel in Appendix C) should be incorporated in forming a lake use plan:

First Steps	Second Steps
Define all problems	Rank and select problems
Set realistic goals	Choose a mission
Evaluate all methods	Form treatment strategies
Set a time table	Seek funding
Assemble into written plan	Monitor and revise

Although complicated by problems bred of diverse uses, lake use planning can actually help solve conflicts by building a consensus among competing interests. The key to accomplishing this is educating the lake community through a strong informational network: the same newsletters, surveys, and other media you use to routinely communicate can be a strong asset in both assessing your lake community's interests and determining the uses of your lake.

A lake association should also consider long-term ecological goals. Think about the effects from lakeshore development, including docks, boathouses, and marinas, and the problems that usually accompany a denser population. How will additional development affect recreational use of the water and water quality? How will the shoreline look? What measures can you take to ensure that new septic systems are installed properly? Think ahead, even if your lake seems healthy today.

Defining & solving problems

Once you understand the influences on your lake and how you want to use it, problems that affect those uses will usually be spelled out as well. Is the focus on algal blooms and nuisance weeds? Septic systems or lawn fertilizers might be at fault.

Or are people worried about powerboating interfering with fishing? Then you are dealing with surface water conflicts.

When your lake develops a problem that is beyond your association's level of expertise, collect data to define the area of concern, hold a meeting to secure member support for future actions, and form a special committee to identify additional information and sources of help. Several suggested resources are listed in Appendices B and C.

Invite your county extension agent to visit your lake and advise you on handling the problem; your local soil and water conservation district and the state Clean Lakes coordinator are also valuable resources. The committee should take advantage of their expertise and also explore similar services and visit with knowledgeable personnel in the city and county governments.

Profile the problem(s) in detail. If the problem is weeds, what type and density are they? Be as thorough and accurate as possible and remember that your indepth research will make the ultimate decisions easier. If the problem seems overly technical, your committee may ask for a general meeting to vote on using funds for a professional evaluation.

Consider the problem's symptoms and causes, and the actions that might have produced them. When developing a plan to manage the problem, put together a set of alternative methods. You may need professional help with this; the guidance and regulations for EPA's Clean Lakes Program can be particularly helpful (see Appendix D).

Determine each method's strengths and weaknesses, cost, and the information needed to implement it properly. How long will it take to implement the plan and how long will it be effective? Some of the best solutions combine both short- and long-term methods. Cover everything thoroughly so you will be using the most effective management technique to solve your problem.

Set realistic objectives and a timetable for each phase of the plan and have one committee or association member be in charge of implementing each step.

Present the plan at an association meeting (if possible, print copies for the membership to read ahead of time) and allow a period for review and discussion. If you have used professional advice, ask the consultant to be on hand to field more technical questions. Have the membership vote on the plan and the budget to put it into action.

Consultants

A consultant is a professional who works independently, with a firm, or with a university or nonprofit organization and is paid for providing specific services, information, or training.

To select a consultant, ask the agencies and people who've helped you define the problem to recommend individuals or firms who are qualified to work on this specific project.

Riprapping a shoreline to prevent bank erosion.

Next, develop a detailed problem statement and work plan and send them to recommended consultants, asking each to submit a proposal.

Before finally selecting your consultant, establish a set of criteria that encompass the following areas:

- Experience and technical competence in the services required,

- Record of performance,

- Ability to do work within a reasonable time,

- Knowledge of the type of problems that are part of your project, and

- References.

Choose your final candidates, have them make separate oral presentations, and then narrow down the field. After you have selected the most qualified applicant, negotiate the scope of the work, budget, and the schedule. Again, rely upon your state Clean Lakes coordinator and local advisors for assistance.

Further information about hiring a consultant is available in *The Lake and Reservoir Restoration Guidance Manual*, second edition, published in 1990 by the U.S. Environmental Protection Agency (see Appendix C).

Making the plan work

Factors vital to the success of your plan:

- A realistic timetable,

- A person or group to oversee the job and carry it out,

- Permits from the proper authorities,

- Accurate records at every stage (photograph the area initially, then on an ongoing basis for newsletters and meetings),

- Periodic evaluations and adjustments as needed, at least annually, and

- Frequent reports to the membership.

Update your plan as needed to keep it current with changing conditions. Once solved, many problems simply need monitoring; others require modifications of how the lake is used.

Funding a plan

Publicly-owned lakes have access to a variety of local, state, and federal grants. Since many require a local match, the fundraising process may be similar for both public and private lakes.

■ **Local funding.** Many voluntary associations fund lake projects by time-honored activities: member dues, auctions, raffles, and flea markets. As described earlier, in some states property owners living on lakes can form lake districts with taxing power.

A private lake association followed a consultant's advice to build this retaining wall.

✔ **Bylaw provisions:** (1) your association may be based on covenants in your deed that permit invoicing members on an annual basis; (2) a one-time, special assessment may also be voted on by the membership or the board of directors; or (3) certain funds may be set aside for such inevitabilities as dam repair (this is especially common in bylaws for privately owned lakes).

Other funding can include private donations, grants from private foundations, and user fees. Call your local planning commission for additional information.

■ **State funding.** Publicly-owned lakes can apply to county and state governments for grants. Most states have their own Clean Lakes programs, usually modeled on the federal program. Large associations have formed task forces with local, state, and government agencies to study the problem and find solutions and funding. You must keep in mind, however, that state sources of funding vary according to the economic climate and that your association will be expected to cost share with the state agency. Your state's environmental or natural resources department can give you additional information on funding sources.

■ **Federal funding.** Publicly-owned lakes can also apply for grants from the federal Clean Lakes Program, which is administered by the U.S. Environmental Protection Agency. EPA enters into these cooperative assistance agreements with states, so your first step here is to contact your state Clean Lakes coordinator. This cooperative assistance is cost shared: the state match may be in-kind services, an option that strongly encourages the involvement of local organizations such as your association. Clean Lakes assistance is offered on three levels:

> ✔ **Phase I** (for a diagnostic feasibility study of a lake's problems) is 70 percent federal/30 percent state-local cost share.

> ✔ **Phase II** (for implementing projects recommended by Phase I) is a 50/50 match.

> ✔ **Phase III** (for monitoring completed restoration projects) is also a 50/50 match.

Other federal agencies also offer grants and advisory services. Contact the local or main offices of the Tennessee Valley Authority and the Departments of Agriculture (Extension Service and Soil Conservation Service), Defense (Army Corps of Engineers), and Interior (Fish and Wildlife Service and Bureau of Reclamation).

Legally protecting your lake

Your association can cooperate with local, state, and federal officials to develop regulations that will protect your lake in three general ways:

• Regulate immediate watershed activities that can cause erosion and pollution;

- Control development to protect the shoreline and general aesthetics; and

- Regulate use of the lake to reduce surface water conflicts.

Most permits and ordinances that relate to watershed activities and land development are the province of the local municipality. The state and federal governments become involved in some projects, such protecting wetlands, shorelands, and floodplains from intensive development.

Know the law — and apply it to your lake's needs. Your association should propose ordinances as well as document problems. It is your responsibility to understand your local codes and regulations and therefore be an intelligent advocate for your association when conferring with local boards.

Because a healthy lake is an aesthetic and economic asset to a community, local governments often divert some tax monies toward stricter enforcement of existing laws or an expanded water quality monitoring program.

Regulating use of the lake can result in many conflicts about surface water use. That's why it is important to assess your community's choices of lake uses. Then you can work purposefully with local government to adopt ordinances that separate activities to different areas or times of day. You may want to institute local regulations through your state or community for:

- Docks, moorings, and boathouses,

- Fisheries,

- Boating (including safety, motor size and speed, uses, and noise levels),

- Public access, or

- Other uses, including those discussed earlier.

Monitoring the status of your lake

You can set up a water quality monitoring program and take simple, effective measurements that can identify the status of your lake's water quality and indicate any changes that might affect the use of your lake. This section of your practical guide will give only an overview of monitoring. For further, indepth information, we refer you to *Volunteer Water Monitoring: A Guide For State Managers* and *Volunteer Lake Monitoring: A Methods Manual*, both published by the U.S. Environmental Protection Agency.

■ **Planning Your Monitoring Program.** You must first set the general goals for your program. What are you primarily interested in:

   ✔ Providing data to local or state agencies,

   ✔ Educating your members or the public about water quality issues, or

   ✔ Building a group of involved association members?

All three goals can be incorporated into your program, but you should decide which has priority.

Next, identify the data users; these can include state and local agencies, universities, and federal agencies such as the U.S. Fish and Wildlife Service. Ask these organizations to participate in a planning committee to help you develop a volunteer monitoring program. Once this group is established, it should meet periodically to evaluate, fine-tune, and update your program.

Establish a regular, ongoing training program for your volunteer monitors. Build that all-important quality assurance and control into the entire monitoring system by insisting that every volunteer exercise responsibility for:

   ✔ being precise, accurate, and thorough in every monitoring action,

   ✔ taking a representative sampling of conditions, and

   ✔ using the same procedures wherever and whenever samples are taken.

Since you can't monitor for every condition found in your lake, focus your efforts on the lake condition that seems most troubling. Some of the most prevalent conditions that are usually induced by human activity are

✔ Increased growth of algae,

✔ Increased growth of rooted aquatic plants,

✔ Lower dissolved oxygen concentrations (particularly near the lake bottom),

✔ Increased turbidity and sediment accumulation,

✔ Decreased clarity of water, and

✔ Decreased water depth.

■ **Monitoring for algae.** Algae are small aquatic plants that occur as single cells, colonies, or filaments and are sometimes known as pond scums. Although an essential link in the lake's food chain, when their growth mushrooms algae can become a nuisance and affect lake use.

An increase in nutrients (such as inflows of fertilizer-laden runoff and nutrients from malfunctioning septic systems) is one of the factors that affect algal growth and produce what are called algal "blooms." This condition can give water an unpleasant color, odor, and taste as well destroy its clarity. Mats of algae can clog water intakes, foul beaches, and generally ruin recreation in the water.

Three parameters are commonly used to measure algal conditions:

✔ Water transparency (by using a Secchi disk),

✔ Chlorophyll a (the green pigment found in algal cells), and

✔ Phosphorus and nitrogen (indicates water fertility).

■ **Monitoring for aquatic plants.** Too many aquatic plants may affect your use and enjoyment of the lake, although some are good habitat and food for fish and wildlife. Submergent, emergent, rooted floating-leaved, and free-floating plants are all important to the ecology of the lake.

Luke Wandell lowers his Secchi disk into Blue Lake, Michigan.

Organic matter and sediment flowing off the watershed stimulate growth of aquatic plants. Often, exotic plants (that originated in other continents) are introduced into the lake and grow profusely, crowding out native species. Aquariums that are dumped into the lake can be a source of these plants. They also move on boats trailered from lake to lake.

You can characterize the aquatic plant conditions in your lake by:

✔ Mapping the plant beds,

✔ Estimating plant density in a selected area, and

✔ Collecting specimens and having them identified by a professional botanist.

■ **Monitoring dissolved oxygen.** The amount of dissolved oxygen in a lake affects the type of organisms that live there and therefore is an indicator of general water quality. Trout need consistently high concentrations of oxygen to survive, so, if you are an angler, you might be especially interested in monitoring for this condition.

A number of factors affect the amount of oxygen in a lake, including:

✔ Climate,

✔ Water temperature,

✔ Wind and waves,

✔ Amount of oxygen being used by algae, aquatic plants, bacteria, invertebrates, and other respiring aquatic life, such as fish,

✔ The rate at which organic matter sinks to the bottom and decomposes,

✔ Oxygen content of incoming groundwater and surface streams,

✔ Human activities in the lake and watershed, and

✔ The shape and depth of the lake's basin.

You can monitor dissolved oxygen by using:

✔ **A dissolved oxygen field kit.** You take a water sample and immediately analyze it by using precise quantitites of several chemicals. To get meaningful results, you must sample according to a strict procedure.

✔ **A submersible oxygen meter.** You may find this a more convenient method. To measure oxygen, you lower a thermistor and oxygen probe on a calibrated cable through the water. At specified intervals, you read and record the temperature and dissolved oxygen concentration.

Field kits take more time to use, but meters are more expensive.

Since monitoring for any of these conditions requires going out on the lake in a boat, you should always use good common sense about weather conditions and boating safety.

Maintaining dams

Most lake associations are responsible for the dam that creates their lake. Dams are typically built of either native soils from the site or concrete. From 1977 through 1981, the U.S. Army Corps of Engineers instituted the National Dam Safety Program to inspect and inventory all existing dams, which were put into three classes corresponding to the hazard potentials if the dam fails:

■ **Class I:** Probable loss of life; excessive economic loss

■ **Class II:** Possible loss of life; appreciable economic loss

■ **Class III:** No loss of life expected; minimal economic loss

After finishing the program, the Corps turned the information over to the states to use in their dam safety programs.

Your state may require a permit to operate your dam that is renewed periodically, depending upon the hazard classification. The initial inspection and frequency of reinspection depends on such factors as condition of the dam and its size, type, location, and the downstream hazard potential. Some states require that a licensed professional engineer perform the inspection.

Most associations have members who check the dam periodically throughout the year and within 24 hours after flooding. Keep an accurate and complete file of all inspections.

You must maintain a dam year-round, not just during the warmer months. At a minimum, maintenance for earthen dams can include

- Checking for excessive seepage or saturation,

- Checking for internal erosion,

- Maintaining principal and emergency spillways,

- Keeping the spillways clear of debris,

- Restoring and reseeding eroded areas and gullies,

- Controlling trees,

- Establishing a good grass cover and routinely mowing.

Concrete dams, which are usually constructed for larger lakes, should be maintained to eliminate

- Concrete deterioration,

- Leaks at construction joints,

- Excessive seepage,

- Settling, and

- Blocked spillways.

If you decide to construct a dam, design procedures, manuals, and criteria are available from the following federal agencies:

- U.S. Army Corps of Engineers;

- U.S. Department of Agriculture, Soil Conservation Service;

- U.S. Department of the Interior, Bureau of Reclamation; and

- U.S. Department of Commerce, National Weather Service.

Be aware that before building a dam you may need to prepare either a state or federal environmental impact statement. This requirement depends primarily on the type of construction, the type of permits needed, and its proposed site (e.g., wetlands or other sensitive areas.)

Dams should be constructed, operated, and maintained to perform safely and effectively during the period of time for which they were proposed and planned. As previously noted, your state may require an operation and maintenance permit. You may also need a permit to significantly alter an existing dam or build a new dam.

Typically, part of any permit application includes filing an emergency action plan that addresses how to evacuate people living below the dam and inform local authorities if dam failure is imminent.

Consult your state dam regulatory agency and your local government and emergency coordinator for information on what permits are required to operate, maintain, construct, or alter your dam. They should also be able to assist you in preparing an emergency action plan.

For information about dam safety regulations for your state, contact the head of its Dam Safety Section. A list of these officials is available from the Association of State Dam Safety Officials at P.O. Box 55270, Lexington, KY 40555; (606) 257-5140. This national organization holds annual conferences that local citizens can attend.

Periodically, dam safety officials also set up regional public awareness workshops, which are great places to get information on all aspects of dam construction and maintenance.

A partial list of publications about dams is given in Appendix C.

CHAPTER 6

Networking with the Lake World

No matter where you live, how big your lake is, or whether it's publicly or privately owned — you're not alone. Somewhere out there, probably in your own state, another group of lakeside property owners faced (and conquered) failing septic tanks or speeding powerboats or a conflict in uses (the list is unending) and in the process, grew stronger as an association. And chances are, they've shared that experience with your state natural resources department, a college or university, or some type of organization. So look around you — you'll find

■ **Individual lake associations:** on all types of lakes— rural, city, private, public.

- **State lake associations:** some, like Maine and Massachusetts, have been around for many years. Others are relatively new, and some of are chapters of the North American Lake Management Society.

- **The North American Lake Management Society:** the only national organization concerned solely with protecting, restoring, and managing lakes and reservoirs.

- **Ontario Cottagers:** ask them for contacts in the other Canadian provinces.

- **Conservation groups:** local units of the Izaak Walton League, Soil Conservation Society of America, National Wildlife Federation, National Audubon Society, Nature Conservancy, American Water Resources Association, and others.

- **Local governmental units:** the Extension Service, your local soil and water conservation district.

- **State programs:** the relatively new Nonpoint Source Management Program, the Clean Lakes Program, fish and wildlife programs.

- **Federal resources:** EPA's Clean Lakes Program, the Army Corps of Engineers, the U.S. Fish and Wildlife Service.

- **Universities and colleges:** institutions within your own state are probably among those researching and teaching limnology (the science of lakes) and other subjects concerned with lakes.

Networking makes sense, not only for sharing knowledge, but also for pooling efforts. Thirty (or even five) lake associations can make a better case before your state legislature than one association working alone. The state of Georgia passed landmark lake protection legislation in 1990 — through an unprecedented coalition that included many of the organizations previously described.

Mount Ranier oversees this sailor on Lake Washington.

You may not need the power leverage, but as your own association takes form, you will soon realize the need to share your experiences and learn from others. So combine the sources listed in Appendix B of this guide with your phone book and build your own information network. In the process, you'll be strengthening the national effort to preserve and protect all our lake resources.

8 Additional
RESOURCES

To find a Certified Lake Management Consultant

Contact the North American Lake Management Society: Dennis Bokemeier, Certification Chairman, Lake Carroll Association, 3200 Association Drive, Lake Carroll, IL 61046; 815/493-2552 ext 12; e-mail: denny_lcpo@yahoo.com

NALMS' web site — www.nalms.org — lists names of certified lake management consultants, and other information of interest to people who live beside lakes.

FOR FURTHER
READING

Burgis, M.J., and P. Morris. 1987. The Natural History of Lakes. Cambridge University Press, New York.

Coker, R.E. 1968. Streams, Lakes, Ponds. Harper Torchbooks, New York.

Cole, G.A. 1979. Textbook of Limnology. C.V. Mosby Company, St. Louis, MO.

Cooke, G. D., E.B. Welch, S.A. Peterson and P.R. Newroth. 1993. Restoration and Management of Lakes and Reservoirs. 2nd ed. Lewis Publishers, Boca Raton, FL.

Dreden, M. and R. Korth. Life on the Edge. University of Wisconsin, Stevens Point.

Hem, J.D. 1985. Study and Interpretation of the Chemical Characteristics of Natural Water. U.S. Geological Survey Water Supply Paper 2254.

Holdren, C., W. Jones and J. Taggart, eds. In prep. Lake and Reservoir Guidance Manual. 3rd. ed. North American Lake Management Society and Terrene Institute, in cooperation with U.S. Environmental Protection Agency, Washington, DC.

Hutchinson, G.E. 1957. A Treatise on Limnology: Vol. 1. Geography, Physics, and Chemistry. John Wiley and Sons, Inc., New York.

Kirschner, R. 1996. McCullom Lake, McHenry, Illinois: A Program for its Restoration and Protection. Northeastern Illinois Planning Commission, Natural Resources Dep., Chicago, IL.

Linsley, R.K. 1958. Hydrology for Engineers. McGraw Hill Publishers, New York.

Moss, B. 1988. Ecology of Fresh Waters: Man and Medium. 2d. ed. Blackwell Science, Ltd. Oxford, England.

New York State Department of Environmental Conservation and Federation of Lake Associations. 1990. Diet for a Small Lake: A New Yorker's Guide to Lake Management. Albany, NY.

Odum, E.P. 1971. Fundamentals of Ecology. W.B. Saunders Company. Philadelphia, PA.

Reid, G.K., and R.D. Wood. 1976. Ecology of Inland Waters and Estuaries. 2nd. ed. D. Van Nostrand Company, New York.

Schueler, T. 1995. Site Planning for Urban Stream Protection. Center for Watershed Protection, Silver Springs, MD.

—————. 1995. The Stream Protection Approach. Metropolitan Washington Council of Governments, Washington, DC.

Terrene Institute. 1995. Local Ordinances; A User's Guide. Terrene Institute, Alexandria, VA.

—————. 1996. A Watershed Approach to Urban Runoff: Handbook for Decisionmakers. Terrene Institute, Alexandria, VA.

U.S. Environmental Protection Agency. 1993. Guidance Specifying Management Measures for Sources of Nonpoint Pollution in Coastal Waters. EPA 840-B-82-002. Office of Water, Washington, DC.

Wetzel, R.G. 1975. Limnology. W.B. Saunders Company, Philadelphia, PA.

NOTES

DARK TIDE

ALSO BY ELIZABETH HAYNES

Into the Darkest Corner

DARK TIDE

Elizabeth Haynes

HarperCollins*Publishers*Ltd

HarperCollins Publishers Ltd.
2 Bloor Street East, 20th Floor
Toronto, Ontario, Canada
M4W 1A8

www.harpercollins.ca

Library and Archives Canada Cataloguing in Publication
information is available upon request.

ISBN 978-1-44341-315-2

Designed by Michael P. Correy

Printed and bound in the United States
RRD 9 8 7 6 5 4 3 2 1

For David

DARK TIDE

Prologue

The smell reminded her of cleaning out the fish tank she'd had as a kid; dead, slimy vegetation, mud, wet stones, and above it the briny tang of the sea carried upriver on a cold wind.

It was all horribly quiet. She should be able to hear sounds by now, music, laughter, something to point the way to the party, which had to be down here somewhere—but there was nothing. The only music was a distant wet sucking, slurping as the river played with its toys at the water's edge.

She picked her way across the potholed parking lot in the darkness, gritting her teeth in concentration, trying to keep her balance on the stupidly high-heeled shoes. Something moving, further down the slope, made her jump, and she stood still for a moment, listening for a voice, a footstep, breathing, something to give substance to that gnawing sense of unease that she felt inside. Large shapes, moving. She peered at them myopically, and then she realized they must be the boats, moored and rising and falling on the water—how silly she was! Jumping at shadows.

Everything that was darkness was suddenly blinding light. She must have triggered some motion-sensitive light, and as she looked up to see where she was going they were there, two of them, and she just had time to register that they were right in front of her, and she opened her mouth to scream as one of them drew back his arm, his hand balling into a fist.

Then she was lying on cold asphalt, gritty under her face,

warm and wet running down her cheek and nose and dripping red onto the ground. She gasped just once and then she felt herself being lifted, her head swinging loosely against fabric, hearing hushed voices, urgent, a whispered argument.

She felt a shrill panic and tried to scream again, but as she opened her mouth she was falling. And then the shock of the freezing water hitting her like concrete. She gasped to take a breath and the water surged in. Walls on either side of her, slippery, nothing for her clawing fingers to grip. And then the walls closed in, squeezing her.

There was a bright flash of pain, beautiful almost, surprisingly peaceful, and then nothing.

Chapter One

It was there when I opened my eyes, that vague feeling of discomfort, the rocking of the boat signaling the receding tide and the wind from the south, blowing upriver, right into the side of the boat.

For a long while I lay in bed, the sound of the waves slapping against the hull next to my head, echoing through the steel and dulled by the wooden siding. The duvet was warm and it was easy to stay there, the rectangle of skylight directly above showing the blackness turning to dark blue, and gray, and then I could see the clouds scudding overhead, giving the odd impression of moving at speed—the boat moving rather than the clouds. And then, that discomfort again.

It wasn't seasickness, or river-sickness, for that matter: I was used to it now, nearly five months after I had left London. Five months living aboard. There was still a momentary shock when my feet hit the solid ground of the path to the parking lot, a few wobbly steps, but it was never long before I felt steady again.

It was a gray sort of a day—not ideal for the get-together later, but that was my own fault for planning a party in September. "Back to school" weather, the wind whistling across the deck when I got up and put my head out of the wheelhouse.

No, it wasn't the tide, or the thought of the mismatched group of people who would be descending on my boat later today. There was something else. I felt as though someone had rubbed my fur the wrong way.

The plan for the day: finish the rest of the wood siding for the second room, the room that was going to be a guest bedroom at some point in the future. Clear away all the carpentry tools and store them in the bow. Sweep out the boat, clean up a bit. Then see if I could bum a ride to the store for party food and beer.

There was one wall left to do, an odd shape, which was why I had left it till last. The room was full of sawdust and wood remnants, scraps of edging and sandpaper. I'd done the measurements last night, but now, frowning at the piece of paper, I decided to recheck it all just to be on the safe side. When I had sided the galley, I'd ended up wasting a load of wood because I'd misread my own measurements.

I put the radio on, turned up loud even though I still couldn't hear it above the miter saw, and got to work.

At nine, I stopped and went back through to the galley for a coffee. I filled the kettle and put it on the gas burner. The boat was a mess. It was only occasionally that I noticed it. Glancing around, I scanned last night's take-out containers hurriedly shoved into a shopping bag ready to go out to the garbage cans. Dirty dishes in the sink. Pans and other items in boxes sitting on one of the dinette seats waiting to be put away, now that I had finally installed cabinet doors in the galley. A black plastic bag of fabric that would one day be curtains and cushion covers. None of it mattered when I was the only one in here, but in a few hours' time this boat would be full of people, and I had promised them that the renovations were almost complete.

Almost complete? That was stretching the truth a little thin. I had finished the bedroom, and the living room wasn't bad. The galley was done, too, but needed cleaning and tidying. The bathroom was—well, the kindest thing that could be said about it was that it was functional. As for the rest of it—the vast space in the bow that would one day be a bigger bathroom with a bath, as well as a true shower instead of a hose; a wide deck garden area with a sliding glass roof (an ambitious plan, but I'd seen one in a magazine and it looked so fantastic that it was the one project I was determined to complete); and maybe a study or an office or another unnamed room that would be wonderful and cozy and magical—for the moment, it worked as storage.

The kettle started a low whistle, and I rinsed a mug under the tap and spooned in some instant coffee, two spoons: I needed the caffeine.

A pair of boots crossed my field of vision through the porthole, level with the dock outside, shortly followed by a call from the deck. "Genevieve?"

"Down here. Kettle's just boiled."

Moments later Joanna trotted down the steps and into the main cabin. She was dressed in a miniskirt, with thick socks and heavy boots, the laces trailing, on the ends of her skinny legs. The top half of her was counterbalanced by one of Liam's sweaters, a navy-blue one, flecked with bits of sawdust and twig and cat hair. Her hair was a tangle of curls and waves of various colors.

"No, thanks, not for me—we're off in a minute. I just came to ask what time we should come over later, and do you want us to bring a lasagna as well as the cheesecake? And Liam says he's got some beers left over from the barbecue, he'll be bringing those."

She had a bruise on her cheek. Joanna didn't wear makeup, wouldn't have known what to do with it, so there it was—livid and purplish, under her left eye.

"What happened to your face?"

"Oh, don't you start. I had a fight with my sister."

"Christ."

"Come up on deck, I need a smoke."

The wind was still whipping, so we sat on the bench by the wheelhouse. The sun was trying to make its way through the scudding clouds but failing. Across the other side of the marina I could see Liam loading boxes and shopping bags into the back of their battered Ford van.

Joanna fished around in the pocket of her skirt and brought forth a pouch of tobacco. "The way I see it," she said, "she should keep her fucking nose out of my business."

"Your sister?"

"She thinks she's all that because she's got herself a mortgage at the age of twenty-two."

"Mortgages aren't all they're cracked up to be."

"Exactly!" Joanna said with emphasis. "That's what I said to her. I've got everything she's got without the burden of debt. And I don't have to mow any lawn."

"So that's what you were fighting about?"

Joanna was quiet for a moment, her eyes wandering over to the parking lot, where Liam stood, hands on his hips, before pointedly looking at his wristwatch and climbing into the driver's seat. Above the sounds of the marina—drilling coming from the workshop, the sound of the radio down in the cabin, the distant roar of the traffic from the highway bridge—the van's diesel rattle started up.

"Fuck it, I'd better go," she said. She shoved the pouch back into her pocket and lit the skinny cigarette she'd just managed to fill. "About seven? Eight? What?"

I shrugged. "I don't know. Sevenish? Lasagna sounds lovely, but don't go to any trouble."

"It's no trouble. Liam's made it."

With a backward wave, Joanna took one quick hop-step down the gangplank and onto the dock, running despite the boots across the grassy bank and up to the parking lot. The van was taking little jumps forward as though it couldn't wait to be gone.

• • •

At four, the cabin was finally finished. A bare shell, but at least now it was a bare wooden shell. The walls were clad, and the berth built along the far wall, under the porthole. Where the mattress would sit, two trapdoors with round finger holes in the board accessed the storage compartment underneath. The rest of it was pale wood in neat paneling, carved pine edging covering the joins and corners. It would look less like a sauna once it got a coat of paint, I thought. By next weekend it would be entirely different.

Clearing away the debris of my most recent foray into carpentry took longer than I thought it would. I had crates for the tools, but I hadn't bothered to put them away into the storage area since I'd started work on the bedroom, months ago.

I lugged the crates forward into the bow, through a hatch and into the cavernous space below. Three steps down, watching my head on the low ceiling, stowing the crates to the side.

It was only when I made the last trip, carrying the black plastic bag of fabric from the dinette and throwing it into the front compartment, that I found myself looking into the darkest of the spaces to see if the box was still there. I could just about see it in the gloomy light from the cabin above; on the side of it was written, in thick black marker: KITCHEN STUFF.

I had a sudden urge to look, to check that the box still held its contents. Of course it did, I told myself. *Nobody's been down here since you put it there.*

Stooping, I crossed the three wooden pallets that served as a floor, braced myself against the sides of the hull, and crouched next to the box. KITCHEN STUFF. The top two-thirds was full of garbage I'd brought from the London flat—spatulas, wooden spoons, a Denby teapot with a crack in the top, a whisk, a blender that didn't work, an ice cream scoop, and various cake pans nested inside one another. Below that was a sheet of cardboard that might, to the casual observer, look sufficiently like the bottom of the box to deter further investigation.

I folded the cardboard top of the box back down and tucked the other flap underneath it.

From the back pocket of my jeans I took out a cell phone. I found the address book and the only number that was saved there: GARLAND. That was all it said. It wasn't even his name. It would be so easy to press the little green button now and call him. What would I say? Maybe I could just ask him if he wanted to come tonight. *"Come to my party, Dylan. It's just a few close friends. I'd love to see you."*

What would he say? He'd be angry, shocked that I'd used the phone when he'd expressly told me not to. It was only there for one purpose, he'd told me. It was only for him to call me, and only when he was ready to make the pickup. Not before. If I ever had a call on it from another number, I shouldn't answer.

I closed my eyes for a moment, for a brief second allowing myself the indulgence of remembering him. Then I put the screen lock back on the phone so it didn't accidentally dial any numbers, least of all his, and I shoved it in my pocket and made my way back to the cabin.

Chapter Two

Malcolm and Josie were the first to arrive, at six. It was an unofficial arrival: they stopped for a chat and didn't leave again. I was on the deck, tipping the ice I'd just gotten from the minimart into a big plastic tub, and Malcolm heard the chink of beer bottles from his narrowboat. Seconds later he was chatting amicably from the dock about this and that, three bottles of French red wine cradled in one arm.

"We've got loads more if you run out, Genevieve," Josie said, when they came aboard. "We went to France last weekend. Stocked up for Christmas, you know."

"I thought you didn't drink wine," I said, handing the bottle opener to Malcolm so he could crack open his first beer.

"Don't, really," Malcolm said. "Don't know why we bought so much of it, tell the truth."

I'd cleaned up as much as possible. It could have been better, but the worst of the mess was out of the way, and the galley wasn't looking too shabby. Maureen had given me a ride to the store and I'd taken a taxi home, with two cases of beer and several bags of ice, jumbo bags of potato chips, and a large block of cheese that had seemed like a good idea at the time. I wasn't very good at party food, to be honest—but at least there was plenty of alcohol.

Josie had brought garlic bread wrapped in tinfoil. "I thought it could go on your stove," she said.

"I wasn't going to light it. I think it's going to be roasting with lots of people in here."

Malcolm, the designated expert in the room who had provided advice on living aboard more times in the last five months than I could remember, snorted. "You'll freeze at night if you haven't got your stove on."

For a moment we all stood contemplating the wood-burning stove that sat on large tiles in the corner of the main cabin. It wasn't cold now, but Malcolm had a point—not good to be lying in bed at four in the morning freezing cold.

"I'll light it, if you like," Malcolm said at last. "You ladies go up on deck and admire the sunset."

On the way past the galley I took hold of the bottle opener and, as I opened two bottles of beer—not as cold as they should be but cold enough—Josie said something about leaving the man to build his fire. "He loves it. We were going to have central heating put in at one point but he kept putting it off and putting it off. He even starts piling up logs in the summer, just in case it gets a bit on the chilly side. One of these days he's going to chop down one of the trees in the park."

I looked down and along the dock to the *Scarisbrick Jean*, the narrowboat Malcolm and Josie shared with their cat, Oswald. Not long after I'd moved in, I had heard them talking about "Aunty Jean" and for a while I'd thought they had a third person living on the boat with them, until I realized that *Aunty Jean* was their affectionate name for the boat itself. A friendly name. Maybe I should think of a pet name for mine.

The first time I saw the *Revenge of the Tide* I knew it was the one. It was above my price range, but my finances had seen a recent improvement and as a result I was looking at boats I'd previously discounted. It needed work, but the hull was sound and the cabin was bearable. I could just about afford to buy it and do the renovations for a year or so, provided I budgeted carefully and did the work myself.

"*Revenge of the Tide*. Odd sort of a name for a boat," I'd said, the day I decided to spend the bulk of my savings on it. Cameron, the marina owner and the broker for boat sales, was standing beside me on the dock. He wasn't a very good sales-man; he was in a hurry to get on with the countless other tasks he had waiting. He was fidgeting from one foot to the other and was clearly only just managing to hold back from saying, *Do you want her or not?* It was a good thing for him that I'd already fallen in love.

The *Revenge of the Tide* was a seventy-five-foot-long steel-hulled barge of a type known as a Hagenaar, named for the canals of The Hague, under whose bridges the boat was low enough to pass. It had been built in 1903 in the Netherlands, a great beast of a boat, a workhorse. The masts had been re-moved and a diesel engine added after the Second World War, and it had been used for transporting goods around the Port of Rotterdam until it was sold in the 1970s and moved across the English Channel. Ever since then, a steady stream of owners had been using it either for moving cargo, for pleasure trips, or as living accommodations, with varying degrees of commit-ment and success.

"The owner bought her just before his second divorce," said Cam. "He managed to con his missus because he bought the boat with all the savings he had stashed away. He wanted to call her just *Revenge*, I think, but it was a bit too obvious so he called her *Revenge of the Tide* instead."

"I might have to change the name," I said as Cam took me into the office to sign the paperwork.

"You don't want to do that. Bad luck to change a boat's name."

"Bad luck? What, worse than having a boat named after a failed marriage?"

Cam grimaced.

"Anyway, the last owner changed the name, didn't he?"

"Yeah. And he's just getting divorced for the third time, and having to sell his boat to pay for it. What does that tell you?"

So I left the name as it was, because I didn't need any more bad luck in my life. Besides, the *Revenge* had character, had a soul; living aboard such a majestic, beautiful boat made me feel a bit safer, a bit less lonely. And it looked after me and hid me away from view. Boats were supposed to be female, but I always thought of the *Revenge* as male: a big, quiet gentleman, someone who would keep me safe.

"So what time are your London friends turning up?" Josie asked.

"Oh, lord knows. Late, probably."

Josie was like a warm cushion, fleecy and brightly colored. There was barely room for the two of us on the narrow bench. Her graying hair was fighting the breeze to escape from her loosely tied ponytail. At least the sun had come out, and the early evening sky overhead was blue, dotted with white clouds.

"What are they going to make of us, do you reckon?"

"I'm more worried about what you'll make of them."

A few days after I'd moved in, I had poked my head out of the wheelhouse to be greeted by the sight of Malcolm sitting on the roof of the *Scarisbrick Jean*, smoking a cigarette and wearing nothing but a pair of boxer shorts. It was early, barely light, and the spring air was so cold that Malcolm's breath came in clouds. His hair stood up on one side of his head as if it had been ironed.

"All right?" he'd called across to me.

"Morning," I'd said, and had almost gone back down below when curiosity got the better of me. "You okay over there?"

"Yeah," he'd said, taking a long, slow drag. "You?" As though it were entirely normal to be sitting on the roof of a narrowboat at five in the morning wearing nothing but your underwear. I hadn't known his name then. I'd seen him coming and going, of course, and we'd exchanged nods and greetings, but it still felt a bit peculiar to be sharing the dawn with a man who was just a scrap of gray flannel away from naked.

"Aren't you cold?"

"Oh," he'd said, with dawning comprehension. "Yeah. Fucking freezing. But I can't go inside: Josie's stunk up the whole boat."

In the first few days and weeks of boat ownership, living in the marina had felt like being in a foreign country. The pace of life was slower. If someone was going to the store they would shout at you and ask if you wanted anything. Some of them turned up unexpectedly and sat on your boat and talked about nothing for three hours and then went away again, sometimes abruptly, as though the flow of conversation had dried up, or some other, more pressing, engagement had surfaced. Sometimes they brought food or drink with them. They helped you fix things, even if it wasn't immediately apparent that the thing in question needed fixing. They gave you advice about which chemicals you should use to keep the toilet working. They laughed a lot.

Some of the boats were owned by people who only showed up at the marina on weekends, or less often if it was rainy. One of them, a narrowboat in a state of considerable disrepair, was owned by a man with wilder hair than Malcolm's. I'd seen him only twice. The first time, I'd called a cheery hello on my way past his boat and gotten a vacant stare in response. The second time, he'd been walking across the parking lot with a shopping bag that looked heavy and chinked as though it was full of glass bottles.

Then there was Carol-Anne. She lived in a cabin cruiser that should by rights not have been moored in the residential marina, but she got away with it because she did actually live there. She was divorced, with three children who lived with their father in Chatham. She would say hello and then try and talk to you for hours about how grim things were and how difficult it was to get by. All the other liveaboards tried to avoid her and, after a couple of weeks, I did, too.

The rest of them were wonderful.

Joanna had turned up with a plateful of dinner once. "Have you eaten? Good, we made too much."

We'd sat together at the dinette, Joanna drinking from a can of lager that she'd found in my fridge, while I tucked into shepherd's pie and peas.

"I'm not used to people bringing me dinner," I'd said when I'd finished.

Joanna had shrugged. "It's no bother. I'm happy not to throw it away."

"People here are very friendly," I'd said, aware at the same time of what an understatement this was. It was like suddenly finding yourself part of a big family.

"Yes. It's the whole boat thing. You get used to it, after a while. Not like living in London, huh?"

Not like living in London, I'd thought, *not at all.*

Mixing London friends with marina friends had the potential to be a recipe for pure disaster: they'd have nothing in common, other than perhaps that Simone occasionally read the *Guardian* on a Saturday. Lucy would show up in her tank-like all-terrain luxury vehicle that did about twelve miles to the gallon and had never been outside the M25; Gavin would be wearing incredibly expensive designer shoes that would be ruined in the muddy puddles around the dock that never seemed to dry.

And then there was Caddy. Would she even come?

At some point in the future, the *Revenge of the Tide* would be a fantastic party boat, big enough for lots of people to socialize in and crash out on—but not yet. If they all showed up, some of them would have to sit on the deck, and some of them would probably never even set foot belowdecks—there simply wouldn't be room. They would all joke about it and then they would walk back up to the main road and go to the pub. The other liveaboards would make some remarks about city dwellers, laugh a lot, drink more beer, and drift back to their own boats in the early hours.

They would be here soon. Josie closed her eyes against the low sun and breathed in, a smile of contentment on her face as though she were sunbathing on a yacht in the Mediterranean instead of on an old Dutch barge on the Medway River.

"We'll love them," she said at last. "We love everyone. Unless they're real snobs."

It had gotten to the point where I didn't actually care what my city friends thought. At the start of this year I had cared very much. It had mattered what I thought, what I wore, what I said, what music I listened to, what pubs I drank in after work, and what I did over the weekend. London was a vast social network where you met people in bars and clubs, at the gym, at work and at events, in parks and at the theater, at salsa dance nights in the local pub. You spent enough time with them to establish whether they were on your wavelength, and eventually decided whether they could be considered friends. People came and went in and out of your life in a transitory fashion, and it never really seemed to matter. There was always someone else to go out with, always an invitation to some party or gathering. So I had plenty of people I knew, and in London they would generally be called friends, or mates. But were they? Were they people you could call on in a crisis? Would they stay with you if you were ill, or in danger? Would they protect you if you needed protecting?

Dylan would.

"They're not snobs, not really. But to be honest, I think it's going to be a bit of a shock for them. I think they're expecting some kind of gorgeous loft apartment squeezed into a boat."

"Bullshit, you've done a fabulous job."

"I've still got a long way to go. And there isn't a single thing on my boat that I've bought new. Unfortunately that lot doesn't really get the recycling ethos."

"Seriously? But your boat's looking fabulous. And you've done it all yourself. Not many of us have done the fitting out on our own."

"At least the tide's coming in."

The hull was currently sitting comfortably on a cushion of mud, the boat steady. When the tide came in, it would rise on the water and, depending on the weather, rock gently for six hours or so, until the tide ebbed again. The boat looked much better when it was floating, and of course the mud didn't always smell particularly nice.

Josie looked across the dock. "Who's this?"

The sight of the shiny 4×4 pulling into the marina parking lot meant that some of the London group had arrived, and in fact it turned out to be most of them. Lucy was first to jump down. She'd made an effort to dress down in jeans and boots, but the boots still had heels on them. Almost immediately she sank down into the ground and from our position on deck we heard her shout some expletive.

From the back came Gavin and Chrissie, and someone else, from the passenger side—at first I couldn't see who it was, and then he came around the front of the big hood and I could see him, in all his glory.

"I don't believe it," I murmured.

"Ooh, he looks nice," said Josie.

"It's Ben."

"What, the gorgeous one?"

"Yes. The one in the jacket is Gavin. I used to work with him. The blond girl is Lucy, and the other one is Chrissie— she's a model."

I stood up on the deck and waved. It was Ben who saw me and returned the wave, and then they all started picking their way across the parking lot toward the marina, carrying various things between them. Gavin was almost hidden behind a huge bunch of flowers. "You'll need a great big vase for those," Josie said under her breath.

"Mm. I think I've got a milk bottle somewhere."

We laughed conspiratorially and for a moment I wondered why I'd decided to hold this party in the first place. It was like a crashing together of two worlds, two different planets that I'd inhabited—one of them had been home before, and the other one was home now. I had a foot in both worlds, and to be honest I wasn't completely comfortable in either.

"Hello!" Lucy had reached the end of the dock and was looking at it uncertainly. "Can I walk on this?"

"Of course you can," said Ben, marching past her. "Can we come aboard?"

He was at the bottom of the narrow gangplank. Even from here I could see how blue his eyes were.

"Sure," I said. "Come up."

He made it onto the deck, taking my hand for balance although he didn't need it. It was enough reason to pull me into a hug. He smelled delicious.

"I didn't know you were coming," I said.

"I didn't know, either. I was at Lucy's and she said I could tag along. You don't mind?"

"Of course not."

"Um, hello? Someone give me a hand?"

Ben held out his hand for Lucy, and she wobbled up the gangplank, followed by Chrissie and Gavin at the end.

"Guys, this is Josie."

Josie stood up, a little awkwardly. "Hi. I live on that boat down there." She pointed down at the *Scarisbrick Jean*, sitting forlorn and slightly at an angle on the mud. Oswald was lazing on the roof, enjoying the early-evening sunshine, one leg elevated elegantly in the air while he licked his behind.

"Oh, cool," said Lucy. "It's—oh. A lovely boat."

There was a pause, and then, just when it was about to get awkward, Malcolm appeared through the door to the wheelhouse, wiping the back of his sooty hand over his sweaty forehead, and said, "I've put the garlic bread on the stove. All right?"

Chapter Three

It got better as the evening wore on, which was a relief. By the time I had given the first tour, Carla and Simone had arrived, and after the second tour the boat and the deck and the dock were full of people, most of them from the marina, outnumbering the London crowd and making the party come alive.

Joanna and Liam came with the lasagna and two whole cheesecakes, Maureen and Pat brought more beer, Roger and Sally brought a keg of their homebrew and a bag full of homemade bread. Diane and Steve came without their children but with a two-way baby monitor, which worked just fine given that their boat was only about ten feet away. Joanna had also brought a present of a couple of strings of Christmas lights, which were duly strung up around the deck and made the boat look pretty and festive as the sun set at last and darkness fell.

There was no sign of Caddy. I wondered if I'd been enthusiastic enough with my invitation. For a long time she had been the closest thing I had to a best friend in London, and I missed her, I wanted to see her again. If I couldn't invite Dylan, there was nothing stopping me from asking Caddy. But she hadn't made it.

I'd spoken to her lonely a few times since I'd left. She still hadn't forgiven me fully for leaving in such a hurry. When I called her, it seemed to take her several minutes to thaw out before we could relax enough to joke around.

"What kind of a party?" she'd asked.

"Oh, you know. Just a party. Maybe to show off the boat."

"Will there be any nice guys there?"

A mental image of Malcolm had flashed through my mind. "Well..."

"Oh, all right, then. I guess so. You'll have to text me the address."

"How's the club?" I'd asked, the way I always did.

"It's all right. Quiet at the moment. New girls started last week, most of them suck. No real competition anymore."

There was a pause. She knew what I was really asking and she always left me hanging. Sometimes she made me ask it; sometimes she took pity on me.

"Dylan hasn't been in the club much. Fitz has him doing something, I think."

"How is he?"

"Grumpy, same as always."

And she'd laughed.

Where *was* she?

I found myself penned into the corner of the dinette by Malcolm and Lucy, somehow involved in a protracted discussion with Lucy about the toilet system and how it worked.

"But what about the shower?" Lucy shouted above the chatter in the cabin. Joanna was heating up bread in the galley, banging cabinet doors open and shut in the vain hope of finding a baking sheet.

"What about it?" Malcolm said, his voice challenging. He had a thing about his hair—he never used shampoo to wash it, which wasn't a problem as far as he was concerned, but he got defensive sometimes.

"Well," said Lucy, "not putting too fine a point on it, it's a hose."

"I know it's a hose," I said. "It won't always be a hose."

Oh, God, I'm drunk, I thought. *I'm drunk already.*

I looked at my watch. Caddy should be here by now. Why wasn't she?

Malcolm said, "Most people have bathrooms on board but, just in case, there's showers near the office. They're kept really clean and nice."

"Oh, you mean like on a campsite?" Lucy said, although the closest she had come to camping was two half-day visits to Glastonbury, and even then she had stayed in a hotel.

"Yeah, kind of. But cleaner," Malcolm said.

"Look, I'm building a bathroom at the end. A real one with a tub," I said, anxious that she wouldn't think I was intending to spend the rest of my life roughing it.

Malcolm coughed.

"I'll have it ready by Christmas, honest. It's going to have a real bath, and after that I'm going to install an outdoor shower in my deck garden."

"Your what?"

"I'm going to put a sliding roof on, beyond the bedroom. There's going to be about ten feet or so of deck that I can open up to the elements, with a shower. Then right at the bow I'll put another room—maybe an office or a study or something."

"It sounds like a lot of hard work," said Joanna with a sympathetic smile.

"It's all right," I said. "I can work at my own pace."

"How's the money side of it? Five months without an income would kill me," said Lucy.

That's because you spend all your money on clothes, I found myself thinking. "It isn't going too badly. I've still got savings."

"I thought you spent it all on the boat."

"Not quite all of it."

There was a pause. I was waiting for her to say something

else—daring her. Malcolm was looking from me to Lucy and back again.

"So what is it you did in London?" he asked.

"Sales," I said, before Lucy could answer. "You heard of ERP software? It stands for 'enterprise resource planning.' It's a big software package: you sell the core system to multinational organizations and then after that you keep trying to sell them bolt-on modules. You know, accounting modules, human resources, that kind of thing."

Malcolm's eyes had glazed over.

"It's sales, basically," I went on. "Doesn't matter what you sell, the same principles apply. Except in our case it was high-pressure because we were dealing with buyers at the boardroom level and trying to persuade them to spend hundreds of thousands of pounds."

"And ninety percent of the time," Lucy chipped in, "we were selling to guys. And the rest of the sales team were all guys. They try and say that sexual inequality is a thing of the past, but let me tell you, it's alive and well in the world of corporate ERP sales."

Malcolm had stopped listening, but Joanna was still with us. "You were the only two women on the sales team? Out of how many?"

"Twenty in total," Lucy said. "And we were the first two they'd ever had. It was like being the first girls allowed to play in the tree house."

"I bet that was tough," Joanna said.

"Still is," Lucy said. "Except now I'm the only girl in the tree house, since Genevieve walked out."

Joanna and Malcolm both looked at me in surprise.

"I'd had enough," I said. "All I wanted was to save up the money for the boat. After that I didn't want to hang around."

"Must have been a good job, though, to earn you enough to buy a boat."

Lucy dove in before I could stop her. "Ah, well, Genevieve had two jobs, didn't you, Gen?"

"Most of the money was from sales," I fibbed.

"Genevieve worked in a club," Lucy said. She was looking directly at me, her expression unreadable.

My face felt hot. Across the other side of the cabin I could see Ben talking to Diane; both of them were laughing. He was so tall that he was almost stooping slightly, even though the ceiling was above six feet. He looked beautiful, and unreachable.

Liam appeared at the top of the steps. "Joanna? Where's that scoopy thing for this cheesecake?"

"What 'scoopy thing'? You mean a spoon?"

"Yeah, spoon, whatever. You got one?"

She got up from the dinette and rifled through the drawer in the galley, banging things about.

"There's a big spoon on that hook there, look," I said.

Joanna unhooked the slotted spoon and, wielding it like a weapon, went up the steps.

"You worked in a club? What, like bar work?" Malcolm asked, animated.

I glared at Lucy, but either she didn't notice or she chose not to.

"Genevieve used to be a dancer," Lucy said, a note of triumph in her voice. "Didn't she tell you? She was really rather good. That's what I heard, though of course I never went in the club where she worked—more of a men-only place, if you get my meaning."

Malcolm's eyes were like saucers. I almost wished I hadn't invited her. And Caddy wasn't coming, clearly, otherwise she'd be here by now. I hadn't realized until that moment that I'd been looking forward to seeing her more than anyone else. And she would have been a useful ally against Lucy in any discussion about the moral or feminist aspects of dancing— nobody would have argued with Caddy.

"Do you ever get that feeling," I said, more to myself than to either of them, "I don't know, sort of like impending doom? Like something bad is about to happen? I've had that all day."

"I get that sometimes," Lucy said. "Usually when it gets to after two in the morning and I'm still drinking and I've got to get to work by seven the next day."

It lightened the mood a little, but even so, I couldn't face sitting here making small talk with Lucy anymore. If she wanted to share more details about my past, she could do so without me. I excused myself and Malcolm moved to let me out of the dinette. Squeezing past all the bodies in the galley, I climbed up to the deck.

I looked across to the parking lot, half-hoping to see Caddy being dropped off by a taxi. But everything was quiet. Josie sat with her back to the wheelhouse, facing Roger and Sally and, of all people, Gavin, who had taken off his jacket and his handmade Italian shoes and was sitting barefoot and cross-legged, telling them the story of when he went traveling and accidentally sold his passport in Thailand. They had the keg of homebrew balanced on a bucket in the middle of their circle and were helping themselves to it.

"Here," said Ben, at my shoulder. He handed me another bottle of beer.

"Oh—thanks."

The evening was starting to feel a bit surreal. We walked to the other side of the wheelhouse and looked to where the lights from the highway bridge reflected in the water. The wind had dropped. From the opposite bank, the distant bass beat from the nightclub throbbed.

"I haven't been drunk for months," I said.

"I haven't been drunk for—oh, I don't know. Days. Hours, more likely," said Ben.

We sat on the roof of the cabin.

"I've missed you," he said.

I laughed at that. "You big liar," I said. "You never miss anyone, or anything."

He looked a little bit hurt, but I knew it was an act. Despite all these people, despite everything that had happened between us in the past, he was just angling to stay the night.

"You've done a great job with the boat," he said.

"Thank you."

"I like the bedroom."

Here we go, I thought.

"I like the skylight. It must be wonderful to lie there at night and look up at the stars."

I smiled. "Actually, it's more of an orange glow. Light pollution isn't just confined to London, you know."

"I was trying to be romantic."

"I know you were, Ben. But you forget I know you too well. It doesn't work on me anymore."

"What happened to you in London? You left so suddenly. Nobody knew where you'd gone. Lucy thought you'd been kidnapped."

"Nothing happened. Don't be so dramatic."

"Genny, you quit your job and walked out. You literally walked out."

"Who told you that?"

"Who do you think? Lucy, of course. She said it was the most exciting thing that had ever happened in your office. She said you marched into the CEO's office while he was having a meeting and threw your letter of resignation on the table. Then you just grabbed your coat and left. She said she had to empty your desk for you, and when she took the box to your flat you were all ready to move out."

I didn't speak for a moment. That feeling was back: the sense of disquiet. The tide had started to rise, and in another few hours it would be at its highest point. Already the boat was moving, just slightly, the comforting feeling of the *Revenge* holding me up and cradling me. And yet, with the boat full of people, it didn't feel quite right.

From the skylight next to us on the roof, I could hear genial conversation coming up from the galley below changing subtly into more heated tones. Joanna and Malcolm, by the sounds of it—and, on the other side of the exchange, Lucy and Simone.

"All I said was—"

"I know what you said, and I know what you meant." That sounded like Joanna.

"You lot are all the same, you haven't got a clue"—and that sounded like Malcolm, the edges of his words blurred and slurred by cheap beer—"you think just 'cause we live on a boat we're somehow inferior, just 'cause you choose to live in a house . . ."

"I didn't say anything of the kind!"

"Well, why were you going on about the bathroom, then? I tell you, when this boat's finished it'll be palatial, and you lot will all be blinded by jealousy."

Lucy laughed. "I don't think so somehow."

On the deck above, I put my head in my hands. "Oh, God. I knew this was a mistake."

Ben put his arm around my shoulders. "They're just drunk, Genny. It'll all be forgotten in the morning."

"Ben! Where the fuck are you?" Lucy was coming up the steps into the wheelhouse, stomping with her high-heeled boots on the varnished pine. "Gavin? Let's go to the pub."

"Want me to stay here?" Ben asked me quietly.

"No," I said. "You go with them, it's fine."

"I could always come back later."

His voice sounded so hopeful that for a moment I looked up. *It would be so easy to say yes*, I thought. *It would be easy to have him here, to share my bed with him tonight and put him on the train to London in the morning.* Would it hurt, one night with Ben? Five months since Dylan, five long months waiting for him to make contact with me again. He obviously wasn't missing me as much as I missed him.

"Where the fuck's Ben?" Lucy said.

"What's up, princess?" Gavin asked, getting to his feet.

"I want to go somewhere else!"

"Have some of this," Roger said soothingly, "it'll make you feel better, I promise."

"What is it?" Lucy sounded suspicious.

"It's magic potion," said Gavin, giggling.

"What?"

"No, seriously, Luce. Give it a try. I've never had anything like it, honestly: it's like drinking the earth and the moon and the stars . . ."

"Gavin, you're so full of shit, you've been smoking dope again, haven't you? I thought you said you hadn't got any left?"

"Rog here gave me a puff. But I tell you what, lovely Princess Lucy Loo, it's not nearly as good as this stuff. Here."

"Eww! It tastes like shit!"

Laughter from the wheelhouse and the deck.

Ben was kissing me. He'd taken my face in his hands and kissed me, before I had a chance to protest, before I could say no, before I could move away. He was good at it. I could feel my barriers, my resolve, and my resistance disappearing. It would be so easy to tell him to come back later on. Nobody would even notice. There was a good chance that the other liveaboards would all disappear back to their own boats in the next hour or so. Once Lucy and the other London group had gone to the pub, then on to Rochester or Maidstone, or even, if they were desperate enough, back to London, the marina would be empty and quiet and nobody would even see him come back; nobody would ever need to know . . .

"Ben! There you are!"

The kiss ended abruptly. Lucy fixed me with a hard stare, as though it was all my fault that she had been irreparably insulted by these river people, the man with the crazy hair and the girl with the black eye; clearly now to find Ben down here in the semidarkness, with his mouth on mine, was pretty much the final straw.

"Are you staying here or are you coming with us?" Lucy asked, her voice chilly.

Before he had a chance to answer, I stood up. "You should go," I said.

"Why?"

Lucy had gone to herd up the rest of them, including Simone and Carla—presumably they were expected to squeeze into the trunk of the car.

I gave a little shrug.

"You've got someone you're seeing here?" he asked.

"I've got a different life."

He tried again, with his best cheeky smile to go with it. "I'm not talking about any sort of commitment, Genny. Just one more night. Come on. You want me, admit it."

Despite myself, I laughed.

"Amazing as the offer sounds, Ben, I would rather be on my own than have you here, even for one night. But thank you."

He gave up. "Suit yourself," he said, and turned his back on me to find Lucy.

They left, with promises to text or phone, hugs, professions of what a fabulous night it was and such a shame it had to come to an end, while I hugged them all in turn, and all the live-aboards continued with the beer and the lively conversation and the last of Liam's lasagna.

As I waved them off and the motion sensors triggered the lights in the parking lot, Lucy tripped over something and fell on her face—fortunately on the grass. Malcolm let out a hooting laugh.

Diane and Steve went soon after that. The baby monitor gave every indication that the children had gotten out of bed and were playing some kind of console game on board their boat—either that or the boat had been stormed by terrorists who were shooting everything in sight.

Downstairs in the main cabin the conversation had turned to milder topics.

Joanna handed me a beer.

"Sit down and join us," she said.

"I'm sorry they were such assholes," I said.

"They weren't assholes."

"I thought they were all right, on the whole," piped up Malcolm, who seemed to have forgiven Lucy already.

"Thanks," I said. "You guys are lovely."

"I think you should have shagged that Ben, though," said Josie with a chuckle.

"What?"

"You think we couldn't hear you? He was begging for it. Absolutely begging."

"Yes, he was, wasn't he?"

She gave me a wink. "I wouldn't have turned him down, if it were me," she said.

"Oy," said Malcolm, "you old hussy. You'll end up sleeping on the roof if you keep that up."

I laughed. "He's not all he's cracked up to be. Ben, I mean."

"Ooh," said Josie, "you've been there before, then?"

"Been there, done that."

"And he's no good? Christ. Who'd have thought? He looks all right to me."

I considered this for a moment. This wasn't a conversation I'd particularly planned to have.

"It's not that he's no good," I said. "It's just that he's not the sort of person I want anymore."

"You got your eye on someone else?" said Joanna.

"Not really. I just think I'm better off on my own for a while, you know? Busy with the boat, and all that."

"Ah, the boat," said Roger. "She's married to the boat already. Happens to us all. You still haven't shown me the new room."

"Help yourself," I said. "Go and have a look."

Malcolm took it upon himself to act as tour guide, taking Roger to see the newly clad room, while I stayed in the main cabin and finished off another bottle of beer. Too many, I thought. The woodstove was burning low and the cabin was warm now that the door to the wheelhouse was closed. We all sat with our feet up, feeling the gentle rock of the boat.

I realized that I hadn't thought about Caddy since Ben had started flirting with me. Where was she? Maybe she'd had to work after all.

"We should do this more often," Josie said drowsily.

"We always say that," said Sally. She was curled like a child into the big, soft sofa, a patchwork blanket I'd bought from a thrift store over her feet.

"I like your boat," said Joanna. "Did you know that? You have one of the best boats out of all of us."

This was a conversation we had regularly—who had the best boat and why. We never seemed to reach a conclusion.

"The *Souvenir* is my favorite," I said.

Sally laughed. "You're just saying that because you're sweet and lovely."

"I like the *Souvenir*, too," said Joanna. "I think the *Souvenir* is the best boat at the moment, but if Genevieve manages to pull off the deck garden with the sliding glass roof, then the *Revenge* will be the best one."

"You're right," said Sally. "We can't top a deck garden."

"What are you going to grow on your deck, Gen? Have you thought?"

I was wondering whether this was Josie's roundabout way of asking me to grow some cannabis for her and Malcolm, but before I had a chance to answer, Malcolm and Roger came back.

"You do realize Liam's asleep on your bed, Genevieve?"

"Shit," said Joanna. "I wondered where he'd gone. I thought he'd gone back to the boat."

She got up and went to try and rouse her partner from his beer-induced slumber.

"We should go," said Malcolm. "Busy day tomorrow."

"Oh?" I said. "What's happening?"

"We're going to look at dresses," said Josie. "My niece is getting married soon, and Malcolm's promised to take me shopping."

"And before you ask," said Malcolm, although none of us had said anything, "I'm having my hair cut before the wedding, all right?"

Chapter Four

Not long after that they all went, off my boat and back onto the dock, swaying back to their boats and the warmth of their respective woodstoves.

I stayed in the main cabin once I'd shut and locked the wheelhouse, gazing unfocusedly at the glow of the fire and finishing off my last bottle of beer. I was trying not to think about Ben. I wondered where they were staying. I didn't have his number, which was a good thing. I probably would have given in and texted him.

The galley was a mess—bottles and glasses and dirty plates everywhere. The floor was scattered with crumbs from the garlic bread. Joanna and Liam's empty lasagna dish filled the sink, burnt-on bits glued to the edge. I wondered how much soaking it would take before I could return it to them, clean.

Something was digging in . . .

I reached into the back pocket of my jeans, and there it was. Dylan's phone. I went through the menus again to the address book. GARLAND. Why that word, of all words? It was just a word, he'd said. It was supposed to be random. It was supposed to be something that nobody would suspect, if the phone got into the wrong hands.

"What if I want to contact you?" I'd said.

"Why would you want to contact me?"

He had no idea, none at all, about how I felt. I wasn't even sure of it myself, right then. I just knew that the concept of not seeing him was a difficult one to grasp.

"What if something goes wrong?" I said.

"Nothing's going to go wrong." He was getting impatient. "It will be fine, I promise you. Nothing will go wrong. When I'm ready, when I've got everything taken care of here, I'll call you and we can meet up somewhere. All right?"

That had been more than five months ago. All that time, I'd kept the phone on me, kept it charged, and I'd never used it. Not once.

I tossed the phone clumsily onto the wooden shelf behind the sofa. There was no point sitting here thinking about Dylan. Wherever he was, he certainly wasn't thinking about me.

The toilet, which I'd emptied only this morning, was full and backed up. None of the liveaboards would have left it like that. I felt desolate, and alone. I should have said yes to Ben. It would have been nice just to have him here. He wasn't Dylan, but he was someone.

I turned the lights off and climbed into bed.

I dreamed about the phone, Dylan's phone. It was ringing, the name GARLAND coming up on the display as if to emphasize further that this was it, this was the call; but every time I pressed the green button to answer, nothing happened.

I was half-awake and half-asleep for most of the night, opening my eyes to see the square of inky blackness above my head. Then Ben was in my dream, too. He was lying here with me.

"You lied about the stars," he said.

I looked up to the skylight and it was full of stars, so bright that they blended together, just one dazzling light shining down on us.

Then I opened my eyes for real, and it was still just dark. There were stars—I could see them—but they were faint.

Alcohol always does this to me, I thought crossly.

I was fully awake, because I needed the toilet. I remembered mine was backed up and I wasn't about to go across to the shower room in the middle of the night, so I crawled into the storage space at the front of the boat and found the bucket I used to mix adhesive. It was clean, which was a bonus. I left the bucket in the bathroom after I'd used it and went back to bed.

For a while I lay there, listening to the lapping of the water against the hull. The tide must be going out by now. Before too long the boat would settle back into the mud and lie still, and then it would start to get light.

As well as the water, there was another sound. It started out as a gentle bump, distant, as though the bow had nudged the dock or one of the bumpers had lifted in a sudden swell and fallen back against the hull. It was easy to ignore at first. But then it came again, and again, rhythmic now—part of the song of the boat, the percussion of the river.

The gentle bumping became a knocking, more insistent. A soft thud, a scrape of something along the hull. I was awake again, listening to the sound and trying to work out what it was. It sounded as though something was trapped between the boat and the dock, just outside my bedroom. And the tide was receding, which meant it was unlikely to be washed clear again. It would stay there, knocking, until the hull of the boat came to rest on the mud. Which was still hours away.

With a sigh, I sat up in bed, listening. It was coming with the rise and the fall of the water, a rhythmic bump. It was nestling against my boat, big enough to make a sound. What could it be? A plastic container, something like that?

Shivering, I pulled my jeans on in the dark, a sweater from the pile of laundry. The boat was cold now; the stove had long since gone out. Just inside the hatch to the storage area was my flashlight, big and powerful and cased in rubber. I'd had a Maglite but I'd dropped it in the water during my first week on the boat and never got it back again. One of the first pearls of wisdom Malcolm had dispensed was: "Put a float on anything important."

I opened the door to the wheelhouse, my teeth chattering. It was bitter up here, freezing, the sky above barely gray. I slipped on the sneakers that were by the wheel; they were cold and damp, but better than bare feet on the wet boards outside.

No sign of anyone. The boats in the marina were all silent and dark, the ones on this dock still rising and falling gently on the outgoing tide, the ones nearer to the shore already sitting on their bank of river mud.

To my surprise, I heard a noise from the direction of the parking lot—a door shutting? Then the noise of an engine starting up, and tires on gravel. A dark shape of a vehicle driving out of the lot. No rear lights, no headlights. Why didn't they put their lights on? And why hadn't the lights come on in the parking lot? They were motion-sensitive. I remembered someone complaining to Cam that the lights shone into their cabin when the foxes were out by the garbage. Solution—the garbage cans were moved. But surely the lights should come on if someone was there?

Silence, apart from the lapping of the water against the bow. Even the highway bridge was silent. Then it came again. A soft bumping, accompanied now by a gentle splashing as a little wave drifted over whatever it was. It must be something big.

I crept along the port side of the gunwale, holding on to the side of the cabin for support. I was still a little bit woozy, the boat's rocking making me nauseated.

For some reason I felt afraid. Out here, away from London, it felt wrong to be awake at this time of the night.

When I got roughly alongside the bedroom, I turned on the flashlight, surprisingly and suddenly bright, a powerful beam shining out from it and hitting the giant conifers that rose behind the marina office. Then I directed the beam down into the space between the *Revenge of the Tide* and the dock.

I couldn't tell what it was, at first.

A bundle. Something covered in fabric.

My first thought, my first crazy, misplaced thought, was of the black plastic bag full of random fabric that I'd thrown carelessly into the storage space in the bow. But it couldn't be that. This was clearly something heavy, judging by its sluggishness, its reluctance to be moved by the water. It was floating, knocking into the side of the hull—right where my bed was.

I went back to the wheelhouse and found my boat hook, a long pole that had come with the boat and to my knowledge never been used, not by me at any rate—the *Revenge* hadn't left this mooring since I'd moved in. The hook was heavy and unwieldy, and for a moment I contemplated leaving everything where it was and going to sleep on the sofa with my duvet, but it was no good. The knocking was regular, but not regular enough—just random enough to slowly but surely drive me crazy.

I tucked the boat hook under my right arm and clutched the flashlight in my left, but the hook was too heavy—it needed both hands. I put the flashlight down on the roof of the cabin, its beam shining across the tops of all the narrowboats and all the way over to the office.

I fished around with the boat hook until it made contact with the object. I jabbed at it. It was solid, and heavy. I tried a couple of times to snare it with the hook but, when it finally connected, the bundle was too heavy for me to lift. I felt it roll, turn, pulling the pole almost out of my grasp, so I wriggled it until it was free and peered over the edge of the gunwale into the darkness below.

Something pale, something shapeless. I got the flashlight, shone it down into the space—and Caddy's face looked back up at me. One eye closed, one eye half-open, gazing up at me in a bizarre, twisted sort of a wink. Her hair, a dark tangle, swirling and washing over her face in the muddy water.

I dropped the boat hook. It clattered at an angle on the gunwale and tipped over onto the dock, rolling to a stop. I was breathing fast and hard and then I found my voice and screamed, screamed louder and harder than I ever had in my life.

Chapter Five

By the time it was daylight, the shock started to kick in.

Josie, who had been a paramedic in her former life, sat with me in the main cabin of the *Souvenir* and was keeping a close eye on me.

The police were on my boat.

Malcolm had called them. He and Josie had been the first ones to get to me, although not long after that the whole marina was awake and milling around in various states of undress, waiting for the police to arrive. They all took turns looking down the side of the boat with the flashlight, at the body. Eventually Malcolm had shouted at everyone that they were contaminating the scene—and most of them went back to their boats.

One police car had arrived, and two patrol officers. We'd met them in the parking lot of the marina. The automatic lights still didn't appear to be working, so it was dark and by that time I was shaking, shaking from head to foot. One of them asked me questions about what I'd seen and heard while the other one went to look.

I hadn't cried. Instead, I'd found myself making a sound that started out like a wail of panic, something I couldn't control, a noise from somewhere inside that came from fear and horror at finding her like that; finding Caddy, of all people, my beautiful Caddy. The noise went on and on, rising and fading again as I ran out of breath, while Josie held me to her chest and shushed me and rocked me, and I held on to her.

When I'd calmed down again, they made me go with Sally and Josie to the *Souvenir*. More police cars came, and a motorboat came up the river with other police on it. They put some kind of net over the end of my boat and tied the other side of it to the dock, presumably so the body didn't float off on the outgoing tide, although it didn't seem to want to go anywhere. Now it was daylight, low tide, and I was sitting in the main cabin with two blankets around me, one around my shoulders and the other across my knees, but even so, I was shaking. I couldn't stop thinking about how filthy my sneakers were, and whether anyone would notice if I took them off.

People kept asking me questions, and to each of them I gave the answer, "I don't know, I don't know." I was only half-aware of all the people in the cabin, and people were talking about me as though I wasn't there at all. In truth, my presence was mostly physical.

Caddy was dead. An accident? Had she tripped, somehow, in the darkness? Had she come to the party earlier, and I hadn't realized? Had she fallen over, stumbled against something and hit her head on one of the posts? Why hadn't I heard anything? Why hadn't I noticed?

"What's happened?" It was Roger. He'd managed to sleep through it all.

"It's a body in the water. Against the boat."

"Is Genevieve all right?" Malcolm's voice.

"She'll be fine, I'm keeping my eye on her. She just needs a bit of peace and quiet for a while, that's all."

"Genevieve?"

"I said leave her alone, Malcolm, all right? Honestly, you should know better."

"I just wanted to ask her if she wants me to talk to the police for her, you know, kind of like a liaison . . ."

"What does she want a liaison for? Honestly, she's perfectly capable of speaking to the police when they need her to. Anyway, she didn't see anything; she just found the body. It could have happened to any of us."

"Her boat's nearest the river. It must have come down the river from Cuxton. Her boat's the one that would catch it first if it came downstream."

"Who says it went in at Cuxton?"

"I never said that. I said it must've come from the Cuxton side, that's all. That's where the last one came from, remember? That guy that got stuck in the mud. Last Christmas."

"You're wrong. The last one was that stupid fool who jumped off Aylesford bridge in the summer."

"That one ended up in Gillingham, not here."

"I *know* that, I was just saying, that was the last body."

"Why are you all arguing about it?"

This last voice was Sally's. She'd been crying, off and on, not noisily but dabbing her eyes with a tissue, mourning someone she didn't know.

They were all silent for a while.

I said, in a voice that sounded somehow different from my own, "Aren't you going shopping?"

It felt as if they were all staring at me, and my face grew hot.

"Oh, don't you worry yourself about that," Josie said. "We can go later."

"Shall I get you a drink, Genny? A cup of tea?" Sally said.

She'd made one for me an hour ago. It was still there on the table, cold.

"I don't know," I said again. "No. I don't think so."

"Wonder who she was," said Malcolm.

"Let's not talk about it anymore," said Josie, patting me on the knee. "Plenty of other things to talk about, after all."

But that didn't work, either. A man came down the stairs from the deck, a man in a suit. He had thinning gray hair cut short, dark eyes, a lined face.

"Morning," he said. "Detective Sergeant Andy Basten. I'm looking for Genevieve Shipley?"

They all looked at him and then at me, despite themselves, and almost imperceptibly they all seemed to move a fraction closer to me as if to afford me some sort of protection.

He showed me his ID and his badge. The badge had rubbed against the card in the ratty leather wallet and you could hardly see his picture, let alone his name. He looked as though he liked a beer or two.

The *Souvenir* was a big boat, but not as big as the *Revenge of the Tide*, and it felt crowded in the main cabin with all these people.

"We'll, er, leave you to it, shall we?" said Malcolm.

"I'm staying here," Josie said, "unless she wants me to leave."

I wanted her to stay. I wanted her to tell him to go away, the policeman; tell them all to go and leave us alone. I wanted to rewind to last night and that terrible, insistent noise and, instead of going to look, turn over and put my hands over my ears and go back to sleep.

"I'm all right, Josie. Honest," I said at last.

They all went up on deck, leaving me there with the policeman.

"This won't take too long," he said. "Must have been a terrible shock for you."

I nodded, rapidly. My head felt wobbly, as though it wasn't connected to my body properly. "I was half-asleep. It woke me up very quickly when I realized what it was."

He sat down on the armchair opposite me and took out a notebook. "I know you've been through all this with the officer earlier. I just want to check we've got things straight. You said you heard a noise?"

"I heard a knocking on the side of the boat. It woke me up. I went to find out what it was."

I was repeating myself already, babbling. My mind wasn't functioning clearly; it was working at least three beats behind my mouth. *Think. Concentrate. Don't say anything. Don't tell him anything.*

"That sort of thing happen often?"

"No. Sometimes garbage gets caught against the boat when the tide goes out. That's what I thought it was."

He nodded. "It's a nice boat," he said. "Live there alone, do you?"

"Yes. I'm renovating it. I had savings from my job in London. I'm taking a year off to fix up the boat. I've been here five months already, I've done most of it by myself. All the siding. The plumbing."

I was rambling now, but he didn't stop me. Just watched me with tired-looking eyes.

"I'm sorry it was such a mess in there. We had a party last night. Why did you need to go in my boat, anyway?"

"We're finished with it now," he said. "Just needed to check it wasn't part of the crime scene, that's all. Birthday party, was it?"

"Kind of a boatwarming, I guess. Some of my friends from London. Lots of people who live here"—I indicated the marina with a vague sweep of my hand.

"I'll need to get you to write me a list. Everyone who was here last night. That okay?"

"Of course."

"And you all had a good time? At the party?"

I nodded.

"The woman you found," he said, "she wasn't one of your party guests?"

I stared at him. "They all left. All the London group. They all went early. I saw them leave the parking lot."

His question had reminded me of something and, before he had a chance to ask me anything else, I said, "There was a car, last night. I've just remembered. In the parking lot. When I went outside to see what the knocking was, I heard a car driving off. I thought it was odd because it didn't have its lights on and it was still dark. And the light's supposed to come on in the parking lot, it's on a motion sensor, and it didn't work. The light didn't come on."

The sergeant was noting all this down, and when I ran out of words he was still writing. "You didn't see what kind of car it was? Registration number? Color?"

"It was dark. I mean the color. That was all I could see."

He nodded slowly, made another note.

"Have you identified the body?" I asked, trying to keep the trembling out of my voice.

"Not yet. Did you recognize her, Genevieve?"

I pulled the blanket tighter across my chest. The wool was scratchy against my arms. "I couldn't really see the face. I just saw that it was a body and I started screaming."

He didn't say anything. He was looking at me curiously, as though he knew something I didn't. As though I'd said something particularly interesting.

He'd written everything down, laboriously, on three sheets of lined paper headed with various official titles, and he handed them to me. I looked at them blankly, at the rounded letters on the page, thinking how his handwriting was girlish, not what I'd expected at all.

"I need you to sign it," he said.

"What is it?"

"Your statement. You need to read it through carefully and check that you agree with everything I've written. Then you need to sign the bottom of each page. There—see? And there."

I read through it. He'd written it on my behalf, as though I'd done it myself. It was odd seeing my words summarized in that curiously rounded script. I signed each page with a rough approximation of my signature and handed it back to him.

"Can I go back to my boat now?"

"Not just yet. We'll come and find you when we're ready, okay? Are you feeling all right?"

"I think so." I unwrapped myself from the blankets slowly, as though I was peeling off bandages. I felt a wave of relief: maybe I'd gotten away with it.

"We'll come and talk to you again, maybe tomorrow," he said. "Can I take your phone number?"

I recited it to him. "I don't think I can tell you any more," I said. "It woke me up, I went to look, and I found it. That's it."

"Yes," he said, giving me his card. DETECTIVE SERGEANT ANDREW BASTEN, MAJOR CRIME. "But you never know. You might remember something else. Like the car in the parking lot. Your brain does funny things when you've had a shock; it's like it only lets you remember one thing at a time."

He led the way up the steps onto the deck of the *Souvenir*. Sally and Josie were sitting on the wooden bench, with Sally's petunias and geraniums, just starting to look autumn-bedraggled, in pots around them.

"You okay?" said Josie when she saw me coming up the steps.

"I'm fine. Thank you."

"You look terribly pale," said Sally.

Basten cleared his throat. "I'll leave you to it," he said. "Let me know if you think of anything else in the meantime."

He didn't head for the parking lot; instead he climbed off the *Souvenir* and headed toward the dock where the *Revenge of the Tide* was moored. There were still lots of people around; crime-scene tape fluttered across the start of the dock and he lifted it and ducked beneath it. At the end of the dock, two figures dressed in white coveralls were on their hands and knees doing something. The whole area was illuminated by lights on metal rigging, as though they were preparing to make a movie. It was daylight, and yet still cloudy enough to make the lights necessary. I thought about what they were illuminating down there and shivered. The space between the end of the dock and the side of the hull was draped in a huge blue tarpaulin.

The tide was out now.

"They've not taken anything away," said Sally. "I think the body must still be down there."

Along with all the other cars in the parking lot, a black van with "Private Ambulance" in gray letters on the side had arrived. At the main gate, two police officers were standing guard to prevent vehicles entering or leaving.

"I heard one of them say they were going to move it soon. Before the tide turns."

We watched the activity as people came and went. The street filled up with spectators and a constable was stationed there to move people on. Then the press arrived and spent the rest of the morning hanging around trying to take pictures of anything interesting. Sally made sandwiches. Josie ate two. I stared at them because I didn't want to look at anything else. In the end I lay on the sofa in the main cabin of the *Souvenir* and tried to sleep. I could hear them talking, on the deck, commenting on the action in the marina. I tried to block out the sound, but it still came through.

What seemed like hours later, I heard Basten on the deck of the *Souvenir*, telling Sally that I could go, if I wanted to.

I went up to the deck but he'd already left.

"He said you can go back," Sally said. "They're still working down there but you can go back if you want to."

I looked doubtfully down to the adjacent dock where the *Revenge* was still surrounded by people in white coveralls. Josie pulled me into a hug. She was big and warm and soft.

"You poor thing," she said into my hair. "Do you want me to come with you?"

"No, thanks," I said. "I think I'll just go back to bed and try and get some sleep. I'm so tired."

I was tired, it was true, but there was no way I was going to be able to sleep. I just needed to be alone. I needed them all to leave me on my own, so I could think. So I could work out what to do, without having to worry about accidentally giving something away.

"All right, then. I'll come and look in on you later."

I stepped off the *Souvenir* gingerly, my legs shaking. I felt as if I'd been ill, or asleep for a long time. The bright lights lit up the scene dramatically; I couldn't think of a time when I'd seen so many people in the marina.

A young policewoman tried to stop me when I got close to my boat.

"He said it would be okay for me to go home," I said, pointing at Basten.

"Oh, it's your boat? Let me just check."

The sergeant was at the end of the dock, talking on his cell phone. The police officer got his attention and pointed back to where I stood, behind the flapping strands of blue-and-white plastic tape.

I heard him say, "Yeah, let her through."

She gave me a smile and beckoned me forward. "Must have been a shock for you," she said, before I had time to reach the gangplank.

"Yes, it was," I agreed. I had no desire whatever to go through all that again.

"Take it easy," was all she said. Her smile was warm.

I stumbled down the steps to the cabin, my legs like jelly.

I picked up Dylan's phone from where I'd thrown it the night before. My hands were shaking as I scrolled through the menus to the address book, selected the only name in there: GARLAND. I pressed Call.

It was ringing. My heart was pounding at the thought of talking to him.

"Yeah?"

Oh, the voice. It had been so long and yet I remembered it instantly, it came flooding back—everything.

"It's me." My voice was low, urgent. I didn't want to risk anyone overhearing.

"Yeah. What do you want?"

I hadn't been expecting an especially enthusiastic response, given his unequivocal instructions never to call him, but I hadn't been prepared for quite such a hostile tone.

"It's about Caddy."

"Caddy?"

"She's dead, Dylan. I found her last night. She was in the water, next to the boat. I heard this noise, and I went to look, and then I found her in the water."

An indrawn breath, a pause. "What a fucking mess. What the hell was she doing there?"

"She was supposed to be coming to my party, and she didn't show up, and—"

"Why the fuck did you invite her to your party?"

It registered somewhere in my foggy brain that he didn't seem that shocked that someone we both knew well had met such a horrible death. And was this somehow my fault—was he blaming me?

"What should I do?" I asked.

"Did you tell them anything?"

"No. Nothing. I didn't say I knew her. What should I do, Dylan? I'm so afraid."

There was a pause. I couldn't hear any sounds in the background, no traffic, no voices. I wondered if he was at home, or in the car. I longed to be there, wherever it was. If I could see him, if I could see his face, this nightmare wouldn't be quite so awful. I felt another lurch of misery, like a jolt.

"Just keep your head down, right? I'll be in touch."

I went to say something else to him, something—what? That I missed him? That I wanted to see him?—but I didn't get the chance. He'd disconnected the call.

I'd waited so long to talk to him again. And of all the conversations I'd imagined, none of them bore any resemblance to this one. Despite the exhaustion, the panic, one thing registered above anything else: he already knew. He knew Caddy was dead.

Chapter Six

The cabin was still a mess. I'd been staring at it for half an hour and not seeing it, my brain trying to process the image of Caddy in the water through a fog of exhaustion and alcohol.

I got started cleaning up, sweeping up the breadcrumbs, soaking the dishes in the sink and then working my way through them methodically, my back to the scene of chaos behind me. The clouds had cleared, and through the porthole above the sink I could see the river, peaceful and sparkling in the bright sunshine. It looked like it did on every other sunny day, and for a moment I could focus on the task at hand and forget about last night.

When everything was washed and dried, I was almost tempted to wash it all again, just so I could stay in the warmth and safety of that moment. I put it all away, leaving the lasagna dish on the table in the dinette. I would take it back to Joanna later on. The bathroom smelled awful, but I had no intention of emptying the toilet cassette while the dock outside was swarming with police officers. I used the bucket again, and closed the door behind me.

The new room was just as I had left it, the woodwork soft with the last of the sanding, a shaft of sunlight dancing with specks of sawdust. It smelled of fresh timber. It would almost be a shame to paint over it all.

The smell of the wood reminded me of my dad, as it always did. Certain smells took me back to his workshop, a large shed behind our house built of corrugated asbestos and breeze blocks: linseed oil, turps, pickled onions, barley sugars, and engine oil. My dad was a practical man. He could fix anything, build anything, and repair anything. He scoured rummage sales for lonely and discarded items that could be recycled, reworked, or otherwise brought back to life with a bit of care and attention. His workshop had rows of old pickle jars half-full of screws, nuts, bolts, nails, capacitors, resistors, and fuses, nailed by their lids to the cobwebby beams overhead. As well as random bits of machinery, he collected cars that now would be called classic: a Ford Escort Mark II, a Citroën 2CV, and a Lotus, which, even with his best effort and constant tinkering, never traveled another mile under its own power. My mother tolerated it all, since it kept him out of the house and out of her way.

I was never excited by the cars. I watched him as he tinkered and fixed, but I never felt that same drive to see those old things working again. But when he got out his workbench and the woodworking tools I was always there, ready to help. I built a chair when I was nine years old. There was something about the transformation from the rough wood to the beautiful, practical lines and curves of the finished article that I found inspiring.

He died the day I took my final exam at university. I'd phoned home when I'd finished, but there'd been nobody there. He had suffered a massive heart attack in the mall at lunchtime. My mother had told me she knew he was dead the moment he fell.

I helped organize the funeral while all my friends were celebrating their summer of freedom. My mother was supported by a lanky, gray-haired man called Richard, whom I'd never met until the day we buried my dad. She married him three months after the funeral, sold the house I'd grown up in, and moved with him to the South of France to renovate a farmhouse. Our contact shrank from sporadic to virtually nonexistent over the course of the next few years, and while I missed my dad every single day, I barely thought about her at all anymore.

I went back into my bedroom, looking for something to do. This was turning into the longest day of my life, and it felt as though I'd been awake for a week. It was too early to go to bed, but it looked so tempting, the duvet thrown back. Just as I had left it last night when I went to investigate that noise.

I took off my jeans and lay down on the bed, pulling the duvet over myself. I was exhausted, my head aching with the remains of what was probably a hangover from all that beer I'd drunk.

I lay there for a while, dry-eyed, wondering why I wasn't crying. Caddy's body was outside, probably less than two yards away from where I was lying, in the mud of the river Medway. Dylan had answered me as though I were the last person on earth he wanted to speak to. There were so many things wrong with this that I couldn't begin to understand what could have happened. Poor Caddy. My poor, dear friend.

Thinking about it made my head hurt. And my heart.

It was impossible to sleep, to rest, even to think. I could hear them talking out on the dock—just the impression of voices at first, but when I sat up in the bed I could make out phrases.

". . . could be worse, at least it hasn't been raining . . ."

". . . get out of here before it starts . . ."

I wanted to know how she'd died. I wondered if they would tell me, if I asked.

She couldn't have been there when the party started. It must have been afterward, after everyone had gone. I'd sat in the main cabin, looking at the mess, and Caddy was—where? Outside, on the dock? In the parking lot?

Had she come for the party after all, slipped, and fallen into the river? No, she hadn't. I remembered that first glance, what I'd seen in the beam of the flashlight, the shock that it was Caddy—and her face had been misshapen, her head—some kind of wound, too deep for an accidental blow—she'd been hit.

Why hadn't I heard anything? Why hadn't she screamed?

She hadn't just fallen in the water. She hadn't floated downriver from Cuxton or anywhere else upstream. Someone had killed her, and dumped her body in the water, next to my boat.

Outside, on the dock, a cell phone rang.

It was no use. There was no way I was going to sleep. I got out of bed and went back to the main cabin, got a clean glass out of the cabinet and ran the tap. The water still didn't take the taste away. Last night's beer, last night's panic.

I heard the sounds of footsteps on the deck above and then a sharp knock on the door to the wheelhouse.

"Yes?"

The door opened and a man in a suit appeared at the top of the steps. But it wasn't Basten; this one was younger, with dark hair and dark eyes and—unexpectedly—a nice smile.

Just as I was thinking how easy it was to spot police officers, I realized he was looking me up and down. Underpants. Cropped T-shirt displaying an expanse of midriff.

"Sorry. Didn't realize you were—er . . ."

"I was just trying to get some sleep," I said, even though I was patently standing in my main cabin and not in the bedroom.

"Miss Shipley?"

"Yes."

"I'm DC Jim Carling." He showed me his badge. Like Basten's, it was scuffed and worn so badly that the image was unrecognizable.

"I already spoke to somebody."

"I know. I just wanted to let you know that they're bringing the body up now. Didn't want you to get another nasty shock."

"Oh," I said, my voice rising. I looked across to the porthole without thinking, at the several pairs of legs that had now gathered on the dock.

He came down the steps into the cabin, so he was on my level. "I'll stay with you for a bit, if you like," he said gently. "Here."

He'd taken the crocheted blanket from the sofa and put it around me, guiding me to the sofa to sit down so my back was to the porthole. For the first time I felt on the brink of tears.

"It's all right, Genevieve," Carling said. "It'll be fine."

He was nice, really, I thought. He had a kind face.

Like Dylan. Dylan had a kind face. A face that only a mother could love, he'd said once. He did look like a bruiser, broken nose from boxing when he was a kid, misshapen ears, shaved head—but then, an unusually sensual mouth, and beautiful eyes, kind eyes. He wasn't what any girl would describe as handsome. Maybe that had been a blessing, otherwise I would have fallen for him sooner than I did, and then everything would have been different.

Carling was in the armchair, looking around the main cabin. I wondered if he'd ever been on board a houseboat before today.

"Do you want to have a look around?" I asked.

"Hm? Oh." He looked curiously embarrassed, as though I'd caught him looking at something he shouldn't. "That's okay. I just—I think it's nice in here. You've done a good job."

"Thank you."

"What made you want to live on a boat, then?"

I smiled at him. "I don't know. Just something I always wanted to do: buy a boat, spend a year fixing it up."

"Did it cost a lot?"

"I had a good job in London for a few years, saved up."

"What are you going to do when the year's up?"

"I don't know. I might stay on the boat, try and find work around here. Or go back to London."

From the dock came noises, shouts. They were hauling up the body. Josie told me afterward that there were four of them down in the mud, wearing waders. Another four on the dock. She watched the whole thing from the safety of *Aunty Jean*. They'd put a tent up, perched on the end of the dock and rocking in the wind because they had nothing to anchor it to, because the parking lot was starting to fill up with press. Cameron was talking to the journalists, while next to my boat they lifted her out of the mud and onto the dock. She was tiny, Caddy, probably weighed no more than a hundred pounds, but it took eight of them to lift her up.

"It will be strange, going back to a nine-to-five after this, won't it?" he asked. His voice was jovial, a little forced. I think he was trying to distract me.

"It will. I don't know if I'll be able to do it. But the money will run out soon enough."

"Does this thing work? I mean—does it go anywhere?"

"It could, I guess. I've never tried the engine but it does have one. That part of it is beyond my technical capability at the moment."

"You should take it on a trip, before the money runs out."

"Maybe I should."

There was an awkward pause. I wanted to ask him about his job, what it was like. I wanted to ask if he was married, what he did when he wasn't working. But none of it would come out. It sounded wrong, to be asking such things, given what was happening outside.

"Would you like a drink, Mr. Carling?" I asked at last. "Coffee?"

He smiled, a warm smile. "That would be great. Thank you. And call me Jim."

"Jim. All right, then." I pushed the blanket to one side and went to the galley, filling the kettle from the sink and putting it on the gas burner. At least I'd managed to clean the kitchen this morning. If he was going to spend time on my boat, he might as well see it at its best.

"It's an odd name for a boat," he said. "Under the circumstances."

"I guess so. It was already called that when I bought it. Apparently it's bad luck to change the name."

I turned from the galley, and the way he was looking made me realize that I still hadn't managed to get dressed again.

"I couldn't be having much worse luck, really, could I?" I said.

"I guess it's not really luck. Your boat is the closest to the river; if it was going to wash up anywhere it would be here."

I wondered at what point Caddy had changed from a "she" to an "it." The thought of it made me want to cry.

Carling stood.

"I think I would really like to look at the rest of the boat. You don't mind?"

"Go ahead," I said.

From here I could see down the hall to the end, to the hatch leading to the storage area at the bow. He wouldn't go in there. If he did, I told myself, he would just see boxes, carpentry tools, tubs of emulsion and paintbrushes. But he wouldn't go in there. Not with his suit on, at any rate.

He stopped at my bedroom and looked inside. "I like the skylight," he called.

"Yes," I said. "It's nice to wake up to. I like it when it's raining."

He said something else, but the kettle was starting to whistle on the stove and I missed it. I poured water in the coffee mugs and left them, and went to find him.

He was in my bedroom, looking up at the skylight.

"I didn't hear what you said, I'm sorry."

He started a little and turned. "Oh, I just said . . . it's cozy."

We stood for a minute, facing each other. My jeans were on the floor by his feet, the duvet a tangle on the bed.

"I should . . . um . . . put my clothes on."

"Oh, yes. Sure. Sorry."

"You could finish making the coffee, if you like."

His cheeks were pink. He squeezed past me and went back to the galley, while I pulled my jeans back on and found a thin sweater, one that didn't make me look like an ancient mariner.

"I wouldn't go in the bathroom," I said as I went back to the galley. "Toilet needs emptying."

"You have to empty the toilet?" he said, handing me a mug.

"Yes. You get used to it. When I redo the bathroom, I'm going to put one in with a bigger cassette, then I won't need to empty it so often. Or maybe a composter."

"It's starting to sound a bit less idyllic," he said.

"I'm not looking forward to the winter, to be honest. It gets really windy here."

A cell phone rang and I nearly jumped out of my skin. Carling fished in his pocket for his phone while my heart raced.

"DC Carling. Okay . . . thanks. No worries. Bye." He drank his coffee. "They're all done out there now," he said. "Will you be all right?"

I nodded. "Yes. Thank you. It was kind of you to stay with me."

"Thank you for the coffee. I'll have to see the rest of your boat another time, maybe." He scribbled his cell number on a scrap of paper. "Call me if you remember anything else."

I wondered if policemen always said that.

When he'd gone, and I'd shut the door of the wheelhouse and locked it behind him, the boat felt very empty, and very big. I stared at the closed door, thinking about what circumstances could bring him back here again, and whether giving him a tour of the rest of the boat was really an option.

I stood for a moment in the silence. I should eat something, I thought, but I had no appetite. My coffee was getting cold and I didn't even have the stomach for that. I should try to sleep, but I knew I would just lie there thinking about it all.

In the end I started by wiping down the woodwork in the new room, getting the dust off everything so that I could paint it. Autopilot kicked in, which was a relief. I put the radio on, which meant I could block out the sound of feet tramping up and down on the dock outside—what were they doing out there? Surely they'd looked at everything, sampled everything, photographed everything?

The boat had been my dad's idea. It was one of our main topics of discussion in his workshop. There was some unspoken understanding that it was only to be mentioned in that sacred space, between us: that if my mother knew of this, she would flip. He shared his dream with me. One day, he said, he would buy a boat and fix it up, then he would take it around the canals and rivers of Britain. We spent hours discussing the merits of the narrowboat over the barge, whether to do just the fitting-out ourselves or whether to buy a rusting shell and tackle the welding, too. He snuck in boat magazines, which he secreted in a box under the workbench, and we pored over the classified ads, choosing our dream boat and then changing our minds, over and over again. We set ourselves imaginary budgets and planned interiors. I had different names for my boat every week, but Dad's was always the same. He was always going to call his boat *Livin' the Dream*. I tried to tell him how cheesy this was, but he didn't care. It was his dream, his decision.

My mother found his magazines when she ventured into the workshop for the first time, two months after the funeral. She'd burned them in the back garden, along with a whole pile of wood that he'd been planning to make into a chest of drawers.

When the woodwork was clean and everything in the room smelled of damp pine, the floor swept and washed, too, I realized it had gotten quiet outside. I stuck my head out of the wheelhouse. There were police cars in the parking lot, and the gates were shut—all the other cars and people outside them. Cameron must have evicted the press. The dock was as it always had been—empty, and starting to move on the rising tide. If there was anything left to find down in the mud, their chance was gone.

I seized the opportunity to head for the disposal tank, and emptied the toilet cassette and the bucket I'd used in the night, cleaned them both and scrubbed the bathroom from top to bottom. Then I took a bagful of wash to the laundry room and stuck it in the washing machine, leaving it to its own devices while I took a hot shower in the shower room. The hose was all right. It had been fine in the summer. But now that the weather was turning chilly I should think about doing the bathroom next; I couldn't keep coming out here when it was getting darker in the evenings.

I felt better once I'd showered, and back at the boat I made myself a fresh cup of coffee. After that I went back to the laundry room and transferred the wash into the dryer. Cameron was in the parking lot, up on a ladder.

"How's it going?" he called.

"Okay, I guess," I said. "Are you fixing the lights?"

"Yeah. Something's snagged the cable."

"Really?"

He climbed down the ladder and showed me the section of cable he'd just replaced. It looked as if it had been caught around something, twisted.

"I guess that means there wasn't any CCTV, either," I said.

Cam shook his head. "The camera one was all right; that

feeds directly into the office. It's only the lights that weren't working. Of course, without the lights the camera's not going to have picked up much, but they might be able to see something. I don't know."

The police cars were still in the parking lot, two of them, but there was no sign of their occupants. The lights were on in the *Souvenir*, and in a couple of the other boats. The sun had gone in and the wind had picked up a little, and the clouds were making the afternoon feel darker and later than it was.

Back on the boat, the woodwork in the new room had dried off and I decided that now would be as good a time as any to paint it. I went to the end of the hall and opened the hatch into the storage area. It was dark in there, and cold. The flashlight I usually kept just inside the doorway was missing. For a moment I hunted around for it, and then I realized it was probably still on the roof of the cabin where I'd left it last night.

I turned on the light in the hallway, one I rarely used, and it shone brightly enough into the cavernous space to show me where the can of primer was, and the brushes in a shopping bag.

The light shone directly into the bow and illuminated the box at the end. I tried not to look at it. If I ignored it long enough, I would forget it was even there. But once I'd got the paint loaded into the tray and started work on the plain pine siding, the thought would not let me be.

I had to get rid of it. I had to get rid of the package.

Dylan should have come to collect it. A few weeks, he'd said, maybe a couple of months. Five months was really pushing his luck. And it couldn't stay where it was. If the police took it upon themselves to search the boat, they would find it and then I would be in big trouble.

I worked fast, splashing paint onto the wood. Missing spots. Going over other places twice.

On my first night on the boat, I'd lain awake on the sofa in the main cabin—the only really habitable space on the boat back then—and thought about all the hiding places, all the options. It had to be somewhere safe. It had to be close by, where I could be certain that it was still there, that it hadn't been tampered with. It had to be dry, and hidden well enough that someone wouldn't accidentally come across it.

The very front of the bow was the place I chose. If I'd realized I was going to have to hide it for all this time, I would have incorporated a better hiding place into one of my projects—a false wall maybe, a hidden compartment behind the siding. Too late for that now.

The porthole was a dark circle, nothing beyond it but black. The boat rocked gently, almost imperceptibly, beneath my feet on the river. The wind was blowing waves up from the inlet, and after a while I heard rain on the skylight in the hallway outside.

I finished painting. It wasn't a very good job. I would put another coat on in the morning, and try harder to concentrate.

I turned the radio off and the quiet was like a blanket that descended on the boat. Just the tickling of the rain on the roof of the cabin, on the skylights. It was a lonely night to be on board a boat this big. I washed the brush out in the sink and thought about making something to eat, a proper meal. I still had no appetite.

I couldn't bring myself to think of it, and yet it was there, all the time. Waking up, still half-drunk. The sound. Caddy's body against the side of my boat. The cable to the automatic light in the parking lot, mangled and snapped. The car, driving away with its lights off.

Chapter Seven

I hadn't expected to be able to sleep, but somehow I did.

I kept both phones by the bed, mine and Dylan's, and neither of them rang. Apart from the rain, which grew heavy, and the gentle rise and fall of the river, nothing stirred all night.

When I looked out of the wheelhouse the next morning, one of the two police cars was still parked in the parking lot. No sign of anyone in it.

It was still raining, so I pulled on my thick waterproof jacket and took a plastic bag over to the laundry room with me. My clothes were in a laundry basket by the side of the dryer, neatly folded. The washing machine and the dryer were both whirring. The room was warm and humid and smelled of fabric softener. As I was transferring my clothes to the plastic bag, Josie came in to check on her clothes.

"Did you fold these?" I said. "That was kind. I'm sorry I didn't take them out of the dryer last night."

"It's no bother. How did you sleep?" She was eyeing me, concerned.

"Not bad, considering. You?"

She laughed. "Oh, I always sleep like a log. Nothing ever wakes me. Good thing, too, with Malcolm's snoring."

"Josie," I began, talking quickly so I didn't have a chance to change my mind, "I was wondering if Malcolm would help me with something on the boat."

"Oh, love, you don't have to ask. You know he'd love to. What is it?"

I hesitated, the momentum gone. "I think—um . . . I think I'd like to see if I can get the engine started."

She stared at me. "What's brought this on?"

I shrugged. "Nothing really. I just thought—you know. It might be nice to take the *Revenge* on a trip one day."

"There's a lot more to it than just getting the engine started—you know that, don't you?"

"Mm. I just thought, it seems a waste to have a boat that never goes anywhere. I need to have a new project, that's all."

"Well," she said uncertainly, "I'll ask him. Maybe if you wanted to go on a trip he could go with you. Where did you want to go?"

This was all starting to get a bit too detailed. I should have asked Malcolm, rather than Josie—he wouldn't have batted an eyelid at the idea.

"Nowhere special. Look—just forget I asked. It's not a problem."

"Genevieve," she said sternly, "are you worried about what happened yesterday? Because I'm sure it was just a one-off. We don't often get bodies washed up here, you know. I know your boat is the one nearest to the river but you don't need to worry about it happening again, really you don't."

I picked up my bag full of laundry. "It's fine, Josie, honest. It was just a thought."

I was putting the laundry away when I heard a knock at the door to the wheelhouse. It was Malcolm.

"Morning," he said cheerily.

"How did the clothes shopping go yesterday? I forgot to ask Josie."

"Ah," he said. "Didn't happen, in the end. Far too much going on here."

He filled the kettle and put it on the stove, as if this were his boat and not mine. I didn't mind, although I probably wasn't at the stage yet where I could stroll onto *Aunty Jean* and help myself to whatever I wanted.

"The police, you mean?"

"Yeah. The gavvers."

"Did they talk to you?"

"Oh, yes. They wanted to come aboard the *Jean*, but I told them it was too cramped and we sat in the office instead. Good thing, too." He gave me a lopsided smile. "I'm not too keen on the gavvers. Although this lot weren't too bad, to tell the truth."

"I thought they were all right."

"Yeah, but see, there's all sorts of things wrong with that body being there. I don't think it was washed downriver, for one thing."

"I've been trying not to think about it, to be honest with you."

"And it didn't just fall in."

"No, I guess not," I said with a sigh.

He helped himself to two mugs from the cabinet, spooned coffee into each. "The police are starting a murder inquiry."

"Really? Are you sure?"

"You don't get that number of cops for a suicide, or even an accidental death. And they don't know who it is. Generally by the time they find a body in the river they know exactly who it is that's missing. That means, either they haven't been reported missing, or they're not from around here. Maybe from London or somewhere, I don't know."

"Why London?"

He made a face. "It's handy here, innit? Straight down the A2. First river you come to. First bit that feels like countryside."

"I guess so."

"What gets me," he said, pointing a teaspoon at me, "is why your boat? Now, that's intriguing me."

I stared at him. "Maybe they just thought it would get washed out to the river if they put it at the end of the dock."

"Maybe," he said. The kettle was starting a low whistle. "Feels to me like it was put there deliberately."

"What?" My voice sounded dull, a long way off.

"You come here from London, yeah?"

"So?" I felt sick all of a sudden. How could I get out of this? How could I wind the clock back, to before the laundry room, before I asked Josie for Malcolm's help? I felt as if I'd managed to give myself away.

"You never mentioned moving the boat before," he said.

"It was just something that policeman said," I replied lamely. "He asked if I'd taken the boat out on any trips. It hadn't really crossed my mind before that. That's all. It's got nothing to do with the body, not really."

He smiled, as though he didn't believe me. Nor should he.

"You shouldn't be scared, Gen."

"I'm not."

"You shouldn't lie to me, either." The kettle screamed its final, loudest note, and he turned off the gas.

Malcolm handed me a mug of coffee and we went to sit in the main cabin. I felt as if I was at a job interview that was going south.

"Well, of course I'm bloody scared," I said lightly. "I came face-to-face with a corpse last night. That kind of thing doesn't happen in Clapham. Not often, anyway."

"When I was in the army I saw all kinds. I saw a lot of bodies, in Bosnia, and other places. It fucks with your head. You think you've dealt with it, but you haven't. It takes years."

"I didn't know you were in the army," I said.

He sniffed. "Don't like to talk about it really."

I sipped my coffee. It was chilly in the main cabin. I wondered whether to ask Malcolm to light the stove again, to give him something to take his mind off the topic of starting the engine.

"I never felt scared here before, never worried about being here alone. This place always felt so safe."

"You're not alone. You've got all of us now."

"Yes, I guess so. I'd still like to try and start the boat, though. Just to see if it works. Will you help?"

Malcolm's whole face brightened. "Of course I'm going to help, you big wuss."

An hour later, Malcolm was up to his armpits in the engine.

I'd looked at the engine when I bought the boat; Cameron had pointed out all the various parts, and I'd nodded and smiled as though I knew what he was talking about. As though I was listening. Thanks to my years of training with my dad in his workshop, I was fully prepared to do all that needed doing on the boat in terms of renovation, and I'd done a lot already: I'd learned as I'd gone along and I'd made the *Revenge* into a habitable, comfortable boat. But the engine was just a step too far.

Of course, Malcolm scarcely stopped talking. It started with a low whistle when we lifted the hatch down to the engine space.

"Nice."

"Is it?"

"Looks good from here," he said. "Maybe it just wants a good clean. Have you tried starting her up?"

My blank expression told him everything. He went up into the wheelhouse and fiddled with various controls. Nothing happened. "Charged the battery?"

Of course I hadn't.

"You've got a decent generator, you know."

"I do?"

"Bloody good thing, too. A new one would cost you a small fortune, and you need a decent generator if you want to take her upriver. What you going to plug her into, otherwise?" He indicated the dock and the electricity and water hookup.

"I hadn't thought about it."

"Lots of things you probably haven't thought. Got a cloth?"

I found him some old rags from the storage and crouched next to him on the deck, watching as he cleaned black gunk away from joints, dials, and levers.

"So," he said cheerfully, leaning back on his heels, "while I'm doing this, you can tell me all about what happened in London."

I hesitated. "There's nothing to tell."

He stopped what he was doing and gave me a pointed look.

"You don't have to tell me," he said. "Just trying to make conversation, that's all."

And he went back to tinkering with the engine.

It wasn't that I didn't want to tell him. Lord knew it would be good to tell someone—it was just where to start.

And then I had a picture of myself, dancing. How it felt to dance. How free.

"Well, you know I used to be a dancer," I said, quietly.

He continued tinkering.

"I started with ballet, when I was young. I kept it up until I was twelve. I got to be good at it, but not quite good enough for ballet school. When I got turned down for that I concentrated on gymnastics instead. I was all right at that, too."

"What happened?" he asked, without turning.

"Well, for a start, my body changed and suddenly I was the wrong shape for it. Then I got too busy with A-levels, then university. That was it, basically. Then, when I was working in London, I started looking for dance classes—something to do to keep fit. I thought, I'd enjoyed it before. And—well—what happened was, I found a pole fitness class."

"What's that?"

"Pole dancing."

"Ah!"

"Yes. You can laugh."

"I'm not laughing. Sounds like a good idea to me. Pass me that wrench? No, the other one."

I watched him for a moment, wondering whether I should continue with this.

"So—you went along? To the class?"

"Yes. It was fun. Not as easy as it looks, you know. You have to be fit, and physically strong—it's not like other dancing classes where you can get away with it if you have a good sense of rhythm. And it was a fitness class really, but I loved it right off."

"I bet you were good at it. What with all that dancing you'd done. And gym, and that."

"Well, I really enjoyed it, that always helps. Have you been to a club where they've done it?"

He coughed a little. "Well, yes. Not very good, though. I bet you were better."

I found myself laughing. "Maybe."

Malcolm said, "Right, that's all I can do until you get the battery charged. We'll have another try tomorrow."

I felt a bit bereft all of a sudden, until I realized that he had no intention of ending our conversation there. He wiped his hands on the dirty rag and handed me his coffee mug. "I think I'd like a cuppa tea this time, if it's all the same to you. I'll just go back to *Aunty Jean* and clean up. Back in a minute."

Ten minutes later we were sitting back in the main cabin, steaming mugs in front of us. I was happy for the warmth of the mug. I'd started the fire in the woodstove but it would be a while before it started throwing off any real heat.

"I loved those classes," I said. "The instructor was a girl called Karina. She'd worked in some of the big clubs, earned loads of money doing it. She said I was better than she'd been. She said I should try it. Dancing in a club, I mean."

"And you did."

"I needed the money," I said. "I'd gotten this idea that I wanted to buy a boat. You know, there were times I loved the sales job—times when I hated it, too—but I knew I couldn't do it forever. It's bloody hard work, very pressured. When everything's going well, it's great, but if things start to slip, then it's just hideous, just like fighting uphill, all the time. And I had a sort of relationship with Ben—that one from the party—that had fizzled. So I wanted out. I wanted something to look forward to, an end to it all. And I decided I was going to take a year off and fix up a boat."

"Bit of a difference from working in London," he said.

"Exactly. I'd saved up money, from bonuses and stuff. But nowhere near enough to buy a boat, and I was getting so sick of it, so sick of the stupid job and the crazy aggressive people I worked with."

"So you were dancing in a club? Like, a strip club?"

This was where it was difficult. "It was a private members' club called the Barclay, near London Bridge. Karina introduced me to the owner. Fitz, his name was. I had no idea what those places were like; I'd never been in one. But it seemed all right. The membership for it was hundreds of pounds. The drinks in the bar were—shit, I don't know—stupid money. The whole place reeked of cash. They had separate rooms, bars. VIP area. It was good money, easy money in a lot of ways."

I was waiting for his reaction. I'd had different ones, from the few people I'd told, or the people who'd found out for themselves. Shock was a common one. Hostility, sometimes. Occasionally I was lucky enough to get a "Good for you" and a pat on the back.

"Well, it's like an art form, innit?" Malcolm said. "That's

what I've always thought, anyway. You have my complete admiration."

"Thank you."

He raised his mug in salute.

"So. That was London." I said it with finality, thinking that might satisfy him. "It's not the kind of thing you can just tell people, after all."

"That's it?"

"I had lots of fun doing it. I earned a ton, more than I was earning in the sales job, just for a few hours on weekends. I saved it up until I had enough to leave my job and buy this boat."

He nodded, slowly. "Makes sense."

"Yes."

"I bet some sketchy stuff went on, though."

"What do you mean?"

"Those places, full of drugs and shit like that."

"I guess so. Some of the girls used to take stuff to keep themselves awake. I kept away from all of that side of it, really. I had better things to do with the money I was making."

He sniffed and finished his tea. "You don't want to be messing with all that stuff, you know. There are some nasty people who run them sorts of clubs."

"Yes," I said.

He looked at his watch. "I better shoot off. I told Josie I'd only be ten minutes."

I felt a huge wave of relief. "Oh, okay. Thanks, for, you know—the engine."

"No worries. I'll have another look tomorrow when you've got the battery charged. She still wants me to take her shopping for this bloody wedding outfit. I don't know why we can't just go as we are; got enough bloody clothes stuffed into that boat as it is."

"Right you are."

At the steps he paused and looked back at me, his lined face serious. "You're not on your own, Gen. You know that, right? We all stick together here. You don't need to worry."

I smiled at him. "Thanks."

I watched from the door of the wheelhouse until he went belowdecks on the *Scarisbrick Jean*. The boat was silent; even the rain had eased off.

Chapter Eight

If it hadn't been for Karina, I would never have met Dylan, or Caddy—for it was Karina who arranged the appointment at the Barclay. An audition, I suppose it was—with Fitz, the owner of the club.

"He's all right," she'd said. "You'll get along with him. And he's gonna love *you*."

He didn't show up very often; he didn't need to. In fact, I found out later that he didn't audition all the girls; he mainly left that up to the club manager, David Norland. For some reason, Fitz had wanted to see me personally.

Karina and I had worked out a rough routine between us. It had been fun dancing around one of five poles in an upstairs studio in Clapham—me, Karina, and several other girls of varying sizes and abilities. It had been fun, even with bruised legs and friction burns on the palms of my hands and the insides of my thighs until I got used to it. Like everything, the more you did it, the easier it got. I'd worked my way through all the basic moves, the intermediate and the advanced, and now I was developing new moves and combinations myself, or trying ones I'd seen on the Internet. It wasn't just fitness, by that stage. It was a challenge. And then I'd had that conversation with Karina.

"You should train to be an instructor," she'd suggested. "You could help me out with classes."

"Nah," I said, pulling my jeans back on after class one evening. The other girls had gone; I'd stayed behind to help her dismantle the poles and put them away in the storage room.

"You're good enough," she said. "You could earn some extra money."

"Thanks for the offer, but I need lots of money. Lots and lots. More than this would give me."

"How come?"

So I told her about my plan. We ended up walking out of the studio together and, without even really discussing it, into the pub next door. It was full of guys, post-work, ties loosened. Sports on the huge flat-screen TVs.

"You should think about dancing for real, then."

"What?"

"In a club. You'd make a killing."

"You mean, like in a strip club?"

"A gentlemen's club, they're called."

"Really? You think I could do that?"

"Of course you could." She was looking at me, her big blue eyes wide.

"How come you don't do it anymore?"

She laughed. "Past my sell-by date," she said. "No—I guess I could still do it. But it's the late nights, you know? Difficult, with the kids."

At the time I laughed it off a bit, finishing my drink and listening to Karina telling me about the clubs, how much fun it was at times, how hard it was at other times, but above all, how much money you could get if you were any good at it.

The week after that, I asked her about it after class. She offered to introduce me to a guy she used to work for, the owner of a club on the South Bank. She made the call on her cell phone, and before I could change my mind she'd made me an appointment to go and see him. Fitz.

To be honest, I hadn't really taken the idea seriously when

Karina had first suggested it. It would be great to have another source of income. I thought it might be fun to spend the night in a posh nightclub and earn money at the same time. But if he'd said no, I would have turned my back on the place and never looked back. That was why I turned up at the club with plain black underwear underneath the skirt and blouse I'd worn to work—nothing special. I can't remember if I was even wearing makeup.

The club wasn't open; it was seven o'clock on a Friday evening. I rang the bell of the main front door of an imposing Georgian townhouse near the river. A man in a suit opened it.

"What?"

"I'm here to see Mr. Fitz," I said, using the same voice I used when I was trying to get put through to a senior buyer. I wondered what he thought of me. He was tall and almost as wide, a tattoo on his neck, unreadable gothic lettering tangled in a swirl of lines. A chunk of his ear was missing.

"You mean Fitz," he said, leading the way up a flight of stairs into a plush, quiet hall. Artwork on the walls. Chandeliers. "Nobody calls him mister."

Fitz was in one of the club offices, talking on a cell phone, his ass perched on the edge of a desk that was bare except for a telephone and a new-looking monitor, wireless keyboard, and mouse.

He waved me in and pointed to a chair in the corner. While he talked in South London gibberish to whoever was on the other end of the call, I took in the expensive suit, the handmade shoes. He had dark hair neatly cut, eyes hidden behind sunglasses. Indoors. I thought he looked like a twat.

"... yeah, mate. Nah. No, I haven't seen it ... Yeah, if you like. Whatever. Right. See ya later, then." And he hung up.

I gave him my best smile.

"You must be the divine Genevieve," he said. His accent lost the Peckham twang with barely a hesitation.

"It's nice to meet you," I said, offering my hand.

"Karina tells me you're something special."

"You should really decide that for yourself."

He nodded, appraisingly. "You haven't done this before?"

"No, I haven't."

"Have you been in a club like this one before?"

I shook my head.

"Very well," he said, offering his hand to help me to my feet. "Let's see what you can do, Genevieve. Afterward I'll ask David to give you the tour. Got any preference for music, or shall we just see what's playing?"

"Whatever's easiest," I said.

We went back downstairs and through a door at the end of the hall, which opened up into the main nightclub. There were private booths, tables, and chairs around the edge of the dance floor, heavy drapes, cushions, discreet lighting. In this bar were three stages, each with a pole. I wondered if he expected me to strip all the way. I hoped not.

He pointed me to the largest of the three. "Off you go."

The opening beats to Elbow's "Grounds for Divorce" came through the speakers at deafening level. I stepped out of my shoes and started by circling the pole with bare feet, my hand on it, before lifting myself up into a curl and swinging around . . . and I was off. I wriggled out of the skirt quickly and did the rest of the routine in my underwear, unbuttoning my shirt and letting it swing around me as I moved. I made my way through the routine I'd worked on with Karina, adjusting it as the music slowed, and after the first half-minute I got into my stride and actually started to enjoy myself. I even added in a few extra cartwheel kicks. The song was over sooner than I expected it to be, and, other than a slight flush to my cheeks, I hadn't really exerted myself.

From the seating area below the stage came a slow handclap. "Very good, my dear. Very good. Different, but not in a bad way. What do you think, David?"

A second man was with him. I hadn't noticed him arrive, but he was seated with Fitz. A sharp gray suit, a thin face, blond hair cut short. "Yeah. She'll do."

"Come and sit with me, lovely Genevieve."

I slipped back into my skirt and stepped down from the stage. I crossed the carpeted floor, buttoning up my work blouse again, and went to sit at the table with the two men. Norland told me the rules.

"Okay, here's how it goes. You can start tonight on a trial basis. If the customers like you, we'll call you back for a full night. That's a minimum of five dances on the stage, more if you get requests. You can do private dances on the pole; that will be in the Blue Room. In between your stage dances you sit with the clients and drink with them—you get commission on that and you get thirty for a lap dance. You don't do extras. You don't take phone numbers, you don't mess around outside the club with customers. If you take guests to the VIP area you get paid for your time, two hundred per hour, plus tips. The house fee is fifty a night. Sound fair?"

"And if I don't like it?"

The men both laughed.

"You're not keen on earning upwards of a grand a night?" said Norland.

"I can earn that in my day job easily enough," I said. It wasn't entirely true, but they would never know. "I'm doing this because I enjoy dancing."

Fitz smiled, a smile that was surprisingly warm. "You'll like it, I promise you. If you don't, then you don't have to come back. All right?"

I nodded. "Thank you."

"Stage name," said Fitz. "What do you reckon, David?"

"I think Genevieve is pretty cool anyway," he answered.

"Don't be a moron," Fitz replied, looking at me steadily. "She can't use her real name. How about Viva?"

"Viva," I repeated.

Norland nodded. "I'll add her to the list for tonight."

When he took me on the tour of the place, I was struck by two things: first, the place was full of money, real money; and second, Norland was a complete prick. He was patronizing and sly and sure of himself. He wore his aftershave like a weapon.

"These are the dressing rooms," he said, leading me through a discreet "Staff Only" door behind the stage. "You can fight with the other girls for a dressing table when you're on."

"Don't we get our own?" I asked. I should have kept my mouth shut.

"There's a lot of girls working here weekends," he said. "We don't have room for egos."

We went back out to the club and down a hall to the side. Away from the dance floor, the carpets were thick and our footsteps were silent. The doors along the right wall of the hall were named: Harem, Justice, Boudoir. Norland stopped outside the last door. On it, a brass plaque: THE BLUE ROOM. It was called that because of the décor, I supposed: rich blue wallpaper and gold fixtures, heavy velvet curtains held back with thick gold braided rope. In the center of the room was a round parquet floor with a gold pole rising from it. The ceiling in this room was higher and the pole went all the way up to the ornate plasterwork cornicing.

"Wow," I said, running my hand up the pole.

Norland smirked.

"Size is everything, huh?"

I didn't respond.

"Can you get up there?" he asked, nodding upward.

"Of course I can," I said coldly.

"Not many of the girls can. In fact, the last one to do it was Karina, and that was five years ago."

I liked the idea of the height in this room. I never felt the poles were enough of a challenge. I liked the idea of working my way to the top of the room and spinning back down. I would have to work out some new combinations to make use of the whole length of the pole.

He showed me around the rest of the Barclay Gentlemen's Club. The two main bars, one of which was downstairs with a separate entrance onto the side street; the reception area; the coat check; the various private booths and VIP rooms around the main dance floor.

"Find something nice to wear later," he said, when we found ourselves back in the foyer. The place looked more like a hotel than a club. "You'll need an evening dress before twelve. Then you can change into something that shows more flesh for your dances. Get yourself some decent underwear."

"All right," I said. The man was a slug.

"Come back any time after ten thirty. When you come tonight, ask for Helena. We'll put you on probably around two, three o'clock. As long as you're here for your dance, you'll be all right. If you're ever late you'll get a fine and you might not get to go on. Got it?"

"Fine," I said, and I was back out on the London sidewalk.

Chapter Nine

I ate toast for dinner. It was the first solid food I'd had in more than twenty-four hours, and even so, it was a struggle. It felt dry and rough and tasted of nothing.

I was sitting at the dinette, looking at the scrap of paper that Carling had given me with his phone number on it. Next to it on the table was Andy Basten's business card. Why didn't Carling have a card like that? And which one should I call, if I needed to? Basten's neat, official card, with the crest of Kent Police? Or Carling's number, handwritten on a scrap of paper, scrawled but legible? Just a cell. I wondered what he did when he was off duty. Did he go home to his wife? Wife . . . and kids, maybe? And a dog. There would have to be a dog. And the wife would have a noble profession, maybe a teacher. Or a nurse. Or maybe she was a police officer, too. And two children at the dining table busy doing their homework when he got in from his hard day chasing criminals. He would kiss the tops of their heads—a boy and a girl—and he would ask his wife what was for dinner, while the dog chased around his feet, wagging its tail with delight. He would open a bottle of wine, and they would finish it—Jim Carling and his wife—when the kids were in bed.

Or he was divorced. He had that pissed-off look about him, I decided. Maybe his wife had run off with someone else— another police officer; they all did it—and left him behind to try and look after a great big house all on his own.

Or he was married, and yet he had affairs now and then, with women like me, women he'd come across in his day job. Victims. He picked ones he liked and got them to sleep with him.

I wasn't a victim, though, was I? Not yet, anyway.

For some reason, my next thought was of Ben. None of the London crew had contacted me since the party. None of them had any idea about the nightmare that had followed their departure. They'd all gone off to the pub, and after that God knows where, back to London in the end. I could just imagine Lucy telling them all how she'd seen it coming, how I'd been on a downward slope since I started stripping for money. I remembered what she'd said to Malcolm, the tone of her voice when Malcolm told her she'd be jealous of my boat one day.

"I don't think so somehow."

I didn't care what she thought about it, anyway. Her opinion had ceased to matter to me a long time ago.

Lucy was one of the people who'd had a real problem with me dancing.

It had been Ben who'd told her, of course; she would never have known about it otherwise. He'd demanded to know where I was going one evening, and I'd told him. Even though he'd claimed to be cool with it, he wasn't, at all. I think he felt he was sharing me, even though our relationship had been casual at best.

Lucy and I were in the pub one Friday after work, drinking big glasses of chilled white wine and dissecting the nightmare of selling high-end software solutions to boardrooms full of men. We took a lot of shit for it. The guys on our team were highly competitive, driven, occasionally downright nasty. Lucy got by because she was the daughter of the managing director, but she was bitter about all the testosterone she had to deal with. I wasn't as put out about the gender thing because I got by through working hard, which usually meant I hit my bonus targets. We had an alliance, of sorts, because Lucy needed someone to commiserate with her. But beyond that we had little in common.

"Ben told me where you were last night."

I drank my wine and looked at her. We'd been out with clients, and I'd disappeared early instead of staying on as we usually did and getting pathetically drunk. I'd begged off with a headache, but in fact I'd gone to the Barclay.

"You're a stripper," she said.

"I'm a dancer."

"You take your clothes off for money."

"Good money."

There was a flicker, I saw it—a moment where I'd almost justified it to her. She knew about money and the pursuit of it. She was about to ask the question: *How much money?* But then the moment passed.

"It's exploitation," she said. "You know how hard we bloody work, twice as hard as some of them, and we still don't get the same recognition."

"That has nothing to do with working in the club. I'm there because I want to be there," I said. "And if anyone's being exploited, it certainly isn't me. Men come in and spend all their money watching me do something I enjoy. It feels great, to be honest."

Just at that moment three of the guys on the sales team had come over and joined us and the conversation turned to the usual topic of who had the biggest car, the biggest sales deal, the biggest set of balls. Lucy had never mentioned it again, not until last night at the party. Despite her supposedly feminist convictions, I couldn't shake the notion that, actually, she was a little bit envious of the money, if not the attention.

Apart from Lucy and Ben, most of my friends hadn't known what I did every Friday and Saturday night, and sometimes Thursdays and Sundays, too. I didn't need to be at the club until eleven, so I kept up with my normal social activity and when they went off clubbing, or back home to bed, I went to the Barclay and earned myself a fortune.

It had crossed my mind to tell them, more than once. If any of them had asked me a direct question, I wouldn't have lied. But none of them seemed interested; when I said I was going somewhere else, they just said things like, "Okay, cool," and waved me goodbye as they disappeared off to some club or other, or back to someone's house, or off to another party.

I was lying awake in bed. The skylight was a square of black that was lighter than the black in the rest of the room. When I closed my eyes, I could still see it. It was like an opening, the entrance to a tomb.

I was physically tired, but my mind was spinning. Malcolm was right: I was scared. During the day it was easy to pretend this wasn't really happening, easy to believe that maybe the body hadn't been Caddy. I'd caught only a glimpse of her face, the dirty water of the Medway washing over it, a flash of white in the beam of my flashlight. It could so easily have been someone else: a body from upstream after all, a suicide, a missing person.

At night, things were very different.

From the first day in the marina, I'd never really felt alone. Even after dark you heard noises from the other boats, the faint voices from someone's television, shouts from Diane and Steve's two children, traffic on the highway, the rattle of the Eurostar or the Javelin rocketing along the high-speed rail link a mile or so away. The other liveaboards were never more than a shout away; I'd proven that last night, I tried to reassure myself. I'd screamed, and in under a minute at least five people had come out of their boats to see what was going on. And yet I couldn't relax.

A cell phone was ringing.

I sat up in bed, my whole body tensed and alert. It sounded

a long way off, as though it were coming from one of the other boats.

I pushed back the duvet and opened the bedroom door. The noise of the ringing grew louder.

In the main cabin, it was louder still. It wasn't my phone, which was charging on the dinette table—it was Dylan's.

Finally I found it, buried down the back of the sofa, where I'd thrown it when Carling came down into the cabin. It was still ringing. The name on the display: GARLAND.

I had a surge of joy, overwhelming relief.

"Hello?"

There was silence on the other end of the phone.

"Is that you?" I said, my voice trembling.

Still nothing. Someone breathing? I was certain someone was there. "Talk to me," I said. "Please, say something. Please."

Nothing.

I disconnected the call and threw the phone back onto the sofa, and cried. I waited a second to see if it would ring again, but it didn't. There was nothing, just the silence of the boat and the sound of my own sobs.

Even though he hadn't said a single word, it felt like a goodbye. He knew about Caddy; he must have some idea of the spinning chaos of my life . . . Why wasn't he here? Why hadn't he called to tell me what to do, to arrange to meet, even? He didn't care about me at all, not really. Whatever it was we'd had, that single night together that I had interpreted as magical, had been nothing to him, nothing.

I went back to bed and buried my face in the pillow until the tears were gone.

Hours later, still lying awake, staring at the skylight, dry-eyed and too tired to move, I had worked my way all around the theory that he didn't care about what happened to me, and found myself in a different place entirely.

He had called, after all. And he hadn't, despite my self-doubt, said goodbye. He'd said nothing at all. Why would he do that? With a rush of fear I wondered if he was in trouble. Had he tried to call but been prevented somehow? Did he need help? And what could I do about it if he did?

Chapter Ten

I'd always prided myself on my ability to adapt to any changes to my working environment, but dancing at the Barclay presented a steep learning curve.

After my audition, I hunted through my closet for something that I thought might be appropriately dramatic and sexy. Eventually I settled on the dark blue velvet dress I'd worn at the last sales conference dinner. A few tops and skirts that I wore out clubbing with my friends. And lingerie. Black lace with a pink ribbon trim.

I had no idea if that was okay.

I was nervous when I went back. The club was already filling with people, the music at a level loud enough that the girls had to lean forward to chat with the guys in the bar but not so loud that they couldn't hear someone calling them over.

I found Helena behind the bar. She was a small woman in her forties with an expression that said *Don't give me any shit.* She never looked happy in the time I worked there; even when she laughed she looked pissed off. She had dark hair piled on her head, which gave her an extra few inches, and sharp heels.

"You worked before?" she said, writing my name on a list behind the bar.

"No," I said. I didn't think she was referring to work in general.

"Did they tell you the rules?"

"I guess so. No fraternizing, that sort of thing?"

She smiled at me, or maybe it was a grimace. " 'No fraternizing.' I like that. If you're any good and they want you back, you have to be here ready and out in the club by eleven. If you're late you get fined."

The dressing room was still crowded even though a lot of the girls were already out in the club. I found a ratty bar stool and dumped my shoulder bag next to it, changing out of my jeans and into my dress while the girls around me ignored me completely. They were all talking at once, laughing, shouting, and the room was a confusing mess of clothing and makeup and clouds of competing perfume.

"Mind if I sit here?" I asked, pulling my bar stool up to the edge of a mirror. A blond girl was finishing off her look with lip gloss.

"Whatever," she said. "I'm done."

I had the mirror to myself. Within a few minutes the room had emptied of everyone except me and another girl. She was shorter than me, even wearing improbably stacked heels; she had long brown hair, big baby-blue eyes.

"You new?" she said.

I nodded. "Is it obvious?"

"Only that you're not out there yet. You're wasting money."

"I'm not on until later."

She laughed. "Christ, you are new, aren't you? Just 'cause you're not onstage doesn't mean you're not working. You should be out there hustling."

I looked at her blankly.

"You go out and chat with men, get them to buy you drinks, do a few dances, try and get them in the VIP area." She took pity on me. I must have looked scared, or lost, or maybe just dumb. "Want me to show you?"

"Yes, please."

"Okay," she said, "but if any of my regulars come in you're on your own, right?"

"Thanks. What's your name?"

"My club name is Kitten," she said. "But back here you can call me Caddy."

"Caddy? Like in *The Sound and the Fury*?"

She looked at me, glossed lips in a perfect O. I thought she was going to ask me what I was talking about, but it turned out we'd underestimated each other. "You read it?"

"Yeah."

"I've never met anyone else who's ever read that book. What's your name?"

"Genevieve. I think they're calling me Viva."

"Viva. Isn't that a type of old car? My dad had one."

We both laughed, and it was the birth of a friendship—Viva and Kitten. The other girls in the club came and went; the Russians and the Polish girls stuck together, hustled in and out of the club, bent the rules in every way they could. Other girls formed cliques and went out with one another on their nights off; but I never got close to them, not the way I did with Caddy.

On that first night she took me out into the club and we strolled around, saying hello, stopping for brief chats. I watched and learned, feeling a bit like the new girl at school.

"Mind if we sit with you for a bit? . . . Special occasion, is it, lads? . . . Ah! Congratulations! Are you going to come and have a dance with me? . . . Yes—this is Viva—she's new. I know! . . . Don't worry, I know you'll look after us, won't you? . . . Ah, I'll have to leave you to it, then—I'll get told off if I sit here too long . . . Well, let's go to the VIP area, then you can have my undivided attention for as long as you like . . . You guys need to be doing shots, especially if it's his birthday . . ."

I felt a bit nauseated, thinking that within the next couple of hours I was going to be taking all my clothes off in front of a room full of complete strangers. It felt surreal, and watching the other girls take their turns on the pole made it somehow worse. I kept one eye on the stage as Caddy and I sat and chatted with the various groups, trying to get some idea of how it all worked. Someone announced the girl onto the stage in a barely intelligible voice that reminded me of the fairgrounds. There would be a ripple of applause, maybe, just audible above the music. She would dance for two tracks, the first with clothes on, then stripping off in the second. The first girl was good, plenty of turns and spins, inverting in her second dance. She got a good cheer when she came off the stage, a little crowd forming around the pole. The second one, by contrast, was no good—just a lot of walking around the pole, a few dips and turns, a halfhearted spin, and then she was done.

That was something of a comfort. Even I could do better than that.

As it turned out, I had to do my first lap dance before I even went on the pole. Thankfully I had the chance to watch Caddy doing one first, and, although mine was a clumsy effort, the young lad I was entertaining was already so drunk he was barely conscious.

"It'll get easier," Caddy said to me as we walked back to the main part of the club to look for our next targets. "The trick is going for the ones who are wasted but not so wasted they've forgotten what they're doing here. It's a fine line."

After that, it was my turn for the pole. My heart was pounding as I stood offstage waiting for my name to be called. At that moment I thought of my dad, wondered what he would say about the fact that I was about to strip my clothes off for a room full of men I didn't know. I tried to picture him, not in the audience but waiting for me outside, a free taxi service home as he'd been on so many nights out with my friends. *I need the money, Dad*, I said to him. *It's a job like any other.* I waited for his response, waited for him to yell at me, to tell me that I should be ashamed. But in life he'd never yelled at me, and he'd always said he was proud of me, not ashamed. All I could picture was his smile, all I could feel was his warmth.

And he understood why I was doing it. It was for the boat. It was all about the boat.

"Give her a big cheer, it's her first night—it's Viva!"

For the first minute or so, nobody was particularly paying attention. I started off with some easy climbs and spins, but that wasn't much fun. Carousel spin into back hook—that got some attention. And then a quick invert, splits at the top. Stripping off my clothes while dancing around the pole wasn't as easy as I'd thought it was going to be—but it didn't seem to matter. By this time the gathering around the stage had grown and I was getting some halfhearted applause. This made me braver. Spin to the floor, little peek-a-boo, knees together, bum out. End of song. I grabbed my clothes and my shoes and skittered off the stage.

Caddy met me as I was coming out of the dressing room a few moments later. "Come and meet Nigel and Tom," she said. "They loved your dance, they want me to introduce you."

I was out of breath and perspiring a little, full of adrenaline. I couldn't keep the smile off my face. I'd done it, and it hadn't been so bad, really—actually, it had been fun. I'd caught glimpses of faces in the crowd, watching me—they liked me, and I'd only just started.

Hours later, so tired I could barely think straight, I was next to Caddy in the dressing room as she peeled the fake lashes off her eyelids. "You did really well," she said, "for a first night."

"Thanks. I wouldn't have had a clue if it hadn't been for you, though."

"No biggie. Want some more advice?"

"Sure."

"Get yourself a decent tan," she said, waving a makeup-caked wipe in my direction. "You're bloody dazzling them under the lights."

I had a lot to thank Caddy for. Most girls tended to look out for themselves—since we were all, in effect, competing for the same limited pot of money in the wallets of the men in the club on any given night, it was horribly similar to my day job. Dancing on the stage was the pitch. You started off showing your skills as a dancer, before moving on to add value to your pitch by showing them that you had a good body to back it up. At the same time, you were scanning the room for potential customers to target later. Once you came off the stage it was all about establishing a rapport with your customers by chatting them up, before closing the deal by getting them into the VIP area, which was the most financially rewarding part of the job, or, failing that, by getting them to pay you for a private dance.

At least I understood how the sales environment worked. Once I applied that to the Barclay, I could start to earn some serious money. As for taking my clothes off, after the first couple of times it didn't bother me. It was acting, just as selling was acting. You spotted the guys who were paying particular attention to you, the ones who made eye contact, prioritizing the ones who were already drinking champagne and shots, and therefore had plenty of money and were already half-drunk. The rest was easy.

"Half the guys in here are expecting you to make them come," Caddy said, "and the other half are expecting you to fall off the pole. That's what we're here for. Entertainment, whichever way you look at it."

Every so often she would come out with corkers like that: classic Caddy quotes that summed up the experience of working in the club in a way I would never have been able to do.

The first night in the Barclay I made two hundred quid, after taking off the house fee. I'd had fun, got a fairly decent workout, and enjoyed chatting with the customers. And I'd made a new friend. *This will be easy*, I remember thinking. *This is going to be a piece of cake.*

I had absolutely no idea.

• • •

When I woke up, it was raining. I'd slept through the dawn, the hours where the brightening of the skylight above my head usually woke me. It was nearly ten.

I got dressed, waterproof jacket on, and took my bag with me down to the office. My bike was in the storage room behind the main building. I unlocked it and headed downtown, the rain falling more heavily and stinging my eyes.

The city of Rochester was beautiful, even in the rain. I left the bike chained to a bike stand and walked past the pubs and the Indian restaurants. Today there was a food festival, and an Italian market was lining the cobbled high street. Some of the stalls had given up, drawing tarpaulins over bowls of olives and baskets of fresh bread. I looked at cheeses and jars of relish and chutneys. At the corner, a stall with a huge pan was selling hot farmhouse sausages in a baguette. The smell was enticing and I bought one, but a few bites in I realized I still had no appetite.

I browsed through thrift shops and secondhand bookshops, looking for things for the boat. I was very careful about what I bought. I didn't have room for piles of junk.

The rain fell steadily and I walked up the hill to the castle, through the castle grounds, and back down to the cathedral. I wanted to walk until I was tired . . . until I was beyond tired.

I felt lonely today. But I didn't want to be with Malcolm, or Josie, lovely as they were. I wanted someone who knew who I was, knew what had happened in London. I needed Dylan. Part of me wanted to phone him again and demand to know exactly what had been going on in the club, how Caddy had looked, what she'd said—everything I'd missed from that last day right up until the moment she'd appeared in the water.

But I couldn't get the sound of his voice out of my head, that tone when I'd called him. I'd disobeyed his instructions. I'd pissed him off. Where was he? If something had happened to him, would I ever find out?

When I got back to the boat, I made a hot drink and sat at the dinette, staring at Dylan's phone, and at the scrap of paper with Carling's number on it.

Fuck it, I thought, and reached for the phone.

But this time it didn't even ring. There wasn't even an option to leave a message.

The number you have dialed is currently unavailable. Please try later.

Chapter Eleven

The first time I met Dylan I was afraid of him, although I was careful not to show it.

I'd been dancing at the Barclay for two weekends already, and I had arranged to meet Caddy for a drink on a Saturday evening. I woke up zinging with such energy that I decided to go to the Barclay first, to practice. It didn't cross my mind that this was something out of the ordinary—it just seemed like the perfect way to spend a few hours, even though I'd only got to sleep at four that morning.

The door to the Barclay was locked. I rang the bell and waited. Then I rang again, and knocked, and sat down on the top step and debated what to do with myself. I had my earphones in and was listening to a playlist of potential dance music and so I didn't actually hear the door open behind me, wasn't aware of his presence until I got a little kick on the bum.

I jumped and looked up, and there he was. A mountain of a man. I pulled the earphones out.

"What do you want?" he said.

I got to my feet and climbed to the top step so at least I was on his level before answering. In fact, he was still at least a foot taller than me but I didn't let that stop me. "Thanks for the welcome. I'm here to practice."

"Practice?" he repeated, and laughed as though I'd said something hilarious.

I ignored him and walked in through the open door, into the main club. The place was empty, though the lights were on. No point bothering with the changing rooms if there was nobody here. I kicked off my boots and wriggled out of my jeans. Pole lessons with Karina had always been barefoot, and the one thing I found difficult was dancing in heels. The first few evenings in the Barclay I'd started off in heels and then kicked them off as soon as I started to do climbs and spins, but nobody else danced without their shoes. So in my bag were a pair of platforms I could just about manage to walk in, with ankle straps, and impressive spike heels that were sturdier than they looked.

The air conditioning was on and it was chilly, so I stretched and jumped up and down a few times to warm up.

Heels on, then. I walked around the room in them to start off with, trying not to look at my feet, trying to be purposeful, trying to "own the room." I felt silly, but better to be doing this here on my own rather than stumbling in front of a club full of potential paying customers.

"You look like you're walking into a boardroom."

He was sitting in one of the booths near the door, almost in darkness. I was getting used to guys watching me, but having him there without my realizing it was just plain creepy.

"Like I said, I need to practice," I replied. "I could do without you watching, thanks all the same."

"Only trying to help."

He didn't move.

Creepy as it was, he had a valid point. I tried to put a bit of a swing into my hips, one foot in front of the other, head up, back straight . . .

"Better, but now you look like you're going to pounce on someone. Try smiling."

I ignored him this time. I was warm enough now, anyway, and I was feeling more confident in the shoes. I climbed up the steps on to the stage and into the glow of the lights. That was better. I couldn't see him.

I walked around the pole a few times to get used to the additional height the heels gave me, both ways, so I didn't get dizzy. The floor seemed a long way down, my heels clomping inelegantly on the laminate stage.

Without warning, a heavy beat started up. He was in the DJ's booth. He turned the volume down to a reasonable thud.

He wanted a show, I thought. Whoever he was. And I realized that actually I was better off with an audience. What was the point of practicing on my own? And the music helped.

I started off with some easy climbs and spins, mixing it with some filler moves and kicks, then I gripped the pole and inverted, my head back against the pole, my ankles crossed and my legs squeezed tightly together to hold me steady. Normally, doing this I had enough grip in my legs that I could let go with my hands, but I didn't know if I could trust my grip with the shoes on, and my legs felt so much heavier with them. It felt very strange. I transferred the grip back to my hands and opened my legs into the splits, spinning slowly to the floor and standing up, snaking my body against the pole. A hook and spin around the pole to get my breath back, then back to an invert, splits, back down into an attitude spin. The trick was allowing those few extra inches to land both feet back on the floor despite the heels. If I spun too far down, it would be harder to stand up, and not very elegant.

I was so engrossed in the shoes and how different it felt moving around the pole with them on, I almost forgot he was there.

"You're a good dancer," he said.

He was near the stage now, sitting to the side at the bar.

"Who *are* you?" I asked, back to the pole, sliding to sit back on my heels before kicking one leg up in front of me. Then a pivot on my hand, holding the pole above my head—bum out, straighten, toss head back.

The song ended and before the next one started I stepped down from the stage and went to stand next to him. Seated precariously on a bar stool, he didn't seem quite as intimidating as he had out on the front doorstep.

"Dylan," he said, holding out a hand like a shovel.

I shook it. "You work here?"

"Sort of."

"Haven't seen you before."

"That's because you're new," he said.

I got a water bottle out of my bag and drank from it, watching him. "You don't have to hang around, you know," I said.

He stayed where he was. It dawned on me that he didn't trust me, that he thought I might be here to steal money from the registers or something. His presence was intimidating and I was here on my own with him.

His cell phone rang then and he answered it, heading for the door of the club. I stood, watching him, until the door shut behind him.

I went back to the pole and tried some more spins. The track was much slower. I concentrated on getting on and off the pole with these stupid shoes on, trying to make it look effortless when it wasn't. Despite the door between us I could hear Dylan's half of the phone conversation and that was also distracting me.

"... I don't see it like that. He said he'd have it for us tonight... It's not good enough, is it? Tell him if he doesn't pull his fucking finger out, he's going to get his head handed to him..."

Inverted, looking up at my feet in those ridiculous shoes, I thought, *I should get a pedicure, a nice bright color that would show up under the lights.* The pole was thicker than the poles I'd learned to dance on. It made it easier for the climb and sit, harder for the hand grip.

"... he doesn't get it, though, does he? You tell him one thing and it's like he's not fucking listening..."

There was no point having routines here. You didn't get to select the music you were dancing to unless you were doing a private dance in the Blue Room. It was better to just get used to going with the flow, building the momentum of your spins if the music was faster, concentrating on snakes and hip circles when it was slower.

". . . no, *you* tell him. Seriously, mate, this is a warning, yeah? My contact is going to be fucking unimpressed. We need it tonight or else he's going to have some big regrets, you got me?"

I was back on my feet, looking toward the door. Being here on my own, half-dressed, with this huge lump of a man didn't seem like such a bright idea right at that moment. The call was over. I saw him through the glass in the door, shaking his head. He still had his back to me.

I kicked off the high heels and put them in my backpack. Jeans on, socks. I was lacing my boots when the door crashed open with a bang, as though he'd kicked it.

When he appeared next to me, he was breathing hard, as if he'd been running.

I gave him a hesitant smile. "I'm off now," I said cheerily. "I'm going to meet Caddy for a drink."

"Are you, now?" he said, raising an eyebrow. "Hope you behave yourselves. Come on, I'll show you out."

The sunshine was bright outside. I turned to say, "See you later," but the door had already been shut firmly behind me. Above the noise of the traffic I heard the sound of the locks turning.

I left both phones on the table and pulled my boots on. I had had enough of being alone.

Joanna was on board the *Painted Lady*. She was watching TV while cleaning out her gerbils' cage and seemed pleased to see me.

"Liam's gone into town about a job," she said. "Hope he gets it."

As far as I knew, Liam worked sporadically and seasonally, building and sometimes painting and decorating, taking cash-in-hand jobs where he could. The *Painted Lady* was a narrowboat like the *Scarisbrick Jean*, clean and tidy but cluttered. As well as the gerbils, two cats lived aboard. I sat at their dinette and folded the pile of washing on the seat next to me, while Joanna emptied damp sawdust onto sheets of newspaper next to me. Behind her the portable TV mounted at head height was showing the news.

"Has it been on the news?" I asked.

She shook her head. "Nah. How are you feeling today?"

"All right," I said. "The boat just seems very quiet. I can't get motivated to do anything."

"It was a good party," she said. "Your friends are interesting."

I laughed, and then she did, too.

"They're not really my friends," I said. "Not anymore. I think I've moved on."

"Good thing, too. You're better off with us."

The gerbils were scratching around in the bottom of a big plastic tub, the same tub that Joanna used for transporting her wash to the laundry room. I could hear rain on the roof of the cabin, a rapid pattering.

"Haven't seen any police for a while," she said. "Do you think they've done everything?"

"I guess. Did they interview you?"

Joanna nodded. "They interviewed all of us. I had a call from Rowena; she hasn't been near her boat for at least a month and they still went to her house and talked to her."

Rowena was one of the people with a boat at the marina that was used sporadically, on the odd weekend. With the cooler weather, she visited it less and less frequently.

"What did they ask you?"

"Oh, you know—what happened at the party, what time we went back to the boat, what we saw, heard. Didn't have much to tell them, to be honest. First we knew about it was when we woke up and heard you yelling."

"Sorry about that," I said.

"Are you kidding? Most exciting thing that's happened here in ages."

One of the cats was peering into the plastic tub. "Jasper, *no*," said Joanna, picking him up under his belly and throwing him up the steps onto the deck, shutting the door. "He's always trying to get at them, poor little things."

"I wonder why they wanted to know about the party," I said.

"Maybe they think it's linked. Can't see how, though."

"When you went back to your boat," I said, "did you notice if there were any strange cars in the parking lot?"

She stopped scooping clean sawdust into the gerbil cage and stared at me. "The police asked us that, too. No, can't say I remember. In fact, to be honest, I don't remember much at all. Too much of that homebrew. It's a wonder I even heard you yelling."

The cage was ready. She crouched over the plastic tub and crooned encouragingly at the gerbils, which squeaked and scrabbled in frantic circles until she managed to grab first one, and then the other.

I was twenty minutes late meeting Caddy in the bar, but she hadn't even noticed. The place was busy already, even though it was early evening, and she was sitting in a booth with a long drink in front of her, playing with her cell phone.

"You missed the excitement," she said, leaning toward me as I slipped into the seat next to her.

"Why? What happened?"

"Chanelle was in here with one of her regulars. She didn't see me, though. They just left a few minutes ago. Probably gone to the hotel around the corner."

I must have looked blank.

"Chanelle. You know—Summer? The one with the tattoo going up the back of her leg?"

"I know the one you mean. What's exciting about seeing her in here, then?"

"Ah," Caddy said, sipping her cocktail through a little straw. "It's not that she was in here. It's who she was with. We're not allowed to meet up with customers. House rules."

"Maybe she's seeing him, or something."

"She's got a boyfriend. He's a schoolteacher, poor bastard."

"They're tough with the rules, then?"

"Pretty tough. It's for our benefit, though. Means we don't have guys trying to take advantage all the time."

"Are you going to tell Fitz?"

"What, that she was in here with a regular? No, of course not. He'd go ballistic. Things like that draw attention to the club. Can you imagine? He has enough trouble with the licensing people as it is. If they started looking into the way he runs the club, there would be absolute hell. And she would take the brunt of it."

I wanted to ask her what she meant by that, but just at that moment two guys came and sat down next to us. Casually dressed, already quite drunk by the look of them. "Ladies," the taller one said, "you need to let us buy you a drink. What are you having?"

The shorter of the two, his blond hair spiked with gel at the front, rested his arm on the back of the seat behind me.

"Do you mind?" I said, my voice frosty. "We're having a private conversation."

"Ah, don't be like that," he said, breathing beery fumes over me. "We were just thinking, you two look like two girls in need of a drink and some sensible conversation . . ."

Caddy laughed at this.

"We can buy our own drinks, thanks all the same," I said.

"And we can manage a sensible conversation on our own, too," Caddy added.

"Seriously, girls," said the one leering at Caddy, "you could be missing out on the chance of a lifetime."

"I'll risk it," Caddy said, to my relief. "Can you please piss off?"

They gave up, and without a further word of protest headed to the bar to look for other prey. We looked at each other and giggled.

"I went to the club to practice this afternoon," I said. "I met this huge guy called Dylan. Wouldn't like to get on the wrong side of him."

"Oh, Dylan's all right," she said. "He's pretty decent, once you get to know him."

"Really?" I was remembering the one-sided telephone conversation—something about someone getting a kicking.

"Yeah. At least he sticks to the rules. The others, and most of the doormen—they take kickbacks from the foreign girls. They turn a blind eye to things in the VIP suite—and they keep an eye out for the regulars, give the girls a nod so they don't miss out."

"Don't they do that anyway?"

"Not unless you give them twenty quid every night."

"Is it worth it? Surely we can keep an eye out for our own regulars?"

"It can give you a boost if you need more cash one month," she said. "And it's not just your regulars. They know who the big spenders are. When the club's busy, if you get stuck talking to someone and you don't notice who's come in . . . or they come over and let you know who's just arrived, who's in the coatroom before any of the other girls see. It gives you a bit of an advantage."

It was looking more and more like sales, and less like a girls' night out.

"But Dylan doesn't do that?"

"Not that I've ever seen. That's why the foreign girls all steer clear of him. Plus, he doesn't serve up drugs to them; they have to go to Gray for that."

"Gray's a drug dealer?"

She laughed. "You're so funny! No, he's not really a dealer. He just gets stuff for you if you need it. They don't hire girls who've got a serious habit, but if you need a bit of a hit to put the sparkle back in your eyes, Gray is the man to see."

"I like Dylan a little more now," I said.

Caddy went to the bar and got us some more drinks, although it didn't look as though she'd had to pay for them, judging by the sweet little flirtatious chat with the barman and the wiggle as she walked back to our table.

"He's a cutie, that guy behind the bar," she said to me.

"I guess he's fair game," I said, "since he's not a customer."

"You think I should give him my number?" she asked, sipping her drink.

"Why not?"

She didn't answer, just glanced back across the room to where the barman was still watching. She looked sad for a moment, thoughtful.

"You've got someone," I said.

"No," she said, quickly. "But it's not easy to keep a relationship going with our line of work. Ask Chanelle."

"How did you get into dancing?" I asked then, curious.

"I started doing it to earn some extra cash," she said. "I was waitressing weekends; one of the girls there started, and after a couple of weeks she left the restaurant. I bumped into her in a bar a few weeks later; she was raving about it and going on about how much money she was making. She made it sound so easy."

"So you started at the Barclay?"

"No," she said. "I started working in a strip pub. Very different from the Barclay. Still fun, just not quite so . . . refined. And you can earn good money because there isn't a house fee. You only pay commission to the bar."

The barman was still looking. Caddy was ignoring him now.

"Anyway, did you seriously show up at the Barclay to practice? What did Dylan say?"

"He was kind of giving me tips," I said.

Caddy laughed, pushing her hair out of her eyes. "I bet he thought all his Christmases had come at once. Did you strip for him?"

"No!" I said, shocked. "I just practiced on the pole. I wanted to try keeping my shoes on."

"And?"

"I'll get there. Feels weird, especially inverting. The shoes make my legs feel heavy."

I thought back a few hours: Dylan sitting by the side of the stage, watching me. His face expressionless, waiting for me to hurry up and finish so he could get back to whatever business he'd been dealing with before I'd rung the doorbell. "What does he actually do?"

"Who?"

"Dylan. Is he a doorman?"

"No. He helps them out sometimes when the club's busy—they all do, if they have to. Dylan works for Fitz, not for the club. He's been with Fitz for years."

"Doing what, exactly?"

Caddy shrugged, smiling at the barman again in preparation for getting us another round. "I guess he's, like, Fitz's enforcer."

Chapter Twelve

After I left Joanna, I went up to the office to check my mailbox. The rain had passed over and the sun was shining. It was almost warm.

Cam was in his office, feet up on the desk, talking to Maureen. She was standing in the doorway with her arms folded. They had conversations like this on a regular basis: Maureen would be complaining about something, Cameron would placate her and do nothing, and so things went on as normal.

"... all I'm saying is, you should be doing something about it, not just sitting there."

"And, as I said, I'll get some quotes. I can't do it overnight."

I turned the key in the lock of the mailbox and Maureen noticed me for the first time.

"Ah, Genevieve! *You* think we need gates that lock, don't you?"

"Um—well, I . . ."

"After what happened. We could all end up murdered in our beds, like that poor girl."

"She wasn't murdered in a bed," Cameron said helpfully.

My mailbox was full of junk, as usual—free newspapers and pizza ads—even though I had a sign on my box that expressly requested mail only. I sifted through them in case something important had slipped in.

"I don't see what the problem is," Maureen said, her voice

rising. "Surely it's a straightforward thing to do. Lord knows we pay enough to live here; the least you can do is make sure we have some degree of security. And that man, last night! Honestly, it's the final straw . . ."

"What man?" I asked.

Maureen turned to me again. "Pat saw a man hanging around in the parking lot yesterday evening. She called the police, but by the time they got here it was pitch-black, there was no sign of him."

"What did he look like?"

"She didn't get a good look. He was standing by the side of the office, just out there, skulking around. Obviously up to no good."

"Probably one of those journalists," Cameron offered.

"It doesn't matter who he was!" Maureen said. "It's that he was there at all, and he had no business to be. If we had decent gates, it wouldn't have happened!"

"What did the police say?" I asked. "Did they have a look around?"

"Well, no, I don't think they did. They were here for about twenty minutes. Then they said they would keep an eye on the place overnight. Not good enough, really, but of course what can they do?"

"I've fixed the lights again," Cameron said, "and I'll ask for some quotes for the gates. These things aren't cheap, you know."

"You can't put a price on safety," Maureen said.

Cameron's cell phone rang then and I thought that would be the end of the discussion, but Maureen showed no signs of moving. While he spoke to someone on the other end of the line about booking the crane for a hull inspection, Maureen turned her attention to me.

"We should put some sort of petition together," she said.

"A petition? To Cameron?"

"To make him get some decent gates!"

I left them to it then, despite Cameron flashing me a pleading look. As I locked my mailbox again he swiveled in his chair to face the wall.

On the dock Oswald the cat was enjoying the sunshine, stretched out, the end of his tail flicking. His eyes were half-closed but I could tell he was watching the young gull sitting on the roof of the *Scarisbrick Jean*. When I approached, the gull flew off and Oswald jumped up and wound himself around my legs, the way he always did whenever anyone came near. I scratched the top of his head.

"Hello, old friend," I said. "Is it nearly dinnertime?"

He followed me to the *Revenge* and sat at the bottom of the gangplank, twisting to lick his shoulder blade.

The cabin was chilly, despite the sun. I put the kettle on the burner and turned on the radio for some company.

Pat had seen a man outside yesterday evening, near the office. Could it have been Dylan? Maybe that was why he hadn't been able to speak when he called me last night. Maybe he had been outside, waiting for the right moment to come to the boat, and instead Pat had called the police and he'd had to take off.

I didn't go back to the Barclay to practice again. I got used to working there, just as I got used to walking and dancing in the heels. I learned the best and quickest ways to make money, too. And I learned that being a good pole dancer opened up opportunities to maximize my income.

For a start, I realized pretty quickly that I was much better on the pole than I was at the lap dances. Caddy was more of an all-rounder, better than me at the lap dances. A lot of the girls had never bothered to learn to pole dance properly, and mostly what they did was walk around the pole, snake against it and do an occasional easy spin.

The real money was to be made on lap dances and in the

VIP area, so for most of the girls, dancing around the pole was a waste of time, tolerated only because they could spot their regulars from the stage and head straight for them as soon as they finished.

But the pole was the best part of it for me, and, although some of the girls thought I was nuts, I got more adventurous as my confidence grew. My pole routines attracted more attention and as a result I found it easier to approach people afterward. I did get better at the lap dances, but I was still no more than average. So I increased my chances of getting private dances by impressing them on the pole.

Two weeks after my afternoon practice session, I saw Dylan again in the club. I was doing my first pole dance of the evening, warming up with some swings and wriggles, waiting for the beat to kick in so I could climb and spin, all the while looking out for the potentially lucrative customers. And there he was—sitting at the back, in one of the VIP booths. I noticed him because he was watching me, and then I realized he was sitting with Fitz, who was busy talking to Gray on his right—the guy with the tattoo on his neck who had let me in when I'd come for the audition. With them were several other men, on the table a bottle of vodka and several ice buckets holding half-empty bottles of champagne.

I hadn't seen Fitz since my first visit to the club.

I got a ripple of applause and a few cheers when I climbed the pole and inverted—I think they all expected me to fall off, to be honest—and then did a split. They loved that one. I was keeping my eye out for one man in particular, someone I'd met here last Friday. Karim had ended up spending the rest of the evening with me in the VIP area, telling me about his business and buying me bottles of champagne and not noticing that he was drinking most of it. At the end of the evening he'd promised to come back.

By the time the music slowed and I went into my second dance, the one where the clothes came off, Fitz and the other guys were paying attention, too. I saw Dylan say something to Fitz, who was nodding.

At one of the other VIP booths, a group of guys in suits were applauding me enthusiastically, much to the disgust of the two girls who were sitting with them. I blew them a kiss, and when the song finished I grabbed my clothes and scooted off to get dressed.

When I came out a few moments later, one of the girls had given up and moved on to try her luck at the bar. I sauntered past Fitz and Dylan, feeling their eyes on me, and put a hand on the shoulder of the nearest, drunkest of the group. "Hi, guys," I said. "Are you having fun?"

"You're good at dancing," one of them said. He was wearing a decent suit. I was getting better at spotting them.

"Thank you," I said. "May I join you?"

I sat down in between two of them. Across the table, another girl, Crystal, was busy chatting up two of the younger guys, laughing with them and swigging down the champagne.

One of them poured me the last of their bottle of champagne, and another bottle was ordered—and I sipped mine while topping up their glasses, pretending to drink more than I was. Crystal wasn't so cautious. Some of the girls knocked it back, then did a couple of lines of coke to sober themselves up every now and again. I aimed not to get drunk in the first place.

"Come and have a dance," I heard her saying to one of the guys.

"I don't have any money left," he protested.

"You're a fibber, Jason, I just saw your wallet! You've got cards."

He made a noise of weak protest, but she was winning him over.

"You can get tokens at the bar. Come on—you know I'm the best," she said, with the good grace to give me a wink.

"We should have a competition," I said to the table in general. "Crystal and Viva, you decide the winner!"

We took them off to the private area one after the other and Crystal and I danced side by side for each of them in turn. An hour or so later we'd depleted their credit cards and the score—thankfully—was determined to be a dead heat.

I got a glass of ice water from the bar and drank it quickly, scanning the room for my next target. Still no sign of Karim.

Dylan appeared beside me, his bulk putting me in shadow. "Fitz wants a word."

I followed him over to the booth. Two other men had joined the group, and Caddy was there, too, sitting on Fitz's right side and sipping champagne. She gave me a smile and a wink.

"Viva! Come and join us," Fitz called when he saw me, patting the seat next to him. "Guys, this is the lovely Viva. She's just been here a couple of weeks."

Fitz poured me a glass of champagne while I said hello to them all. I wondered if any of them were Caddy's regulars. I didn't want to tread on her toes.

"So, are you enjoying yourself, Viva?" Fitz asked.

"Oh, definitely," I said. "It's like having a fantastic night out with your friends every week."

I wasn't exaggerating. I'd had fun every night I'd worked so far, particularly when I was working with Caddy. The downside was that it was a bitch to get up for work on a Monday morning, but other than that I was having the time of my life. And earning money doing it.

"That's good," Fitz said. "I like to know my girls are happy."

"Viva," Caddy said, "your friend's just turned up."

I followed her gaze and saw Karim at the bar. He was watching me and I felt a fizz of excitement. I gave him a little wave. "Would you excuse me?"

"Of course," Fitz said. "We mustn't keep you."

I stood and went over to the bar, smiling my best Viva smile.

Karim was my first "regular." Over the following weeks, I collected quite a few more, but he was the one who earned me the most. Some of them, Karim included, became friends: people I liked and trusted and respected. And, as Caddy had said, having regulars was the key to making big money.

Chapter Thirteen

In the middle of January the club was quiet and I found myself bored for the first time.

There were so few customers that the girls almost outnumbered them. I was sitting at the bar, talking to one of Caddy's regulars, trying to persuade him to come for a lap dance with me. He was so drunk he could barely stand, and making conversation with him was hard work.

"So where's Kitten tonight?" he asked for the third time, breathing over me.

"She's on vacation," I explained again. "She'll be back next week, though, Pete. And in the meantime I promised her I would take good care of you if you came in . . ."

"What about . . . Summer?" he said, hesitating over the name, as though he was struggling to bring it to mind.

I struggled myself for a moment, then I had a flashback to the drink I'd had with Caddy, and her explaining to me about Chanelle meeting up with one of her customers. I hadn't seen her since then, but I worked only on weekends. She might have been working different shifts than me and our paths would never have crossed.

"I think she's away, too," I said.

I saw Dylan out of the corner of my eye, crossing the floor of the club directly toward me. He stood on the other side of Pete at the bar, and Tracey put a drink in front of him.

"Dylan," I said, "Pete was asking about Summer—is she working a different night?"

He didn't turn to look at me and for a moment I thought he hadn't heard. But then he glanced at Pete and said something I couldn't hear.

A few moments later, Pete stumbled off in the direction of the men's room and I turned back to my glass of water.

"What did you say to him?" I asked, moving up to fill the space that Pete had vacated.

"Summer's gone," he said.

"Gone where?"

He knocked back the last of his drink. "No idea. Dancers come and go all the time."

"It's so quiet in here tonight," I said.

"It's always like this in January," he said in reply. "Won't get any stags in till they get paid. Anyway, I came to find you. Fitz wants a word."

I wondered if I was in trouble. I followed Dylan up the stairs, struggling to keep up in my heels. I heard voices and laughter from up the hall, faint, deadened by the heavy fabric and thick carpets.

". . . like he said, he needs to learn who's in charge . . ."

". . . not this time, not after what happened . . ."

". . . look, boss, we can fucking do it in an hour. Just give us the nod, all right?"

". . . lads, lads. All I'm saying is, he owes me, right? It's not about the money. It's about the respect."

Dylan was at the door. "Fitz."

"Genevieve! Come in, come in."

I gave him a wide, innocent smile that would have fooled no one, least of all him. He put an arm around my bare shoulder and drew me into the office. It smelled of whiskey and testosterone.

They were all in there, comfortably lolling in armchairs and sofas. The desk held a bottle of aged malt, three-quarters gone, and piles of cash in bundles.

"Nicks, Gray, this is our new star, Genevieve. You know Dylan already, of course."

I recognized Gray. He was the one who'd let me in when I'd come for the audition. The guy next to him must have been Nicks—smart suit, leaner than Dylan and Gray, but his eyes said he wasn't someone you should consider messing with.

Fitz had been drinking; I could tell by how unsteady he was on his feet.

"Did you want me to wait outside for a minute?" I said to him.

"Not at all, my dear, we were just finishing anyway. Have a seat. Drink?"

"I'd like a glass of water, please."

It was Dylan who was sent up to the bar to get me water. I watched him retreat from the room, pulling a face as he did so. He was built like a tank.

"I wanted to put a proposition to you, Genevieve," said Fitz. He was behind the desk now, fingers steepled. The other men were talking among themselves.

"Oh?"

"I wondered if you'd be interested in earning some extra money."

"I'm always interested in that, Fitz. What did you have in mind?"

He regarded me steadily, as though still uncertain whether I could be trusted. Dylan came back with a tray on which sat a frosty glass bottle of mineral water, an iced glass with a slice of lemon on a small silver dish, and a matching silver bowl of ice. He placed it on the table next to my seat. I looked at him but he didn't meet my gaze, a face carved out of solid stone.

"I'm entertaining some clients at home next weekend, a private evening—just a few select guests. I wondered if you'd dance for us."

"What's the room like?" I asked. I didn't much care about the room, to be honest; I was stalling for time, to think about whether this was a good idea. Decide how badly I needed the money. I poured some water into the glass, squeezed the lemon, licked my fingers delicately.

He nodded as though this was a legitimate question: I was showing my professionalism, and he appreciated it.

"It's good," he said. "You could come and check it out first, if you like. The guys would be close by, the lighting brighter than it is in the club, but the normal club rules apply: no touching, no messing around. My guests are all wealthy individuals. I can guarantee you would get good tips if you agreed to do it."

"How much?"

"Two grand, for the night. As many dances as they want, although we'll be talking business, too, so I don't reckon there would be time for more than four or five. Tips on top of that— you might be looking at doubling the pay."

I looked into his eyes, saying nothing. One of my favorite sales techniques. He met my gaze resolutely for a few moments, and then laughed. "You're good," he said. "Very cute. And cheeky."

I smiled my best cheeky smile.

"All right," he said, "I give up. Two and a half, plus tips. Final offer."

I'd reached his best price. "What about Caddy?"

"What about her?"

"Is Caddy doing it, too?"

Fitz looked at me for a moment, considering. "Nah."

"Why not?"

"Caddy probably won't want to do it," he said. "Think she thinks it's beneath her these days. You can ask her if you want;

I don't mind paying for two as long as she's prepared to work for it."

I thought about it, sipping from my glass of water. Something about it made me uneasy. As I'd found this week, as much as I was getting used to working and dancing at the Barclay, it wasn't nearly so much fun without my friend. But then, the money . . .

"I'd love to," I said at last. "What would you like me to wear?"

When I went to go back downstairs to see if Pete was still around, Dylan walked with me, in silence. I hadn't asked for him to accompany me, and to my knowledge nor had Fitz; maybe there had been a private nod from him behind my back, some signal. He walked a pace behind me, like my shadow. I wondered if there was something going on in the office, some extra part of the meeting that I wasn't allowed to hear.

"Thanks," I said to him, when I was back outside the dressing room.

He smiled at me, looked me in the eyes for the first time. "You're welcome," he said.

When he smiled, he was a different person. I decided he was all right, in the same way that I'd decided Norland was a piece of shit.

He hesitated at the doorway.

"What?"

"Just wanted to say," he said, "I'll be there. Next weekend. I'll make sure there isn't any trouble."

"Thank you," I said.

He walked off down the hall and I found myself wondering whether I should have been expecting trouble. I hadn't factored that into the calculations, but, to be fair, I couldn't really expect two and a half grand for an evening's work without there being some additional drama to deal with.

• • •

When Caddy got back from St. Lucia a week later, I told her about my meeting with Fitz. We were in the dressing room, and I was waiting for her to finish getting ready so we could go out into the club.

"He wants us to dance at a party at his house," I said. "He wants both of us—you and me."

She stared at me for a moment, then let out a short laugh. "Really? Why didn't he ask me himself?"

"You were away," I said, hoping that this would sound plausible. "What do you think? Go on, it'll be a hoot if you're there."

She set her mouth in a firm line. "I don't know, Gen. Too much hassle," she said. "I've done them in the past. Don't really want to do them anymore."

"Hassle? How come?"

She didn't answer, pulling on a pair of sandals and tugging at the strap.

"I thought it would be good for the money," I said.

"Yeah. It's just what you have to do for it."

"Fitz said—"

"I know, I know . . . same rules. All of that shit. Just be prepared, is what I'm saying. Think about what you're willing to do for it. If you don't want to do anything, he'll be okay with it, but you won't be the top dog after that."

"What? You mean he's going to ask me to fuck his friends?"

She laughed. "No, not you. He'll just bend the rules a bit, that's all."

We were both ready to go but neither of us moved. It felt as if there was something she wasn't telling me.

"He doesn't seem to be here that often," I said, changing the subject. "What's he like?"

"He's all right, as long as you don't piss him off."

"What happens if you piss him off?"

She didn't answer but looked at her foot, and then swore and tugged at the sole of her sandal, which had started to come off.

"Chanelle's gone, did you know? Dylan told me."

She had taken both her shoes off and thrown them into her bag in disgust. I wondered if she'd even heard me.

"Over a hundred quid, they were! Bloody rip-off. Well, I'm taking them back."

"You can fix them," I said, ever the cheapskate. "Won't cost much to get them resoled."

"That's not the point."

She sat down again, having rooted through her bag for some low-heeled pumps. Her cheeks were flushed.

"Did you tell Fitz that we saw Chanelle?"

Her eyes narrowed. "Of course not. Did you?"

"No!"

"Well, someone else must've."

"Maybe she just left. Maybe she's gone to another club."

Caddy shook her head. "Not without telling us."

"So . . . what do you think?"

Caddy stood up abruptly. Nicks was at the door. I wondered how long he'd been there, listening.

Chapter Fourteen

I couldn't get the thought of the man Pat had seen by the office out of my head. The more I considered it, the more convinced I became that it was Dylan. Who else could it have been? I tried to call him for the third time in as many minutes, but still the same result:

The number you have dialed is currently unavailable. Please try later.

In the end I put a second coat of paint on the spare room. With another coat, the paint job on the siding was looking less patchy and more like a reasonable coverage. I would make curtains next, put in a chrome bar at the bottom to tuck the curtain into so that it didn't swing when the tide came in and the boat rocked. I would build a shelf unit for the walls, use it for books. I might even build a cabinet for bed linens and towels.

I turned the radio up and thought again about the process of building the deck garden, wondered how much it would cost to get a glass roof custom-made, and whether it was something I could actually make myself or if it was beyond my level of expertise. I needed something waterproof for the bad weather, with a reasonable degree of insulation, so that even in the dead of winter my plants would survive.

As hard as I tried to distract myself, the thought of Dylan kept coming back to me. Where the hell was he? Why wasn't he answering the phone?

By the time I was at the sink, cleaning the brushes again, it was dark outside and the marina was quiet. Tomorrow I would start planning the bathroom. I'd put it off long enough, finishing the easy jobs first. It would be a new project, something to sink my teeth into; something that would take all of my time and tire me out every day.

The radio was still blaring in the spare room. I should turn it off; it was getting late to be playing music so loud. The instant the radio went off, the silence descended again.

Something was wrong.

A sound, from overhead—on the deck? No, on the roof of the cabin, directly above my head.

I froze, listening with my whole body. No sound, nothing—just the waves lapping against the side of the hull.

A scrabbling, a scattering sound. It was probably a bird, I thought, exhaling. A gull . . . sometimes they landed on the docks and on the boats, especially when it was windy.

I went back to the sink and rinsed it with bleach, trying to cover up the smell of the paint. After that I decided to have a beer, maybe two. My nerves were jangling, and alcohol might numb them a little. Was every night going to be like this from now on? Waiting to get tired enough to go to bed and sleep?

I heard another noise from outside just as I opened my third beer. It wasn't on the deck, and it wasn't a bird, I was sure of it. It was an animal noise, a yowl, a yelp. Maybe Oswald was having an argument with the foxes.

Alcohol made me brave.

I unlocked the door to the wheelhouse, which made a noise, and took enough time to scare whoever was out there away.

I stepped outside.

"Hello?" No one on the dock. The marina was in darkness all the way up to the parking lot, a brisk wind blowing from the water, bringing with it the smell of rain.

I took a step forward onto the deck and stood for a moment, looking across the water to the lights on the opposite bank. I looked down onto the dock and I could see a dark shape lying on the wood at the end of it. Whatever it was hadn't been there this afternoon. I went down the gangplank, trying to get a closer look, my arms folded across my chest against the chill of the wind.

The dock was completely dark. Even standing right next to the object, staring down, I couldn't make out what it was. I nudged it with my foot and it moved—something soft. I crouched low, reaching out with my hand.

Fur, soft fur. Cold. Wet. I stood and lifted my hand to the little light that came from the highway bridge. I could see dark on my fingers.

"Oh my God, oh my God," I found myself muttering under my breath. Again, looking out across the dock, over to the office, the parking lot. There was no sign of anyone.

I went back up the gangplank and turned on the light in the wheelhouse, the one I never bothered using because it attracted moths in the summer—and when I went back to the dock I saw what it was. A bundle of fur, black. Blood on my hand.

It was Oswald. Malcolm and Josie's cat. Someone had killed him and thrown him onto the dock.

I bit back a scream, my breathing shallow and fast. I had a sudden notion that whoever had thrown the cat onto the dock had had no time to leave the marina and was probably hiding somewhere in the darkness, just out of sight.

I ran back up the gangplank, turned off the light in the wheelhouse and jumped down the steps into the cabin, slamming the door and locking it as fast as I could.

From outside came the sound of footsteps, someone walking away quickly, fading and then louder again on the gravel in the parking lot. Whoever it was had been just on the other side of the *Scarisbrick Jean*.

I stood in the galley in a panic. Everywhere I turned were the black circles of the portholes. Anyone outside on the dock would have been able to see in, to see me. I washed my hands in the sink, rinsing the blood away and scrubbing with soap, tears pouring down my cheeks.

Whom could I call? Whom could I talk to? I tried Dylan's number again. The same message.

I kept coming back to the same, reluctant thought. He was probably at the club.

I didn't even stop to think about what I was going to say to him. I put Dylan's phone back down and picked up mine. I dialed the office number for the Barclay and waited an age for it to be answered.

"Hello?"

I could hear the music, a low, thumping bass in the background. It sounded like Helena's voice, but I couldn't be sure.

"Can I talk to Dylan, please?"

"He's not here."

"Do you know where he is?"

"Who is this?"

"Genevieve."

"Who?"

"Genevieve. Viva. I used to work there?"

"Hold on."

The music cut out and was replaced by an "on hold" bleep. I waited. *This is ridiculous*, I thought. *What am I even going to say to him if he's there?* What could I say about Caddy? Was he grieving for her, or had he not given her death a second thought?

"Genevieve." Fitz's voice was loud and took me by surprise.

I swallowed. I should have disconnected the call the moment the woman had told me Dylan wasn't there. I just hadn't quite believed her.

"Hi," I said, as cheerfully as I could manage. "How are you?"

"Well, this is an unexpected treat. What can I do for you?"

"I just—just wanted to see how you all are. And I wanted to say I'm sorry—about what happened to Caddy."

There was an awkward silence, a long one. I could hear him breathing and, muffled this time, the low percussion of the music.

"You don't really want to know about everyone, do you? You were asking for Dylan. He's not here, though. You want me to pass on a message?"

"No, no," I said, too quickly. "Is he in tomorrow? I could try then. It's not urgent."

"Yeah, all right. I'll tell him you phoned, shall I?"

"Whatever," I said, hoping that I didn't sound as panicky as I felt. "If you like."

"So what are you up to, these days?" he asked then.

"Oh—nothing much. I moved out of the city," I said.

"How'd you hear about Caddy?" he asked, his tone casual.

I had no idea what to say. My hands were shaking and then I felt the tears starting at the horror of it, the shock at finding the cat, covered in blood, and the lunacy of calling the Barclay and ending up with Fitz, of all people—and that Dylan was obviously fine, still happily working there and deliberately not answering my calls.

I couldn't think of anything to say and the prolonged silence had become too much to deal with. I disconnected the call. Cut him off. *Well*, I thought, *that was an unbelievably stupid thing to do.*

There was only one place left to turn. I took the scrap of paper with Carling's number on it from the table and turned all the lights off in the galley and the main cabin. I went through to my bedroom and scrambled onto the bed, to the far corner, tucked into the side of the hull. Above me, the skylight— someone looking in would not be able to see me, here, in the shadows—but I would see them, outlined against the dark sky.

I huddled in the corner and dialed the number.

It rang for ages and I thought he wasn't going to answer.

And then: "Hello."

It took a long moment for me to find my voice, so long in fact that he said, "Hello?" a second time.

"Is that Jim Carling?"

"Yes. Who's this?"

"It's Genevieve."

There was a pause. I wondered if he was trying to remember who I was.

"Hi. How are you?"

"I'm sorry to call you so late," I said. My voice was hoarse. "I'm . . . I'm afraid. Something's happened."

"What is it?"

"I was here on my own and I heard noises outside. I heard a bump on the deck. I went up to look, and . . . and . . ."

"It's okay," he said gently. "Take your time."

"Someone's killed Oswald. I found him outside. I don't know what to do."

"Oswald?"

"The cat. My friends' cat. He's lying outside and I'm afraid, I'm so scared. Please help me."

There was a pause. I realized that maybe I should have just dialed the number for the police, whatever it was. Called the main switchboard.

"I'm sorry. I didn't even ask if you were on duty. You said I could call you."

"To be fair," he said, wearily, "I did say to call me if you remembered anything else, not if you found a dead cat."

I felt very small and suitably chastised.

"I'm coming over," he said.

"Really?"

"Yes. Don't go anywhere, okay? I'll give you a call on your

cell when I get to the marina, so you won't get a fright when I knock on your door. All right?"

"Thank you," I said. "Thank you so much."

I shrank back into the corner in the darkness and waited. On the deck above my head I could hear more noises. Bumps, scrapes. As though someone was crawling over the roof of the cabin. I stared and stared at the skylight, but all I saw was the dark, stormy sky.

Chapter Fifteen

I didn't even have to get myself to the venue for Fitz's private party: he arranged for Dylan to pick me up. It meant I had to be ready early, of course, but, on the other hand, getting a lift was certainly preferable to public transportation.

Dylan rang the bell for the flat, and when I went down-stairs he was holding the rear door of the car open for me.

I laughed. "Are you my chauffeur, Dylan?"

"Something like that," he growled, and climbed in the driver's seat.

"Does Fitz not trust me to get there on time, do you suppose?" I asked, as we headed toward the main street.

"Don't ask me. I think he thinks this is a perk."

"A perk for you, or for me?" I asked cheekily, then instantly regretted it. He gave me a look in the rearview mirror, a look that said, *Don't mess around.*

The busy streets of London gave way to the leafy, dark suburbs. I had no idea where we were; I hadn't been paying attention. And that, I thought with a sudden understanding, was probably the real reason I was being driven—so I wouldn't know where I was going.

"So, how long have you worked for Fitz?" I asked.

"Years."

"You like working for him?"

A brief shrug of the shoulders. A few moments later he turned up the music, loud enough to prevent further conversation. I looked out the window and watched the world gliding past.

About half an hour later we pulled into a driveway and tall wooden gates swung open automatically. The driveway continued ahead of them, and we drove for several more moments before the car stopped in front of a large house, mock Tudor. *If I didn't know we'd headed west*, I thought, *I'd have sworn we were in Essex.*

Fitz was home. His guests hadn't arrived yet, he told me. He showed me the downstairs, the wide living room with the huge leather sofas and abstract artwork on the walls, the white carpet, glass everywhere, crystal. Through a heavy door to the left was the room I'd be dancing in. There were several comfortable chairs and sofas grouped around the center, and the pole. I went across to test it, trying a few gentle swings to see if it felt solid. It did. I kicked off my shoes and climbed it, one hand over the other, and flipped over at the top, spinning back down to the bottom. Not easy, wearing jeans. It would be a piece of cake with bare legs.

Fitz watched all this with an expression that was hard to read. He shook his head gently. "Does me in," he said, "when you do that."

He took me into the kitchen to wait. Dylan was leaning against the counter, arms folded across his immense chest.

"Have you eaten?" Fitz asked. "Want something to drink?"

I didn't want to eat or drink—neither was particularly good just before cavorting around a pole—so I sat on a stool at the marble-topped breakfast bar, talking to Dylan until the guests started arriving.

"So am I the only one here?" I said in a hushed tone.

"You're the only one dancing, put it that way," he said.

"What does that mean?"

"There's other girls here. You're the only one dancing."

Dylan was eating from a bowl of olives, removing them delicately between finger and thumb and placing the pits into a little dish on the marble surface.

"Why don't the girls in the club like him?"

"No idea."

"Do you like him?"

He stopped chewing and looked at me. "You're full of questions today," he said. "What am I supposed to say to that?"

"The truth?" I suggested.

At least that made him laugh. "He's all right," he said. "Don't fuck with him and he's fine."

Almost the same thing Caddy had said to me. I wondered what happened to people who didn't follow that advice.

I watched Dylan eating for a moment. He had a glass in front of him, like mine, except mine contained water, his vodka.

"So," I said, trying to lighten the mood a little, "who's coming to this party? Anyone I know?"

I'd been at the club long enough by this time to recognize some of the regulars, many of them friends of Fitz's.

"Doubt it."

"Who are they?"

"Seriously, Genevieve, you ask too many questions."

I laughed. His tone wasn't as hostile as the words implied. "Well, you're not exactly a natural conversationalist, Dylan. I'd rather not sit here waiting in silence."

"Nor would I."

"So you ask me some questions. Balance it out a bit."

He gave me a smile and again I was struck by how much less threatening he looked when he smiled.

"All right. I've got a question for you. What are you doing with all this money?"

"What?" He'd taken me completely by surprise.

"You're raking it in," he said. "You take twice as much in tips as Lara, and she's always been the best dancer we've had. She's got a whole fan club of guys who've come to see her every weekend for the last four years, and since you started at the Barclay you've made her income look like a pittance. So what are you doing with it?"

I flushed. I didn't really have an answer for him. Telling him about my dream, to renovate a boat, sounded ridiculous in this context.

"You're not a druggie," he said.

"How do you know?"

"Oh, give me a break. I know everything there is to know about drug addicts, believe me."

"Well, you're right. I don't do drugs."

"So what are you spending it on?"

"I'm not spending it. I'm saving."

"You're *saving*?" As though he'd never heard the word before.

From the hallway came the sounds of guests arriving. The caterers started moving platters of food into the dining room and all of a sudden the kitchen was a hive of activity.

I nodded. "I can't stand my job much longer. I hate it, in fact. I'm just waiting until I've got enough, then I'm going to hand in my resignation and take a year off."

His face lit up. "Traveling?"

I stood up. "Maybe. I'm not sure. Just as long as I don't have to do that job forever, that's all. I need something to look forward to."

Afterward, of course, I had a different perspective on that cozy little chat with Dylan in the kitchen of Fitz's enormous house. He'd stuck with me because he'd been told to keep an eye on me. He wasn't eating olives with me at the breakfast bar out of choice. He was my minder, just in case I decided to go snooping into other rooms.

And he'd asked the question he needed to ask. Not for Fitz, but for himself. I didn't know it then, but Dylan had an agenda of his own.

Chapter Sixteen

When the phone rang, I jumped out of my skin. I didn't recognize the number, and for a moment I hesitated before answering.

"Hello?"

"Genevieve? It's Jim Carling. I'm in the parking lot, I'll be two minutes. Okay?"

I went to unlock the door to the wheelhouse. It was still pitch-black out there, so I turned on the light. I could just make out the tangled pile of black fur lying on the dock. I would have to do something with the body: wrap it up in a cloth or a towel, or put it in a bag.

I saw a figure making its way down the dock toward the boat. I couldn't see it was definitely him until he was right at the gangplank.

"Evening," he said with a smile.

"It's there," I said. "Look."

He turned back to where I was pointing. "All right. Go inside, I'll be in in a minute. Put the kettle on, okay?"

I did as I was told. I presumed he was having a look at the body, trying to determine how Oswald had met his end, or doing whatever it was that detectives did. He was such a lovely cat, so friendly, I couldn't see why anyone would want to hurt him. But they had. I thought of the man Pat had seen last night, the man I'd stupidly been convinced was Dylan. It couldn't have been him, after all.

The kettle was boiling when the wheelhouse door finally opened and Carling came in. He was dressed in jeans and sneakers, with a dark waterproof jacket on top. He looked very different out of the suit, younger. He went to the sink and washed his hands.

"I'm sorry to call you. I didn't know what else to do," I said, putting two mugs of coffee down on the table in the dinette.

"That's all right. I wasn't doing anything particularly exciting."

"It must be hard on the home life, this job," I said. Unsubtle. I felt my cheeks coloring.

"It can be," was all he said in reply.

We drank our coffee.

"What do you think happened? To Oswald, I mean?"

"Difficult to say," he said. "Not easy to see any injuries in the dark. Have you told the owners?"

I shook my head. "I had a feeling that someone was on the dock. I didn't want to go out, in case they were still there."

"Who's 'they'?"

I stared at him. "Whoever it was that killed Oswald."

He sighed, and ran a hand through his hair. "See, I get the distinct impression that there's stuff going on that you're not telling me about, Genevieve. And it's very difficult for me to help you when I don't know the full story. Do you understand?"

I nodded. "Really," I said. "There's nothing going on. I'm just scared. I've just been shaken up since I found—you know—the body."

"Candace Smith," he said.

"What?"

"That's her name, Candace Smith. We've identified the body."

"Was she—local?"

Carling shook his head. "From London. We still don't know what she was doing down here."

"So she drowned?"

"The cause of death was drowning, but the postmortem showed a head wound. If she'd been outside the water she would have died of the fractured skull soon enough."

I turned away, thinking about Caddy and her face, her lovely face, shattered and swollen, the muddy water washing over it. I felt sick at the thought of what had happened to her, and my eyes filled with tears. I wiped them away with the back of my hand, took a deep breath in.

"You think she hit her head on the dock? Like, she fell over, or something?"

His look said it all.

There was a silence. I fought back the tears. She had been so lovely—and so kind to me. And I was never going to see her again.

"I'm scared. I'm afraid to be on my own."

"You know I can't stay," he said.

"Oh, of course. I hope you didn't think . . ."

"Didn't think what?"

"That it was some sort of . . . I don't know . . . come-on."

He smiled, warmly. "That's a shame. I was rather hoping it was. Never mind—in either case, I can't stay. It just wouldn't be right."

"Are you married? Or seeing someone?" I asked, his flirting making me bold.

"No. Are you?"

"No. It's just me and the boat."

"Right." He finished his coffee. "I've wrapped up the cat in an old towel I had in the back of the car," he said. "Have you thought about what you're going to do?"

"I'll have to go and see Malcolm and Josie in the morning. They'll be beside themselves."

"I'm not sure if it might not be kinder to tell them the cat was run over, to be honest."

"Would I get away with that? I mean, does it look like he's been run over?"

"Maybe they won't look too closely."

I felt sick. "Who would do something like this? Seriously, what sort of sick fucker?"

"The same sort of sick fucker who fractured Candace Smith's skull, I expect."

I looked at my hands. They were trembling. I crossed my arms and tucked my hands tightly under my armpits.

"Look," he said, "I can't force you to tell me. But whoever killed that girl seemed to deliberately put her next to your boat. And now it looks as if someone's left another very unpleasant message for you to find. And you seriously have no idea who's behind it?"

He was looking at me, studying my face. I wondered how it was that I was giving away secrets without telling him anything. My cheeks flushed and I stood up, uncomfortable, took my mug to the sink, and poured the last of my coffee down the drain. Behind me he made a sound, like a sigh that turned into a low growl of frustration.

Carling stood up and brought his mug over to me. Without saying anything, I took it and washed it in the sink.

"Candace Smith was a stripper. She worked in a nightclub in London, a place called the Barclay. Have you ever heard of it?"

I tried to stay as relaxed as I could. This was not something I wanted to talk about, not with Carling.

"I'm scared, Jim," I said.

"I know you are." He put a hand on my shoulder.

I turned away from the sink to face him. He'd been about to say something else and he stopped himself. He was very close. I could have moved away but there was something about him, something about his nearness. I could feel warmth from him.

"You don't have to be scared," he said, so quietly I barely heard him.

He took a step toward me and kissed me. Despite his near-ness, it took me by surprise. For a second it was gentle, and then he pushed me back against the sink and the kiss was force-ful, demanding. I should have resisted, I thought vaguely, at the same time realizing that it felt good and there was no way on earth I was going to do anything other than kiss him back, just as hard, and maybe even a bit harder.

When we parted, I whispered, "I'm sorry," as though I'd assaulted him. As though it had been my idea.

"I can't help you," he said softly, "unless you tell me."

"I can't," I said. "I just can't."

"Right." He took a step back from me. "It's late," he said.

"I know, I'm sorry."

And then, as though there was some kind of magnetic field pulling him back, he kissed me again, his arm around me, his hand in my hair. I could feel how hard he was. For a moment I thought, *Is he going to want to stay? Is that what I'm hoping for?* And then he pulled away from me again, right away this time. He backed off and leaned against the dinette.

"Shit," he said. "Sorry about that."

"Don't apologize, Jim," I said. The expression on his face made me laugh. How the hell had we ended up going at it like a couple of teenagers?

"I should go," he said.

"Sure," I said.

"Do you want me to stay?"

I thought about this. I thought about Dylan and my heart gave a lurch. I'd waited five months, and now it was clear he wasn't interested.

"Look," he said, "I don't want to make things worse for you. Do you want me to stay until you fall asleep?"

That did sound like a very good compromise to me—and while he was here, at least, I was safe.

"Yes," I said. "That would be very kind."

He took me into my bedroom. I took my jeans off and got into bed. He pulled the duvet up around me and sat on the edge of the bed. After a moment I said to him, "You can lie down if you like."

"I don't want to fall asleep," he said, but he lay down anyway. We lay together on the bed, side by side, looking up at the skylight. He was holding my hand. I could feel the tension in him through his skin.

"When you're asleep, I'll go. You'll be all right. I'll call you tomorrow, is that okay?"

"Yes," I whispered.

The clouds had cleared and above us was the night sky, black like a blanket, a few tiny stars like pinpricks of light. I closed my eyes, afraid that I'd see a face or a shape in the dark rectangle. Despite myself I felt sleepy. I felt his bulk beside me, his warmth. I wanted to snuggle up to him, to throw my arm over his middle so that he would not be able to slip away without me noticing.

"I'm glad you called me," he said.

"I thought you'd be angry. Or, actually, no—I didn't think. I just knew I wanted to see you. I knew you'd make me feel better."

"I can't believe I kissed you."

"I can't believe it, either."

"I've been thinking about kissing you since I first saw you."

"Really?"

"You know . . ."

"What?"

"You know this can't happen, don't you? Not now. Not with the investigation and everything."

"Do police officers never find themselves being tempted into immoral situations by witnesses, then? Does this never happen?"

He laughed. "Not to me, no," he said. His fingers were

stroking the skin on the back of my hand. It was soothing, so gentle.

"I like you," I murmured.

"I like you, too."

We were silent for a while and I wondered if I kept quiet long enough maybe he would fall asleep, too; maybe I'd wake up and he would still be here and daylight would be showing through the skylight instead of darkness.

But what happened was quite the opposite: I fell asleep, and when I woke up he was gone.

Chapter Seventeen

In total, I estimated that there were no more than five actual guests at Fitz's party. They were vastly outnumbered by caterers, a waitress, heavies they'd brought with them who weren't officially participating, and by Fitz's entourage, including various other men, Gray, Nicks, Dylan, and me.

I got changed in a downstairs bathroom before my first dance. Dylan had taken a CD with all my favorite music, plus some extras, and uploaded it to Fitz's sound system.

I'd gone to town on the outfit, although it never consisted of much more than underwear with something stretchy over the top that I could remove in the course of the dance.

In fact, I'd spent most on the shoes—two hundred pounds on a pair of sandals that buckled with thin straps all the way up to just below the knee. The heels on them were five inches. I'd had to practice dancing with them on, as much of my grip came from the skin on my calves down to the ankles, but when I tested them out it was fine. The only danger would be if one of the buckles snagged on the other when my legs were crossed at the ankle.

Dylan came to fetch me. Despite my attire he didn't so much as look at me twice. "You're on," he said.

The first dance went well. I opened to my favorite dancing track, the one I'd had at my audition with Fitz—Elbow's "Grounds for Divorce."

I swung around the pole at full force to start off with, and it was my first chance to have a look at the men grouped on the chairs and sofas. They were well dressed, and they'd all had a drink or two—including Fitz—but they weren't drunk yet and I needed a spectacular start to get their attention. They were still talking and laughing among themselves when I started, but they stopped within the first ten seconds of my routine and then I had their undivided attention—vertical, upside-down splits with a spin, my hair flying around in an arc so fast that they should have been able to feel a breeze from it.

Fitz watched me, and looked at his guests, glancing from them back to me with an expression that was hard to read. Approval, definitely. Arousal? I could never tell, not with him.

The next morning I went to the *Aunty Jean* to see Malcolm and Josie, but the boat was empty and the hatch shut and locked. Liam was on the deck of the *Painted Lady*, tinkering with something. He waved at me, and I went across the dock.

"Morning," he said.

"How are you doing?"

He pointed, with the screwdriver he was holding, toward the office. The ladder was resting against the wall. "That light's out again. Maureen's just been out there having a go at Cam."

"Out again? What do you mean?"

"Someone's cut the cable. Maureen said Cam should put electronic gates on the parking lot and keep them locked at night. She's trying to get a residents' meeting together for tonight. Hasn't she been by to see you yet?"

I shook my head. "I saw her yesterday; she was going on about it then, too. Liam, have you seen Malcolm and Josie?"

"They went to the supermarket, 'bout half an hour ago."

"Oh. Thanks."

I still had no idea what to say to them about Oswald. I'd tucked him inside a cotton tote bag, wrapped in Carling's towel, and put him in the wheelhouse so he wouldn't get wet if it rained. He would need to be buried—maybe at the playground? It all seemed so unspeakably horrible.

I couldn't get Carling out of my head. He knew where Caddy worked. Which meant it was only a matter of time before he found out that I'd been a dancer there, too, that we were friends. I needed Dylan, needed him so badly. Why wasn't he answering his phone? And then Carling—lying on my bed next to me. This morning the memory of last night just felt awkward.

"What did Cam say about the gates?" I asked.

Liam laughed. "You know Maureen. Maybe she just asked in the wrong way."

I went back to the boat and spread my plans and notes out on the dinette table. If I was going to do the bathroom, I would need to lose the storage space at the bow. I would need to start with the deck garden and the sliding roof—in theory a straightforward project; in practice quite difficult.

I called a local glass company and tried to describe what I wanted. I'd done this before, with other companies, and had received a mixed response, including one telling me to my face that I didn't know what I was doing and I would be better off leaving the boat alone and getting myself a nice house.

The local independent glazing company was much better. I spoke to a guy called Kev who promised to stop by and have a look.

At some point I was going to need to get the MIG welder and the saws out again and cut a hole in the cabin roof. I'd done it before with the skylights, and each time it had made me nervous. But when Kev turned up an hour later, he was more helpful than I'd expected, and he offered to help fit the sliding roof as well as supply it. His father owned a boat and he'd helped out on it. Nothing this dramatic, mind you, but he looked at my plans and at the article I'd clipped out of *Waterways World* magazine that had a boat with a similar sliding roof, and he agreed that it could be done. He even had tracks in stock that we could use to make the mechanism for the slide.

I started to get excited about it again. "How long would it be before we can do it, if I order everything now?"

"Six weeks, maybe less," Kev said. "When they're ready, we could pick some good-weather days, and I'll help you out with the roof."

I felt much better with a plan. I wrote a check for the deposit, and when I waved Kev off in his van, the sun came out.

Malcolm and Josie were back.

I went to board the *Scarisbrick Jean*, knocking on the hatch. A shout came from below; it might have been "come aboard," or it might just have been "piss off." Either way, I opened the door and climbed down the three steps into the cabin.

Josie was packing shopping away in the galley.

"I've got some bad news," I said.

Her face fell and she stared at me. "Is it Oswald?"

I nodded, and went forward to hug her as she started to sob.

"I knew it, I knew something had happened to him. I told Malcolm, I said—"

At that moment Malcolm came in from the bedroom. "What's going on?"

I looked at him over Josie's shoulder. "I found Oswald."

"Aw, shit. He's dead? I knew it; he always comes home. Run over, was he? Bastards on that road, they speed up and down."

I didn't say anything else. I should have told them what had happened, but I was afraid they would blame me. I'd done this: I'd brought this to the marina, this nightmare.

"Where is he?" Josie whispered. Malcolm was hugging her now, stroking her back with his huge, bony hands.

"I've got him in my wheelhouse," I said. "I've wrapped him up a bit."

Malcolm nodded. "I'll come and get him."

I said to Josie, "Do you want me to stay with you?"

She shook her head. "I just need a minute," she said, her shoulders shaking. "I just need to be on my own for a minute. You—you go with Malc."

We got to the wheelhouse and I showed him the tote bag, neatly wrapped. Malcolm said to me, "Is there anything you want to tell me?"

The sun shone fiercely on the back of my neck. Just for a moment, it was warm. "He wasn't run over," I said. "I'm so sorry."

"Right," he said. "We won't say anything to Josie."

"No."

"What happened?"

"Last night," I said, "I heard a noise. Like a thump. When I went outside to have a look, Oswald was lying on the dock."

"You didn't see anyone?"

I shook my head. "Did you know someone's cut the cable to the light again? Liam told me that Cam was up there trying to fix it again this morning."

"Yeah. Maureen was bending my ear about electronic gates when I went shopping earlier. Like that's going to solve anything."

He picked up the bundle, cradling it gently as though Oswald were still alive. "I'd better take him back," he said.

"Can I help? With—you know. Digging a hole."

He smiled. "No. I'll do it later. I'll be fine."

He left me alone on the deck, taking Oswald with him. I felt so bad for them both, and Malcolm was so kind. Even though it was all my fault.

I earned nearly five thousand pounds for one night's effort at Fitz's party. I did work for it, in truth—I lost count of the songs I danced to on the pole, and then lap dances for each of them. Worth it for the tips.

By three, most of Fitz's guests had gone. One guy was left—hand-stitched suit, silk shirt, open at the neck. Bling on his wrist. Serious money. I'd been talking to him for a while, pouring him drinks and laughing at his stupid attempts at humor. His name was Kenny. I had an appalling memory, but I'd trained myself at the day job by repeating people's names back to them constantly until they stuck. It felt clumsy to me, but I'd never met a man who'd commented on it. They all seemed to love the sound of their own names.

The flirting ramped up a notch. The same lines, variations of which I heard most weekends at the club.

"Seriously, you're the best dancer I've ever seen. And I've seen a few. What's your name?"

"You know—it's Viva."

"No, your real name. What is it?"

"Ah, if I told you that it would spoil the magic, Kenny. You'll just have to trust me."

"You have an incredible body, Viva."

"Thank you, Kenny."

"No, seriously. You deserve better than this. Why don't you come out with me? Go on, say yes. I can give you the best time ever."

"I'm sure you could," I said, smiling.

"Will you? Let me take you away somewhere. I've got a place in Spain—come with me for a weekend . . ." He was slurring his words. He wouldn't have been able to stand up without assistance. I topped up his glass.

Behind him, in the darkened room, Dylan looked at me and then at his watch.

"Ah, I can't. I'd love to, but I've got to work . . ."

"I can pay you," he said. "You just tell me how much it is you need and I'll take care of it."

"It's not the money," I fibbed. "I love my job. I get to meet gorgeous guys like you, Kenny."

He sighed heavily, as though admitting defeat. Dylan took a step forward.

"What about one last dance?" Kenny said, leaning forward unsteadily. "One last dance, just you and me. You know."

Dylan appeared at his side. "It's getting late," was all he said.

The man said, "Where's Fitz?"

I took advantage of the distraction and excused myself, and went to the bathroom to get changed. A few moments later Fitz opened the door, without knocking. I was folding up clothes and packing them away into my bag.

"Viva," he said. "I need to ask you a favor."

I stopped what I was doing and gave him a look. It had been a long night.

He came over to me and stroked the back of his hand over my bare arm. "See?" he said. "Touching's not so bad, is it?"

"That's not the part he wants to touch, is it?"

"Viva. This guy—he's going to be very helpful to me. I need to keep him sweet. He really likes you; he's never been interested in any of the girls before . . ."

"I'll dance as many times as you want, Fitz. That was what we agreed. You promised me that there would be nothing like this. You want to change the deal, you have to pay for it."

"How much?"

I told him I would do it for a grand, I would choose my own music, and there was an extra condition: that Dylan was waiting at the door. Fitz was torn, as though I was screwing him over, and at the same time as though he'd just been given the keys to the candy store.

"Seriously, a grand? Who do you think you are?"

He was quite drunk, unsteady. I waited patiently.

He looked at me for several moments, then said, "All right. A grand. You're pushing your luck, you know that, don't you?"

A thousand pounds. I'd better make it worth his money.

The music had already started when I went into the room. Donna Summer's "Love to Love You Baby"—the extended version, all sixteen minutes of it, complete with Summer's orgasmic moans and cries. Not the three-minute track I'd chosen. Should I make a fuss? I wondered. But it seemed easier to just get it over with.

He was waiting in the chair, reclining. He looked half-conscious; he would wake up pretty damn soon. I came up behind him, stroked my hand across his shoulders, down his arms. One last look behind me. Dylan was standing at the open door, his face in shadow.

I didn't make him wait too long for the dress to come off. The song made me hot anyway. He'd paid, or rather Fitz probably had, for just about everything he wanted. Even though I knew he wanted me to be close, I was going to start on the pole, since it was what made my dances special. So I spun and swirled and kicked, vaguely aware of Dylan at the back of the room. If he'd been watching a soccer match he would probably have shown more emotion.

As I had more skin to play with, I was adventurous with my dance and experimented with some new moves. I tried some back flips and twists that I hadn't done since my gymnastic days, although doing it in heels was a different story. When the music slowed and pulsed, I came off the pole and went over to Kenny, and I danced for him. I let him have my best moves, up close. At first he didn't touch, then a hand on my ass. I pushed backward encouragingly. After that, there was no stopping him. When his fingers got too insistent, I backed off, smiling as though I was enjoying it, as though he was turning me on. And when I was astride his lap, rubbing the side of my knee against the bulge in his expensive dress pants, I glanced up to the shadows. Dylan was still there. Unmoving.

There was a lot of touching. Some of it clumsy, uncomfortable. I had a moment where I thought, *Why am I doing this? This can't be right. I don't give a fuck about this guy, I don't even like him, and he's got his hand on me and the other in his open fly and I'm pretending I'm enjoying it. Is it worth the money? Is it really worth a grand?*

The song came to an end, like all things, both good and bad.

Dylan came forward with a large, soft towel and held it out for me as though I'd just swum the channel.

"Goodnight," I said to Kenny. "Thank you, that was fun."

He tipped me an extra two hundred quid, and asked again for my number. I smiled at him and said he should come and see me next weekend in the club. It was a compromise, potentially lucrative—although if I never saw him again I would be secretly relieved. I kissed his cheek and he made a clumsy grab at my breast. I took his hand off me and kissed it. I wondered where his money came from.

Dylan waited for me to get dressed, then he drove me home in silence. I had the feeling he was somehow pissed off at me. He kept his eyes on the road ahead.

"You must be tired," I said at last, fed up with looking out of the window into the bleak grayness of the early morning.

"Not really," he said.

"Got far to go home?"

He just shrugged.

"Have I done something to upset you, Dylan?"

Even then, he didn't look in the rearview mirror. He was made of stone. "No."

"Thanks for getting me that towel, it was kind of you."

Silence.

When we got back to my flat, I half-expected him to come out and open the door for me, but instead he stayed where he was, the engine running, staring straight ahead.

"Thank you," I said.

He waited for me to get to the door of the flat, and then the car sped off into the dawn.

Chapter Eighteen

I'd almost forgotten that Carling said he was going to call me until the phone rang on the table in the cabin.

I'd been trying to call Dylan again, but his phone was still off. It was easy to become obsessive about it, to call every few minutes in the hope that he would have turned the phone on by pure chance since I'd last called.

My phone rang at just past nine. I was doing dishes at the sink in the galley, wondering if it was too early to go to bed and whether I would be able to sleep if I did.

"Hello?"

"Genevieve? It's Jim Carling."

I should really program his number into the phone so I would know it was him, instead of answering it with such trepidation, I thought.

"Hi, Jim," I said, my face coloring even though nobody was here to see it. Last night he'd kissed me and pushed his body against mine. He'd lain next to me on my bed and held my hand until I slept, and yet this morning once again the only person I could think about was Dylan.

"I'm sorry it's so late," he said. "I meant to call you earlier, but it got busy. This is the first chance I've had."

"That's okay," I said. "Thanks again for coming over last night," as though he'd come over to fix a leaking tap or hang a picture. "It was really kind of you."

"How did it go with Malcolm and Josie?" he asked.

"They were very upset," I said. "I think Malcolm's buried the cat somewhere."

"Did you tell them what had happened?"

"I didn't say much to Josie, she was devastated. Malcolm's no fool."

"No," he said. "I got that impression when I spoke to him the other day."

There was a little pause.

"Are you still at work?" I asked.

"Yes. Going to be late finishing tonight."

"You poor thing, you must be exhausted."

He laughed. "I am a bit. Funny, that. Anyway, I was just calling to check that you're okay. You know where I am if you need me, right? Or you can always call the main number. They'll send someone out quickly."

"Thanks," I said. Was that it?

"I'll see you soon," he said. "Sleep well."

I finished the pots and got ready for bed, brushing my teeth in the bathroom. I left all the lights on in the cabin, and I'd left the radio on since the afternoon, too, the noise from it blocking out the silence. It was the quiet moments that were worst, I'd decided, once the marina had gone to sleep, darkness had fallen over the Medway, and the only sounds were those of the wind and the water lapping at the sides of the hull as the tide rose and floated the *Revenge of the Tide* away from the muddy riverbed. I never wanted to hear that bumping noise again. If I had to leave the radio on every night, I would do it.

I turned off all the lights and crawled into bed. I left the radio on the timer, with it set to turn off at one in the morning. There was no way I would still be awake by then, I thought. I would drift off to sleep to the peaceful sounds of Classic FM, and I would wake up to bright daylight. Nothing to worry about. No stupid gulls marching up and down the roof of the cabin above my head. No footsteps outside on the dock. Nothing bumping against the side of the hull.

I slept, and I think I was dreaming about Dylan. He was there, in any case, on my boat the way he'd never been in real life. He was saying, "You did a good job with all that money, Genevieve." I thought then that maybe he wasn't paid as much as me by Fitz. It was a sudden realization that the time he'd driven me home from Fitz's private party he was probably pissed off because of all the money I'd earned for not doing very much at all. Whereas he'd done so much that evening, watching out for me and ferrying me around, and stopping me from going upstairs and seeing all the other things that were going on at the party without me having a clue—and he'd likely earned less than I'd taken home in cash.

It was dirty money, I realized that now. But it was all just cash, to me. It was beautiful cash that I could put toward my boat. And I'd been wrong about Dylan, of course. I'd been wrong about just about everything, back then.

The Sunday morning after my appearance at Fitz's private party, I slept late.

When I woke up, it was to banging on the door. Half-asleep, I answered it—a delivery of a hand-tied bouquet of roses and lilies, so big that I could hardly see the delivery person behind them.

I managed to get them through the door and into the kitchen, and read the card. It said, simply:

Thanks
You were great

I smiled as I rummaged around for vases and spent the next half hour or so arranging the flowers. I'd enjoyed myself, money or no money, even the last dance for Kenny. Nakedness was just a state of mind, after all. And the clumsy fingers, the grabbing hands? Nothing that a nice hot shower wouldn't wash away. He wasn't that bad; in fact, if he hadn't been quite so drunk I might even have found him attractive.

I wondered if Fitz liked me. Was that why he'd asked me to do the party? No, of course not—he had guests to entertain, and I was the best dancer he had—he'd told me that often enough, and Dylan had said something similar earlier in the evening, hadn't he?

One thing was for certain: Dylan definitely didn't like me. In fact, he'd barely been able to look at me on the drive home this morning. The thought of the tension in his shoulders, the way he'd looked steadily ahead as though I weren't even there, made me feel sad. I wanted him to look. I wanted him to smile when he saw me dance. And I had no idea why. It wasn't even as if he was my type. He was taciturn, monosyllabic . . . a moody shit, in other words. But when he smiled, he was a different man.

When I got up, it was a beautiful day. It reminded me of summer, a huge blue sky overhead, so bright that it hurt my eyes to look at it, scored with vapor trails and the occasional wisp of cloud. It was still, the river sparkling. The cabin was warm, even though the stove had gone out, the ashes cold.

The door to the wheelhouse was sticking. The damp weather was warping the wood. That would be my job for today, something to take my mind off it all. It was cold outside, but the air so fresh and clear I took deep breaths of it for several moments.

The marina was at peace, all the boats quiet. The parking lot was still; Joanna and Liam's van was there, and Maureen and Pat's Fiesta. Another I didn't recognize. The door to the office was open. Everything looked as it should. I'd been half-expecting something else to happen in the night, some new horror to deal with, but this morning was so normal and right that I almost felt silly for my apprehension.

I went back into the cabin to get a sweater, and while I was there I put the kettle on the stove to make coffee. The cool air flooded in from the open door and the steam from the kettle rose in clouds.

I sanded the edge of the wheelhouse door, watching the dust dancing and whirling in the sunshine, as the marina came to life around me. Maureen emerged first, shopping bags in hand. She called to me across the decks of the boats.

"Need anything?"

"Where are you going?"

"Market!"

"No, thanks! Have fun."

She waved at me and headed off to the parking lot.

The door was better, but still sticking. I debated getting my workbench out and planing the surface. It wasn't that bad, not yet. I went back to sanding and lost track of time. My shoulder was starting to ache.

The door to Joanna's cabin opened with a bang. Music drifted out. I recognized it right away, faint as it was—the Velvet Underground, "Venus in Furs." I used to dance to this, a lifetime ago.

I could smell bacon cooking, too. I wondered if it was Joanna's. I stopped sanding for a moment to stretch my arms over my head, then I drank my coffee. It was cold, flecks of sawdust floating on the surface.

I'd finished working on the wheelhouse, and the cabin was full of dust. I couldn't worry about that now. I left things as they were, went over to the *Painted Lady* just as Joanna came up on deck with a steaming mug and a plate.

She saw me and waved.

"You want some? Liam's making."

I shook my head. "No, thanks."

"Help yourself to a coffee, then."

I went down the steps into their cabin. Liam was standing in the galley, dressed in a pair of jeans. He was shaking a frying pan that was sizzling furiously, filmy smoke in the air. I was pleased to see that their cabin was in a state of even more riotous abandon than mine.

"Morning," he said cheerfully. He looked as though he hadn't slept.

"Hi," I said. "How are you?"

"Not bad. Bit of a bender. It was Manda's birthday."

"Oh, okay." I helped myself to the last remaining clean mug and poured myself a coffee from the pot. I left it black and took it upstairs onto the deck. Joanna was sitting with her face to the sun, hamster cheeks full of bacon sandwich.

"I hear you had a good night. Who's Manda?"

"Sister," she mumbled, through a mouthful.

"Oh. You made up, then?"

"Different sister."

Her bruise was fading to yellow already, a smear under her eye that might have been mistaken for exhaustion. The sound of an engine out on the river trundled and rattled closer and then faded again as it passed. The sun was warm on our faces.

"That policeman seems very nice," she said eventually.

I looked at her. She had a mischievous smile on her face.

"You mean Jim Carling? He is nice. I like him. So where did you go last night?"

"Oh, just in town. George Vaults, a few other places."

"What time did you get back?"

"Not sure. Late. Why?"

"I just wondered if you saw anything last night. Anyone. In the parking lot, I mean."

She looked blank.

When I went back to the *Revenge*, Malcolm was sitting on the dock at the stern of the *Scarisbrick Jean*, doing something to the water pipe that connected the boat to the mains. He was bashing at the connection with a wrench, making a loud clanking noise that sounded dramatic, echoing off the walls of the office. His face was pink, and beads of sweat stood out on his forehead.

When he saw me, he stopped.

"That looks serious," I said.

"I think there's a blockage," he said. "Water pressure sucks."

I felt like saying that whacking the connection probably wasn't going to improve things much, but he looked so depressed I held it back. "How about a cup of tea?" I asked instead.

His face lit up. "Got any beer left?"

"Sure. Might be a bit warm."

We were on the sunny side of the deck, where I'd sat with Ben nearly a week ago, drinking our beers.

"How's Josie?"

"All right, considering," he said. "She didn't sleep much, so she's having a nap."

"I'm really sorry," I said.

"What I don't get," he said, "is why Oswald? And what were they doing in the middle of the night, killing cats? It doesn't make sense."

"I know."

"Bastards."

"I heard someone running away."

"You didn't see them?"

"No."

He shook his head, took a big gulp of beer, and let out a long, soundless belch.

"Why was he left next to your boat, though?"

I shrugged. If I could have thought of a different topic of conversation to turn to, I would have.

"I reckon you must have pissed someone off back in London."

"Not me," I said, attempting a laugh.

"You didn't make off with the takings, or anything like that?"

"Nah."

"Ah," he said, "I reckon there's a lot more to it. These London gangsters, they don't mess around, you know. You've obviously done something to piss them off. Or you've got something they want."

His voice trailed off, and I looked out across the river, taking big gulps of beer and trying to swallow it without choking. I hadn't even thought about it—Dylan's stupid package. Of course that was it. Of course that was what all this was about.

"You all right?" He was looking at me with concern.

I didn't answer for a moment. Malcolm was eyeing the beer bottle I was holding against my knee. I looked at it, wondering why it was dancing up and down, and then I realized it was my hand shaking.

I put the bottle down by my feet and spread my palms on my knees, rubbing them on the denim to try and keep them steady.

"I've got something," I said, my voice unsteady.

"What?"

I stood up and took a deep breath, trying to stop the panic that was rising inside my throat. I put a hand over my mouth.

"Gen? What is it?"

"It's—it's just a package. Someone gave it to me to look after, when I left London."

"What's in it? Drugs? A gun?"

Fuck—a gun? I hadn't even thought about its being a gun. It was drugs, it had to be, even though I'd done my best not to think about it, even though I'd just hidden it away and pushed it to the back of my mind, even though I'd pretended it didn't even exist, not really. It wasn't what was inside it that was important—it was just his package. It could have been anything.

"I don't know; I didn't like to ask too many questions. I just promised I'd look after it, that's all."

"Jesus. Well, that explains a lot, don't it?"

"It might not be that," I said, at the same time knowing that it was.

"You need to get rid of it," he said.

"Yeah, thanks for that! I've been trying to get hold of the person that gave it to me. No luck so far."

"You want me to—take care of it?"

"What?"

"Well, we could find somewhere else to hide it. We could bury it at the playground."

"No. It's all right where it is. Thanks, though." It was still Dylan's package, and I was supposed to be looking after it. What if he turned up to collect it, despite everything, and I'd gotten rid of it? He'd be furious.

We sat in silence for a few moments, watching as a small motorboat chugged upstream. The woman sitting in the back of it was wearing a bikini top. Surely it wasn't warm enough for that? I was starting to calm down a bit now. The breeze was fresh, blowing in gusts under the Medway bridge. The woman on the boat waved at us. Malcolm raised his bottle of beer in salute.

"You worked at that club a long time?" he asked then.

"Six or seven months, altogether."

"You miss it?"

"Sometimes. It was fun."

"Why did you leave?"

"I got enough money for the boat."

He looked at me and laughed. "That can't be the only reason. Why not work there and fix up a boat at the same time?"

He was right, of course. There was a moment when it had

all started to go horribly wrong, when things began to un-ravel. They'd unraveled at the Barclay at just about the same time that my night job collided with the day job, and it had all started the night I recognized my boss in the crowd of custom-ers at the Barclay.

Chapter Nineteen

His name was Ian Dunkerley, a well-built man with small-man syndrome. His way of working was to make you look like an idiot in front of your colleagues, so that you were left not trusting your friends, and despising him.

He'd taken over the line management for the sales team only a few months before. At the time I was one of the top performers, but not *the* top, and that made me a target. Everyone who wasn't actually top of the performance tables was a target. The idea, I suppose, was to encourage us all to be hungry for profit, or at least to make us want to be the favored one who didn't get picked on or abused, but in practice it pissed everyone off.

Of all the people to see at the Barclay.

I didn't notice Dunkerley at first, as I was concentrating on the moves, but when I was pausing in a particularly provocative pose, getting my breath back for the next gymnastic flip, I scanned the room, as I always did, looking for my regulars, for new customers, for guys who looked reasonably well-oiled.

And there he was.

I was so shocked I nearly fell off the pole. I had to do an extra spin, which put me one beat off.

He was sitting in one of the VIP booths with a number of other men—quite casually dressed, I noticed; I was surprised they'd been let in—laughing and joking with a couple of the girls and fortunately paying no attention whatsoever to the action onstage.

When I'd finished the routine and run back to the dressing room, flushed, breathless, I contemplated going home sick. I hadn't missed a single dance since Fitz took me on, but the thought of going out there and dancing in front of that odious man made me feel physically ill.

"Are you all right?" Kay asked me.

Kay was new to the Barclay, a pole dance specialist like me. She had been sent over from one of Fitz's other clubs because she put on a "challenging" show, mainly due to her outfits, which had more than a hint of S&M about them. Her dance name was Mistress Bliss, but since that was a bit of a mouthful we were allowed to call her Kay, as long as it wasn't in earshot of any of the customers.

"Yes. Thanks—I just . . . I thought I saw someone I know."

"What? A customer?"

"Yes."

She laughed. "I get that all the time. I saw my old math teacher when I was working at the Diamond."

"Really?"

"Yeah. There he was, Mr. O'Brien, in the front row, drooling. It was hilarious. Who've you seen out there, then?"

I grimaced. "My boss."

"From the day job?"

Not all of us had day jobs. We never mentioned them here, in any case. I had no idea what the other girls I worked with did. "Yes."

"Ooh, shit. He doesn't know about this, then?"

"You must be kidding. What makes it worse is that he's not even nice. He's a complete, total douche bag. What am I going to do, Kay?"

She patted me on the upper arm. "Do you dress like this at work? What's the chances he's going to recognize you? Lord knows Mr. O'Brien didn't recognize me. Hope not, anyway."

"I feel sick."

"Go home, then. Don't ask Norland—go and see Helena. You'll be all right."

"I'm not a quitter."

"Then you're going to have to go out there and face him."

It crossed my mind to ask one of the other girls for help, to distract Dunkerley for me. But, except for Kay, none of the girls on tonight were particularly friendly. Caddy wasn't here to ask. There were a bunch of Eastern European girls who stuck together; they worked the room hard and concentrated on the lap dances, putting in a halfhearted show on the pole and then doing their best to hustle in the club. If I asked them for help, they'd be less likely to oblige by providing a distraction and more likely to use it as an opportunity to get one over me by deliberately pointing me out to him.

I sat miserably, putting makeup on in the hope that it would work as a disguise, borrowing someone's curling iron to put a few loose curls into my normally straight hair. Kay was probably right. The chances of him recognizing me, with my hair down, wearing these clothes, in the dark, in that context in fact . . . it was all a bit unlikely.

And yet, he was a sharp little fucker. I wouldn't put anything past him.

My next dance was slower—Portishead's "All Mine." The lights in the club were low and I could almost hear the conversations going on around me as I danced. I loved this song, it made it easy to block him out, to take myself off to a private space where I was alone and dancing for myself.

When I looked over to the table where he'd been sitting, toward the end of the song, he was gone.

· · ·

Malcolm went back to the *Scarisbrick Jean* after two beers. Josie had popped her head up and seen us sitting together, feet up on the gunwale, laughing about something. I waved at her but she was already on her way back down.

"Better go," he said, downing the last of his beer. He slid the empty bottle into the crate outside the wheelhouse and hopped down the gangplank. When he got to the deck of the *Jean*, he waved. "Cheers, Gen," he said.

When I stood up, a little unsteadily, thinking that it was probably a bad idea to be drinking beer in the middle of the day, I caught sight of something down in the mud. I put both my hands on the gunwale and peered over the edge.

The mud was disturbed, churned up, around the boat. When I looked closely, I realized there were footprints, deep holes with trails between them as though someone had pulled their feet from one step to another, stumbling, leaving a muddy wake with each step. To my left the trail ended in a mess of mud, debris and river weed.

The footprints led away from the boat to the grassy waste-land between the marina and the great concrete legs of the Medway bridge. I followed them with my eyes all the way to an old dock, half-submerged in the mud, which was made out of old pallets lashed together with pieces of rope. There, more churned mud and footprints on the wooden pallets leading up to the tussocky grass, the marshy land under the bridge.

Someone had walked from there, down to my boat. They must have struggled in the deep mud, and, judging by the mess, they had probably lost their balance once or twice and fallen over. There was no sign of anyone—nothing moved in the marina, no cars in the parking lot. In the bushes under the bridge, the only movement was the leaves and branches stirring in the breeze.

This morning I'd felt relief that the night had passed without incident. I'd chastised myself for being foolish, for expecting more horrors when I had no reason to expect any. But as it turned out, I'd been right—someone had been here. Someone who hadn't wanted to be seen by anyone at the marina and so had approached my boat from the river, across the mud.

I leaned over a bit further, dizzy with the beer and with a sudden waft of stinking silt, until I could see that the footprints were right underneath the porthole. The porthole that looked in on my cabin.

Chapter Twenty

I didn't see Dunkerley on Monday morning. He was out at meetings, and as usual it was a hectic day. By the time I got home, I was starting to feel relief where previously I'd been feeling dread, panic. Lord knew he made my life hellish enough as it was. He didn't need any additional weapon to fire at me.

Tuesday was our regular team meeting. Usually this was the time he laid into one of us, the one he perceived to be performing badly and needing a boost. We all dreaded it, every week.

But this Tuesday was different. He scanned the room to see if anyone was missing. I felt his eyes brush over me like an unwelcome grope on a crowded Underground train.

But there was no public humiliation, not for me or for anyone else. He was quiet, taking notes, his bald head pink and shiny with perspiration. He asked for updates on workload, on profits. As soon as that was over he called the meeting to a close and scuttled off.

"What the fuck? What's happened to him?" asked Alan.

We all celebrated our first gentle meeting since Dunkerley had arrived, with a coffee and a prolonged discussion about what could possibly have come over him. I had a horrible feeling it might have been related to our encounter in the club, but I kept quiet.

Dunkerley avoided me at work after that, and I started to relax. Maybe he'd been embarrassed by it; maybe he was worried that I would tell everyone he'd been seen in a lap dancing club. I was almost able to enjoy work again, for the first time in ages, without that constant pressure.

Of course, it all changed the following weekend at the Barclay.

He was there early, on his own this time. He managed to snag himself a table right at the front of the main stage, and he was sitting there looking up with a kind of joyous anticipation, like a kid at his first puppet show.

I stared at his ugly mug, the door to the dressing rooms open just a crack.

Well, there was no doubt in my mind what he'd come to see, and I had no way of getting out of it.

He was there for all my dances. He only ever moved when I went offstage. I did my best, as I always did, but the force of his stare was off-putting. In my second dance I slipped and only just recovered in time. Even so, he laughed. The bastard laughed.

After that the rest of my routine was powerful, and faultless. I would show him.

I was half-expecting him to ask for a dance with me, and it was no surprise when Helena came to see me in the dressing room when I still had at least two dances left.

"There's a customer for you," she said.

"I thought there might be."

"Thing is, he said he wants a private pole dance with you for free. I told him that wasn't an option. He said I should ask you. Someone you know, is it?"

"Yes. The man's a complete idiot."

"I take it you don't want to dance for him, then?"

I gave her a look that said it all.

"Is he giving you any shit?"

"Yeah, a little. He's sitting at the front and he's making me nervous, to be honest with you."

"Right," she said, and marched out again.

When I went back out into the club, he was gone.

I asked Helena, when I got a chance to talk to her. They'd escorted him out. He wasn't welcome, she said.

I could have kissed her.

I spent the afternoon keeping busy, anything to take my mind away from the churned-up mud under the porthole, but even so, the thought of it kept returning. Whoever it was had been there at low tide, which meant first thing this morning. I'd been asleep in bed.

The cabin was still full of dust from the sanding I'd done earlier, so I spent a long time wiping everything down with a damp cloth. I kept glancing across to the porthole as I did it, as though I was expecting to see a face appearing there. In the end it got dark and then all I could see when I looked up was a blank, black circle.

When I'd finished wiping down the cabin, I rinsed the cloth and left it out to dry. It was early, but I was exhausted. I got ready for bed, and as I drifted off into an uneasy sleep, the tide ebbed away once more and left behind it a clean, smooth surface on the mud outside the porthole, as if those footprints had never been there at all.

The week after he'd been chucked out of the Barclay, Ian Dunkerley avoided me. I thought that I'd escaped somehow, that maybe the heavies at the club ejecting him had put an end to it.

Of course I was wrong.

It was one of the regular Friday-night after-work drinking sessions that I'd participated in with rather less frequency since I'd been dancing; most of my team went, got smashed every Friday, on the company's tab, and then either staggered home to nurse their heads, or went off into town and got drunker and drunker at their own expense.

Dunkerley didn't come along often; he'd told one of the supervisors that he felt it was important to allow the team to relax without him, it helped foster an atmosphere of independence. Bullshit to that. It was because he knew we all hated him and if any of us saw him away from company property there was a strong chance one of us would punch him in the face, especially when lubricated by several bottles of wine.

This time, he was in the Highwayman, working on a large glass of red wine, when I made it in there at a little before eight. I'd been working hard to set up appointments for the following week, something I liked to do on a Friday because then I could draw a line under the day job and concentrate on getting ready for the Barclay.

He was already a bit wasted, I noticed, his bald, fat head shiny in the lights from the bar. Of course, what I should have done was turn on my heel and leave immediately, but I was tired and I'd been looking forward to my two glasses of wine for most of the afternoon.

"Genevieve," he said, holding out his arm in an arc, as though he expected me to snuggle into his sweaty armpit and embrace him.

"Ian," I said in reply. "Special occasion?"

He tried to laugh but snorted instead, which made him look like a drunken idiot.

"I was just thinking I'd have a few drinks with my team," he said in general, and then, in a comic stage whisper directed at me, "I might go on somewhere else later. Anywhere you recommend?"

"I recommend you go home," I said.

Dunkerley gave me a foul look; clearly, I'd made a mistake.

"Sorry," I said, with a tight smile. "It's been a hectic day."

I got myself a glass of burgundy and took a big sip. One glass, I thought. One glass and I'd be on my way. I tried talking to some of the other guys on the team, but they kept looking over my shoulder at Dunkerley as though he might erupt at any moment.

"He's been acting really weird," Gavin said. "It's like he's disturbed or something."

I still hadn't told anyone at work about the Barclay. I wasn't sure any of them would believe me if I did.

A few minutes later I finished my glass of wine. "I'm off," I said to Gavin.

"What? You can't go yet!"

I winked at him. "I'm afraid I've got a hot date," I said. Only something of that magnitude would satisfy him.

"Really? Who is it?"

"I'll tell you all about it on Monday," I said, recognizing that by the time Monday rolled around Gavin was likely to have consumed enough alcohol to have killed off all the brain cells that were currently engaged in our conversation.

I kissed him on the cheek and headed for the door.

Dunkerley followed. I hadn't realized until I'd reached the Underground, and there he was, pressed against me from behind in the crush to get on the District Line. It was still the tail end of rush hour, I'd left the bar so early.

"Where are you off to?" he asked into my ear, breathing wine fumes and cheese-flavored snack all over me.

"Home," I said. "Why don't you go back to the bar, Ian? They'll be wondering where you've gone."

I recognized that this was a dangerous situation, despite the crowd of people. I had to be pleasant to him, when all I wanted to do was throw him on the tracks.

"Are you dancing tonight?" he asked, as though to put to bed any lingering doubts I might have had over his recognizing me.

"Not tonight," I lied.

"Shame," he said. "I was going to try again for another private dance."

The woman standing next to us on the platform looked at me, and him, and then focused on the advertisement for coffee on the far wall.

"I don't think they'll let you in, Ian."

His voice rose, just slightly. "And who do I have to thank for that, eh? You sarcastic bitch."

That did it. "I beg your pardon?"

"I said you're a sarcastic bitch!" His voice got louder and louder, and by the last two words they were a full-on shout.

The other platform occupants were torn between staring or looking pointedly in the opposite direction. No one intervened. He could have put his hand up my skirt and not a single person would have said or done anything.

I felt a gust of wind heading toward us through the tunnel. I turned and started to walk away. As I thought he would, he followed. I had to push my way through the crowd that was surging forward to try and get on the train.

"Where the fuck are you going?" he shouted over people's heads.

I didn't answer. I was going to get a cab home. He couldn't follow me there, after all. I had a sudden vision of being crammed against him in the train, feeling his skinny little erection pressing into my ass. *I'd rather die*, I thought. *I really would.*

Outside the station, though, there were no cabs anywhere. It had started raining, and everywhere I looked were people patently ignoring this wanker who was standing within my personal space, bleating something about my being a stuck-up bitch who needed to get a grip.

"Leave me alone," I said. "Seriously, Ian, fuck off back to the pub. This is getting embarrassing."

That didn't work, either; in fact, it seemed to make him even more mad. "Look," he said, "you're moonlighting. You could lose your job. I could fire you."

"Yeah, course you could. And how would you explain how you found out what I do in my spare time, huh?"

It threw him for a second, but he rallied. "I don't need to explain myself. If anyone asks, I'll say I got a tip-off."

"You can't fire someone on hearsay. And in any case, you know what? I don't give a fuck. Do what the hell you want, just leave me alone, okay?" I was getting angry and raising my voice, and of course now people were starting to take an interest. Fortunately for me, at that moment a cab came into view with its light still on, and I waved at it and stepped into the street to force it to stop. I got in and told the driver to go, fast, please just go . . . just as Dunkerley reached for the door handle—and had it snatched away from him as we sped off.

I cried in the cab. I had been afraid of him, the wanker; if I'd been in a different place, with fewer people around, what would he have done? Would he have tried to be more physical with me? Would he have hurt me?

"You all right, love?" the cab driver asked me.

"I'm okay," I sniffed. "Thanks."

He drove me home and even though my savings were building up by this stage, it was the principle of it, that I'd had to spend money on a cab because of that man, that made me even more mad.

I sensed that wasn't the final confrontation between us. Things would not get better, they would get worse from now on. He'd make every day at work a misery for me, until I left. I needed more money. I needed enough money to get out, and soon.

I woke up, with a start—my heart pounding—without really knowing why.

I sat up in bed and shrank back into the corner, away from the skylight, even though it was still dark overhead—gray clouds. Too early to be awake.

Something must have woken me up—what? I strained to

listen, but there was nothing, except the gentle rise and fall of the boat, the musical rhythms of the water. I could distantly hear something else—a car maybe?

And then, a sound, directly overhead. On the roof of the cabin. I froze, my heart thumping with panic. I thought of my cell phone—both of them, mine and Dylan's—on the table of the dinette. Fat lot of good they were there—what if I needed them? I would bring them both to bed with me tomorrow . . .

In the perfect rectangle of the skylight, framed against the gray sky, I saw the figure of a man.

I took in a sudden gasp of breath and pushed myself back even further into the corner. From here I could just see the dark shape outlined against the sky. I could see him moving as he tried to peer in. And then I heard something else, a voice—but not clear enough to make it out—and a footstep on the deck.

Seconds later and there was a figure in the doorway to the bedroom.

Daddy, I thought. *I want my dad.*

I tried to scream but it was too late. He saw me in the corner and lunged for me, grabbing my pillow and ramming it against my face. My head hit the wall behind the bed and for a second I saw stars. Then I started struggling and kicking, fighting as hard as I could.

"Stop it," he hissed. "Stop it, you stupid bitch."

I kicked harder, and he put one hand across my throat until I couldn't get any air. I really panicked then.

"You going to stop struggling?"

I tried to speak but couldn't get a word out with his hand over my throat, so I nodded, hoping he could see me in the darkness. Someone else came into the room.

"What the fuck are you doing?"

"She was going nuts on me," said the first man in a low

whisper. He took his hand away from my throat and I gasped and choked, pulling air into my lungs.

He pushed me over onto my front and between them they grabbed my wrists and fastened them with something, pulled it tight, the plastic biting into my skin.

"Genevieve," said a voice—the second man. "You want to tell us what the fuck's going on?"

"What? What do you mean?" I shouted. They were whispering, but I had no intention of doing that on my own boat.

He lifted my head by my hair and flung it back on the pillow so my teeth knocked against my lip. I felt blood in my mouth and spat it away.

"Don't make it worse. Tell us what you're up to, and get it over with, or we'll just fucking shut you up and have plenty of time to look around the boat. What's it going to be?"

"Fuck off," I said. "My boyfriend's coming over when he's finished work. He'll be here in a minute."

He laughed. "Like fuck he is. You mean your boyfriend Mr. Carling? He's tucked up at home with Mrs. Carling. He's certainly not on his way here. Oh, Genevieve, you're hilarious."

There was a breeze a fraction of a second before his fist connected with the side of my head, just behind my ear, once, twice—hard. I felt dizzy and sick.

"Don't be stupid. Okay?"

I could hear buzzing, a ringing, and for a second I wondered what it was, until I realized it was coming from inside my own head.

"I don't know," I said, my voice muffled by sobs and the pillow, "what you're talking about."

Someone else was on the boat. They were throwing things around in the galley.

I recognized the voice of the second man, the one who had

stopped the first from strangling me. It was Nicks, Robby Nicks, one of Fitz's men.

"Nicks?" I said.

There was silence in the room, broken only by the noises from the main cabin and the galley.

"Will you shut up, you stupid fucking bitch," he hissed.

There was a bang like fireworks going off in my head, and the room disappeared, and everything in it.

Chapter Twenty-One

After the episode with Dunkerley, I spent some time counting up the money I'd saved. Realistically, I needed eighty to a hundred grand for a barge in a reasonable condition. I could have gotten a narrowboat for much less, but I found them a little claustrophobic. I wanted the same space I could get in a house, on a boat. After all, I was going to live on it, not spend summer weekends there. And then I would need cash to fix it up—say another twenty or thirty grand, assuming a worst-case scenario, a boat with some sort of structural problems or one that needed taking out of the water and welding. On top of that, I'd need enough to live on for at least twelve months, although it was in the back of my mind that I could get a part-time job if I had to, once the process had started.

I had about two-thirds of the amount I needed, and most of that had come from equity from my flat, which I'd sold a year ago. Nowhere near enough to be able to leave the job now. Part of the trouble was that, as much as I earned from dancing, there were expenses, too: clothes, shoes, cosmetics—even being frugal and cheekily borrowing stuff from Caddy whenever she would let me, I was spending a small fortune on makeup every month. So: another six months at work, assuming I didn't get the opportunity to do any more of Fitz's private parties, and I should have enough money to be able to resign.

I didn't know if I could stand it that long.

Dunkerley went back to keeping out of my way, but he had also returned to his usual dreadful self. Performance targets had been published—increased demands on all of us. We were already working as hard as we could. Where the extra was supposed to come from, none of us had any idea. The only reason I stayed was because of the money. Other organizations in our sector were actively downsizing. I didn't hold out much hope of getting another job if I chose to leave now, especially since Dunkerley would be the one writing my reference.

No, I decided: I would have to stay, and just try and manage Dunkerley the best I could.

It was a week after the incident on the Underground, Friday again, that I first had an indication that Dunkerley was not prepared to let things lie. I opened my desk drawer, and inside, on top of my papers, was a flyer for a lap dancing club.

I took hold of it and marched into Dunkerley's office. He was in there on his own, pretending to be busy. I slammed the leaflet on his desk.

"What is this all about?" I said, furious.

He grinned. "I have no idea what you're talking about," he said. "What's that—applying for another job, are we?"

"Why are you doing this?" I asked, quieter.

His face changed.

"You know why. You had me chucked out of that club. It was humiliating."

"I didn't do anything of the kind," I said, embellishing the truth a little. "The manager told me you'd asked for a private dance for free. They don't like that kind of thing, as I'm sure you realize. You don't get anything for free in that place, and if you ask, they take it as an insult. So that's why you were chucked out."

"So if you weren't in the club, would you have given me a private dance for free?"

"No, of course not," I said.

"Why not?"

"Because you're an odious little shit. Besides the fact that you're my manager and it's inappropriate on just about every level."

"You complete bitch," he said. "Get the fuck out of my office!"

I went to see the Human Resources manager. If he was going to get nasty on me, then I could play the same game. I sat in her office, breathless and flustered and teary, and told her his behavior toward me amounted to sexual harassment and I was sick of it. She listened sympathetically while I explained that I'd seen him in a nightclub and he'd hit on me, and ever since then he had been making inappropriate suggestions. I showed her the leaflet.

"He put this in my drawer," I said.

"How do you know it was him?" she asked.

"I went to ask him. He denied it at first and then he—he said something about how I should dance for him."

"I see."

She asked me to write her a report detailing all the incidents I could remember, all the times when he had said things to me or done things that I considered inappropriate. I was still anxious, stressed by the whole thing, and she said I should take the rest of the day off and she would take care of it.

I had work to do, and, realistically, I should have gone back to my desk, especially considering the new targets we were working toward. But the thought of having to face Dunkerley again was making me feel sick, so I did as I was told and went home.

I was looking forward to the weekend. Assuming they wouldn't let my prick of a boss through the door at the Barclay, I was going to have a great weekend dancing, seeing my regulars, getting some good exercise, and earning money in the bargain.

• • •

I opened my eyes and almost immediately closed them again, because the light was too bright and everything hurt—everything, from my head to my feet.

It took me a second to realize where I was, then I saw I was on the floor and someone was talking to me, only I couldn't hear them clearly. It was like being underwater—I could hear my own breathing, my heart, the blood rushing through my veins.

"Gen? Oh, thank God . . ."

"Malc?"

He went off somewhere, saying something—"Where's the fucking scissors?"

In the drawer in the galley, I wanted to say. Why couldn't I move my hands? Then it started coming back to me—there had been men in here, in my bedroom, on my boat . . .

I started to panic, and struggle, and then Malcolm was back. "Hold on, hold on. You've got a cable tie on your hands. I can't find any effing scissors, it's a bit of a mess back there."

"There's a pair of pliers in the hatch . . . in the box of tools."

The hatch was a mess, too, apparently. That told me everything. They must have found the package. It was a miracle they'd left me alive.

He found the pliers under one of the pallets in the storage room. It hurt like hell, levering the jaw of the tool under the cable tie, digging into my swollen flesh, and then one snip and the plastic tie came free and I let out a scream of pain as my arms were released and the blood started rushing back to my hands and fingers.

For a moment I couldn't move, I just lay on my bedroom floor crying my heart out. How did I get into this stupid, crazy mess? What had I done to deserve all this shit?

Malcolm was sitting on the floor, resting with his back

against my bed, watching me steadily. "Take your time," he said. "When you want to sit up, I'll give you a hand."

I gasped and sobbed into the carpet. My hands were in agony. "Oh, God, Malc . . . I was so scared . . ."

"Did you see who it was?" he asked.

I shook my head and tried to push myself up from the floor. He stood, and hooked his hands under my armpits, pulling me upright and then helping me to sit on the bed.

"It was dark . . . Oh, God. Have they trashed it, Malcolm? Have they damaged the boat?"

"It's not so bad," he said. "I think they've just thrown stuff around. If it was my boat you wouldn't even notice they'd been in. Perhaps I should ask them to stop by *Aunty Jean* next time; they might actually straighten it up."

I smiled despite myself.

"Do you want me to call the gavvers?" he asked, in a tone that suggested complete unwillingness to do anything of the kind.

I shook my head again. "I can't."

"This is shit, Gen, you know," he said.

"What—not calling the police?"

"No. What they're doing. It must be that fucking package you told me about." He was shaking his head, running a hand through his hair. "They could come back any time, couldn't they? They could start on us, too; they could be threatening us next if they can't get what they want from you, and Josie—"

"Calm down, Malcolm. I'm not even sure that's what they were after."

"Of course it fucking is! Why else would a bunch of heavies suddenly start searching your boat and beating you up?"

I wished I hadn't told him about the stupid package. He was raising his voice now, pacing up and down.

"Look," I said, "they've gone, right?"

"How do you know they haven't taken your package?"

"I don't know. They might've. But I somehow think they didn't find it."

"You want me to check for you?"

"No, I don't!" I was losing patience with him now—always this bloody need to help, to interfere. "Thanks. Honestly, I'll be fine. I'll have a look in a minute, okay? I need to—work some things out first. I need to tidy up a bit. Will you come by later?"

"Yeah, if you want," he said.

He looked peeved. He shuffled his feet, clearly not ready to go just yet.

"I wanted to tell you we buried Oswald," he said gruffly. "We found a nice quiet corner of the park. He used to bring us back presents from there—you know, even a baby rabbit once. He'd like it, where we put him."

"Is Josie all right?"

"She'll be okay in a week or so. Right as rain. She's already talking about going to the RSPCA over the weekend, look for another rescue cat."

"That's a good sign."

He nodded, and then stood. "Are you sure you don't want me to help you tidy up?"

"I'll be fine, honest," I said.

"I'll see you later, then," he said.

"Malcolm—thank you."

He shrugged. "Would have come over sooner if I'd known you were lying here bloody well tied up and unconscious," he said with a smile.

What did he mean? I looked at the clock as he left. I'd been out of it for hours. No wonder I ached all over.

I got up slowly, finding my feet, feeling the room wobble even though the tide was out and the boat was back to resting on the soft mud below.

The cabin was such a mess that I cried out. Paperwork everywhere, my drawings and measurements for the deck garden, scattered all over the floor. The drawers in the galley had been pulled out and emptied. The cabinet doors had been ripped off. The dinette seats had been removed and the storage space beneath, which was full of odds and ends, bedding, ropes, rigging, spare parts for the engine, had been emptied.

I looked back at the hatch. Malcolm had left the door open and I could see a black space. Was it even worth checking? I knew it had been turned over.

They'd even opened a can of paint, but thoughtfully emptied it down one side of the hull, presumably so they didn't get any on their clothes and shoes. All the boxes had been tipped up. And the one at the end? The one helpfully marked KITCHEN STUFF?

I crawled painfully over the pallets to the corner, over tools and pieces of hardware and the cordless drill and spare lengths of wood I'd been keeping just in case. Some of them had been broken.

The box was upside down, but as soon as I lifted it I realized that it hadn't been fully emptied. The false bottom hadn't been touched. They had just kicked the box over, seen the kitchen things spilling out of it, and moved on.

They hadn't found it. And at least now I knew who it was, targeting my boat: Fitz. And Caddy must have been coming to warn me. She must have known Fitz had found out about Dylan's package, and they'd stopped her before she could get to me. She'd died because of me.

Chapter Twenty-Two

That night at the Barclay, Fitz turned up in time for my last dance. The club had been quieter than usual, and although the other girls were all busy, I'd just been doing my turn on the stage, interspersed with the occasional lap dance. None of my regulars had shown up. It was cold outside, a chilly February night, but inside the club the atmosphere was sensual.

I was enjoying the workout, getting a thrill out of watching the guys at the front of the stage watching me. Sometimes we had bachelor parties come in, but given the prices in this club they weren't common. There was a group in tonight, however. The giveaway was the age range, considerably younger than the Barclay's usual clientele. The young man who was about to plight his troth was probably the son of one of our club members. He and his friends were all suitably attired in suits, grouped around the stages and enjoying the show. One or two of them had had dances with some of the other pole dancers, but I suspected they were starting to run out of money.

I put on my best show for them, even blew the groom-to-be a kiss at the end. His friends liked that.

As I was leaving the stage, I saw Fitz in one of the VIP booths, surrounded by his usual mix of steroid-pumped associates: Nicks, Gray, and the others. Dylan wasn't with them. Not then.

In the dressing room, I freshened up, and then I went back into the club to look for customers to entice. And maybe I was looking for Fitz, too.

He was still in the VIP booth, and to my delight when he saw me he smiled and waved me over. "Viva! Come over here, gorgeous."

He waved away the two girls who had positioned themselves on either side of him and patted the seat encouragingly. The girls went off in search of other game, leaving me with Fitz. They hadn't been talking business just now, judging by how relaxed they all appeared to be.

I sat neatly on the red-velvet cushions, next to Fitz. I'd half-expected him to touch me, maybe just a hand on my thigh, an arm around my shoulders, but he didn't.

"I wanted to say thank you for the flowers," I said, when the next dance started and the attention of the men was drawn to the stage. "I haven't seen you since then or I'd have thanked you sooner."

"Ah," he said. "You liked them?"

"They were beautiful. I appreciated them."

"Well, you know," he said with a smile. "You did a good job. Especially that last dance."

"Do you think he got his money's worth?"

"You know he did."

"I wouldn't have done it for anyone else, Fitz. Only you."

He laughed. "And a grand."

Dylan was waiting for me in the dressing room.

"Are you allowed in here?" I said, looking around at the other girls, who were busy either disrobing or getting dressed again, depending where they'd been.

"Aw, leave him alone!" shouted Kay from the table next to mine. "He's all right, aren't you, Dyl?"

"I'm allowed anywhere," he said to me.

He was sitting in the seat by my bags. I waited for him to move, but he didn't. I wondered if he was still pissed off at me for some reason. I hadn't seen him since the night he'd driven me home from the party.

"Come for a drink," he said.

"What?" I replied. I didn't know if he meant now, in the club, or . . . on a date. That would have been just bizarre.

He stood and offered me his arm.

"I've—er—got to be back onstage in twenty minutes," I said.

"Liar. You've done your share, right? And the club's nearly closing. So come on."

Blushing, I took his arm and let myself be steered out of the room, with wolf whistles and catcalls following me out. He took me downstairs to the public bar, of all places. Dances didn't happen in here, but sometimes the girls came down if it was quiet, to try and tempt the regular members of the public into the more exclusive, and more expensive, areas inside the club. They didn't let just anyone in here, but there was always a line outside, and the bar was usually full of people.

"You're costing me money, you know," I said. I was only half-joking.

"Get over yourself. You can afford five minutes off."

There were no free tables or seats anywhere from what I could tell, but Dylan gave a nod to one of the door staff and a few moments later some drunk-looking lads in suits were being escorted out the door while Dylan guided me into their warm booth.

"What would you like?" he asked me.

"Just water, please," I said.

"I'll have a vodka," he said to the waitress, who had appeared the moment we'd sat down. Dylan wasn't Fitz, but even so, his presence held a lot of weight in this place. I wondered what it would be like to spend the whole evening on Fitz's arm.

I'd been half-expecting him to squeeze into the booth next to me but instead he sat on the stool opposite. I was used to being stared at here. I had no illusions about it, since I never got this kind of attention in my day job, apart from that infernal idiot Dunkerley, and, after all, that was only because he'd seen me here. He'd seen Viva. But Dylan was immune to Viva's charms.

"This is a nice surprise," I said cheerfully. It was noisy, and I had to speak up so he could hear me.

Our drinks arrived. I squeezed the slice of lemon into my water and licked my fingers, watching his face.

He was completely unimpressed. In fact, he laughed. "It doesn't work with me," he said.

"What?" I asked, my face a picture of innocence.

Dylan was serious again, quickly. "You need to be careful, you know."

"What do you mean?"

He leaned across the table so he could speak normally. "Fitz."

"What about him?"

"You know exactly what I'm talking about. Don't get involved."

"He likes me. You know he does."

"Yes, I know he likes you. I'm not blind, or stupid. Just be careful."

"Why are you telling me this?"

He sighed, took a long swig of vodka, with a grimace to follow it. "Because you're smarter than the rest of them. You've got a future, and I don't mean in here. Don't get too close to Fitz. And don't piss him off."

I sat back. He was warning me away. Whatever his motives, he wasn't doing it out of jealousy—all the more reason why I should listen to what he was saying.

"I don't get you, Dylan," I said.

"You don't have to get me. Just think about it. It's not a good idea."

I sipped my water. It was icy cold and if I drank it too fast it would make my teeth hurt.

"Dylan—remember you asked me what the money was for?"

He nodded.

"You still want to know?"

"If you want to tell me," he said.

"Just between us, right? Nobody else would . . . understand."

He shrugged, as though it made no difference to him either way, but I knew I could trust him. I wasn't sure why, but I knew. After all, nobody else had warned me off Fitz. And he had no clear motive for doing so.

"I'm going to buy a boat," I said.

To his credit, he didn't laugh or make some joke about a ship called *Dignity*, or any of that shit. "A boat? What sort of a boat?"

"A barge, preferably—you know, like a houseboat. I want to buy a boat and spend a year fixing it up."

"Why?"

"It's just something I've always wanted. And now everything's starting to go wrong here, so I want to get the money together as quickly as I can."

His expression changed then. "Hold on. What's going wrong here? You're the top earner in this place, you know that. I thought you liked it."

I shook my head. "I don't mean here, Dylan. At my day job. Three or four weeks ago my stupid boss showed up in the club and recognized me. He's been giving me shit ever since."

"Really?"

"Yes. He followed me out of a pub the other weekend; he was making a scene down on the tube platform. I had to go and get a cab in the end. Now he's started being all suggestive at work. I have to make sure there's always someone there when I see him, that I'm never on my own with him."

"What's he want?"

"What do you think he wants, Dylan? He wants the same thing they all want. Apart from you."

"You want me to take care of him?" he said. He was smiling but that didn't mean he was joking.

"No, of course not."

He finished his vodka, throwing it down the back of his throat as if it were water and he was dying of thirst. "Well, just say the word. I've dealt with pricks like that before. Thinking they own you just because you flashed your panties at them. Piece of shit."

Dylan waved at the waitress who came straight over, despite the crush of people waiting to be served. "Another vodka. Viva?"

"I'm fine, thank you," I said.

"So," he said, when the waitress had gone. "A boat, eh? And how much are you short?"

"Quite a lot," I said, wondering why he was so interested.

"And this is why you're dancing? To get the money together?"

I sighed and drank some water. This was getting torturous; I almost wished I'd never told him. "I have a good job—during the day, I mean. It pays well. I thought I would be able to save up enough to buy the boat at some point, take a year's sabbatical maybe. But it's hard work, high-pressure, so I started doing this—dancing—for kicks, for some exercise . . . And what do you know? I'm really enjoying it. I can earn money doing something that to me is like a workout. So now I've got two jobs, the money's coming in faster and faster, and the more money I make, the closer I get to my dream. Now, instead of two years away, I could be on my boat by Christmas. And it's making me hungry for it, especially now I've got all the shit with my boss hanging over my head. So, yes, I'm earning money, and I want to make more money. And Fitz has lots of it. Doesn't he?"

"Fitz could buy Parliament," he said slowly.

"Exactly. And he likes me. What's fifty grand to him? Nothing. He could give me that and he almost wouldn't even notice. I'm just not brave enough to come out with it and ask."

The waitress appeared with Dylan's second vodka. By the time she'd turned to go, he'd drunk half of it in one gulp, then inhaled and looked me straight in the eye. "Have you ever thought where he gets his money from?"

"Of course I have; I wasn't born yesterday."

"And?"

"I know it's sketchy, if that's what you're asking. And I don't care, personally."

He smiled—a slow smile, one of the ones that made him look beautiful. I felt as if I'd crossed some kind of line—as though I'd given the right answer, somehow.

"And," I added, "if he asks me to do another private party, I will. I know you think I'm a slut for what I did the other weekend; I don't really care about that. I want my boat. I want to be away from London. I've had enough of it."

"I don't think you're a slut at all."

"Why were you so pissed off at me in the car on the way home, then?"

He didn't answer at first; when he did, he looked away. "I have my reasons."

"Anyway, why do you care what I spend my money on?" I asked.

He shrugged. "I think of you and me as friends," he said.

"What?"

"I don't have many friends, to be honest with you. I like you. I think you're clever, and witty, and you don't sell yourself like some of them do here. When you dance, you do it as a job, and yet you look as though you do it because it's all you want to do in the world. What I'm saying to you is, I respect you as a person who does a good job no matter what the circumstances. You're committed. And you don't interfere."

"Interfere?"

"That party," he said, leaning over the table again, "was a test. Did you know that?"

"I thought I was just there to dance for his private guests," I said.

"It was a test to see if you could be trusted."

"With what?"

"With Fitz's business."

I was confused. "I wasn't there when they were discussing business. What do you mean?"

"Exactly. You did your job, you did it well, you put your heart and soul into it, and you weren't nosy about what was going on upstairs, or what Fitz was talking about with his 'private guests,' as you call them."

Light was starting to dawn in my head, as well as through the windows to the street outside. "I don't give a shit what he does," I said.

"Good," Dylan said quietly. The bar was beginning to empty. We were getting near closing time. "Because the minute you do is the minute you start to become a risk. And that's why I want you to be careful around Fitz."

"Right," I said.

"He's going to ask you to do another private party," he said.

I felt a sudden rush of elation. I wasn't sure if it was the money, or the thought of dancing in front of Fitz and watching his face as I danced, that was making me feel so excited.

"You'll say yes?"

"Of course. What do you think?"

"If you do," he said, "ask for more cash. And now you've

set a precedent, you'll probably have to do more intimate stuff. You know that, though, don't you?"

"Oh," I said.

"So, if you do it, he'll make it worth your while. But remember what I said about being careful."

"Will you be there?"

He smiled at me again. I wished he smiled like that all the time. "If I have to."

The waitress appeared again. "Can I get you anything else, Dylan? We're just starting to close . . ."

"It's all right, Tina. We're going back upstairs."

I followed him up the carpeted stairs to the club, and when we got to the top he left me to go to the dressing room by myself. We'd spent long enough in each other's company. There was no doubt it would have been noted, and it would get back to Fitz. My head was swimming. How could Dylan be loyal to Fitz and have told me so much about him?

And yet, his smile.

I made a start on tidying, beginning at the front of the boat and working my way back. I put all the spatulas, spoons, and various gadgets back in the KITCHEN STUFF box and set it back in its place at the very point of the bow.

Some of the other boxes of tools I refilled and positioned around the box, a rather halfhearted attempt to disguise its significance. Where was the best place to hide a box but in among other boxes, after all?

This wasn't the ideal place for it, I knew that. In a few weeks' time it would have to be moved, in any case, as Kev and I would be taking the roof off this section of the boat and my cavernous storage compartment would become a deck garden, plus another room at the end, which I could use as a junk room until I'd moved on to the final part of the project. Even so, it would be more exposed.

What I should do, of course, was get the damn thing off my boat.

What I didn't understand in all of this was why the hell Fitz wanted Dylan's package—unless Dylan had stolen it from Fitz in the first place. It seemed so unlikely. Dylan wasn't a thief. He was a bruiser, an enforcer, but not a thief.

So if Dylan had decided to branch out in business for himself, how had Fitz found out? And why would he believe he was entitled to come here and take something Dylan had left in my care?

Unless it wasn't about the package after all.

What if they thought Dylan and I had some other scheme going? What if someone else had stolen something from Fitz, and they'd assumed, because we'd become friends, because he'd protected me, that I was in on it?

All that time, five months, that I had no contact from Dylan and I'd so desperately wanted to talk to him, to see him again . . . He should have worked things out with Fitz—that was the plan, after all.

Maybe Fitz assumed we were working together. If it wasn't the package, what on earth were they looking for?

My brain wasn't functioning properly—I had a lump on the side of my head and a headache the likes of which I'd never experienced. I left the bow storage area. The paint that had been thrown over the wall could stay there. I was going to clad over it with wood paneling anyway, one of these days.

The state of the kitchen and the cabin brought on a fresh round of tears. That, and my aching head. I picked up all the papers, rearranged them into some semblance of order. I replaced everything in the storage area under the dinette, then put the cushions back. Already it looked a lot better, more like my usual mess than an actual burglary.

The only things that were broken in the kitchen were a mug from Dover Castle and the cabinet doors. I didn't tend to buy many fragile things, since it would only have taken a rough spell at high tide for things to get knocked about in the cabin. Everything breakable was either behind a rail or, in the case of the television and music system, bolted to the wall. Most of my plates were melamine.

In a pile on the floor I found some Tylenol that had been in one of the galley drawers. I took three and swilled them down with a handful of water from the sink.

When Jim Carling called me, at eight thirty, I was already drunk.

I'd finished the beer and most of a bottle of wine, sitting by myself in the main cabin waiting for night to fall. I thought it would be easier to deal with if I was wasted.

I answered the phone the third time it rang, having ignored the first two. I couldn't think of anyone I really wanted to talk to, except for Dylan, but his phone was still turned off. "Hello," I said at last.

"Genevieve. Why didn't you answer the phone?"

He didn't say, "It's Carling," I noticed. He sounded pissed off.

"I was out on the deck," I lied.

"Are you okay?" he asked.

"I've had a few drinks," I said, by way of explanation.

"Ah. Sounds like a good state to be in. I need to catch up," he said.

I didn't answer, my thoughts drifting away from the phone conversation.

"So," he went on, "I was wondering if I could come and see you."

"Yes," I said.

"Have you eaten?"

I was going to say that I couldn't remember, which would have been the truth. But that would sound as if I wasn't taking care of myself, and I couldn't face a scolding. "Um . . . not yet. Why?"

"I could bring takeout."

"That would be great. Thank you."

"I'll be over in half an hour or so, then," he said. "Don't go anywhere, will you?"

As soon as he'd hung up, I tried Dylan's number again.

The number you have dialed is currently unavailable. Please try later.

I tried to tidy up a bit more, halfheartedly, my senses dulled by the alcohol and by the exhaustion. My body still ached; everything hurt. If I had a real bathroom, I told myself crossly, I could be soaking in a nice hot bath right now. Instead, it was a choice between a shower in the shower room beside the office, and the hose.

I took clean clothes over to the shower room with me. The sky was darkening, the lights across the river reflecting patterns on the water.

The parking lot had filled up since I'd last looked this afternoon. Joanna and Liam's Ford van was there, and Maureen and Pat's Fiesta. I didn't see any cars I didn't recognize.

I had a hot shower and it made me feel better, more awake, although I kept dropping things. There were marks around my wrists where I'd spent most of the night tied up, and when I washed my hair I felt the big lump on the side of my head, above my ear. I tried pressing it experimentally, but only once because the pain was sudden and sharp and brutal. Fortunately no blood, no broken bones. With any luck Carling might not notice.

I had no idea how long I'd been in the shower, but when I came out it was completely dark. I waited for the light to come on in the parking lot, but it stayed resolutely off. *Surely it should trigger,* I thought, standing under the sensor in my sweatpants and sneakers. Maybe they'd cut it again last night. Maybe they cut it every night, and Cam repaired it every morning. Maybe he wasn't bothering to repair it anymore.

I started walking back to the boat, my feet unsteady on the moving dock.

The lights were on in my boat. I tried to remember whether I'd left the lights on or not, and couldn't decide. My brain felt as though it were full of cotton balls.

I went down the steps into the cabin and nearly jumped out of my skin—Carling was standing at the kitchen sink, about to fill the kettle.

"Fuck!" I said. "You gave me a heart attack."

"You should lock your door when you leave the boat."

"I only went for a shower."

He came up to me and took me in his arms. It hurt, and felt good at the same time. He kissed me after that. It felt slightly awkward, not like the kiss we'd shared before.

For a moment, I thought about Dylan.

"Are you okay?" he asked, his expression concerned.

"I'm still a bit drunk," I said, as if this explained it all. "I'm sorry. I was feeling blue, and I felt like getting so drunk the world would go away."

On the table in the dinette was a big paper bag with two containers of french fries. I grabbed ketchup, salt, and vinegar from the kitchen cabinets.

"I brought more alcohol," he said. "I thought you might be running low."

Two bottles of wine, one white, one red. They looked very tempting. I smiled at him, my best drunken smile.

"You open it," I said, handing him the corkscrew. "I've completely forgotten how."

We ate our fries sitting at the dinette. It was only when I started eating that I realized how hungry I was. I ate all my fries, every one, scraping the remnants of ketchup from the paper. He ate his at a more sedate pace, sipping wine elegantly as though he were at a restaurant and not sitting on a worn velvet cushion in a half-finished Dutch barge on the Medway.

"So," he said at last, "why were you feeling blue?"

I shrugged. I was feeling a little less drunk but still vulnerable. "I guess I felt alone, that's all. I don't want you to feel sorry for me. I don't get lonely very often, but I did today."

"Well, not anymore. We can be alone together."

"Why are you looking so sad?" I said.

He laughed, but without mirth, and topped up my wineglass. "I'm not sad. Just getting old."

"You're not old."

"I'm older than you."

"So what?"

"All right, then, I feel old today. Which is also a good excuse for getting drunk."

I smiled at him, starting to really enjoy his company. "We need shots," I said.

"Funny you should say that," he said. From a gym bag that lay just beside the steps up to the wheelhouse he brought out a bottle of vodka. "I hope you like this stuff."

"Hell," I said, "it's better than rubbing alcohol."

After that, everything seemed funny, to him and to me, and we drank shots while listening to jazz on the radio, which neither of us really liked. Every time one of us grimaced at a discordant note, we had to drink. And so we both got drunker and drunker.

The bag and the bottle of vodka told me he was planning to stay the night. He was going to stay the whole night, and judging by how much of the vodka he was downing he didn't need to get up early tomorrow to go to work, either. And once that had filtered into my poor, drunken, battered brain, I realized that tonight, at least, I could relax.

They wouldn't be breaking into my boat again, not tonight. Dylan's package was safe.

Chapter Twenty-Three

It was a Friday, again, the next time Dunkerley stepped over the line.

I was looking forward to dancing, and, although it had been an incredibly busy week at work, it was nearly over and I couldn't wait to get to the Barclay later and loosen up.

There was an afternoon performance progress meeting, one of the things Dunkerley had initiated that was universally unpopular with my team. On this Friday, to my great misfortune, nobody showed up except me. I'd been so busy during the day that I'd hardly noticed that most of the team was out of the office. Two of them were out sick. Gavin was in Tenerife. Lucy had taken the afternoon off to get her nails done. So that left me and Dunkerley.

I think he'd been told to stay out of my way by Human Resources, while they investigated my allegations. Either way, I'd hardly seen him since that argument we'd had in his office. But now, here he was, sitting across the boardroom table from me, staring blatantly in a way that was making me feel increasingly uncomfortable.

We waited in silence, until, ten minutes after the meeting was supposed to start, Dunkerley cleared his throat and said, "Well, Genevieve. Looks as if it's just you and me today."

"Looks like it," I said.

"So, what have you got to report?"

I looked down at the performance report I'd printed in preparation and passed it across the table toward him. I was top this month. It had nearly killed me, but I had never been so motivated in my life.

He read over it quickly and nodded. "See," he said, "what you can do if you try?"

I didn't say anything. I couldn't trust myself to speak.

"Look," he said, "I think you may have misunderstood my intentions toward you."

I raised an eyebrow at him. "Really? And what were your intentions, exactly?"

"My intentions were to get you to sleep with me."

Whatever I'd expected him to say, it wasn't that. I must have looked shocked.

He laughed at my discomfort. "You can't have been surprised. Not in the line of work you do. I mean, your other work, of course."

"If that's the end of the meeting," I said, "I'd really like to go and finish what I was working on."

"You're a very hard worker, Genevieve."

"You know you shouldn't be saying this. How do you know I'm not taping this conversation?"

"Because you're not as clever as you think you are."

I was getting angry now. I wondered if he realized that he had found the right button to push to get a reaction. "You're a shit, you know that?"

"Yes, probably. So, are you going to do it?"

"Do what? Fuck you? In your dreams."

"Not that. Are you going to drop your complaint against me?"

"No," I said. "Why should I? If anything, you're just giving me more to report."

"I think you should drop your complaint before everyone else finds out what you do on the side."

"You know what? Tell them. I really don't give a shit. In fact, I might just tell them myself. I might just invite them all to the club as my guests and see what they think. Shall I do that? I'll invite everybody—except you."

I stood up abruptly, the chair rocking behind me, and left the room, slamming the door behind me.

We'd finished the first bottle of wine and were a quarter of the way through the vodka before he kissed me again. We were on the sofa together, laughing about something that wasn't even funny, and somehow I collapsed against him and mumbled, "Sorry," as he took my face in both his hands, as though he might miss otherwise, and that made me laugh, too, and then I couldn't say anything because his mouth was on mine.

While he was kissing me I climbed onto his lap and straddled him so I could control this, even though I was so drunk I was having trouble balancing. He held me steady, his hands on my waist. *Oh, God*, I thought, *this was probably a mistake.*

At last I stopped to give him a chance to breathe.

"I seem to remember saying this shouldn't happen," he said.

"Well, I'm not very good at following instructions."

"Even more so because we're both drunk."

"You've never had drunken sex before?"

"Of course I have. Is that what's happening, then?"

"What?"

"Drunken sex."

"Well, maybe we'll sober up eventually. Then we can have sober sex, too."

It was dark in my bedroom, and chilly: the heat from the stove had warmed the main cabin and the alcohol had warmed us from the inside, but going into the cold room I found myself shivering. I undressed as quickly as I could and got under the clean duvet. Carling took longer to get undressed, folding his clothes and leaving them in a neat pile on the chair onto which I'd already thrown my clothes with far less care. He was thinking about it too much, and maybe I wasn't thinking about it enough.

He had a good body. Even in my drunken state I could tell: he was warm and solid and had kept himself in shape, athletic rather than muscular, long-limbed, taut. He climbed in bed with me and immediately pulled me against him. The skylight over our heads bugged me. I still remembered the shock of seeing that face, framed against the dark sky. Was that only last night? It felt like a long, long time ago.

It was drunken sex, but it was still good. Tangled in the darkness, unfamiliar bodies reacting in unfamiliar ways; breathing hard, and sweaty limbs against each other in a sort of desperate dance to which neither of us was certain of the correct steps. The conclusion of it was something of a relief for both of us. He fell asleep right away, not snoring but breathing heavily, his body securely between me and the door of the bedroom. If they came for me tonight, they would have to get past him first. Even if it took a lot to wake him from his drunken sleep.

I liked him, that was true. Was it enough? Was it wrong of me to have fucked him when my feelings for him amounted to less than what I felt for most of the people who lived on the marina? God, I suppose I was even fonder of Malcolm than I was of Carling—though I wouldn't have fucked Malcolm if he was the last man alive.

I thought about Dylan, wherever he was. What he would say if he knew what I'd just done. I could almost picture myself saying it. Him standing there in front of me with his arms folded across his massive chest.

I fucked that policeman.

He would raise one eyebrow at me as if to say, *So?* And he would pull that face that implied he had somehow expected better.

• • •

I was still angry, hours later, when I finally got to the Barclay.

The club was packed: more than one bachelor party group by the look of it as I made my way toward the dressing rooms. I saw no sign of Fitz, but that meant nothing; it was early. Maybe he'd show up later.

Dylan was talking to Nicks, by the largest stage. They seemed to be deep in conversation, but Dylan looked up as I passed, gave me a nod.

I got changed for my first dance and did some stretches to warm up. Not for the first time, I wished I could choose my own music. I needed something fast, something brutal. Something to work off the aggression so that I could calm down for my routines later in the evening. When I got onto the stage for my first dance, fortunately it was "Sexy Bitch" by David Guetta and Akon. That would do the trick. Not exactly girl power, but I would embed my stilettos into the crotch of any man who felt like challenging me about my attitude tonight.

Fifteen minutes later, and my first routine was over. I'd put effort into it, done some high twirls and spins and an upside-down split against the pole that I'd tried only a couple of times before. It looked inelegant if it wasn't done right. The last time I'd tried it had been at Fitz's party.

I watched the faces of the men gathered around the stage when I finished and I knew I'd done a good job.

In the dressing room I drank water and cleaned up. I scarcely noticed Dylan until I'd finished, and only then because Crystal called out, "Dylan! You're perving over Viva—stop it."

He wasn't perving, of course; he was standing in the doorway like a brick wall, his face impassive. When he'd finally gotten my attention, he said, "Fitz wants to see you."

I checked the clock over the dressing table. I didn't want to waste time; I could be out there in the club, earning money.

Dylan walked up the stairs to the offices and I hurried after him, tottering on those ridiculous heels. "What's it about, do you know?"

"Don't ask me," he said.

I was half-expecting to see several guys gathered in the office as usual, but today Fitz was alone. Despite the warmth I'd generated dancing, I felt a shiver. I wondered what it meant that he was on his own, if I had cause to be afraid.

"Viva. Can I get you anything?"

I wasn't really thirsty but I needed a reason for Dylan to come back. "Water, please."

Dylan was dismissed from the room with a nod from Fitz. He crossed the room and shut the door.

I smiled at him.

"Have a seat, my dear," he said, indicating the sofa.

I did as I was told. No wonder I was shivering—the window behind me was open, the heavy curtain moving gently as the breeze stirred it. I could hear the noise of the traffic in the street below.

"So," he said at last, "you enjoyed the party the other week?"

"Yes," I said. "It was a good night."

"Would you like to do it again?"

"Sure."

"Next weekend?"

Was that it? He could have asked at closing time, or sent a message through Dylan.

He was standing in front of me, his legs slightly apart, hands thrust into the pockets of his expensive silk suit. There was a knock at the door and a few seconds later Dylan opened it. He brought a tray with water on it, exactly as he had done the last time. Ice and a slice of lemon on a silver dish. He set it down on the table next to the sofa and left the room again without a word, or a look at Fitz, or at me. He shut the door behind him.

Fitz cast a glance behind him at the door and turned back to me, head cocked to one side as though he were considering something. "He likes you," he remarked.

"Could have fooled me," I said. "He never so much as gives me a second glance."

"You had a nice long chat with him last weekend," he said. "What was that all about?"

"He was asking me for advice on some girl he likes," I said, without missing a beat. Whatever I'd said would have been a lie and I was sure he would have seen straight through it, but I wasn't about to drop Dylan in the shit.

To my profound relief, Fitz laughed. "Sly old dog," he said. "I still think it's you he likes. Maybe it was some kind of double-bluff."

I laughed, too, and Fitz went to his cocktail tray. He poured himself something that could have been whiskey, a tumblerful.

He came and sat next to me on the sofa. Next to me, but with a discreet distance between us. "See," he said, "I have a problem with that."

"With what?" I said, feeling uncomfortable again.

"With him liking you."

"Why's that?"

Fitz drank from his glass, then he sighed heavily and put the glass down on the table, reaching across me as he did so. "Because, my dear Viva, I like you, too. And that big bastard is better-looking than me."

I smiled at him. "You like me, Fitz?"

He was watching me coyly from his end of the sofa. "Come on. You know I do."

I drank my water to give myself a few seconds to consider how to play this. "I didn't think you had any free time for girls," I said at last. "You're a very busy man."

He looked at me steadily, as though he was evaluating my response. "You're different from the others," he said. "That's why I like you. You're not going to fuck around with me, are you, Genevieve?"

"Depends what you mean by that," I said. "I work for you and I'm very proud of what I do. I don't want to stop dancing, Fitz. And, whatever happens, I don't want anything to interfere with work. Do you understand what I mean?"

"Well," he said at last. "You are different from the others. You really are."

"I need to go," I said. "They're busy downstairs."

"Yes," he said, "I wouldn't want to come between you and your dancing."

He stood and held out a hand to help me to my feet.

At the door he kissed my hand gently. "I don't do casual fucks, Genevieve," he said. "If I can't have your heart, I'll have to make do with having you as a valued employee."

"Thank you," I said.

I half-walked, half-ran back down to the dressing room, feeling as though I'd been in the lion's den and come out again without so much as a scratch. Could that have gone any better? Only if I'd managed to renegotiate my payment for the next private function—the question of remuneration had somehow failed to come up in the light of the other revelations.

Dylan was waiting for me outside the dressing room and he walked back with me to the door to the club. "Well?" he said.

I smiled at him. "He thinks you like me," I said.

Dylan laughed, and I went off to find some nice gentlemen to chat up.

I woke up and my head was splitting with pain even before I opened my eyes.

I was alone—Carling was gone. My head fell back onto the pillow, and that hurt, too, the bump on the side of my head jarring with the impact.

I needed water.

I dragged myself upright and found a T-shirt on the floor, pulling it over my head as I went into the bathroom. I drank from the tap, ran my hand under it and over my hair, holding a cupped hand of cold water against the bump on the side of my head.

I washed my face and finally looked in the mirror. I'd looked worse, I thought. It would have to do.

It was cold, so I went back into the bedroom and pulled on some jeans and socks. Then I went through to the kitchen.

He hadn't left, after all. He was at the table in the dinette, flicking through a copy of *Waterways World* that he must have found on the bookshelf, a steaming cup of coffee in front of him. He was sitting in a shaft of sunlight from the skylight overhead, almost as though he was about to be transfigured. He looked a hell of a lot better than I did.

"Morning," he said cheerfully.

I cleared my throat. "Hello," I said.

He put the kettle back on the stove while I sat down on the other side of the dinette. I thought about the Tylenol in the drawer and wondered if I could muster the energy to stand up again to get it.

"You look as if you need to go back to bed," he said with a laugh.

"Thanks," I said. "I'll be all right in a minute."

"Oh," he said, pouring the water into the mug, "I just met your neighbor. Again. I think he was quite surprised to see me."

"Which one?"

"I remember seeing him last weekend. Fiftyish. Wild gray hair."

"Malcolm? What did he say?"

"He just said, 'Oh,' and I said you'd be around later if he wanted you. And he said, 'Thanks,' and then he went away."

We sat sipping our coffee for a few minutes. I wondered

why he was still here, torn between liking the feeling of not getting up to a lonely, empty boat and not enjoying the thought of having to make conversation. Although I liked that he stopped reading now that I was here.

"I'm glad you stayed," I said.

He looked surprised, and pleased. "Oh, good. I was hoping I hadn't outstayed my welcome."

"Don't you have to work today?"

"I've got a day off today, and tomorrow. I was going to head out and do all the stuff I don't get a chance to do during the week—you know, shopping, laundry, all kinds of exciting stuff. How about you? What do you have planned?"

"I was going to go and look at bathtubs," I said.

"You mean like in a showroom?"

"Not unless I have to. Salvage yards, that kind of place. If I can't find an old bathtub I like I'll have to go for a new one. Most of them aren't really designed for boats, though."

A pause. I wondered if he was hungry, and if I actually had any food in the house that hadn't gone bad.

"I wanted to ask you something," he said.

"That sounds ominous."

"I'm going to ask once, and if you don't want to give me an answer you don't have to. All right?"

"Sure."

"What happened to your wrists?"

I looked down at my hands on the table of the dinette. I hadn't thought to put a sweater on to cover up the marks. Thin scabs had formed in arcs around both wrists, not all the way around but in those sections where the skin had been broken by the cable tie. It looked almost as though I was wearing bracelets, threads of pink. I put my hands on my lap, out of sight.

"If I told you, you wouldn't believe me."

"Try me."

I shrugged, still a little drunk, and too tired to argue or

fight it. "Some men broke into the boat when I was asleep. They tied me up. That's about it."

"When was this?"

"Night before last."

"Didn't you call the police?"

I shook my head. "Malcolm found me in the morning and cut the ties. By that time there didn't seem to be any point calling anyone."

He was staring at me.

"What?"

"I can't believe you're so casual about being attacked."

"What am I supposed to do—lie down and cry?"

"Aren't you afraid they'll come back?"

"Of course I am," I said. "But what can I do about it?"

"Genevieve. You can't not report things like this. If anything happens again, you've got to promise me you'll dial 999."

"Sure," I said, feeling a bit chilled that he'd suddenly become all official.

He rubbed a hand through his hair. "I shouldn't be here," he said. "I shouldn't be doing this."

"I'm not keeping you prisoner," I said, turning my back on him and heading for the bedroom. "Shut the door on your way out."

I stretched out on my bed again, listening for the sound of his feet on the steps up to the wheelhouse, waiting for the sound of the door slamming behind him, and hearing only silence. At least the room wasn't spinning anymore. There was just a hint of nausea, and the headache grinding behind my eyes. If I could catch up on some sleep, everything would be fine. An hour or so of sleep, and then I would go out in the fresh air, get on my bike and go and look at bathtubs.

He appeared in the doorway a few moments later. I turned my head to look at him, thinking that maybe I should apologize; thinking that I should get up, at least say something.

Instead, I watched as he came back into the room, pulling his shirt over his head as he approached the bed. This time he didn't bother folding up his clothes, putting them in a neat pile. He got them off as quickly as he possibly could and left them where they fell.

I bumped into Caddy on the way back down the stairs. "What did he want?" she asked, an urgent whisper above the thumping bass from the main room.

"Another party," I said.

She looked upset.

"I thought you didn't want to do them?" I said.

"It's not that. It's just . . ."

"What?"

Dylan passed us, heading back up toward the offices. He gave me a pointed stare, and a quick glance up at the CCTV cameras.

"Look," I said, "let's talk later."

Caddy looked at me as though she was about to refuse, then shook her head. "Whatever."

I had three private dances booked in the Blue Room before the end of Friday evening. The final appointment came as a surprise, to say the least. I went into the room and found that the only person sitting in there was Dunkerley.

He looked pleased with himself, lounging on one of the sofas as if he owned the place.

I wanted to turn around and leave, but if he was in here he must have paid. If he'd paid, then I was going to make myself very unpopular by asking to have him thrown out.

"Good evening," I said. "What brings you here?"

"I wanted to see you," he said, a smug smile on his face. I had to fight the urge to smack it away.

"That's nice," I said. "Would you like a fast dance, or a slow dance?"

"Mm," he said. "Surprise me."

I went through my list of music quickly, trying to find something that was even vaguely appropriate to dance to for the benefit of a man I couldn't stand. All the music was in this list because I liked it, and I had routines worked out for all of them. Whichever one I picked I probably wouldn't use again because it would always remind me of dancing for this asshole.

I found one. The Pussycat Dolls' "Don't Cha." It wasn't one they appreciated in the club as a rule—it was a little over-used.

I did the dance; I even did some of my most intense moves, before winding down by gyrating in front of him, spinning, and twisting. I watched his self-satisfied smug-ugly face change. At the end, he applauded.

I went straight from the Blue Room upstairs to the offices. Nicks was standing guard at the top of the stairs. Dancers didn't usually come up here unless they'd been summoned, and then only with a chaperone.

"I'd like to see Fitz," I said to him.

"I'll ask him," he said. "You wait here."

I waited. I felt hot and uncomfortable, not even sure what I thought I was doing. But knowing I had to do it anyway.

A few moments later Fitz emerged from the main office, at the end of the hall on the right. He shut the door behind him and came over to me.

"I'm sorry," I said, giving him my best Viva smile. "I wanted to ask you something."

"Come with me," he said. He led me to the far end of the carpeted hall. I'd never been down here before. It was a smaller sitting room, almost like a waiting room—chairs and sofas around the edges of the room, a potted plant in the corner. A desk near the door. Fitz sat on one of the chairs and I sank gratefully down into the chair next to his.

"I've been having some problems with a guy at work," I

began. "He recognized me here a few weeks ago, and he's been making it really difficult for me there."

Fitz's face was impassive. He was waiting for me to get to the part where it became his problem.

"He wanted me to do a private dance for him but he wasn't prepared to pay for it, so Helena got him to leave. I didn't think he'd come back, but he's here, now."

Still no response. I was starting to feel like I was making a huge mistake.

"He just booked me for a dance and I did it, so I guess he's changed his mind about paying. But he's staying in the club, he's hanging around, and I don't like it. I think he's going to try and follow me home."

I had nothing to support this theory, but nevertheless I'd finally gotten to the part that concerned Fitz. While I was working for him, I was his responsibility, and anyone seeking to disrupt that easy relationship was not going to be allowed to continue.

"What's he look like?" he asked.

"Tall, bald, fat, light gray suit, glasses."

"Sounds like a charmer."

I smiled and looked down at my bare knees. "I'm not easily scared, Fitz. I can take care of myself normally. I don't like asking for help."

"I know that," he said softly. "But this is bad for business, whether he's paid up or not. I can't have him distracting you while you're at work here. I'll make sure he doesn't follow you home. All right?"

I nodded gratefully and stood. "Thank you," I said. "I'm sorry if I interrupted your meeting."

"No worries."

I went back to the end of the hall and turned at the top of the stairs. He was watching me go. Checking me out, or making sure I wasn't going to try and nose around some of the other rooms? I still wasn't sure he trusted me.

I was just in time for my last dance. I was tired, so I made it a slow one, erotic, taking it about as far as it was possible to go without another person. There, at the front of the audience, looking pink and sweaty, stood Dunkerley. At the back, in one of the VIP booths, Fitz, Nicks, and Dylan. They were talking, helping themselves from what looked like a half-full bottle of Russian import vodka and watching me.

When it was over, I blew a kiss to the few men who were still sitting over to the left, despite the fact that it was nearly dawn and they should have been at home long ago, tucked up in their beds next to their wives. I went back into the dressing room and got changed into my jeans and sneakers and fleece, wiped off the makeup, and tied my hair in a ponytail behind my head. I said goodnight to the other girls who were still there, and let myself out the back way.

The backstreet was quiet and gray with the approaching dawn. There was no sign of Dunkerley, or anyone else for that matter. I'd been kind of hoping for an escort to take me safely home, maybe Dylan, or even Fitz—maybe I'd even have been all right with Nicks, under the circumstances—but there was nobody.

I walked around to the front to find a cab.

At work on Monday, they told us Dunkerley was out sick, that he was going to be out of work for a while. There was a lot of gossip about it, of course. I heard a suggestion that Human Resources had put him on leave for some sort of harassment, and that he'd been asked to resign. There was even a rumor going around that he was genuinely ill, seriously ill, and that he might not be able to come back.

All I knew was that I didn't have to see his smug fat face again, and for that I was profoundly grateful.

Chapter Twenty-Four

Jim Carling came with me to look for bathtubs. I was thankful for this; despite the sharp words in the morning, I was starting to really like Jim. Aside from ferrying me cheerfully everywhere I wanted to go, he kept up the conversation about boat ownership and whether it would be possible to make your way around the world in a boat of this size, and, if so, where would you go? We had fun with that one. Jim wanted to go to the Far East. I said I wasn't going to go anywhere in the Indian Ocean because of the threat of Somali pirates. All of this was arbitrary anyway because I had never driven a boat before, much less negotiated the open sea.

We didn't come back with a tub, although there were some reasonable ones in a salvage yard in Sittingbourne. I was on the lookout for a hip bathtub, maybe even a genuine Victorian one, something I could manage to connect to the boat's plumbing without too much hassle.

We stopped and had lunch in a café at a garden center—baked potato for me, salad for him—with pots of tea. It felt very domestic, shopping together on a weekend.

"Is there anywhere else you need to go?" he asked.

I laughed. "You don't have to be my taxi," I said. "It's very kind of you, but I wouldn't want to take advantage."

We drove home to the marina, and, because it seemed like

the most appropriate thing to do with the fading afternoon, we went back to bed. The boat was chilly. I took him by the hand and into the bedroom. He was skillful and patient, his big hands decisive and firm.

By the time we'd tired ourselves out, it was dark. I went to the galley and lit the stove to warm the boat up, and then came back to bed. I thought for a moment he was asleep but he moved to let me under the covers, and pulled me against him.

"It should start to warm up soon," I said. "The stove's really efficient when it gets going."

"Mm," he said. "I should think about going home."

"Really?"

"I don't have any clean clothes. And I need to do stuff at home—laundry, you know."

"Oh."

He was kissing my arm, making the hairs on it rise in anticipation. "You could come home and stay with me."

"No," I said.

"Why?"

I laughed. "I don't sleep well on dry land."

"You don't have to actually sleep."

It was at that moment that I realized. I wanted to tell him. Maybe not all of it, but enough to make him understand.

"I have to stay on the boat."

"Why?"

"The men who came on the boat and tied me up—I think they were looking for something. If I leave the boat, they'll come back."

"What were they looking for?"

"I'm not sure. I just know that they turned the boat upside down, and I assume that means they were looking for something."

He sat up in bed, bunching the pillows behind him, and turned on the light overhead. "If you don't know what they were looking for," he said with impeccable logic, "how do you know they didn't find it?"

I blinked at him.

"You have to tell me, Genevieve."

"No, I don't."

He shook his head slowly. "God," he said, more to himself than to me, "why am I even here? This is fucking crazy."

"Look," I said, trying to comfort him, "I'm not scared of them. Not really. They are bad people, but I've dealt with them before. I just need to figure out a way to get whatever it is off my boat so that I'm not a target for them anymore."

"Caddy Smith," he said, "you knew her, didn't you?"

I nodded my head.

"Why didn't you tell me before?"

"You said her name was Candace."

"Don't play dumb, Genevieve. You knew it was her when you saw her in the water. You lied in your statement."

"No, I didn't. It was dark. I saw a body. It looked like her, but I wasn't sure."

"You've got to tell me, Genevieve. What do you mean, 'you've dealt with them before'? Who are they? What do they want from you?"

I didn't answer.

He got out of bed and started to collect his clothes, which, once again, were scattered all over my bedroom floor. I watched him silently, wondering which part of the whole bloody mess had sparked off this sudden change in mood. Just because I didn't want to make everything worse? Just because I didn't want to tell him about all the shit at the Barclay? What was he planning to do, anyway—go and ask Fitz nicely to leave me alone?

He was nearly fully dressed now, pulling his sweater over his head.

"What are you going to do?" I asked.

"I'm going home," he said. "Crazy as it is, the offer's still there if you want to come with me. But I'm guessing you won't." He was so angry. And maybe he was disappointed in me, too. When he'd finished dressing, he came over to the bed and kissed me hard, fiercely, as if it might be the last time. I put my arms around his neck and tried to pull him back to bed but he wasn't having any of that.

It was a kiss goodbye.

It was on my second visit to Fitz's house that everything began to change, for all of us: for Fitz, for Dylan, for Caddy, and for me.

I'd been looking forward to it all week, not just because these weekends were going to be giving such an impressive boost to my savings, even if I hadn't managed to negotiate a better pay deal for it—this time, Caddy had agreed to do the party with me.

Added to which, not having to deal with Dunkerley at work was a bonus. Gavin had been made our temporary manager, and it was pretty much like working for your best friend: we got on with things as we always had, but it felt more as though we were laughing about it instead of stepping over each other's twitching bodies in the desperate fight to close deals.

It wasn't Dylan who collected me that evening, but Nicks. He sat in the car outside until I was ready and stayed there; I let myself into the backseat and then we drove off into the traffic.

"Where's Caddy?" I asked.

He moved his shoulders in some kind of lazy shrug and then barely said a word to me the whole trip. I plugged into my music and went over my moves in my head, planning where I could make tweaks, considering what I would do if the option arose for Fitz to bend the rules again. I'd kind of set the precedent now by doing it once; it was more or less accepted that I would be asked to do it again. No matter. The money was the important thing. If it got me closer to the boat, I was prepared to do it. And if he wanted me to go further still? No point worrying about it now. I would decide when the time came.

We pulled up to the rear of the house this time, and I went straight in through the back door to the kitchen. As before, the caterers were busy preparing food, a sit-down meal by the look of it.

I found a comfy chair in the corner and kept myself busy with a notebook I'd brought with me, full of plans and clippings from various boat magazines. I was so engrossed in it that I didn't even notice Dylan until he was standing right beside me, eclipsing the light from the kitchen.

"Hi!" I said, removing an earbud. "I didn't know you were here."

He looked at me without expression. "You're not on till later. They're having dinner in the dining room in half an hour. Fitz wants to know if you'd like to join them."

"You're kidding?"

"Nope."

"Just me?"

"You and a few others. There's a seating plan."

"Oh. Dylan, do you know where Caddy is? She's supposed to be here, too."

"She's upstairs, I think."

I accepted this without comment, pissed off that my evening of entertainment with my best buddy was not turning out quite the way I'd hoped.

"Am I sitting next to someone I should know about?" I said.

"You're between Fitz and Leon Arnold."

I dropped my voice to a whisper. "Who's Leon Arnold?"

He looked at me as though I'd asked the wrong question. "Owns a yacht. You'll get on well with him. And if you don't, you should pretend to. And be careful with him."

"What do you mean, 'be careful'?"

He took a moment to reply. "Don't worry about it. I'll keep an eye on him."

There was no point pressing him for a more specific answer. It was another test, I realized. Good thing I'd brought enough outfits with me so that I could select something suitable for an evening meal. I went to the downstairs bathroom and got changed, put makeup on, and twisted my hair up into french pleat that I hoped looked classically elegant.

The dining room was empty but the table was laid for ten; through open doors on the other side I heard sounds of polite conversation, a woman's laugh, so I went to the door cautiously and looked through.

They were all in there—Fitz and some other men, one of whom I recognized from the last party. There were women in there, too; I recognized a girl from the Barclay—Stella? She'd danced there a few times, but usually she worked at one of Fitz's other clubs. And standing next to Fitz, resplendent in a jeweled black cocktail dress and a pair of killer heels, was Caddy. She gave me a little wave.

Three of the girls were on their own in a corner, giggling over some private joke. I saw Fitz cast a displeased glance over to them before resuming his conversation with the man to his right. I went over to the girls with a glass of champagne I'd lifted from the tray of a passing waitress and said to them quietly, "Ladies, aren't you supposed to be mingling?"

Two of them looked worried, but one of them—an acid blonde with pale blue eyes—said, "Fuck's it got to do with you?"

I treated her to a warm smile. "It doesn't pay to piss Fitz off," I said sweetly, "and he's already shooting daggers at you. Just a bit of friendly advice."

As I left them and headed for Fitz, the girls seemed to come to their senses and split from their cozy huddle, making their way toward the remaining guests.

"Viva," Fitz said to me as I approached. "Come and meet Leon."

Fitz slipped an arm around my waist and kissed my cheek as I shook Leon Arnold's hand. He was maybe fifty, the same height as me, with a shaved head and capped teeth. A good suit, a diamond stud in one earlobe.

"I'm pleased to meet you," I said. "I understand I'm the lucky girl who gets to sit next to you at dinner."

He looked as though he might take a little warming up, but what the hell? I was already thinking of my potential bonus for taking care of Fitz's girls and for softening up Mr. Arnold for whatever scheme Fitz had planned for him. What I hadn't figured on, though, was the look Caddy was giving me. She wasn't smiling. She was looking at me as though I were something she'd found on the sole of her shoe.

"Hey," I said to her, as we filed in to dinner, "I was wondering where you were."

"You're sitting next to Fitz," she said.

"Yes," I said. "Dylan told me."

I read something in her eyes, something she wasn't telling me.

"What?" I said.

"Don't get too close to them," she said. "Don't get close to either of them. Understand?"

"What's that supposed to mean?"

She didn't seem to hear me. Whatever. This wasn't the time or the place.

Over dinner, the topic of business seemed to be strictly off-limits. Stella told everybody about an audition she'd had to dance in a music video; one of the other men, a younger version of Fitz, told her he was looking for girls to appear as extras in a film he was producing. After that they were all over him.

I chatted with Leon Arnold over dinner, asked him about

his yacht, about cruising around the islands in the Mediterranean. More than once I cast a glance in Fitz's direction to
check I was doing the right thing. He gave me a smile, which
reassured me. The rest of the time he was busy talking to the
man who was sitting on the other side of him, an older man
with a neatly trimmed gray beard. Caddy seemed to have been
tasked with entertaining him—she kept her focus on him and
away from me.

I managed to eat most of the soup and then picked at my
dinner, pushing it around the plate even though it looked
delicious—in any other circumstances I would have wolfed
it and asked for seconds. Not eating allowed me to devote all
my attention to Leon, who, despite his yacht and his Rolex
Oyster and his unconscionable amount of money, was de-
cidedly dull.

Stella was sitting on the other side of Leon, and when her
attempts at enlivening the conversation with the dark-haired
man on her right failed, she turned her attention to Leon and
left me momentarily free to check out the men I'd be dancing
for later.

"How's your food?" Fitz asked me.

I felt my face flush a little. "It's delicious," I said. "I'm hoping
there might be some leftovers for when I've finished dancing."

He smiled and under the table his hand made contact with
my thigh.

"What time do you want us to start?" I asked.

He shrugged. "We've got business to discuss, so . . . after
that. I'll send one of the lads for you when we're ready. Kitten's
going to do some private dances, if they want them."

"Caddy isn't pole dancing?"

He gave me an amused smile. "No, Viva. You're here for that."

I tried a different tack. "Thank you for inviting me for dinner," I said.

"You're good at this," he said.

"At what?"

"At knowing what they like. And you worked things out with the girls earlier. I appreciate that."

I glanced down the table at the three blondes, who were animatedly discussing their potential careers in the music industry with the three young men.

The girls were all there for sex, I realized. It came to me in a moment, even though I'd probably known it all along. When Dylan had said to me last time, "You're the only one dancing," I'd thought that meant there would be girls from the club serving drinks, maybe doing lap dances, but when I hadn't seen any other girls, I didn't give it another thought. Now, I realized, they'd all been upstairs; and the last time, while I was being felt up by Kenny and dancing for the other clients of Fitz's who'd gathered here, the remaining men had probably been upstairs being entertained by the other girls.

"You know," I said to Fitz, "you should think about diversifying the club a bit."

Another amused smile. "Diversifying?"

"You could do a couple of ladies' nights—get some men in to dance as well as girls. And maybe a burlesque night, something with a bit more"—I searched for the most appropriate word—"widespread appeal."

"Ah, but widespread appeal means reduced profits."

"But you must admit, you're serving a very limited pool of customers at the moment," I said. "Think about all the people who wouldn't dream of setting foot in the club as it is now. Couples. Girls' nights out. Bacherlorette parties, if you like."

Leon Arnold leaned over me, one arm heavy across my shoulders. He smelled of whiskey and aftershave. "You want to watch yourself with this one, Fitz, old boy," he said. "She's gonna take over your empire."

My reply was swift. "No, I want to stick to what I'm good at—dancing for gorgeous men like you, Leon."

Fitz laughed then, and Caddy gave me a sharp look from the other side of the table.

As soon as dinner was over and I could excuse myself, I went back to the kitchen, found a bottle of water to try to dilute the half-glass of champagne and the half-glass of red wine I'd drunk, and took it with me to the downstairs bathroom. Dylan was waiting at the breakfast bar, munching on a dish of nachos.

"Don't they feed you properly?" I asked cheekily.

He looked up. "I thought they were going to take you upstairs, with the rest of the tramps," he teased back.

"I'd better get changed," I said. "Come in and talk to me if you like."

Dylan shook his head. "Fitz wouldn't like that," he said.

"What?"

"Us having a private chat."

I thought back to what Fitz had said about having a problem with Dylan liking me. And I remembered the part about someone having noticed us talking in the club.

"Fitz is busy," I said.

There was nobody else around; the caterers had packed up their stuff and gone already. He followed me into the bathroom and sat on the easy chair while I stripped off the evening gown and replaced it with a sparkly cutaway dress in electric blue.

"Do you know what's up with Caddy?" I asked. She'd gone right into the lounge with Fitz and Arnold, arm in arm with both of them, leaving me no chance to take her aside.

"What do you mean?" he said.

"She's giving me filthy looks. I don't know what I've done to upset her."

He stared at me and then a slow smile crossed his face.

"What?" I asked. "What's going on, Dylan?"

"You were getting cozy with Fitz," he said.

"So what? And anyway, I wasn't 'getting cozy.' I was socializing, which is what I think I'm being paid for."

"Calm down," he said. "I just meant that she wouldn't like you being cozy with Fitz, because she's got a thing for him."

"Caddy and Fitz? They're a couple?"

He smiled again. "Well, in her dreams maybe."

Lots of things were starting to make sense. "But he's not so keen on her?"

"He fucked her once or twice. He used to fuck all the girls, the ones that would let him, that is. Then he had a couple of them go a bit nuts on him and he realized it was a bad idea. One of them got pregnant. Trouble is, he didn't exactly finish with Caddy, not in any official sort of way, so she still thinks she's got a shot."

"Why doesn't he just tell her he's not interested?"

"I don't think he has the faintest clue how she feels. And if she told him straight out, he'd get rid of her. He doesn't like his girls clingy, not anymore."

"No wonder she was shooting daggers at me," I said, remembering Fitz's arm around my waist, his wet whiskey-kiss on my cheek.

"What do you make of Leon Arnold?" he asked me then.

"Seems all right," I said. "Why?"

Dylan scratched his jaw line thoughtfully. "He's a big player, that's all. Last time you were here, the guys Fitz was talking to, that was all about setting up this meeting with Arnold."

"Really?" I said. "I'm glad I didn't know that earlier. I'd have been nervous."

"I never met him before. Heard of him, of course."

"You think this deal is a bad idea?"

"Fitz knows what he's doing."

"What's he want?"

"With Arnold? Same as always—earn his fortune. Like

you." His tone suggested that this was the end of the discussion. "Just better do a good job dancing, is all."

I pulled my hair out of the pleat, shaking it free, and took off the low-heeled sandals that were useful for socializing with men who were shorter than me. In my bag I had a pair of high-heeled patent shoes with a velvet ribbon that crisscrossed around my ankle and reminded me of the ballet lessons I'd had when I was nine years old.

"I'm glad you're here," I said.

He shrugged.

"Nothing gets to you, does it, Dylan?"

"What's that mean?"

"I don't know. You must care about something. There must be someone who really means something to you. You married?"

He didn't answer, which I took to mean that he was.

"Come on," I said. "I thought we were friends. I thought you said you trusted me."

"I was with someone," he said. "Not anymore."

"Any kids?"

There was a long pause. This was like pulling teeth.

"I've got a daughter. Lauren. She's fourteen."

"You see her often?"

"Not often enough. She lives in Spain, with her mother."

"Oh. Spain—that must be hard on you."

"Yeah, anyway, are you ready?" The conversation was clearly at an end.

"Will you be watching?" I asked him.

"Don't have much choice," he said.

I went to wait in the kitchen like a good girl, while Dylan headed upstairs to the sitting room to check that the other girls weren't getting too drunk.

•   •   •

When Carling had gone, I got dressed in my jeans and fleece and went to the *Scarisbrick Jean*. Malcolm and Josie were just finishing their dinner: pasta with some kind of sauce that smelled of garlic.

"You hungry?" Josie asked me cheerfully. She looked pale despite her colorful sweater. She'd had her hair done in preparation for the wedding—was it her niece's?—and in place of the usual dark threaded with silver it was a warm chocolate color. It made her look years younger.

"No, no," I lied, "I've just eaten."

"Nonsense," she said, "we've got leftovers."

She spooned some tagliatelle and sauce onto a plate and I sat down at their dinette. "Your hair looks gorgeous," I said.

I saw a pointed look pass between Malcolm and Josie. Malcolm's hair, I noticed, remained resolutely wild.

"Thank you," she said firmly, as if making a point. I wondered if Malcolm had failed to notice and was somehow living in purgatory as a result. He wasn't looking particularly cheerful.

"How have you been?" I asked Josie quietly.

"Oh, you know. Up and down." There were tears in her eyes but she blinked them away with a deep breath. She took her plate and Malcolm's to the sink in the galley and started doing the dishes, banging and crashing cabinet doors with enough gusto to drown out the rest of the conversation.

"My battery's charged," I said to Malcolm between mouthfuls.

He looked up then. "Yeah. Probably is."

"And they didn't take it. You know."

"Right."

"What's up?" I asked, realizing the distinct displeasure in his tone was directed at me.

"You," he said. "Fraternizing with the gavvers."

"You mean Carling? He's all right. He helped me look for a tub."

He looked at me for a moment as though he didn't know quite what to make of me, and then he laughed out loud, his head back.

"Look," I said, when he'd finished sniggering at the thought of me and a police officer looking at bathtubs, "I needed protection last night, all right? He was happy to stay. So this morning I'm still alive."

"Whatever," he said, wiping a tear from his eye.

"I need to move the boat, Malcolm. Those people will probably come back for another go."

"Tomorrow, we'll do it tomorrow. All right? Too dark now to do anything. You can sleep here tonight, if you don't want to be in that boat on your own."

I looked up and down the length of the boat. "Sleep where?"

He tapped a bony finger against the side of his nose. "Aha," he said. "You'll need a duvet or something; we don't have anywhere to keep spares."

"I can't leave the boat, Malcolm. What if they come back tonight?"

"You could bring it with you. This package of yours."

"Don't be silly. Then I'd be putting you and Josie in danger, too. Besides, it's obviously well hidden where it is, right?"

He stared at me for a moment, deep in thought. Then he said, "I've got an idea."

I went back to the *Revenge of the Tide* and collected the duvet, a pillow, and my toothbrush, as well as my cell phones. When I came back to the *Aunty Jean*, Malcolm was out on the dock with some fine-grade steel wire and a pair of pliers.

"What's he doing out there?" Josie asked as I climbed down into the cabin with armfuls of duvet.

"Oh, I don't know—fixing something, I guess," I said.

"It's going to be lovely having you here. Like a sleepover."

I had no idea what she thought I was doing, sleeping on their boat when mine was just ten feet or so farther up the dock. Malcolm had told her something about the stove needing looking at and that had seemed to satisfy any curiosity.

When all the dishes had been cleared away, Josie showed me the hidden single bed that slid out from under the dinette like a giant drawer. Of course, while it was out they would need to step over me if they wanted to get from the dinette to the galley or back again, but the likelihood of that in the middle of the night was fortunately quite slim.

Outside, Malcolm was putting the finishing touches to the elaborate set of trip wires he had fixed at ankle-height across our dock. If Nicks or any of Fitz's men came to have another go at the boat tonight they would make enough noise to wake up the whole marina.

Once I got started, things progressed pretty much as they had for my first visit to Fitz's house.

For the first dance, all the men were present except for Fitz and Arnold. I got the distinct impression that I was there to babysit the other men while they took care of whatever business they had to discuss, in private.

True to his word, Dylan stood in the doorway, watching as I did my routine, monitoring me and keeping an eye on the guests, as he had been told to do. He blended into the background, motionless and silent.

I'd just finished when the door opened and Fitz and Arnold came in, bringing Caddy with them. She was a little unsteady on her feet. I gave her a warm smile, which she did not return.

"Aw, look, Leon—we've just missed the first dance," Fitz said, pouring two large glasses of whiskey from the liquor cabinet.

I blew a kiss to Leon. "I'll be back soon," I said to him. "Don't miss the next one."

I skipped out of the room and Dylan shut the door behind me. Just enough time for a very quick change in the bathroom, and some makeup repair.

The bathroom wasn't empty; two of the blond girls from dinner were in there doing lines of coke on the polished marble countertop. They shut up as I opened the door and almost immediately started arguing again when they saw it was only me.

"Well, you can fuck right off," the taller one said. She was wearing a terry-cloth robe and acrylic-heeled stilettos, and most likely not very much else.

"Don't give me that," came the reply, high-pitched, close to tears. "It was your fucking idea. Don't back out now, come on!"

"What's up?" I asked casually.

They both stared at me as though suddenly united in their concern that I was going to get involved and therefore somehow want to share the last two lines of powder that were still on the vanity unit.

"She," said the younger one, pointing with a shaking, manicured finger at the blonde in the robe, "said we should try and get Leon in for a threesome and we could split the tip, and I said yeah, and now she's changed her mind!"

There was a sigh and a hand on the hip in a gesture of defiance. "It wasn't like that, Bella, you know it wasn't, I was fucking joking, honestly."

"Could be passing up a very lucrative opportunity," I said, reapplying lip gloss.

"That's exactly what I said!" exclaimed Bella.

"But, seriously, it would take a lot of fucking money for me to do him on my own, never mind with someone else to fucking worry about."

"It's called taking one for the team. Don't expect you've ever heard of that, before, have you, Diane?"

"I've had enough of this shit. Are we doing this line or what?"

Differences set aside in the interest of ingesting drugs, the two girls bent for their second lines in turn and paused for a moment before continuing the argument.

"Would you do it?" Diane asked. It took me a second to realize that she was talking to me.

"Why are you two down here, anyway?" I said. "Shouldn't you both be entertaining the guests?"

"Oh, don't you start. You're worse than fucking Dylan."

"He's always bloody nagging us. We came down here to get a moment's peace—you know," said Bella, nodding toward the smear of white residue before wiping it off the counter with a moistened finger and rubbing it on her gums.

"Come on, Bel," said Diane, "let's go and find somewhere warmer. Bit frosty in here."

They left the bathroom to me, and I had a quick check through my bag to make sure my purse and phone were still there. I wouldn't have trusted them with any of my belongings and I wasn't surprised to find my bag unzipped. They'd probably gone in there to see if I had a stash of coke myself.

When the door opened again, I was about to tell them to fuck off and leave me alone, but this time it was Dylan.

"Hello," I said, turning back to the mirror. "Don't bother to knock or anything civilized like that, will you?"

"Seen it all before," he said in reply. He sat himself down on the chair and regarded me thoughtfully.

"What?" I said at last, to his reflection in the mirror.

"Fitz is pissed off," he said.

"Oh," I said. "That's not good."

"The deal's not going down."

"Why not?"

"Some of Arnold's lads have been sharing the samples with the girls upstairs."

"That'll explain why two of them were in here a minute ago powdering their noses."

Dylan ran a weary hand over his forehead. "Fuck's sake. They're a fucking liability." He stood up and headed toward the door with a sigh.

"Dylan?"

"What?"

"Anything I can do to help?"

He laughed. "You can cheer Fitz up, for starters. If anyone can put a smile back on his face, it's you."

"What about Caddy?"

"She's upstairs. Sulking."

I woke up before it was fully light.

For a second I had no idea where I was, only that I wasn't in my bed; the boat was rocking alarmingly from side to side and, moments later, I heard footsteps near my head. I sat up with alarm.

"Go back to sleep," came an urgent whisper. "It's only me."

"Malcolm? What's going on?"

"I heard a noise outside," he whispered, crouching down next to the pull-out mattress. "Think it's just a fox or something, by the garbage. Nobody out there."

"Oh."

I lay back down on the bed and pulled the duvet up around my ears.

It was chilly now, light enough to see the outline of the cabin and the shapes of the galley cabinets, the woodstove, burned out and cold. I guessed it was about four or five, the same time of day that I'd found Caddy's body in the water.

I thought of all those trip wires outside on the dock and hoped to God I would remember they were there when I went back to the *Revenge of the Tide*, otherwise I was likely to take a dip in the mud myself, headfirst, duvet and all.

I listened to the noise of the birds and the gulls and the distant roar of the traffic heading up the M2 toward London, and I was just drifting off to sleep when a sudden thought struck me. Malcolm had been fully dressed.

Chapter Twenty-Five

When I headed back toward the lounge, I became aware that something wasn't right. The door was open and through it I could see Arnold sprawled on the sofa with two of his men; there was no sign of Fitz, or Dylan, or any of the girls.

From somewhere upstairs I could hear raised voices, the sound of something heavy falling.

I put on my best Viva smile and entered the room, closing the door discreetly behind me. "Gentlemen," I said, "can I get anyone a drink?"

Waitressing wasn't, strictly speaking, part of my duties, but they didn't know this, and one by one I served them various spirits, mostly neat.

I sat on the arm of Arnold's chair. He put his hand on my ass and gave it a friendly pat.

"While we're waiting," I said, "would you like me to dance, or would you prefer it if I left you to continue your conversation?"

"A dance would be good," Arnold said. "Especially since I missed the last one. I've heard some very good things about you, Viva."

"In that case," I said, working my way through the list of music on the laptop, "I'll have to make sure you get something very special indeed."

I didn't know if they were expecting me to be naked, or to strip, but if they were disappointed that I kept my skimpy black dress on they didn't show it. Especially given that they could have trotted off upstairs and sampled something far more tactile if they'd chosen to do so. Instead, they sat and watched, and I held their undivided attention until, four tracks and twenty-two minutes later, the door opened and Fitz and Dylan came in.

Fitz was surprised to see me and for a moment he stood there in the doorway, hands in his pockets, as though he'd forgotten what he came in for. He looked lost, his shoulders slumped. My heart sank for him. He looked so defeated. Much as I didn't want to know what this deal was all about, I wanted it to work out for him.

There must be something I can do to help, I thought. *Something to give his confidence a boost . . .*

Arnold and the others didn't even stir. Now that I had some extra audience members I upped the game a little bit more, until the song finished.

Dylan made his way over to the laptop and hit pause, and I took Fitz by the hand and said, "Can I have a word?" while Dylan turned to the assembled men and asked them if they wanted another drink.

I steered Fitz out of the door into the hallway and, casting a quick glance to make sure we were alone, I pushed him firmly back against the wall and kissed him.

Just at the moment that he started to respond, I backed away.

He was staring at me, his breathing fast, the beginnings of a smile.

"You can do this," I whispered.

"What?" he asked.

"Whatever you want to. With Arnold. You can get the deal. Just go and do it."

He stroked my cheek gently. "Do you have any idea?"

"What?"

He just shook his head.

"Fitz," I said, "go and work it out. This is exactly what you're good at, you know it is. Go on."

He went back into the lounge and I closed the door behind him. Dylan was in the act of topping up Arnold's glass with whiskey.

He looked up at me, and for a moment I thought I saw something unguarded in that look. And then the shutters came down again, and it was gone.

They did their deal. I didn't know what it was exactly, had no wish to, but the likelihood was some importation, or a big supply. Nothing I wanted any involvement in.

After the discussions had finished, Arnold and his associates left in several cars; at about four thirty Gray called taxis for the girls—three cabs turned up at the back of the house at five and they all went. All except Caddy. She was sitting in the kitchen.

"Caddy," I said, touching her arm.

"What do you want?" she asked, in a tone of voice that suggested she wasn't interested in my response.

"You know there's nothing going on between me and Fitz, don't you?"

She looked up at me then, looked me in the eyes for the first time since we'd been having drinks before dinner and Fitz had kissed me on the cheek. Looked at me as though she couldn't trust me, didn't believe me, and would be happy if I'd just fuck off and leave her the hell alone.

"I don't give a shit what you do with Fitz, personally," she said with emphasis.

"Why are you pissed off at me, then?"

An exaggerated, drunken shrug.

"I thought you were my friend, Caddy."

Dylan was watching all this with the merest flicker of amusement behind his usually implacable blue eyes.

"I know what he's like," she said miserably. "You don't realize it 'cause you're new. I know the signs."

"What signs? What are you talking about?"

"He wants you. Since you arrived, he hasn't looked at me twice. Know how much that hurts? Any idea?"

"Caddy, this is ridiculous. I don't have any intention of doing anything with him."

I saw her eyes narrow and felt the venom when she next spoke. "You would if he paid you enough."

It hurt more because she was right. I knew it and so did she. And then, in Fitz's multimillion-pound house, in his marble kitchen, I felt cheap and ashamed of myself for the first time since I'd started down this road. What was I doing? It was a boat, it was just a boat. I was in a hurry to get the money together because I'd become greedy and mean and single-minded. I'd slipped into a dangerous spiral of consequences, wanting to buy the boat to escape from all this, and getting into it deeper still in the process.

Gray came into the kitchen then, started banging around making coffee, and Dylan went to join Nicks in the lounge.

I went back to the bathroom to get my stuff together, leaving Caddy in the kitchen. Fitz was in the hallway, at a big glass table, counting money and stuffing it into envelopes. We exchanged looks. Then he followed me, bringing one of the envelopes with him. My pay for the evening. He put it on the top of my bag. It looked fatter than last time. I felt sick at the sight of it, and at the same time felt a shiver of excitement. I could hardly wait to get home so I could count it all.

"You were great tonight," he said. He shut the door behind him and sat down on the chair, watching me while I packed away makeup, towels, dresses, and shoes.

"I enjoyed it," I said. "I'm glad it turned out okay."

"You know that's just between us, don't you?"

"Of course."

"I trust you," he said, nodding.

I was nearly done, zipping up the case and standing it up on its wheels. I was looking forward to going home and sleeping for the rest of the day.

He stood up, between me and the door. I waited. He was buzzing; he could hardly keep still. I wondered what he'd taken.

"I was thinking," he said, taking a step toward me and running a finger quickly up my arm, "about our discussion the other day."

"Yes?"

"You want to hang around for a while?"

"Now?"

"The guys will be going soon. You could stay. We could—er—have some fun. What do you think?"

If it hadn't been for Caddy, I might have said yes. Despite the exhaustion, if I'd just taken a moment to consider, staying here with Fitz—he wasn't bad-looking after all—I would have done it, and maybe everything that happened after that would have been different.

But my head was heavy with the night and the need to lie down, alone, undisturbed.

"I'd like to," I said, "but, honestly, I'm so tired. I just need to go home and sleep. Another time, maybe?"

"I've got some good stuff here, you know—something to wake you up a bit?"

"No, thank you. I just want to go home."

He looked at the floor, a muscle moving in his cheek. "Yeah." He stepped back and opened the door for me. "I'll get Nicks to drive you."

When I finally left Fitz's house, it was broad daylight. Thank God it was a Sunday and there wasn't much traffic. I would be home within an hour.

Chapter Twenty-Six

Josie and I were sitting on the old bench in the shelter of the wheelhouse, listening to the sounds of Malcolm tinkering with the engine of the boat. Other than his unexpected appearance in the early hours, the night had passed without incident. The trip wire hadn't been necessary.

"Did I ever tell you," she said, "about the time he set fire to the boat?"

"No," I said, sipping my coffee.

She chuckled at the thought of it.

"He was welding a porthole shut. Only he'd decided to weld it shut just after he'd finished all the siding inside. He had the full face mask on, you know, and he was sitting on the dock, welding away quite happily, oblivious to the clouds of smoke billowing off the boat. Liam had to pat him on the back and tell him the boat was on fire. Liam told him to go and look for something to put water in to douse it and he was in such a panic he came out with the top from his shaving cream. He said he hadn't wanted to use any of my china cups."

I laughed. "Presumably you've got a fire extinguisher in there now."

"You've got that right," she said. "No idea where it is, though."

Malcolm had undone his elaborate system of trip wires before Josie woke up, winding the wire back into neat coils. He'd offered to redo this every night before bed, but I'd declined—Murphy's law dictated that some innocent person would fall over it.

"He's a flaming liability," she added, although this almost went without saying.

A shout came up from the hatch under the wheelhouse. "Right, try starting it!"

I went over and peered down at Malcolm's grubby gray T-shirt hunched over the engine, then turned the key.

A rumble from the engine, a shudder, a series of congested coughs, and the whole boat shook itself alive. From the stern came the sound of splashing and churning water.

"Right, that's enough, turn it off!"

I turned the key again. "What do you think? Is it okay?" I called down.

"Oh, yeah," he said brightly. "Needs an oil change, filters, basic service. There's no leaks or anything. In fact, she's in good shape, considering."

I left him to it and went back to sit with Josie.

"He seems happy," I said.

"Yes," Josie said, "he loves all this. You just need to check him for stupid mistakes—like for instance it's just pure luck that he got you to start the engine with the tide in. Can you imagine if the prop had started spinning at low tide? Mud everywhere. Not pretty."

"I didn't realize he was quite so accident prone," I said.

"It's not that he's accident prone, just that he doesn't think. When we first moved on to the boat, he dropped his keys down the side into the water. Did he tell you about that?"

"He told me to always make sure my stuff had a float on it."

"Ha!"

"So what happened? Did he get the keys back?"

"The tide was coming in and it was just over waist height. So he went down in the water and stood with his ankles in the mud and of course he couldn't quite reach the bottom, even with his arm in up to the shoulder. So he had to get a broom and force himself down the handle headfirst until he found the keys."

"Lord. Was he all right?"

"He smelled foul. And he was puking all night. Doesn't do you any good to put your face in this river, truth be told."

"I can hear you!" came a shout from inside the wheelhouse.

We laughed at this. I felt more relaxed than I had for ages.

"Why are you wanting to get the boat started, then?" Josie asked, giving me a gentle dig in the ribs. "You moving on?"

I blushed. "No, nothing like that. Well, not yet, anyway. It just seemed like the next step in the process."

"I thought the bathroom was the next step in the process."

"Yeah, that. Or the deck garden. I keep changing my mind."

I slept in the back of the car, jolting awake every time it turned, braked, or accelerated. I couldn't bring myself to make small talk, and I was so exhausted I found it hard to think straight about all the things that had gone on.

The main thing was that it had ended well. The deal had been done, and when Arnold left, kissing me delicately on the inside of my wrist, he had given me a smile and shaken Fitz's hand warmly. And, of course, I was financially one step closer to the boat. Maybe I could have another talk with Caddy when she was sober, try and get our friendship back on track.

I was planning to take Thursday and Friday off to visit boatyards in Kent, on the Medway River. There were a couple of boats for sale at one residential marina, then a much larger marina farther up the river had several more. The Medway seemed as good a place as any. Near enough to London to be able to come back if I wanted a night out, and yet far enough away that I could escape from the city and from all the shit that came with the job. I also had it in the back of my mind that, if I wanted to find another job at the end of the year, being a short train ride away from London would be a bonus. I might not have to sell the boat after the year was up. I might even be able to keep on living on my boat and work in the city again if the money ran out.

I had enough money to buy a boat, preferably one that was at least partly fitted out, so that I could live on it while I was refinishing it. I probably had enough cash to at least start the renovation, as well. As things stood at the moment, I would have to continue working, or at least find a part-time job, to be able to keep myself going while I worked on the boat.

I wished I could fast-forward, speed through the last few months of earning, saving, dancing, struggling for bonuses at work.

I was ready for this all to come to an end.

I opened my eyes and glanced out of the window to see a familiar row of stores. Nearly home, at last.

"Thanks for the lift," I said as I got out of the car and took my wheelie case from the trunk.

As soon as I slammed the trunk shut he sped off toward the main road.

An hour later and Malcolm declared the *Revenge of the Tide* fit to travel. Of course, by that time the tide had gone out and there was no hope of trying it out today.

"You can't do it tomorrow, either," said Josie.

"Why not?" asked Malcolm, looking disappointed.

"Because we've got things to do!" said Josie, smacking him around the shoulder. "Anyway, what's the great rush all of a sudden?"

"Well, the boat's fixed," I said. "I'd love to just go for a little motor upriver, just to see what's there."

"Well, you can wait until after the weekend," said Josie firmly, and that appeared to be that.

She went up to the laundry room to unload the machine, leaving Malcolm packing up his various tools into a filthy canvas bag. When he was done, he sat back on the bench with me. The smell of him reminded me of my dad—engine oil, sweat, effort.

"Thank you," I said.

"What for?"

"Fixing the boat, of course. You've been great."

"Ah, it's nothing," he said. "Be good to get her out for a motor, anyway."

As though the *Revenge* were a little pleasure boat and not a hulking great seventy-five-foot-long barge with all my worldly possessions on it. But it was what I needed to do, after all. I just wished he weren't quite so casual about it all.

Josie was heading back down the slope to the dock, a plastic laundry bag weighing her down. When she'd nearly reached the *Scarisbrick Jean*, Malcolm eased himself up and went down the gangplank to help her. When they'd gone into the cabin, I went inside to wash the mugs and the plates from the sandwiches we'd had at lunchtime.

On the table, the two cell phones were lying side by side. I hadn't remembered them being there, like that. They were in the bag I'd taken to the *Aunty Jean* the night before. Had I taken them out of my bag? I couldn't remember.

I checked the phones and saw two missed calls.

On one phone, a missed call from Carling's number—an hour ago.

On the other, a missed call from Garland. I hit redial.

The number you have dialed is currently unavailable. Please try later.

I shouted at it in frustration, threw it onto the sofa. Why the fuck couldn't he leave his phone on? Was I ever going to speak to him again? At least it meant he was still alive, still out there somewhere. And he hadn't entirely forgotten about me.

Chapter Twenty-Seven

The following Saturday night, the Barclay was busy, busier than I'd ever seen it. Norland and Helena were both in, but there was no sign of Fitz when I arrived. Caddy was there, too, already out on the floor with some of her regulars as I went into the dressing room to get ready.

The club was packed: bachelor parties, groups of men crowded at the bar and around the stage. I had private dances in the Blue Room booked, and even the VIP area was full. Dylan, Nicks, and Gray were there, too, but they were busy—the crowd was rowdy and they ended up helping out the door staff with removing those who had drunk too much.

The atmosphere in the club felt very different. Maybe I should have seen it as a warning; maybe I should have felt it. It reminded me of one of the first weekends I'd danced in the club, when Caddy had steered me away from a group of men in suits who were already tanked up on champagne and vodka.

"Not them, Gen. They're no good."

"Why not?"

"They're discussing business."

"How do you know?"

"You get to know these things. They'll call us over when they're ready. And when they do, be careful with them, all right? Just in case I'm otherwise engaged."

"Be careful how?"

Caddy had taken a deep breath and spouted one of her classics. "This club is full of men who think of themselves as dangerous. In reality, very few of them are. But you want to be able to spot them."

I'd steered well clear, left the group to the other girls who were watching them from a distance and waiting for them to finish their business deals. Besides, I had plenty of other guys to entertain.

Tonight the club smelled of danger.

By two thirty it was beginning to quiet down; the rowdy ones had all been ejected or had run out of money and gone home. Those who were left were a mixture of regulars and tired-looking businessmen. I wound down with some slower moves. I was tired tonight; I had hardly had time to drink water between dances and I was starting to get a headache.

During my last dance I recognized two of the men who had been with Arnold at Fitz's house last weekend. They were in a booth. I made eye contact with one of them and gave him a smile and a wink while I gyrated and swung around the pole.

At the end of the routine, when the last bars of Portishead's "Glory Box" were fading, I saw Leon Arnold. He was talking to Caddy and Norland at the bar, and he was watching me over Norland's shoulder. I considered going over to join them, thought about whether I could get Caddy on her own to try and straighten things out.

I had a ripple of applause from the remaining audience as I handed over control of the stage to Crystal, who was coming on for her last dance.

The dressing room was almost empty; many of the girls had already finished and left. I started to pull off my shoes, looking forward to putting my jeans on and going home, when the door opened.

It was Norland. "You've got another private dance," he said.

"What? You're joking," I groaned. "I'm worn out."

"I'm not fucking joking. Get on with it."

I was half-inclined to leave it, to slip away and pretend that Norland hadn't told me. But I put some lip gloss on and made my way down the hall to the Blue Room, thinking about the money, always the money—it was the only thing that made all this worthwhile.

I didn't know who I'd been expecting—one of my regulars perhaps—but in the room were Leon Arnold and the two men I'd seen in the VIP booth earlier on. One of them closed the door behind me.

I felt uncomfortable for a moment but he gave me a warm smile and they didn't seem to be drunk. I cast a quick glance up, to the corner of the room, the CCTV camera, hoping that someone was in the office upstairs keeping an eye on me.

"Hi, guys," I said, trying to look and sound as if I'd just started work and was ready to give them their money's worth and more besides, "take a seat."

I'd said this to the guy who was still standing by the door, but he ignored me.

I was too tired to mess around so I left the music selection screen and went over to the doorway. "What's your name?" I asked him. He was standing the way Dylan did, still and impassive, as though he were there for my protection. I didn't feel protected.

"His name's Markus," said Arnold, amused.

"Come and sit down, Markus. You won't get much of a view from there."

He looked at Arnold, who was sitting on the sofa with his feet up. I raised a questioning eyebrow at him, and there was a nod in response—either to me, or to Markus.

Whatever. Markus left his post on the door and went to sit on the other side of Arnold.

I went back to staring at the screen, wondering what I'd

already danced to this evening . . . then I had it. Madonna—I definitely hadn't done any Madonna for a long time.

I started my routine by getting as high up the pole as I could, then spinning slowly back down to the floor.

Arnold was paying attention, thankfully. The other two were talking between themselves—nothing they hadn't seen before. I was going to have to do something really spectacular to get them going. The question was whether I had enough energy left, and whether I could be bothered. It wasn't them I was interested in, and it certainly wasn't their money paying for my time—so I turned my full focus on Arnold. I wondered why he wanted them there. He would have had to pay for them, too.

Before the song finished, some signal must have been given that I wasn't aware of, or didn't notice, but Markus and the other guy got up and left the room.

I got to my feet for my final twirl and felt a grip of alarm. Arnold wanted me to himself.

I held out my hand to him and he kissed it, but he didn't let go. "Come and sit with me for a minute," he said.

The music automatically switched over to the lower volume, slow-time background noise that they left running in here when there weren't any dances. I picked up my clothes from the floor and slipped back into them as quickly as I could. "I need to go and get changed," I said in a voice that I hoped left no room for discussion, "but thank you. It's been lovely to see you again."

"Sit down," he said again.

I sat, at the other end of the sofa. Without a word he moved closer to me, his thigh touching mine. I wriggled out and tried to stand, but suddenly, before I really realized what was going on, he was on top of me, his hand up my dress, pulling at my underwear, his mouth on mine.

I pushed him off with a shove and screamed as hard as I

could, kicking out with my heels and making contact with something, a shin maybe.

"Get off me!"

"Ow, you fuckin' bitch!" One hand on my shoulder, his knee in my groin, he pinned me to the sofa by my own stupid dress. "No need to be so unfriendly," he said.

"There's CCTV," I said. "They'll be in here in a minute . . ."

"No, they won't," he said, breathing hard.

His hands were all over me and I couldn't think what to do. I'd been groped before, I'd had men shouting disgusting suggestions to me while I'd been onstage, and all I'd ever had to do was say something like, "Please don't speak to me like that," or look over to one of the guys, and before you knew it they would be carried off toward the exit.

Now I was on my own.

In the back of my head I was replaying the previous weekend, wondering if I'd said or done anything that might have given Leon Arnold the idea that I wanted this, that I wanted to be on my own with him. Or if this was some kind of setup, that Fitz had told him I'd be okay with it, having neglected to mention it to me before or since . . .

"Leon," I said in a voice that I hoped was both calm and firm, "please—this isn't right."

"Shut up," he said mildly, trying to kiss me while I turned my head left and right and crossed my arms over my chest to try to stop him getting so close, so horribly close.

I looked up again at the camera, praying for someone to come and help me. That was my only hope. Even if I screamed or shouted, nobody would hear me. The noise from the club was too loud.

"Please," I said, "you really need to stop this. If you want to see me this isn't the way to go about it."

He was hurting me now, his hand gripped around the fabric of my dress, pulling it tighter and tighter against my skin.

In a moment it would tear away. Where were they? Surely there was someone watching the CCTV monitors? Surely someone would come? I started to panic, writhing and trying to bring my knees up to throw him off. He covered my mouth with his free hand, pressing me down, pushing my head into the sofa cushions so I was fighting for breath while I clawed at him, trying to find skin that I could scratch. The panic was rising inside me, making me shake, weakening my efforts to get free of him.

I heard a muffled sound, like a bang, and seconds later felt clean air above me as Arnold was pulled away. There was shouting, but I couldn't make out words . . . I found myself taking long gasps of air, as though I'd been drowning. My chest hurt.

I managed to sit up, and the room was empty. I was shaking, my hands tingling, my knees knocking together. I tried to push myself up but my legs wouldn't support my weight.

The audio system was still playing at low volume and in front of me the pole rose from the laminate floor, shiny in the lights, gleaming and innocent, oblivious to what had just happened.

I sobbed then, trembling on the sofa, thinking about how they'd made such a big thing about the girls being safe here and how, actually, we weren't safe at all.

And then Dylan was there, hands twitching into fists by his sides, breathing hard.

He held out a hand and pulled me to my feet, then he put his huge arms around me and held me. Inside the circle of his arms I was sobbing and shaking. He patted me reassuringly on the back. "Come on," he said, "you're all right now. Let's get you to the dressing room."

There was nobody in there, nobody in the hall on the way to the dressing room, either.

"Where is he?" I asked, when I could speak.

Dylan was sitting on the stool next to me, waiting patiently for me to stop crying. "He's gone."

"And the others?"

"They're gone, too."

"What happened, Dylan?"

He shrugged. "He thought he could get away with it, I guess."

"What about the CCTV? Isn't someone supposed to be watching it all the time?"

He grimaced. "Supposed to be."

"It's not fucking good enough."

"No."

The door opened and Norland came in.

"Don't you ever fucking knock?" I demanded, finding myself angry, furious, where seconds ago I'd been falling apart.

"What's up with you?" Norland asked with a sneer.

Dylan had got to his feet and moved between me and Norland. He looked twice as big as he usually did, and Norland, who was scrawny in comparison, looked alarmed and took an awkward step backward.

"She just got roughed up," Dylan said, his voice dangerously quiet.

"By Leon Arnold? You're joking."

"Do I look like I'm laughing? Why weren't you watching the cameras?"

"I had stuff to do," he said.

"Where's Fitz?" I said. "I want to talk to Fitz!"

"Fuck off," Norland said, "he's not here. And in any case, do you think he's gonna listen to your whining? Who do you think you are?"

Without warning, Dylan launched himself at Norland, propelling him backward out of the doorway and off down the corridor. I got to my feet, but by the time I reached the doorway they were down the stairs and out of sight. "Dylan!" I shouted, following them on unsteady feet. "Dylan!"

He appeared at the foot of the stairs. There was no sign of Norland. He gave me a smile that was almost reassuring.

"Come on," he said. "I'll call you a cab."

He left me to get changed into my jeans and sweater and when I went downstairs he was there, sitting at one of the empty tables in the bar with a glass on the table in front of him.

"Dylan," I said.

He looked up.

"Thank you."

"No problem," he said. "Cab'll be here in a minute. You want a drink?"

"Vodka," I said.

He helped himself behind the bar and poured me a glass. In deference to my femininity he shoved a handful of ice and a slice of lemon in there, too.

I drank two big gulps, intending to finish it off in one go but not quite managing it before it started to burn my throat.

"I don't know if I can do this anymore," I said.

"It's a rough business sometimes. You know that."

"It's not like he was just a regular customer, Dylan. It's Leon Arnold. What the fuck's Fitz going to say?"

"That's not your problem," he said. "Let them fight it out among themselves."

On the street outside, a black cab pulled up to the curb and I got to my feet. "Thanks again," I said.

By the time I got home I was too exhausted to think but I felt grubby, so I ran a bath while I sat at my dining table, drinking cold water. I was aching all over, head to foot, as though I'd been beaten up rather than simply held down, and my head was pounding.

I opened my bag to look for some Tylenol, and as I did so

I felt my phone vibrate, an incoming text. Not a number I recognized.

Meet me 6pm Monday upstairs food area Victoria Station

I felt a momentary panic. Who the hell had sent that text? My first thought was that it must be Arnold, wanting to get me on my own somehow . . . But then why would he want to meet me in such a public place?

I sent a text back:

Who is this?

But there was no reply.

Chapter Twenty-Eight

I slept badly, worrying about Arnold and wondering what I was going to say to Fitz the next time I saw him. I had dreams about Victoria Station, about meeting some faceless person who meant to do me harm. I got to work even more exhausted than I usually was on a Monday morning, not looking forward to working my way through the day. To my surprise, Gavin was in the main office, sitting at his old desk, with Lucy next to him.

"What's going on?" I asked.

"He's back," Lucy said.

"Who's back?"

The door to the manager's office opened then, and to my horror Ian Dunkerley came out. He'd lost weight, but his smug expression hadn't changed. He fixed me with a defiant stare that looked as though it had required some effort to produce.

"Genevieve," he said. "When you have a moment?"

I stared at him, mouth open, while he collected papers from the printer and went back into his office, leaving the door ajar.

Oh, God. Not him, not him again.

"Don't keep him waiting, whatever you do," Gavin said helpfully. "He's not in the best of moods."

I didn't even put down my bag or take off my coat. I went into Dunkerley's office and stood in the doorway.

He was behind the desk, tapping away at his keyboard as if he'd never been away. "Shut the door," he said.

"I'd rather leave it open, if it's all the same to you."

"You're half an hour late," he said. "Why's that?"

I didn't reply. It felt as though the world was caving in around me.

He stood up, straightened his pants, and came around the desk toward me. I took a step back, away from him, at the same moment wondering why I was afraid of him. If anything, he should be afraid of me.

"You thought I was gone for good, huh?" he said, so quietly I could barely hear. He was close enough for me to feel the warmth from him, smell his noxious aftershave.

"I hoped you were," I said.

"Well, unlike you, I am a professional. I take my career very seriously. And I should point out that I have been working with the police to prosecute your—*friends*—for their assault on me. And the police have been very interested in you, too."

I bit my lip. He had to be lying. Whatever else he was, Dunkerley wasn't stupid—there was no way he'd report the incident to the police, not after the warning he'd had.

"Now, I suggest you get back to work." He turned and went back to his desk.

I felt sick to my stomach as I left the room, closing the door behind me. Gavin and Lucy had gone out somewhere, and the main office was empty. I sat down at my desk and logged onto the network, my head in my hands as I waited for the emails to load. I looked at the list of unread messages in the inbox: four or five from customers, relating to contracts I was working on. And then twelve emails from Ian Dunkerley, one after the other, starting at 7:24 this morning. The subjects of the emails included "New working practice"; three titled, simply, "Meeting"; one at 9:01 titled "Timekeeping"; and, finally, a thirteenth: "Office dress code."

I closed the email window without reading any of them and opened a new Word document.

Ten minutes later, Gavin and Lucy returned with their lattes from the coffee shop on the ground floor, laughing about something and chatting without a care in the world.

"Everything okay?" Lucy asked, seeing my face.

"Not really," I said, retrieving the single sheet from the printer.

"What's up?"

I couldn't even bring myself to answer her. I folded the letter, not bothering to put it in an envelope, and took it with me along with my bag and my coat to the CEO's office on the next floor. There was a meeting going on.

"Will it take long?" I asked.

Linda, the receptionist, looked at me blankly. "Could be ages," she said. "Anything I can do?"

"I'll wait, if that's okay," I said. I couldn't face going back downstairs; the thought of having to see Dunkerley again, or even of explaining any of this to Lucy and Gavin, was almost too much.

I watched the little hand on the clock above Linda's head creep slowly around. Was I really going to do this? Surely this wasn't me—I'd never given up on anything in my whole life. Was I going to let that horrible man get the better of me? I should be fighting this. And yet, the thought of having to keep going . . .

Ten minutes.

The elevator doors opened and Lucy emerged. She looked at me and handed over some reports to Linda.

I don't know if it was Lucy's presence that made me move, or simply that I couldn't stand being there a minute longer. I got up and went to the office door, opened it wide. Simon Lewis, the CEO, was sitting at his conference table with three other people, one of whom was a client I'd worked with on a major project last year. The conversation stopped abruptly and they all turned to look at me. I strode over to them and put the folded letter on the table in front of Simon.

"Genevieve? What's going on?" he said, and despite my dramatic and unannounced visit his voice was so kind I almost regretted it, almost took the letter back and apologized for the intrusion.

"I'm sorry," I said. "I've got to go."

I shut the door behind me and walked straight past Lucy, who was standing by Linda's desk with her mouth open. I took the stairs, and by the time I got to the ground floor I was almost running. I went out of the building through the lobby and, despite my heart thudding with the enormity of it all, the relief I felt knowing that I would never be going back there was sudden, and immense.

The cab took me straight home. I had a hot bath and, after lying awake for a while, thinking about everything that had happened in the last two days, I finally managed to sleep. When I woke up in the afternoon, I put on a skirt and sandals with a denim jacket and headed out with my sunglasses to catch the bus to Victoria Station.

It was busy, packed with commuters making their way home. I took the escalators to Victoria Place, and then up again to the part of the mall where various food and drink outlets circled a central, open-plan eating area.

I looked around but there was no sign of Arnold, or anyone else I recognized. Not sitting anywhere obvious, anyway. I bought a coffee from the burger place and sat down on a hard plastic seat bolted to the table where I could see the escalators and anyone coming up them. I was still early.

A few seconds later, someone tapped me on the shoulder and I looked around, startled.

To my surprise and relief, it was Dylan. I barely recognized him; he was wearing jeans and boots, an unbuttoned Oxford, with a dark gray T-shirt underneath. I'd never seen him in anything other than a suit.

"Come with me," he said.

I took my coffee and my bag and followed him around to the other side of the complex to a few tables and chairs that were tucked away behind a coffee kiosk.

"This is a nice surprise," I said, sliding down into a seat opposite him.

He nodded. "Yeah. Never seen you in daylight before."

"And?"

"You could do with getting out in the sun."

"Thanks. And you look like you could do with laying off the vodka for a while."

It was true, he looked rough, his skin lined and his eyes red and tired. He hadn't shaved and there was a rasp of stubble over his face as well as over his head, showing the shape of where his hairline would have been, if he'd ever let it grow.

"What can I say? It was a late night."

I couldn't get over how different he looked, how—normal. He was like any other guy out having a coffee on a Monday afternoon.

"How do you feel?" he asked.

"I've felt better," I answered. "I've had such a shitty few days." The skin around my mouth felt tender. My arms were sore, too, where Arnold had held me down, but nothing you could see.

"How's the boat-buying going?"

"I went to look at some last week," I said, "thank you for asking."

"So you've got enough money, then?"

"No. I've got just about enough to buy the boat, but not

enough to renovate it properly and take time off, which is all part of it. I can't do one without the other. So I need to do a bit more saving. I'll have to ask Norland if he'll increase my hours. Or maybe Fitz will ask me to do another one of his parties."

He was watching me steadily, evaluating.

"What?" I said at last, feeling worried about the intense expression on his face.

"I could help you," he said, his voice low.

"Help me with what?"

"Help you with the money side of it."

I ran through the possibilities. Whatever we were doing here, it wasn't something he wanted to discuss in front of Fitz. Which meant he was taking a huge risk.

"What do you mean?"

"How much would you need to be able to leave London by, say, the end of this month?"

Two weeks away. "At least fifty grand," I said, after a moment, feeling my cheeks flush.

"I can do that," he said, without hesitation.

I wondered what I'd gotten myself into. If it hadn't been for Dunkerley, I probably would have said no. "So?"

"I need you to look after something for me."

"What?"

"It's a package. Not very big. I need someone to hide it for a couple of months. Maybe not even that long. You're the best person I know."

"That's it?"

"Just hide it and don't let anyone get it. That's it."

"And for that I get fifty grand? Like, to keep?"

"Yours to keep."

"What's the catch?"

"The catch is, it's not something you want to be caught in possession of. And after you leave, you won't be able to come back. You'll have to walk away from the club for good. You get me?"

I paused, drank the last of my coffee while I considered his offer. He watched me without blinking. He wasn't nervous at all, which made me wonder what was at stake here.

"Where are you going to keep your boat, anyway?"

I shrugged. "Depends where it is when I buy it, I guess. The boats I saw on Thursday were in Kent. There was one I quite liked."

He nodded. "Kent. That'd be all right."

"Does that make a difference?"

"Far enough away for it to be safe, near enough for me to come and collect it from you."

"When will you collect it?"

"I don't know. I'll give you a phone. When I'm ready to come and get it, I'll call you to arrange a meeting. Is it a yes, then?"

It was a yes from the moment he'd agreed to fifty grand.

"I guess it is, Dylan."

He smiled his best Dylan smile and offered me his huge meaty hand to shake. "Deal."

I felt a curious sense of release, as though I'd been holding on to a thread somewhere that had finally snapped. I could go. I could afford to buy a boat, and I had enough money to take a year off, maybe even more than a year.

Chapter Twenty-Nine

I was back to planning my fantasy bathroom on the table in the dinette when I heard steps on the dock, followed by steps on the deck, and a woman's voice that called out, "Genevieve Shipley? Hello? Can you come up, please?"

I went up to the wheelhouse.

On my deck were two people, a man and a woman, both of them wearing suits. The woman showed me her card. "I am DS Beverley Davies; this is my colleague, DC Jamie Newman. I wonder if you have a few moments to talk to us." She spoke fast, as if she was in an extreme hurry and had no time for explanation or dissent.

"What's it about?"

"It would be good if you could come with us, Genevieve. We need to have a talk."

"What—now?"

"Yes, right now."

"Where did you say you were from?"

"We're from the Metropolitan Police Serious Crime Directorate."

"But . . . Jim Carling—"

"DC Carling knows we are here. He told us where to find you. He did say you wouldn't mind helping us out with a few questions, Genevieve. It won't take long."

I guessed she was trying her hardest to be encouraging, but

all I could think of was how I could persuade her to fuck off and leave me alone.

It wouldn't work, though. Maybe if I went along with her and answered her stupid questions they would go away and not come back.

"I'll just get my shoes," I said.

"Mind if I come with you?" Jamie Newman asked me. "I'd like to see your boat."

"Sure," I said, and went down the steps into the cabin, leaving the door open for him to follow me.

He stood there watching me while I pulled on my boots and did up the laces. He wasn't interested in the boat at all, for other than a cursory glance around the cabin he hadn't taken his eyes off me.

They knew about the package, I thought. Or at least, they knew I had something here to hide. Carling had told them. Newman was watching me to make sure I didn't move or destroy whatever it was.

I gave him a tight smile, grabbed my keys and the two cell phones from the dinette table, and went back up to the wheelhouse.

"Two phones?" he asked, while I locked the door.

"One of them's got a shitty signal on the boat, the other one's got a shitty signal everywhere else," I said.

"Where are we going?" I asked from the backseat of their Volvo. I'd never been inside a police car before, marked or unmarked.

"Medway police station," Newman said. "They've kindly offered to let us use one of their interview rooms. Saves us a trip back to town with you."

"Oh," I said. "Couldn't we just have had a chat on the boat?"

They didn't answer. I wondered if they had other people onboard now, searching it.

I watched the streets of Rochester as they passed, thinking of the boat and the package and what it could possibly be. Something I didn't want to be caught in possession of, he'd said. Which meant drugs, several kilos of them, hidden on my boat and waiting to be found.

The following weekend at the Barclay was my last. The traces of the bruising Arnold's hands had left were finally fading.

It wasn't even a full weekend, just Saturday night, and even that was cut dramatically short.

All week I'd been working up my courage to go back, telling myself that Arnold wouldn't be there, that I'd be careful about private dances from now on, I'd check that someone was in the CCTV room when I was dancing, I'd ask who it was who had booked me—all of that shit. In reality I was going to hand in my notice. I was working up to that, too.

The club was quieter, as it often was toward the middle of the month. Some of my regulars were in, men for whom payday was a bit irrelevant, and I knew I'd be getting some private bookings later on. Would I be able to dance for them without freaking out? Dylan had said he would keep an eye on me, but I hadn't seen him. What if he wasn't even here? Who would watch out for me, then?

When I had a spare moment between my dances, I went to the bar to find Helena. They were short-staffed and Helena was doing some waitressing. If that was what you called it—there was an awful lot of socializing going on at the same time.

"Is Fitz in tonight?" I asked.

She shrugged. "Haven't seen him. Go upstairs and ask Nicks, he's in the office, I think."

I was halfway up the stairs when Nicks appeared at the top.

Someone was watching the CCTV monitors, at least, I thought with irony, looking at the camera that covered the staircase.

"What's up?" he asked, folding his arms across his chest.

"I'd like to see Fitz," I said.

"He doesn't want to see you."

The answer came back so quickly, I was shocked. He didn't want to see me? Had Arnold said something to him? Had someone seen me meeting Dylan at Victoria Station?

My heart started thumping with alarm. "Why doesn't he want to see me?"

Nicks shrugged and didn't answer.

"Could you go and ask him? I only want a minute."

The wall of muscle didn't move. I looked behind him, down the hall. All the office doors were shut. If I tried to get past him, he would stop me. There was no way I'd be able to get up there, not now.

Nicks gave me a look that invited me to try. Clearly he would enjoy throwing me down the stairs.

I turned around, but instead of heading for the dressing rooms, I went into the main part of the club, scanning the VIP booths for Fitz, in case he was down here after all. No sign of him. Then, to my relief, Dylan came upstairs from the public bar. He was dressed smartly again, freshly shaved, immaculate.

He saw me and hesitated, as though he was unsure whether he should talk to me or not. I gave him a smile I hoped was encouraging. He smiled back and his eyes traveled upward very briefly to the CCTV camera above our heads.

The meaning was clear. We were being watched.

I walked over to him and said sweetly, "I'd like to see Fitz, but Nicks won't let me in. Would you ask him for me, when you get a minute?"

"Sure," he said in reply, and then he was gone, into the crowds of suits, heading for the bar. If they'd watched that little exchange they wouldn't have found anything unusual in it. I hoped not, anyway.

After that I felt odd, panicky. I sat by myself at the end of the bar, ostensibly scanning for customers but at the same time trying to avoid them all. Across the club, in one of the booths, I could see Stephen Penrose. He was the owner of a chain of realty offices: I knew this only because I recognized him from an interview he'd given to the *Financial Times* a few months ago. Here I knew him as Steve, and I would never have let on that I knew exactly who he was. He was staring at me, smiling.

I was on the list for the pole, but for some reason I wasn't called, or, if I was, I hadn't heard it. It wasn't the thought of Dylan's money, that sudden pile of cash that made everything seem so much harder; since Arnold's attack, being here wasn't fun anymore. The few people I recognized, even the ones I liked, the ones I had joked around with week after week—they all looked different tonight, sinister, intimidating. *I can't do this anymore*, I thought. *I don't want to be here.*

Stephen Penrose, a man who wouldn't hurt a fly, who paid me double for our private dances in the Blue Room and always sat there rigid, his hand over his crotch like a small boy who needed a wee, was staring at me, his smile of encouragement fading a little each time I cast a glance in his direction. In normal circumstances he would not have had to wait; I would have been by his side the moment I'd seen he was here. He probably thought I was waiting for someone, waiting for a better prospect than him.

He was safe, surely? Why wasn't I over there, talking to him, easing him out of his working-week shell, making him feel wanted and happy and attractive?

When he stood up and crossed the club toward me, weaving his way through groups of people, I got up off my bar stool and headed toward the door, walking with purpose, and almost breaking into a run. If he called my name, I didn't hear it. I went straight to the stairs, and this time there was no Nicks standing guard at the top. Maybe I'd taken them by surprise; maybe they hadn't considered I would have the audacity to do this; or perhaps they'd all gone out somewhere and I'd find the doors locked.

I was almost expecting that to be the case, so when I reached Fitz's office door I didn't even knock, just tried the door and to my surprise it opened easily, propelling me into the room.

They were all in there. Fitz, Dylan, Nicks, Gray, even Norland, who looked skinny and pathetic next to this group of tough men. I had a second to take in the picture—Norland, Nicks, and Gray sitting on the sofas, cash on the desk, in bundles, a carryall on the floor, Fitz perched on the edge of the desk, Dylan standing as if about to leave.

Nicks stood up abruptly and took a step toward me.

"Oh," I said.

"Viva," Fitz said, holding up a hand, which stopped Nicks in his tracks. "Might be nice if you could think about knocking next time."

"I'm sorry," I said, not looking at the others, deliberately not making eye contact with Dylan. "I just need to have a word with you. It's important."

Fitz was watching me steadily. I stared him down, feigning a confidence I did not feel. My heart was thumping with panic, the need to get this over and done with so I could get out of here.

"All right," he said. "What is it?"

"In private," I said.

He laughed, a single laugh of disbelief at my nerve, but even so, he looked at the others and said, "Gentlemen, would you give us a minute?"

They all left. Dylan was the last to go. He hesitated in the doorway, and for a moment I had the terrible thought that he was going to say something, do something. Fitz gave him a nod, and then he went.

I took a deep breath. "Did you know Leon Arnold was here last weekend?"

He shrugged. "No. And?"

"He attacked me. He booked a private dance and then got his two heavies—Markus and the other one—to wait outside while he jumped me."

At last Fitz looked up and met my eyes. And he laughed. "Did he really? Sly old git."

So it was true, then. I'd seriously pissed him off somehow.

Maybe Dylan had been followed to Victoria Station? No, he was far too careful for that.

"There was nobody watching the monitors, Fitz. He could have killed me."

"He didn't, though, did he? You're still here, aren't you? Toughen up, princess."

"Fitz—"

"You should go downstairs," he said.

"One more thing," I said. "I'm sorry. I need to give you my notice." I knew I was pushing my luck but it just came out.

He didn't even look up from the paperwork this time. "Talk to Dave or Helena about that."

He didn't seem remotely surprised. I got to my feet, left the office, and shut the door quietly behind it.

I went to see Helena in the bar. She didn't seem surprised, either. I'd been there longer than a lot of the girls—some of them stayed only a couple of weeks, especially if they hadn't managed to get themselves any regulars in that time—but even so, I was expendable. I hadn't even made the house fee tonight, so I had to get some money out of my bag in the dressing room. And then I was free to go.

I walked away from the Barclay feeling unexpectedly re-lieved. I hadn't realized quite how afraid I'd been, how tense, since Arnold had attacked me. I'd thought Fitz was someone who cared about what happened to his employees, maybe even cared for me, but I'd been wrong.

It was definitely time to go. I had something to look forward to now: Kent, the Medway River, and the *Revenge of the Tide*.

Chapter Thirty

The police station was new, a big modern building that could have been an office block, a school, or a college.

I was shown into an interview room that contained a table and four padded reception chairs, a wall-mounted video recorder, and a window that was just about too high to see out of. It was bright, though. And very small.

I sat there on my own for half an hour before Beverley Davies and Jamie Newman came in and sat down in front of me. All the interview rooms I'd ever seen on TV had been cavernous by comparison, shadowy, with light from above illuminating the interviewers' faces in a suitably dramatic fashion. This felt more like a job interview. I straightened in my seat. *Concentrate. Think about everything.*

"Sorry about the wait," DS Davies said. "Do you want a drink or anything? Water? Coffee?"

"No, thank you. Am I under arrest for something?"

Jamie Newman stepped in. "No, you're not under arrest. We just need to ask you some questions, and it's easier if we do it officially. That's all."

Beverley Davies continued. "We want to talk to you about Candace Smith, the woman who was found dead in the river next to your boat."

"Yes."

"You told my colleagues that you didn't recognize her, is that correct?"

"It was dark and I had just woken up. I didn't really see much other than a body, a face. It was afterward that I thought it looked like Caddy."

"But you didn't share this information with DC Carling or any of the officers from Kent Police?"

"No. It was just a thought. I didn't want to mislead them. When DC Carling told me it was Caddy, it gave me a bit of a shock to realize it was someone I knew after all."

"Can you tell us how you knew Candace?"

"I met her through work."

"What work is that?"

I looked from one of them to the other, at their calm, impassive faces gazing back at me. Waiting for me to slip up, to tell them something they didn't already know. It was nerve-racking, trying to second-guess them.

"I used to do some dancing—in my spare time. She was one of the other dancers in the club I worked in."

"The name of this club?"

"It was the Barclay."

"How long did you work there?"

"About seven months."

Jamie Newman was writing, the notepad on his lap so I couldn't see it. He held the pen with his fist scrunched around it. "Were you friends with Candace?"

I hesitated, just for a moment. "I guess so. Not really the kind of place you make friends, though. People come and go all the time."

"Some men attacked you on your boat," Davies said, after a few moments.

"Yes." I wondered if Carling had told her everything, whether he'd relayed our conversation word for word, if he'd even been making notes or recording it. Did she know about him staying the night? Would he have managed to keep that part to himself, at least?

"What do you think they wanted from you?"

"I don't know."

"You must have some idea."

"I thought they were looking for something, maybe. But I don't know what."

"Why did you think that?"

I took a deep breath in, trying to stay calm, trying to feel as though I was still in control.

"Because they turned the boat upside down, that's why. They came on board and threw everything around. So either they were looking for something and they didn't find it, or they just felt like making a mess."

"Why didn't you report it?" Davies asked.

I had no answer. I knew now why the window was so high up. If it had been any lower, I would have been able to see out, to see trees and fresh air and people going about their normal business; but all I could see was a small patch of darkening sky. I wanted to be out there. If the window had been at normal height I might have considered throwing myself out of it. I guessed I wasn't the first person to sit in here and contemplate something like that.

"Why didn't you report it, Genevieve? Could you answer the question?"

"I don't know. There didn't seem to be any point. They were long gone, whoever they were."

"After you left London, did you keep in touch with Candace Smith?"

"I spoke to her a couple of times. I asked her if she wanted to come to a party I was having. She said she'd think about it, but then she didn't show up."

"When was this party?"

"It was—the night I found the body next to the boat."

They looked at each other then, Newman and Davies. I wondered what they were thinking. My heart was beating fast. I wiped my palms down my jeans and then clasped my hands together to keep them still.

"Right. Let's just go back a bit. You invited Candace to your boat? When did you ask her?"

"I don't know. A few weeks ago, I think."

"And how did she seem, when you talked to her?"

"All right. Normal, really."

"So she was planning to come?"

"I told her when and where. She said she'd think about it. I don't think I really expected her to show up."

"Why not?"

"Like I said, we weren't really friends. She was just someone I knew from the club."

"Did you invite anyone else from the club?"

"No."

"So what made you invite Candace?"

"It was a spur-of-the-moment thing. I was talking to her, and thinking about the party, and I asked if she wanted to come along."

"Did you phone her, or did she phone you?"

"I can't remember."

I must have answered her too quickly.

"You said you weren't in contact with her very often, so speaking to her would have been unusual, wouldn't it? So think again. Did you phone her, or did she phone you?"

"I guess I phoned her."

"What did you call her for?"

"Just to see how she was."

There was another pause. Newman was still taking notes on his pad, to my right. I could hear the scratching of his pen on the notepad. He might have been doodling for all I knew.

"You said that Candace didn't show up."

"That's right."

"Are you sure? I mean, if you were busy with the party—talking to your guests, drinking, that sort of thing—maybe she showed up and you didn't realize?"

I considered this for a moment.

"It's not a very big boat. Lots of people were up on the deck. Someone would have seen if she'd been there. Someone would have told me."

"We'll need you to give us a list of everyone who was there that night, with their contact details."

"I already gave it to that guy—the one who interviewed me—I can't remember his name."

"Even so, I'd like you to write another list."

She tore a sheet of paper off the top of a lined pad that was on the table behind her and pushed it and a ballpoint pen over the desk toward me. I stared at it for a few moments and made two headings: "Marina" and "Other." As I wrote each name, I thought about how they'd all react to being questioned by the police. Lucy, Gavin, Ben.

When I'd finished, she gave me a smile, the first time she'd softened. "What was Caddy like?"

"She was nice. She helped me out a bit when I first started working there."

"She looked after you?"

"Yes, you could say that."

"Took you under her wing?"

"I guess so."

"Did you see much of her outside work?"

"Not really."

"Did she have any other close friends?"

"I don't know. Nobody I knew."

"Boyfriends?"

"I don't know."

"You never talked about it? About guys you liked?"

I shook my head. "No."

I hadn't lied to them, not directly. Not yet.

"What about Fitz?"

"What about him?" My heart was thudding at the sound of his name, my cheeks coloring.

"You knew him?"

"Of course. He was the owner of the club."

"Did you get along with him?"

"I didn't see him very often. He was usually at his other clubs when I was there."

"What did Candace think of him?"

"She told me that he was okay unless you pissed him off."

"What do you think she meant by that?"

"Just that I shouldn't piss him off. I don't know. As I said, I didn't see him very often."

"Did she ever say what happened if anyone did 'piss him off'?"

"No."

"Did you ever see anyone else cross him?"

"No."

"Were you afraid of him?"

"No. I didn't know him. I just did my job and went home."

"Were the other dancers afraid of him?"

"Not that I saw. If they were, they would have left, wouldn't they?"

"Why did you leave, Genevieve?"

"I was only working there to save up enough money to buy a boat. I'd saved up enough, so I handed in my notice and left."

"When was this?"

"It was the middle of April."

"And you never went back for a visit?"

"No." I still wasn't lying. Not directly. I tried to keep my breathing steady, even though my cheeks were burning, my hands icy cold, as if I had a fever.

"How long had you worked there?"

"You already asked me that question."

"Even so, I'd like you to answer it."

"About seven months."

There was silence, except for Newman writing his notes. Davies was staring at me curiously, as though I were some kind of unusual animal in a zoo and she was expecting more from me, something more interesting, more entertaining.

"These men who attacked you on your boat—did you recognize them?"

"No." The first real lie. It felt as if I were shouting. Had I answered too quickly? Surely they must realize? I swallowed the lump in my throat, took a deep, steadying breath.

"Aren't you afraid they'll come back?"

"Of course I am. Look," I said, "Malcolm—my neighbor— he's been helping me service the engine. I was planning to take the boat upstream a bit. Just somewhere out of the way. I haven't told anyone."

"I see."

"I was going to call DC Carling and let him know. In fact, it was his idea."

"It was his idea?"

"He asked me if I'd ever taken the boat on a trip any- where. I said I hadn't. But that gave me the idea. I mean, it's not like living in a house, is it? Why live on a boat and never move it?"

After that they ended the interview and left the room. I didn't ask how long it was going to be before I could go home, but I wasn't under arrest. I could have walked out if I'd wanted to, but there was no point. I could stay and answer their ques- tions until they were as bored of it as I was.

But they came back after ten minutes and said I could go. The Metropolitan Police Serious Crime Directorate had asked me all they needed to, for now, anyway.

I was packing up boxes in the flat I was renting and drinking a cup of cold coffee when there was a knock at the door.

I'd been expecting Dylan for so many days that I'd almost given up. I was afraid he'd changed his mind about the package, about the fifty grand. I didn't know what I was going to do if he didn't come through with the money, but there was no going back: I'd left work, given notice on the flat, handed over a substantial deposit plus marina fees to Cameron. I had to go, whatever happened.

"Can I come in?" he said.

About bloody time, I wanted to say. I wanted to smack him and ask where the fuck he'd been, why he'd left me waiting without so much as a phone call. He was wearing his non-work disguise, jeans and a shirt, navy blue this time, with a ratty-looking jacket over the top of it. He wasn't carrying a bag, which made my heart sink. He must have changed his mind.

He followed me into my kitchen and I moved a box off the chair to let him sit. "You're moving out already, huh?" he said.

"I'm putting most of it in storage," I said.

"I came to see how you were."

"Oh. I'm all right, thanks. How's Caddy?"

He smiled at me. "Same as usual. Sometimes happy as a clam, sometimes a grumpy little fucker."

I wondered if I should offer him a drink. Did he ever have anything other than vodka? I had no idea where the kettle was, in any case.

"So—you found yourself a boat, then?"

I smiled happily. "Yes, I have. It's called the *Revenge of the Tide*."

"No kidding? Weird name."

"It suits it. You should come and have a look."

"Is it one of the ones you were looking at? In Kent?"

"Yes. In Rochester."

He nodded approvingly. Then, "I thought Fitz might have given you a hard time."

"Not really," I said. "I think I overestimated my own importance."

"He never said you'd left. He never mentioned you after you burst into the office that night."

"I think he was pissed off because I complained to him about Arnold jumping me."

"Ah. That would do it, yeah. And probably coming into the office without an invite didn't help."

There was a strange silence for a moment. He filled the room with his bulk, even sitting down.

"So—you still want to do it?"

"Yes." There was no question about what it was I was still willing to do. Mentioning the package would have been a waste of breath.

"Okay," he said. "You got a car?"

"No. I'm renting a van tomorrow, though. To take all my things down to the boat."

"All right, then," he said, "You know Brands Hatch, the racetrack? There's a hotel there, the Thistle. On the A20. Think you can find it?"

"Sure."

"I'll meet you in the bar of the hotel. Nine o'clock tomorrow night."

"All right. What if something happens? I mean, what if I get held up?"

"I'll wait till you get there."

He stood up to go and I had a sudden urge to ask him to stay for a while. But he didn't hesitate or give me time to ask. He didn't even look back.

Chapter Thirty-One

I was ten minutes late getting to Brands Hatch, mainly because I approached it from the wrong direction and had to exit the road to turn the van around.

It had been a hectic day, and I was tired out with moving more stuff into storage, supervising some moving men who had taken a load down to the boat—mainly furniture. Now it was just me and a van packed to the roof with boxes.

Dylan was in the bar, strategically positioned to the side where he could watch the entrance without making it obvious that he was waiting for someone. I bought a bottle of beer and slid into the armchair opposite his seat.

He gave me one of his best Dylan smiles. He looked so different when he smiled. "Thought you weren't coming," he said.

"Sorry," I said. "I took a slight detour on the highway."

He nodded slowly. On the sofa next to him was a big plastic shopping bag. He placed a hand on it. I wondered what it was. Cocaine? Heroin? It was best not to think about it too hard, so I thought about the money instead.

"It's all in there," he said. "With a cell phone."

"Okay," I said.

"The phone has one number saved in it, under the name Garland. When I'm going to come and pick up the package, I'll call you on that number. Only answer the phone if you see that the caller ID says Garland."

"Why Garland?"

"It's just a word."

"Is it your name?" He'd never told me. I only ever knew him as Dylan.

"No."

"Can I use the phone to call you?"

"No."

"What if there's an emergency?"

"There won't be an emergency. Nothing is going to happen. You just need to put the package somewhere safe, keep the phone charged, and within a couple of months I'll call you on that number and arrange to come and pick it up. Yeah?"

"All right."

The feeling crept up on me before I realized what it was. I wasn't going to see him anymore. It was going to be that one call, that one meeting to hand over the package, and that would be it. Somehow I'd just assumed that we would still be friends. The thought of not seeing him was making me feel uncomfortable—no, more than that. Desolate.

"What's the matter?" he asked.

I had no reason not to tell him the truth. "I'm going to miss you," I said.

Dylan laughed at that, and it hurt me. Maybe I was just tired, maybe it had just been a traumatic couple of weeks, but the tears were falling down my cheeks before I realized, and I rubbed them away crossly with my sleeve.

"It's not funny," I said quietly.

"You won't miss me, Genevieve. I'll be lucky if you remember where you've left the phone after a couple of hours."

"That's not fair. You're always thinking the worst of me, Dylan."

He sighed as though I were just some troublesome female he was going to have to deal with, then picked up the shopping bag and put it on the floor by his feet, making space on the sofa next to him. "Come and sit here," he said, and his voice was softer, almost gentle.

When I got to my feet and sank onto the cushions next to him he put his arm around my back, awkwardly patting my shoulder. I moved closer to him, against him, feeling his bulk, instantly comforted. It reminded me of the moment he'd held me after he'd gotten rid of Leon Arnold. Whatever had been wrong had disappeared and everything was all right again.

We stayed like that for a long time and I relaxed into him. His hand, his huge hand that had been patting me on the shoulder like an inexperienced father trying to burp a new baby, had changed pace and was stroking my upper arm, slowly. And then it was just the tips of his fingers, running from my shoulder to my elbow, and back again.

At last he said, "We should go."

I pushed myself up off the sofa and away from him and he brought the bag and walked with me out of the main entrance and across the parking lot to my van. I unlocked it and opened the door for him to put the bag inside, on the passenger seat, but he didn't move. I turned to face him, about to say, *What are you waiting for?* but the words died in my throat because of the way he was looking at me. He placed the shopping bag carefully at his feet, and without taking his eyes off me pushed the door of the van shut, not with force but with a kind of purpose. He moved forward and with no other warning kissed me, one hand around my back, pulling me against him, the other cradling my neck, his thumb on my jawline.

Oh, it felt so good, that kiss. It was as though I'd been waiting for it, waiting for the longest time without realizing, and now that it was finally happening my legs were giving way under me and he pushed me gently back against the side of the van to steady me.

When he finally moved away, I couldn't see his face in the darkness but I heard his voice, the emotion in it. He said, "You want to stay?"

I nodded. I wasn't even sure what he meant then, but I did want to stay if the alternative was going to the boat on my own, or going anywhere that wasn't with him.

We walked back to the hotel and I waited by the elevators while Dylan went to the front desk to see if he could get a room for us. All I could think was that I needed a shower: I'd been lugging boxes and furniture around all day and I felt filthy. But not tired anymore—I was energized by that kiss, breathing from the very top of my lungs, fizzing with anticipation.

We went upstairs and along a hall that went on and on, me following Dylan, who was carrying that stupid bag, which looked heavier by the minute and was probably full of cocaine.

He was walking fast and I struggled to keep up with him, until he stopped abruptly and I almost ran into his back. He opened the door to a room and we went inside; he dropped the bag on the floor, pushed it with the toe of his boot into the bottom of the open closet, and closed the door with the other hand, putting on the security chain.

I was already taking my clothes off, my top tangled around my arms, trying to kick my boots off without undoing the laces, jeans around my knees; anyone would think I had no idea how to strip in an erotic and beguiling fashion.

"I need a shower, I'm sorry," I said, my voice muffled by fabric as I felt his mouth on my skin, his tongue on my naked stomach.

"Like I care," he said.

That was all he said.

I was made breathless by how much I wanted him. His physique was powerful, the tailored suits he wore hid the muscles, not to mention the tattoos that covered his left arm and both shoulders: a black dragon snaking around and across the back of his neck; a tribal pattern, a sun, all black ink, intricate and lovely on his nocturnal skin. And how pale and small my fingers looked, gripping the inked skin of his shoulder.

It was the way he looked at me, so differently from the way he'd looked at me in the Barclay. It was as though he'd opened his eyes and was seeing me for the first time. And I'd been waiting, waiting unknowing for him to look at me in exactly that way. Why hadn't I realized it before? Why hadn't I seen him as he really was, this beautiful quiet man who looked out for me? His body fit against mine seamlessly; everything he did was at the right moment, just the right pace, just the right pressure. I loved how he tried so hard to make everything perfect and slow and sensual, and then, the way he lost control.

And hours, hours later . . . we'd fucked and showered and had a drink from the minibar, and fucked all over again; I was so tired my body felt as though it was separate from me . . . It was starting to get light and I was lying stretched against him, fingers threaded through his. He was so quiet and still, I thought he was asleep.

I couldn't stop smiling. It felt as though my life had lurched back onto the right track; as if everything that had been wrong was suddenly, magically right. I would live on the boat, and during the week, when the club was quiet, Dylan could come and visit me. He could help me with the renovations, and if he didn't want to do that we would get quietly drunk together sitting on the deck of my boat, watching the sunset, and then go down into my cabin and make love for hours and hours. Maybe in a few months' time he would give up working in London and move down to be with me on the boat . . .

"This was a bad idea," he said.

The sound of his voice after hours without speaking almost made me jump. "Don't say that," I whispered.

He kissed the back of my neck slowly and ran his hand from my thigh over my hip to my waist to my back and my shoulder and my face, and I turned my head to look at him again, and he kissed me.

"You could come and visit me," I said, hopefully, but even before I'd finished the sentence he was shaking his head.

"That's exactly what I meant when I said it was a bad idea," he said.

"But why, Dylan?" I said, my voice hoarse.

"Because of the package," he said.

"So give it to someone else!"

He pushed me away and sat on the edge of the bed. "I'm just trying to keep you safe," he said.

"Safe from what?" I asked.

He didn't answer.

"You're getting me involved in your sketchy deal, whatever it is, asking me to hide stuff for you. How's that going to keep me safe?"

"It's not what you think," he said.

"You're ripping off Fitz? Is that what this is about?"

He stood up and started to find his clothes where they were scattered, and I wished I'd kept my big mouth shut so I could hold on to him for a few moments longer. The pain I'd felt last night at the thought of leaving him was back, but it was worse now, much worse, because of what we'd done. He was probably right. It had been a bad idea. I could feel the anger coming off him like a scent, bristling like an electric charge.

I tried again. "I'll be safe wherever you are," I said.

"No, you won't."

"I don't understand," I said, sitting up in bed.

He already had his pants on. "Exactly," he said. "You don't understand. You don't understand any of it. Remember when you let that guy touch you while you were dancing, at Fitz's house, and I was pissed off at you afterward? You didn't understand about that, either, did you?"

He was looking at me with so much hurt in his eyes, as though I was wounding him still, just by sitting there, just by existing.

"You made me watch," he said. "You said you'd do it on condition that I was there. You made me stand there and watch you."

I think my mouth dropped open with surprise. "I did that because I thought you were my friend," I said. "I thought you'd look out for me."

"I had to stand there and watch him with hands all over you," he said.

"You were looking at me as if I was a piece of furniture."

"I had no choice. If Fitz had had any idea how I felt about you it would have been all over."

"He said you liked me, so it seems he knew anyway."

"Yes," he said. "And now look at us. Fitz doesn't trust me anymore, Genevieve, because he knows how I feel about you. It makes me a liability as far as he's concerned, especially now you've left. He's going to be watching me like a hawk. And I need him to trust me."

"You never told me how you felt. How was I supposed to know?"

"I need to work at straightening things out with Fitz," he said, "and you need to forget this happened, okay?"

"Dylan!"

He was tying his shoelaces, his boots resting on the edge of the bed. Ten minutes ago we had been lying here naked, locked together as if we would never be able to be apart. How could we go from such bliss to conflict in such a short space of time?

When he was dressed, I thought he was just going to go, to

walk out without so much as casting a glance back at me, but he came back to the bed and took me in his arms and held me against him fiercely. I was crying by then. I tried to touch him, to kiss him, but he was holding me too tightly to move.

"Keep yourself safe," he said. "Be careful who you trust. Understand?"

I nodded, sniffing, my face buried in his shirt.

"It might be okay. In a few months, if it works out. If you can wait that long. All right?"

"I can wait," I said.

He pulled back and wiped my tears away with his thumb. "Just keep safe," he said. "Hide that package somewhere. Be safe. And I'll come and find you."

Then he left me. He grabbed his jacket and he was gone.

Later, when I had showered again and dressed, I looked in the bag and saw what it contained. A rectangular package, wrapped in a heavy-duty gray plastic bag and bound tightly and neatly with black electrical tape. A small black cell phone, new, and a charger. And two thick bundles of fifty-pound notes. I'd never seen so much cash in my life, but even so, I stared at it with no emotion.

In the space of a few hours he'd gone from being a friend, someone I was doing a favor for, to breaking my heart by leaving me behind.

Chapter Thirty-Two

I had almost gotten as far as the town center when the rain started—big, heavy drops that threatened to soak me. I made a dash across the pedestrian crossing near the bus station and nearly ran into the back of a silver car that had stopped right in front of me. I went to pass it and the driver's window slid down.

"Genevieve!"

It was Jim. He looked as though he'd had a busy day already: tired eyes, sleeves folded back to his forearms, tie loosened.

"What are you doing here?"

"Thought you might need a ride."

"No, thanks."

I stood in the rain, staring at him. A car behind him honked, making me jump.

I got in the car. It was warm, and almost as soon as I was inside the car started to mist up. He switched on the air-conditioning. I was already starting to shiver, my hair dripping. I wasn't angry at him, not really. He had a job to do like everyone else. I'd forgotten that police were never off duty and so nothing you told them would ever be considered private.

We sat in the car, staring at the traffic, waiting for the light to change, the windshield wipers scraping noisily back and forth across the rain-spattered glass. The multistory parking lot looked as if it were sagging under the weight of its own ugliness. I bit my lip, my shoulders rigid, resolutely looking out the window at the rain.

"Everything all right?"

I didn't answer. What possible answer was there?

"Genevieve," he said, "I had to tell them. You know that."

"Did you tell them you slept with me?" I said with venom. "No, I didn't think so. Funny the part you left out."

I glanced across at him. His cheeks were pink. "There are good reasons why I can't tell them that. Reasons that have nothing to do with you."

"What the hell's that supposed to mean?"

There was an awkward silence, broken only by the noise of the rain, the wipers squealing across the windscreen.

"Did they tell you what I said to them?" I asked, at last.

Carling shook his head. "It's their investigation now. Nothing to do with me."

"Why?"

"Candace Smith was from London, so she's their victim. It's complicated. You're the only thing linking her to Kent, so they've come down here to tick you off their list."

"Oh. You know, I thought they were going to arrest me."

"They probably would have, a couple of days ago. But they've got two people in custody, and they've just charged them, which makes things a bit different. It's about evidence-gathering now."

"They have people in custody?" I asked. "Who?"

He shrugged, as if to say he didn't know, but what he probably meant was, he couldn't tell me. For a horrible moment I wondered if they'd arrested Dylan. Maybe that was why he wasn't answering his phone—maybe he was in some nasty London police station, locked in a cell.

"So what did you say to them?" he asked.

"They wanted to know how I knew her. I told them I met

her when I was living in London. I worked weekends at a club—the Barclay. Caddy worked there, too. That's about it."

"I know the Barclay."

"Do you?"

"Were you a dancer?"

I looked at him sharply, but his eyes remained on the road. "Have you ever been there?" I asked. "To the Barclay, I mean."

He shook his head. "No, some of my friends went for a bachelor party and I heard all about it. Couldn't afford it at the time. Bastards went without me."

I hesitated and then said, "Yes, I was a dancer. That's how I managed to buy the boat."

"You have a dancer's body," he said.

"I haven't done it for a long time," I said.

The line of traffic was creeping forward, a few feet at a time.

"Look, I can walk if it's easier," I said. "We might be stuck here for ages."

"This place," he said. "It's pretty much guaranteed we'll be stuck here for ages. It's not even as if there's any real traffic, it's just the bloody lights slowing us down. There must be ten sets of lights along this one stupid stretch of road, all timed wrong, so it just brings everything to a standstill. I mean, what sort of arses think that changing a town designed entirely around a one-way traffic system into a two-way system is a good idea?"

I thought for a moment that he'd finished and I nodded in agreement, but he was only pausing to get his breath.

"You hope that when the government starts cutting costs, the people making these kinds of stupid decisions will be the ones to go, but no, there's always enough money to keep a bunch of retarded planners employed so that they can deploy their million traffic cones for a short stretch of construction... And even if they do ever finish it, no one in their right mind is going to want to come here anyway."

"Finished?"

"Sorry," he said. "I was coming this way anyway, to be honest, despite the bloody construction. And besides, I wanted to see you again."

I took a deep breath. "I do like you, Jim. But it's no good pretending that this is going to work."

"Whoa," he said, at the sudden change of tone.

"You can't get involved with me when they still aren't sure if I'm a suspect or not."

"I'm aware of that."

"And afterward, well . . ."

"Well?"

"By then you might have met a nice girl, or changed your mind about me, or . . . well, anything could happen. I'm just saying."

"You've got someone else," he said. As though there could be no other possible explanation for my rejection of him.

"No. I just—there was someone, but I haven't seen him for months, since I moved here. I don't even know if he still thinks about me."

"What's his name?"

I pretended I hadn't heard his question, looking out of the window at the dirty, rainy streets. I couldn't believe it was so dark in the middle of the afternoon. The sidewalks were full of Saturday shoppers, umbrellas, gray coats, and soaking pants clinging to wet legs.

"What was she like?" Carling asked.

"Who?"

"Caddy."

I didn't answer at first, wondering how I could do her justice in just a few words. I thought back to some of the good nights we'd had together, dancing and working, yes, but having as much fun as if we were on a girls' night out at the same time. I pictured her laughing, doubled over, because one of the

Russian girls was trying to chat up some lad from Streatham who thought she was from Scotland. Patting tears out of the corners of her eyes and flapping her hand in front of her face to give herself some air.

"She was beautiful, clever, funny . . . And she was kind to me. Despite everything. She was kind."

"Despite everything?"

"She thought—" I said, and stopped short.

"She thought what?"

He was sitting there, looking casual, looking as though he didn't care very much what I was about to say, but I could tell he was paying attention to every single word.

"Is this an interview?" I asked.

"No, of course not." His response was quick. "You don't have to answer. I was just interested in her."

"She thought I was trying to steal her boyfriend," I said at last, watching Carling's face for his reaction.

He looked back at me, his expression hard to read.

"And were you?"

Two weeks after I'd started living aboard the *Revenge*, I went back to London.

Caddy lived in a flat in Walworth, not all that far from my old place in Clapham. I found it easily enough, taking my time about it, not even sure if being there was the right thing to do. It was a Sunday afternoon. There was no telling if she'd be awake, but it was a reasonably civilized hour for a visit, even for a nocturnal person like Caddy.

To my surprise she answered the door quickly. She was dressed in jeans and a gray T-shirt that showed off her chest and narrow waist.

"Oh," she said.

She looked completely different with her hair loose, wavy down her back, no makeup. She looked young. I realized I'd never actually asked her how old she was, just assumed she was about my age, but, looking at her in the bright light of an April Sunday, she looked almost like a teenager.

I thought for a moment she was going to shut the door in my face, but curiosity seemed to get the better of her and she stood aside to let me in.

Her flat was spotlessly clean, and I must have interrupted the process of making it cleaner: a mop and bucket were in the kitchen and the tiled floor was wet. The wide, bright main room smelled faintly of bleach. A small balcony was visible through the open patio doors. From below, faint noise of traffic from the South Circular.

"You want a drink or something?"

"That would be nice, thanks. Water would be fine."

I perched on the edge of a white corner sofa, looking at the wallpaper, a dramatic black-and-white design. It was starting to make me feel dizzy.

"Fitz was mad that you left," she said, handing me a glass of water with two chunks of ice clinking in it.

"He didn't seem that concerned when I told him."

"You don't know Fitz, then. Good thing you didn't hang around." She sat opposite me, her legs crossed, her bare foot flexing and circling. "So what happened? Why did you just take off like that?"

"I'd just . . . had enough, I guess. I bought a boat."

She laughed. "What—like a yacht?"

"No. It's a barge. I'm going to live on it."

She was looking at me, shaking her head slowly. "You always were full of surprises."

"So were you. I just wanted to come and say that I'm sorry if things were bad between us there at the end. I thought of you as a good friend. I don't want to lose touch with you." There. I'd said it. I'd apologized for whatever it was she thought I'd done.

She pulled her feet up onto the chair so that she was cross-legged, biting at her lower lip. "This is all weird."

"Weird how?"

"You leaving. Did you hear about the raid?"

"The what?"

"Last Friday. The club got raided, loads of police all over the place. It was a fucking nightmare. We didn't get to leave until ten in the morning."

"Shit! Did they find anything? What happened?"

"I don't know. Nobody tells me anything anymore. The club was closed Saturday night—we all got the night off and a pathetic handout from Norland to compensate us. Then business as usual on Sunday."

All I could think about was Dylan. No wonder he hadn't called. If there had been a raid at the club, he would have been preoccupied, to say the least.

"You know Fitz was joking about it: how you left and the next minute the club got raided. He thought it was you."

She laughed as she said it, but even so my whole body felt suddenly cold.

"He's always suspicious about something," I said.

"Yeah."

"You love him," I said, trying for a subtle change of subject.

"Yeah, well, I do make that a bit obvious sometimes. Stupid."

"He doesn't know what he's doing," I said. "You deserve so much better than that."

"Unrequited love," she said. "It sucks."

She stretched one leg in front of her, looking at her impeccably pedicured toes as though they could do with a new polish. And then, out of the blue: "You remember Chanelle?"

"The one who you saw in the bar that time we met up?"

She nodded, perfect teeth biting her lower lip.

"What about her?"

"She's dead. Her mum called me. She'd found my number in Chanelle's address book. They don't know what happened to her phone."

"Dead? What happened?"

Caddy sighed. "Overdose."

There was something in the way she said it, as though the manner of her death had been entirely predictable.

"Was she a heavy user, then? I thought Fitz didn't like girls using too much."

"Exactly. He didn't. And, no, she wasn't a heavy user. Not when I knew her, anyway."

"You mean Fitz had something to do with it?"

She stared at me for a moment and then relaxed a little. "You know where Chanelle went, when she left the Barclay?"

"No."

"She went to work for Leon Arnold."

"Doing what?"

"No idea. But he's not someone I'd want to work for."

"He attacked me," I said. "In the club. Nobody was monitoring the CCTV."

"Yeah."

My head was spinning with all this information. There was plenty she wasn't telling me. All through my time at the Barclay I'd deliberately avoided knowing Fitz's business, closed my ears to overheard conversations, looked away.

"So you think Arnold—"

"He's more dangerous than Fitz," she said, interrupting.

"The man you're in love with," I reminded her, "who is still unpredictable and dangerous."

Caddy laughed. "He wouldn't hurt me, though. Not Fitz. Leon Arnold, however, I'd steer clear of."

I felt a light dawning somewhere. "Is that why you were so angry with me at that party? Because I was talking to Leon Arnold? You tried to warn me . . ."

"I was pissed off because you were flirting with Fitz. And because you were too stupid to listen to me telling you to be careful of Arnold."

I drank the last of my water and thought about leaving. I'd come here to straighten things out with her, to make sure she was all right, and I'd achieved that.

"Anyway, you're not in any sort of position to judge me about how I feel about Fitz. What about Dylan?" she said.

"What about him?"

"Well. Me and Fitz, you and Dylan. Don't tell me you didn't know he likes you."

I couldn't answer that one.

"He's very careful, Dylan, about not giving anything away. But you could tell by the way he looked out for you. And by the way he watched you when you weren't looking."

"Really?"

"Absolutely. And he's been fucking miserable since you left."

"Poor Dylan," I said. "He needs someone to look after him."

We both laughed—the thought of Dylan needing to be taken care of was ludicrous.

Then she said, "I think about leaving sometimes. I thought about it when I heard you'd gone, in fact. Trouble is, girls leave but they always end up coming back. You get used to the money, you know?"

"I've been saving up," I said.

"Yeah. That's why you were always borrowing my stuff, huh?"

I got up, taking my glass through to her kitchenette.

"You can come and visit me," I said. "When I've got the boat straightened out. Come and stay."

"Sure," she said. "I'd like to."

"I'll have a boatwarming party," I said. "I'll give you a call."

She walked me to the door of the flat and gave me a hug. Without her heels on she was tiny.

"I'm glad you came by," she said.

"I want to tell you to keep yourself safe," I said. For some reason I felt on the verge of tears.

"I can look after myself," she said.

"I know. But they're—you know. They're doing all kinds of stuff on the side. The place got raided, Caddy. The police must realize something's going on. It's only a matter of time before Fitz gets caught doing some deal or other."

"You think I don't know that? I just do what you did— keep my nose out of it. It's the only way."

Once we'd reached New Road, the traffic started to ease up. It slowed again for all the traffic lights in Corporation Street, at the back of Rochester High Street, and finally we turned left onto the Esplanade before the bridge. Jim had gotten very quiet. Eventually, he pulled into the parking lot and sat, waiting for me to get out.

I was staring at the wipers, wondering what to say.

"Thanks for the lift, it was very kind of you."

"No problem."

"You want to come in for a coffee or something?"

He hesitated, clearly debating with himself, and then: "I don't think it would be a good idea."

I gave him a half-smile, but he wasn't looking at me. I got out of the car and shut the door, ran down toward the dock, splashing through the puddles, expecting the car to roar off up the hill to the main road, but it didn't. When I got to the boat and looked back, he'd parked the car properly and was follow-ing me, hands shoved in the pockets of his pants, head down.

"Changed my mind," he said gruffly, when he'd caught up.

The boat was freezing cold. I busied myself with the stove while he brewed coffee. I glanced around the cabin when I thought he wasn't watching. The boat looked the same as it always had—untidy, cobwebby in places, but not as though it had been searched.

The fire crackled and spat, the flames brightening the room. I shut the glass door and watched the fire for a moment.

"You should think about putting in central heating," said Carling.

"I know," I said. "It didn't seem that important in the summer. It's crazy really: the weather's turning, I should be taking care of the bathroom, but the next thing that's going to get done is the deck garden."

"I'll help you with the bathroom, if you like."

I smiled. "Thanks. That's a kind offer."

He put two mugs of coffee on the table and sat down with a sigh.

"I'm just going to get changed," I said. My jeans were soaked.

I left him in the main cabin and padded down to the bedroom. Waited for a second, then continued on to the hatch—just to see the box, if nothing else . . . I just needed to look. I could check properly later.

The space was cavernous and dark. I opened the door enough and stood away a little to let the light shine in. I could see the shape of the box at the end. Had it moved? Was it more visible than it had been? I'd thought the other boxes had been grouped around it, hiding it, but from here I could just about make out the words written on the side . . .

"Everything okay?"

"Yes, yes, fine," I said quickly, shutting the hatch door with a bang. "I was just—um—looking for something."

I must have looked about as guilty as it was possible to be.

He gazed at me steadily, then a quick but deliberate up and down my body, taking in my wet socks and my wet jeans and my wet top. Then he said, "Your coffee's getting cold," and turned to go back to the main cabin.

I went into the bedroom, with my heart thumping in my chest. I would have to be careful. I'd almost given it away just then—so stupid. He wasn't crazy, he must know there was so much I hadn't told him. And Dylan, too—I'd almost told him about Dylan . . .

I wrestled my sodden jeans down my legs, then got my socked foot caught on the hem of the other leg of the jeans and before I knew what had happened I'd slipped and landed with a crash and a yelp against the chest of drawers.

Jim was in the doorway within a second; he stood there looking at me for a moment, in a heap with my jeans bunched up around my knees, and then he laughed.

"It's not funny, you piece of shit!"

He crouched down next to me. "Yes, it is," he said, still laughing.

I couldn't help laughing, too, even though my back hurt from landing against the drawers. He offered me his hand and hauled me to my feet. "Come and sit down, I'll give you a hand."

He helped me shuffle over to the bed, and while I sat on the edge he pulled my jeans down. They were so wet, the denim was glued to my skin. He tugged and heaved, and I held on to the edge of the bed, but not tightly enough because the next thing I knew he'd pulled me right off the bed and I landed with a thump with my ass on the floor.

I was laughing and crying at the same time, and he could hardly move, his shoulders shaking. "Oh, God . . . I'm sorry . . . are you all right?"

I nodded and shook my head, and then before I could say anything he was kissing me, hard, catching his breath, pulling me against him.

"You are so sexy," he said quickly, "so sexy. You don't even know what you do to me . . ."

I was lying on my back, looking at the dark night sky through the skylight over my head, and feeling the *Revenge of the Tide* moving gently as the water rose up the inlet from the sea and lifted the boat from its muddy cradle.

Jim had woken me, climbing out of bed. I watched him turn left out of the door, heading for the bathroom, and turned over in bed, pulling the covers up.

I dozed for a while, and when I opened my eyes again he had not come back. I wondered if he'd gone home, then I caught the sound of his voice—where? On deck?

The skylight was gray now, light enough in the room to see Jim's T-shirt and sweater on the chair, his jeans missing. I sat up in bed and strained to hear. Silence. And then—a few words. A laugh?

Just as I was considering getting up and going to see if I could hear any better from the doorway, I heard his footsteps in the cabin and I lay back down again quickly, covers up. I listened to the sounds of him taking off his jeans, the chink of the belt buckle as he folded them and put them back on the chair. Then the creak of the bed as he lifted the covers and got back in beside me. His cold hand slid over my stomach. "I know you're not asleep," he said softly. "I can tell."

"How can you tell?" I murmured, still half pretending.

"From how you breathe." He was kissing my neck, my throat, my shoulder, pulling me toward him.

"Who were you talking to?" I asked, my voice muffled against his skin.

"Work."

"Mm. What do they want at this time of the morning? Your hands are cold."

He didn't answer my question. I straddled him, reached up to the wood siding over my head, put both my hands flat against the ceiling to give me balance, and he cupped my breasts with his hands and watched me move, and let out a sound that might have been a word, or might just have been a groan.

Chapter Thirty-Three

The sunlight streaming through the skylight onto my face woke me up. The bed was empty. I squinted across to the chair. Jim's clothes were gone.

I lay still for a few moments, enjoying the warmth of the sun, remembering what we'd done the night before. He was good at it. He was getting better and better, in fact.

I heard noises coming from the galley—washing-up noises. Then the radio went on, the sound down low. Just enough for me to hear the music.

I got up and found some clothes, ran a hand through my hair to flatten the bits that were sticking up.

When he saw me, he put the kettle back on the stove. "Morning," he said.

"Good morning to you, too." I leaned over him and kissed his jawline. He smelled of warmth and yesterday's aftershave.

I took a dish towel from the handle on the door of the stove and dried the cups he'd washed, putting them away in the cabinet. I felt all domesticated, the sunshine streaming in through the skylights, creating shafts of light and warmth. I loved my boat. Even the wooden boards under my bare feet were warm.

He poured me out a coffee and put the mug on the table.

"I could use a shower," he said.

"You could go and have one over by the office."

"By the office?"

"There's a shower room. It's quite nice, and clean. Better than my hose, anyway."

"I should really go home. I need clean clothes, and I'm back at work this afternoon."

"Oh. All right."

He was staring at me, his dark eyes unfathomable.

"What?" I said, thinking I might have said or done something wrong.

"I don't want to go."

I smiled, kissed him again. "I don't want you to go, either."

"How about," he said into my throat, his hands up under my top, "I go and have a quick shower now, and later I can just dash home and get changed on the way to work?"

I made a noise that might have been assent; it was enough to satisfy him. When he let me go, I went to find him a clean towel and some shower gel. He took it and climbed the steps to the wheelhouse.

"Want me to come with you?" I asked.

"Not unless you're going to shower with me," he said.

I let him go.

I went back to the bedroom and made the bed, shaking the tangled duvet over the creased bottom sheet. I opened the skylight to let in some fresh air. I was brushing my teeth a few moments later when I heard it—a buzzing noise. Toothbrush sticking out of the corner of my mouth, I went into the main cabin. It was louder in here.

On the seat of the dinette, a cell phone on vibrate was buzzing and flashing. I picked it up and my first instinct was to answer it, but it wasn't my phone. It was Jim's.

I stared at the phone in my hand, at the number that was illuminated on the display. The name that showed up on the screen was simply: D. On the table was a pile of papers, envelopes, receipts. I grabbed a pen from a broken-handled mug on the shelf in the galley and wrote down the number on the back of my credit card bill just as the phone stopped vibrating.

One missed call.

I put the phone on the seat, chewing my toothbrush thoughtfully. I went back to my poor excuse for a bathroom and rinsed my mouth. In the mirror above the sink I caught the look in my eyes. My heart was pounding.

I found yesterday's jeans in the bedroom and, in the back pocket, Dylan's phone. I scrolled through to the address book. Looked at the number for GARLAND. And then at the number written on the back of the credit card envelope.

I jumped up the steps to the wheelhouse and peered across the boats toward the office. No sign of anyone. The marina was deserted, the boats bathed in bright sunshine. I couldn't see the door to the shower room from here, but there was no sign of Jim.

Back in the cabin, I picked up Jim's phone, activated the screen. He didn't have a password.

One missed call.

I worked my way through unfamiliar menus—Call History? That was it—and there it was . . . Missed Calls. And the last number, the one I recognized.

I selected the icon that looked like a handset and within a few moments I heard a ringing tone as the call connected.

And then—

"Yeah?"

I stood there immobile, the phone pressed to my ear. Just that one word—could I be certain?

"Dylan?"

"Who is this?"

It was him; all my doubts vanished with those three words. "It's me."

There was silence on the other end. I half-expected him to ask, *Who?* but he didn't. He knew my voice as well as I knew his.

"Where's Jim?" he asked.

"Hang on—how the hell do you know Jim? And why is your phone off all the time? And where the hell are you? And what am I supposed to do with this . . . this package you left here?"

I heard him sigh, above the noise of the wind blowing across the phone.

"You're supposed to trust me," he said.

"How can I trust you when you never answer your bloody phone? Some men broke in. They tied me up."

There was a pause before he answered. He probably already knew, after all. He spent enough time with Nicks and the others; he knew everything that was going on in Fitz's world. Still, he played dumb.

"What do you mean, they tied you up? Are you all right?"

"I am now. But I've been really afraid, Dylan! What am I supposed to do? What do you want me to do?"

"Is Jim there?" he asked then.

"No, he isn't!"

"Get him to call me when he gets back," he said.

"Dylan! What's going on?"

But he had disconnected the call.

There was something—a noise—some small sound behind me. Jim was standing at the foot of the steps, hair damp, towel in one hand and his shoes in the other. He was looking at me with an expression that might have been reproach.

"What the fuck's going on?" I demanded.

"Is that my phone?"

He took a step forward, took it from my hand, fiddled with the buttons. I thought he was going to say something, shout back at me, but instead he held the phone up to his ear.

"Yeah, it's me," he said, as the call connected. "I know. Where are you? . . . Yes, you know you can . . ."

He looked up at me then. I could hear Dylan's voice through the phone but couldn't make out the words.

"She's all right. No, of course not. It's what we said, yeah? When? . . . All right. I'll work something out. Okay. Bye for now." All through this he didn't take his eyes off me. All my righteous anger at having been somehow set up, made a fool of, was dissolving into feelings of unqualified guilt at picking up his phone in the first place. And what made it all worse was that he was standing in my cabin, his jeans unbuttoned, his hair wet.

"Genevieve—" he said.

"No," I said. "This is all wrong. Why?"

He shook his head.

"You're using me," I said.

"No."

"You're using me to get to Dylan."

"How? Don't be ridiculous. Who did he phone just now, you or me?"

That hurt, more than if he'd slapped me across the face. "You shit. You complete bastard." Tears stung my eyes, my hands balling into fists.

"Genevieve. I didn't mean it like that . . ."

"Why doesn't anybody ever tell me the truth about what's going on?"

I couldn't stand to look at him anymore. I went back to the bedroom, pushed the door shut behind me. But he caught it, caught me by one arm, pulled me to him.

"Don't walk away," he said.

His face was close to mine. I could feel his breath on my cheek.

I struggled against him, but he held me tighter, bruising my arm. "Let me go!"

He released his grip. And I stood there like an idiot, looking up at his impassive face, tears of fury and misery pouring down my hot cheeks. "You didn't tell me you knew Dylan," I said, sobs catching every other word.

"Neither did you." He was so calm, so infuriating, I wanted to smack him.

"You knew about me and Dylan. You knew all along . . ."

"I didn't know how you felt about him."

"Did he tell you about me?"

He nodded.

"What did he say?"

"He asked me to look after you."

"What?" I said. I was so angry I could barely get the words out. "When?"

"He called me when he heard about Caddy's body being found here. He asked me to keep an eye out for you, because he knew—I mean, he thought that things might get difficult for you. After that he turned his phone off and went out of contact."

"Why?"

He looked at me for a moment, as if debating how much of this he was prepared to share with me. "He's done this before. When things get a bit tricky, he turns his phone off. He's a pain in the ass sometimes, you know that, don't you?"

"So you came here and thought it would be a good idea to fuck me, yeah? Is that what you thought he meant by looking after me? Give me something to take my mind off him?"

"It wasn't like that."

"Why are you here? What do you want from me?"

He looked at me and didn't reply at first, then he ran a hand through his hair and turned away from me, took a few steps. Then he seemed to find the most appropriate answer.

"I was looking for Dylan. When he turned his phone off after he told me about Caddy, I thought he might have still been in touch with you."

"I don't understand. He just called your phone, didn't he?"

"He's only called me twice since that day. Both times, he was in a public place, somewhere busy, impossible to get a trace. The rest of the time his phone's off."

"Well, I think that means he doesn't want to talk to you, doesn't it?"

"Or you, it seems," he said.

I bit my lip and glared at him.

"Genevieve . . ." He touched my bare arm, running his hand up under the sleeve of my T-shirt to my shoulder.

"Please don't touch me," I said, pulling away.

"Look," he said, "he always thinks he knows what he's doing, right? He does things his way. As hard as I try to help him out, try to get him to play by the rules, he's always done it like this. Despite that, I trust him, and you should, too."

He took a step toward me again. I wanted to move away but I couldn't. There was something different in his eyes now. I wanted to believe every word, but it was so hard.

"You should have told me all this before," I said, trying not to sound imploring. I wanted to sound cold. But instead, through sniffs and tears, it sounded weak.

"I didn't think this was going to happen."

"What?"

"You know what I'm talking about; don't play games."

I raised an eyebrow at him. "You still should have told me that you knew Dylan."

"I don't have to tell you about anything, much less something related to an investigation."

"Oh, seriously! You're investigating Dylan? Think it's a good idea to be fucking me, then, do you?"

"Of course it's not a good idea!"

"So—what? You were just going to wait for Dylan to show up, and then take off and leave me behind?"

"I hadn't thought that far ahead."

I grabbed my jeans from the chair and pulled them on roughly. They were still damp but I didn't care.

"Where are you going?" he asked.

"Just—just leave me alone."

He caught up with me just as I was about to go up the steps to the wheelhouse. Both arms around my waist. He pulled me back, pulled me tight against him, and as I struggled he held me tighter.

"Genevieve," he said, his voice just a whisper against the back of my neck. "Don't."

I felt myself melting, softening against him. He held me. And I turned in the circle of his arms and put my arms around his neck and rested my face into his chest, breathing him in. He pulled my T-shirt out where it had been tucked into my jeans and pressed his hands into the small of my back. Without thinking about what I was doing, I slid my hands under the waistband of his jeans, pulling him closer. His mouth was an inch away from mine, his warm breath on me. I could have moved a fraction toward him and our mouths would have met. But I wasn't about to give in. He leaned toward me. I moved back—just slightly. He hesitated, his breath quickening. I could feel him, hard against my body. Inside his jeans, my hand squeezed his ass, my nails digging in. Then he moved one of his hands from my back to my neck, holding my head so I couldn't pull away.

He pushed me back, stumbling, against the steps. My hand felt for a step I could perch on as he pulled my jeans down, then his. When he pushed inside me, I gasped, my head back against the top step. For a second the thrill of it held me steady, but there was something wrong with this position, frustrating—I kept slipping down. I pushed him, and when he didn't respond immediately I pushed him harder, pushed him away so I could turn around, kick my jeans off and kneel on the third step, presenting him with my rear view at exactly the right height. He didn't pause but slid inside me, gentler this time, but for just a second. And then it was hard and fast and powerful, pushing me against the steps with his whole body. It didn't take very long. When he came inside me, he let out a sound against the back of my neck, through gritted teeth.

For a moment neither of us moved. Nothing but the sound of his breathing against my hair, the pounding of my blood through my ears.

He slid away from me. I turned awkwardly on the stairs, my knee aching from where it had been scraped against the siding by the force of him driving into me. He pulled his jeans back up.

He held out his hand to me. "Come with me."

I took his hand and he led me back to bed, took his clothes off again and climbed in beside me, pulling me close. For a long time we kissed and didn't speak. Eventually his hand between my thighs made me forget everything: the anger, the million questions buzzing around my head, the sound of Dylan's voice on the other end of Jim's phone.

Over our heads the skylight showed clouds across the deep blue of the sky; white clouds, then gray . . . darkening to an ominous black that threatened rain.

Jim was holding my hand against his chest. I thought he might be falling asleep. I thought about getting up, getting dressed.

"You're still angry," he said. He was stroking his thumb against the back of my hand. "I can tell. You're so tense."

"I feel like everyone's been using me," I said.

"I prefer to think that we're just helping each other out."

I moved, sat up in bed, hugged my knees. I wanted to be able to see his face. "Why did Dylan call you to tell you about Caddy? I don't understand. Didn't you know already?"

He took a deep breath, ran his hand over his forehead. "I'm not—well—I'm not part of the investigation team."

"So who are you, then? You mean you're not police?"

"I am a police officer. I just work on different things, and I'm Met Police, not Kent."

This didn't make sense. "How come you're allowed to show up and interfere with an investigation you're not a part of? Don't you have to do what you're told?"

He smiled. "I'm not, strictly speaking, interfering. And if you're going to get pedantic, I'm not actually on duty at the moment."

"Does Dylan have something to do with Caddy's death? Is that why he's not answering his phone?"

He didn't answer.

"He wouldn't do that," I said. "He wouldn't have hurt Caddy."

There was something in his expression, something that he tried to hide.

"You think he killed her?" I said.

"I don't think he killed her," he replied. "But I don't know why he's been out of contact for so long. Do you know?"

I shrank back a little, unprepared for the focus to be turned in my direction. "I have no idea."

"You knew Dylan from the Barclay," he said. "You must have some feeling about what he was like."

"Dylan was different: he wasn't like the others. He was kind. Well, he was kind to me, anyway."

Jim grinned. "I've never heard him described quite like that."

"Well, maybe you don't know him as well as you think you do."

He must have noticed the edge in my voice because he sat up then. He didn't pull the duvet up around himself, and he was sitting there, on my bed, arrogant in his nakedness, totally at ease with his body.

"I don't want to fight with you anymore," he said.

"We shouldn't talk about it, then."

"I'm just trying to keep you safe, Genevieve."

"Bullshit you are. You're trying to find Dylan. And I don't need anyone to keep me safe, thank you very much."

He laughed at that, and it stung.

"Another thing that's been bothering me. How do you know Dylan? I mean—he doesn't exactly move in police circles, does he?"

He got out of bed, abruptly, and pulled his clothes on. I watched him, wondering if I'd hit a nerve. He didn't answer right away, which made me think he'd lied to me and he wasn't friends with Dylan after all. What if he was trying to find him because he was going to arrest him? What if that was why Dylan was keeping away from me? Was Jim using me as bait?

"We were at school together," he said. "We've gone our separate ways over the years, but we're still friends."

"Where?" I said, trying to catch him out. Not that I knew the answer. "Where were you at school?"

"Don't, Genevieve," he answered. "You're just going to have to trust me."

"Why should I trust you, when you kept something that important from me?"

He looked me straight in the eye. "You're still keeping important things from me," he said, "and I trust you."

I stared at him, furious.

"I'd better go," he said, pulling his socks on.

I didn't answer.

"You know what your trouble is?" he said, looking back over his shoulder at me briefly and then turning back to pull on his other sock.

He was clearly going to tell me anyway, so I didn't see the need to respond.

"You don't have a clue what you're mixed up in. You're

flitting around the edge of this—mess—not knowing just how fucking dangerous it is. You think you can take care of yourself, but actually, you have no idea. No fucking idea."

I glared at him. He was right: I had no fucking idea—but that was because nobody ever fucking told me anything. A few moments later he was putting his shoes on in the galley, and after that there was a bang as he pulled the door of the wheel-house shut behind him.

Chapter Thirty-Four

It would have been easy just to go to bed, to hide under the covers and cry, for what was left of the day if I needed to. But instead I went and had a shower, got dressed, and tried to get a fire going. It gave me something to concentrate on, with my shaking hands, then sitting in front of the open door, watching it in case it died down, feeding it until it grew strong enough for me to build the wood around it. And then I shut the door to the stove and sat looking at the flames and the logs starting to glow.

I was still sitting there an hour later when I heard a noise outside, and a few moments later a knock at the door of the wheelhouse.

It was Malcolm, complete with his grubby canvas bag of tools. I looked at it doubtfully.

"I thought I'd take a look at your generator," he said.

"I've got tools, you know," I said indignantly.

"Yeah. So—er—what happened to your new fella? Saw him earlier, didn't look too happy."

"Oh, he's fine. He had to go to work."

Malcolm gave me a look that said he didn't believe me. He lifted the hatch in the wheelhouse that accessed the engine and peered down into the engine space.

"The batteries should be all charged," he said. "Then once I reconnect them you can transfer over—here—like this . . ."

Elizabeth Haynes

I looked and tried to pay attention while he showed me a series of buttons and switches.

"The generator will run off your fuel supply so that'll go down quicker than normal. But you won't need to use it all the time, like, during the day and stuff. You've still got gas bottles for the stove, haven't you?"

I nodded. "And I've got the wood-burning stove."

"Exactly. Electricity is overrated," he said with a smile.

He went back to tinkering with the generator, connecting wires and tubes and bashing things. I clambered over him and went down into the cabin.

"I need to turn the power off," Malcolm shouted down the steps.

"All right," I called back.

The main cabin was nice and warm now. I sat in front of it, hugging my knees, trying not to think about Dylan and Jim, but thinking about nothing else. I'd thought about Dylan every day since that last time, but not like this. I wanted him to come back for me. I wanted him to be here, with me. I wanted it so badly it was like an ache, like a void inside me.

And Jim—what was I supposed to do about Jim? The thought of him made me shiver. There was something irresistible about him, some force that made me lose my senses and want him, no matter what he said or did. And he was maddening at the same time.

I would call him tomorrow, once I'd had a chance to catch up on some sleep and get my head straightened out.

"Genevieve!" Malcolm shouted from the deck.

"What?"

"It's all connected." He came down into the cabin.

I didn't turn around. It must have looked a bit odd, me sitting there on the floor facing the stove.

"You all right?" he said.

I didn't answer and he came to sit on the sofa. "Gen? What's the matter?"

"It's been a tough day," I said.

"What happened? Is it that policeman? He been bothering you?"

"No. He's been fine, Malcolm, honest."

"Maybe you should go and stay with him for a bit, then, till it all quiets down again."

"I'm not leaving the boat."

"No one else been around—you know, like before?"

"No."

"I haven't seen anybody," he said, quickly.

I looked at him then, turned my head slowly. He was sitting on the edge of my sofa, hands hanging between his knees. He looked wired. His left knee was jiggling up and down.

"Malcolm?"

"What?"

"What's happened?"

"Nothing, nothing." He looked almost afraid, just for a moment.

"Hey," I said.

He looked back at me. There was something in his expression; I should have been able to tell what it was. But I was too tired and too numb to think hard enough about it.

"I just wanted to say thanks, for helping with everything."

"Okay," he said.

We stood awkwardly in the cabin, Malcolm shifting his weight from one leg to the other. "You know, I used to live in London," he said at last.

"I didn't know that," I said.

"Before I met Josie. I lived all over, but for a while I lived in Leytonstone. In a squat. Well, digs. I guess it was a kind of a squat, anyway, since we didn't pay anyone any rent. But still."

"What were you doing in London?" I asked, wondering where this was going.

"Oh, this and that, you know—some construction work, some plastering sometimes when someone would take me on. Just earning enough for beer, really. It was all right."

He looked at me sideways.

"What is it, Malcolm? What are you getting at?"

"Well, I knew of this Fitz. The one you mentioned, the one who was your boss at that club."

"You knew Fitz?"

"I never said that. I said I knew *of* him. Some guys I knew from the pub, they was talking about stuff one night, where to score drugs mostly, and they was complaining about the quality of the gear on the streets at the moment, and they said it was because Fitz had moved on to something else."

"Something else?"

"Like he wasn't supplying anymore. Or he'd moved on to supplying different gear."

"Oh," I said, sitting back. "Doesn't mean it was the same Fitz, though."

"He used to hang around with this guy, Ian Gray. He was a hard guy, like his protection, you know? His muscle."

"Gray?"

"Big guy, tattoo on his neck. He was missing half his earlobe."

That was Gray, all right. No wonder Malcolm had been so interested in hearing about life at the Barclay.

"I should have said something earlier," he said.

"Yes, you should," I said.

"I was thinking—you know—I might be able to call a few people, find out who it is who's putting the pressure on you. Tell them to lay off."

"Are you kidding? If you know of Fitz, then you know these people aren't going to lay off just because some nice guy calls them and asks them to."

"Yeah, all right!" he said, affronted. "I'm not a complete moron. I just meant—you know—I could do some digging for you."

"I somehow doubt that's going to help," I said. "But thanks anyway. They might just get bored."

"Or they might come along tonight and kill you."

"If they were going to do that, they would've done it by now," I said.

"Yeah, you say that. But they never got their hands on that package of yours, did they?"

"No," I said.

"I'd better go," he said, heading for the steps. "You just shout for me if you need anything."

"Are we still going to move the boat?" I said. "How about tomorrow?"

"Sure, yeah," he said. He was already at the door, and moments later he'd waved goodbye and disappeared.

I looked at my phone and thought about calling Jim. I sat in front of the stove for a while, allowing the warmth from it to take the chill out of my bones. I couldn't stop thinking about Caddy. I kept coming back to Caddy's last moments, how she must have felt. Had it hurt? Had she had time to feel pain, fear? Had she known she was about to die? And all the time I was so close by—and I'd had no idea she was even there.

I got to my feet and stretched. Everything felt achy, my neck so stiff I could hardly turn my head. I turned off the lights and locked the wheelhouse door and went to bed.

Chapter Thirty-Five

I woke up early and lay still in the graying light from the skylight, wondering what had woken me. And then the scrabble on the deck above, and the cry of a gull, fading as it took off. I tried to go back to sleep but couldn't, and the boat felt too quiet to be lying still, waiting for morning.

I got up, dressed, and lit the woodstove while I was waiting for the kettle to boil, the crackling of the logs keeping me company while I made coffee. I looked for something to eat for breakfast and made a piece of toast with the last of the bread that was on the verge of being stale. I definitely needed to go shopping later.

I wondered if there was anything I could do to the boat that didn't involve power tools this early in the morning, and I thought about the black plastic bag full of fabric I'd thrown into the storage compartment when I was tidying up for the party. Maybe I could make some curtains for the portholes, something to cover over those black circles that had never bothered me much before.

When I finished my coffee, I put the mug in the sink and went to retrieve the bag of fabric. I opened the hatch and in the darkness crawled down the three steps, along the pallets to the bow, until I was sitting next to the box. I pushed the box with my finger. It moved. I pushed it again, and it tilted.

No, no! That wasn't right at all.

Without a second's thought I grabbed hold of the box and tipped it upside down, the contents spilling all over my lap, over the pallet, some falling through the gap into the smooth curved space of the hull.

The false bottom of the box came away, and with it—nothing.

It was gone. The package was gone.

I pushed the empty box to one side and sat there in the semi-darkness, trying to think. My brain felt fried with exhaustion, fear making me irrational. Who had been in here? I tried to think when I'd last checked the hatch before Saturday night—whether I'd actually felt the box or just seen it, like last time when Jim was here, and thought it was fine. It was Thursday, I was pretty sure, and today was Monday, so it might have been empty for several days. Could it have been the police? If they'd found it, why the hell hadn't they arrested me?

I crawled out of the bow again and shut the door firmly behind me. I went back to the main cabin, found Dylan's phone and dialed the number. I didn't expect it to ring, and I got the same voice telling me that the phone was off. Damn him!

I paced up and down in the cabin, waiting for dawn, wondering what to do next. Dylan had given me the package to look after, and it was gone. Someone had taken it. Someone had come onto the boat, maybe when I'd been at the police station, or maybe last night when I'd been sleeping, and taken it. I'd let Dylan down. It was all a mess, a complete hideous mess.

I thought again about phoning Jim, but what would that achieve? I couldn't tell him the package was missing, because to do so would be to admit to its existence, to implicate myself in whatever it contained.

I wanted to get off the boat. It was daylight now. I needed fresh air, to be outside in the real world where shitty things like missing packages full of cocaine did not exist. It would be a good idea to go shopping and get some food. I couldn't live on stale bread forever. Anyway, there was nothing left on the boat that needed my protection.

I took my jacket and hat and went up to the parking lot. Cameron came out of the office. I didn't want to talk to him but he waved to me and shouted hello. "How's it going?" I asked.

"Not bad," he said. "What's this Malc was telling me about you going for a trip?"

"Yeah. I just thought I'd try taking the boat out for a bit."

He stood there, a full head taller than me, kicking at a tuft of grass that was growing up through the asphalt. "Just be careful out there, won't you?"

"Oh, don't worry. Malcolm's going to help me. I wouldn't go out on my own."

"Technically you can't take the boat out without a license. It's really easy to run aground," he said, "especially if the tide's on the way out. And it's not easy steering a boat the size of yours. I know Malcolm thinks he knows what he's doing, but your boat's fifteen feet longer than his."

"Malcolm's licensed, isn't he? And he's taken the *Scaris-brick Jean* out for trips?"

"Not for a while."

"Is there something you're not telling me?" I said with a smile.

"No, no," he said. He looked shifty. "I just—I think you need to be careful, that's all."

"Of Malcolm?"

Cameron's cheeks were coloring. "No, Malc's all right, you know that. He just . . . sometimes he does things without thinking through the consequences. You get my drift?"

"Would you help me move the boat, then?"

"If you really wanted to, sure. But I don't see why you need to go anywhere."

"It's a long story," I said. "Really, it's just because—I don't know—it seems a bit silly having a boat and never going out on the river. And I want to have a look upstream before the winter comes. That's why."

"Have the police been hassling you?"

The dramatic change of topic was unsettling. He was standing there with his back to the office door, arms folded across his chest. I wondered what this was leading to.

"No, not really. Why?"

"I saw them come to see you, day before yesterday. Those two from London."

"Do you know them, then?"

"No, they called at the office. They were asking after you."

I looked at my feet. "They were okay. That body I found—turns out she was from London. They're doing the investigation."

"Right."

"Look," I said, "I'm going to go shopping. Want me to get anything for you?"

"Just that there's been a lot of strange things happening since then, hasn't there?"

"What do you mean?"

"Like the cable to the light being cut."

I stared at him for a moment. I couldn't think what to say, and the conversation was taking an awkward turn.

"Just saying," he said. "Thanks. Don't need anything." He turned and went back into the office.

I got my bike out of the storage room and pedaled forcefully out of the gate and up the hill.

The supermarket was just opening, a small crowd of early birds gathered around the entrance, waiting for the shutters to rise. I wandered up and down the aisles distractedly, bought the bare minimum of provisions and stuffed my purchases into my backpack.

When I got back to the marina, it was deserted. The office was closed; even the door to the laundry room, usually hanging ajar, was firmly shut.

I stepped aboard the *Aunty Jean* to see if Malcolm and Josie were home, but their hatch was locked. The tide was going out, a dark tide, the brown, silty water caressing the hulls of our boats.

That was it, then, I was all on my own. I went back to the *Revenge of the Tide* and stoked the remains of the fire that was smoldering in the stove. While I waited for it to warm up I looked once more for the package. I started in the storage space, with my flashlight this time, opening boxes and moving them methodically from one side to the other, lifting things out of the way, taking it slowly, to make sure—of what? That I hadn't accidentally misplaced it, that I hadn't absentmindedly moved it myself?

It was pointless. The package was gone.

Nevertheless I kept looking, organizing as I did so, putting things into some kind of order so that when I next came in here I could find what I was looking for. The bag of fabric and the cans of paint near the door mocked me and I decided that it would be better if I just kept busy. My hands were trembling slightly. Not good for sewing: painting was a much better option.

By the time I'd emerged again, the boat was sitting on the mud. I went to look at the spare room. It was just as I'd left it: two coats of paint. The walls looked pale and almost transparent in the gray afternoon light.

I got the paint and brushes out of the hatch and levered the lid off the can of paint with my gooey screwdriver. There wasn't a lot of paint left. Even if the cans claimed to be the same color, on wooden siding like this the slightest variation in shade would show. I would start with the berth; that way if I ran out of paint I could always do the final coat of the walls with a different can and it wouldn't look as odd as if one wall were a slightly different shade.

The rest of the can just about lasted for the berth. By the time I'd finished I was wiping the inside of the can with my brush, dragging every last drip of paint from the sides.

When I was washing the brushes in the galley sink, I heard noises outside. I went up the steps and opened the wheelhouse door. Malcolm was on the deck of the *Scarisbrick Jean*. He saw me and ducked out of sight. I didn't have to ask where he'd been. He looked as though he'd had an argument with a lawn mower, his scalp showing pink through the short gray spikes.

"Malcolm!" I shouted. "I like your hair."

His face popped up again and looked so depressed I thought he might actually cry. "Never again," he said.

I went down the gangplank and over to the *Scarisbrick Jean* so I wouldn't have to shout. He stayed where he was, one foot on the step down into the cabin, right hand on the roof.

"Is this Josie's revenge for the fact that you didn't notice her hair the other day?"

"Let's not mention that," he said. He was gripping the roof of the cabin so hard that his knuckles were white.

"How is Josie?" I asked. "Does she have a hangover?"

"Yeah. She's having a nap."

"Oh," I said. Then I added, "Is everything all right, Malcolm?"

"Yeah," he said.

I didn't believe him.

"Sounds like you're a bit busy today, then . . ."

"I am a bit, yeah."

"Maybe we could move the boat tomorrow?"

"Maybe, yeah."

I tried not to look disappointed, but lack of sleep and general misery at the situation was starting to get to me. Malcolm was watching me intently, his body blocking the doorway, his whole bony posture rigid.

"All right, then," I said. "Tell Josie I said hi."

I left him and went back up the gangplank to the *Revenge.* When I turned to shut the wheelhouse door, he was still standing exactly as I'd left him, fixed and motionless, staring straight ahead.

The boat was quiet, and still.

I went back to washing the brushes, and when they were clean, I stood them on their ends in an empty jam jar to dry. I should really go back to bed, I thought, try to sleep for a little while. I felt numb and empty. I felt as if I were waiting.

The sound of the cell phone ringing, loud and discordant, made me jump. The phone was on the shelf behind the dinette, under some papers. It took me two rings to find it.

GARLAND.

"Hello?"

"Genevieve?"

The relief, at hearing his voice. "Yes! Dylan?"

"Yeah. You need to get out, now. Right now."

"What?"

"Get off the boat. Take your phone. Call Jim—understand?"

"What's going on?"

"They've been watching you. But they've gone, I don't know how long for. Fitz is on his way to meet them. Get off the boat. NOW!"

Chapter Thirty-Six

I grabbed my fleece, the keys, and my two phones. Jumped up the steps to the wheelhouse, locked the door behind me, as if that was going to stop anyone who wanted to get in. I ran across the dock to the storage room and unlocked my bike.

Pulling it from the rack, I heard sounds from outside. I stopped what I was doing. I hid behind the door of the storage room in case someone was coming inside. Snatches of conversation. Through the crack in the hinge I could see two men standing at the closed door of the office. One of them had a cell phone in his hand.

I didn't recognize either of them. They were both wearing jeans, one with a gray sweater, the other with a black leather jacket. Both of them were over six foot and quite wide, with standard "enforcer" haircuts. They were engaged in some fervent conversation that I couldn't make out. The bigger one, with the leather jacket, seemed to be giving the one in the gray sweater a telling off. In between the verbal assaults and finger-pointing, he would rock back on his heels slightly so he could see around the corner of the office—down toward the water. Toward the *Revenge*.

I didn't hear the phone ring but just then the bigger man held the phone to his ear, ordering the other into silence with a raised finger.

I held my breath. I still couldn't hear what he was saying, just the tone of it. Urgent. Angry.

He ended the call, shaking his head with frustration. The gray sweater was asking him something. More head-shaking.

Without any further discussion they turned and started to walk away from the office. I shrank back against the wall of the storage room, into the shadows, hoping that they would not hear my breathing, my heart thumping.

As they passed, I heard one of them say, "He needs to fucking decide, that's all. I've fucking had it with being pissed about . . ."

And, getting softer as they walked around the side of the building, the other: ". . . been here for days already . . ."

I stood there for a moment. My legs were shaking, and my hands. I looked around the storage room, which was just as it always was—boxes that belonged to Roger and Sally, a chest freezer, an old tent packed into canvas bags that had been here so long nobody really knew who owned it, and, in the corner, Cameron's ancient Triumph motorbike—he was supposed to be fixing it, but none of us had ever seen him go near it.

The familiarity of it all brought reassurance and my legs were starting to feel steadier. I peered through the gap in the hinge of the door—nobody in sight. I couldn't hear anything other than the distant traffic. I moved to the doorway, then out onto the rough path outside. No one there. The door at the bottom was shut, the office in darkness. Beyond, the boats lay silent, sleeping on their muddy beds.

The men had gone to the left. I followed them, crept around the corner of the building in case they were just on the other side. Nothing. I went to the corner. The parking lot was empty.

They had gone.

I went back to the storage room and got my bike. For a moment it crossed my mind that I could go back to the boat, collect some clothes and a few other things that I might need. *Get off the boat*, he'd said. *NOW!*

I biked up the hill toward the main road, looking out all the while for the men, for parked cars. But until I got to the road there was nothing, no one.

I got as far as the castle, the outer wall clad in fiery Virginia creeper like lava pouring from the battlements. I carried my bike up the steps and into the castle grounds, and found a bench. Took both phones out of my pocket. I wanted to call Dylan again, but something told me that his phone would be turned off. Instead, on my phone, I called Jim.

It took him awhile to answer.

"Hello, Genevieve."

"Hi." He sounded as if he was still angry with me.

"Dylan called me."

"What did he say?"

"He told me to get off the boat. He said they were watching me, and that I should get off the boat and call you. So, I'm calling you."

"Where are you?"

"Rochester Castle. I've got my bike. Can I . . . can I meet you somewhere?"

There was a pause, a muffled noise as though he was holding the phone against his shoulder.

"Gen, I'm working; it's going to be difficult to get away. Are you safe right now? Are you sure you weren't followed?"

"I didn't see anyone. There's nobody here. Nobody suspicious, anyway," I said, looking out at the couple walking across the green, pushing a stroller. By the steps to the castle, an elderly couple sitting on a bench. The woman was laughing, clutching her chest. A few students with matching backpacks were sprawled on the grass. I could hear faintly the tinny noise of music, played through a cell phone.

"I'm going to send someone to get you, all right?"

"You don't need to do that. I'm all right here, there's loads of people," I said. "Jim, what the fuck's going on?"

"I don't know for sure. Just keep your head down, I'll get to you as soon as I can. Keep your phone with you. Stay where you can see other people, and, if you need to, call 999. All right?"

"Sure," I said.

He hung up.

I sat on the bench, feeling the beginnings of righteous anger bubbling up inside me. Fury at being told what to do, where to go.

Well, safe or not, I wasn't going to stay here waiting for my hero to come and rescue me. I got back on the bike and pedaled down the hill, into the flow of traffic.

Chapter Thirty-Seven

Rochester High Street was deserted, streamers fluttering in the narrow space between the historic buildings the way they always were, heralding the next festival or mourning the end of the last. My bike tires bumped over the brick road.

I propped the bike up against the side of the Dot café, ordered a latte and a bacon sandwich, and sat at one of the metal tables outside, tucking the bike behind my seat. It was breezy and I was the only one sitting out here, but it gave me some fresh air and time to think.

I hadn't told Dylan that his package was gone. I wondered why he hadn't asked me to bring it with me. Maybe he already knew. I couldn't shake the feeling that he might have been on the boat and taken it back.

The waitress brought my sandwich outside to me and I ate it, big mouthfuls that filled my cheeks. I hadn't realized how hungry I was until my stomach growled and churned at the prospect of hot food. It was delicious, and hardly touched the sides, as my dad used to say. I washed it down with the coffee. I kept looking up and down the high street, half-expecting to see the two guys who'd been at the marina.

I realized my phone was ringing. I pulled it out of my pocket; the display told me it was Jim Carling.

"Hello?"

"Gen, it's me. Where are you?"

"Rochester High Street. Where are you?"

"I'm still in London. I'm coming to get you now, but it will take me awhile to get there. Are you okay?"

"I'm fine."

"You could wait for me at the police station."

"No, thanks," I said. I could think of better places to hang around.

He sighed as though I was being difficult.

"Is my boat in danger?"

"What?"

"Dylan told me to get off the boat. Are they going to torch it or something?"

"No, of course not," he said, far too quickly.

"You mean you don't know."

He didn't answer right away. Then: "I've got to go. Don't go back to the boat, all right? Promise me?"

"Would you please tell me what the fuck is going on?"

"I don't know, all right? If I knew, I would tell you."

"Right."

"I'll see you in a bit, okay? I'll get there as soon as I can."

I walked up the high street toward the cathedral, pushing my bike beside me, wondering how I was going to fill the next few hours. I was at the end of the high street. The bridge stretched out in front of me, traffic flowing across it toward Strood, a train rattling on its way to London. I was finding it hard to think straight. Everything in me wanted to go back to the boat. I had a longing for it now, a need to be back there, as though I'd been away for months instead of half an hour. A need to go home. I could jump on my bike and be there in ten minutes, maybe less.

The doors to the Crown were open, inviting me in. I thought about going inside and getting wasted; that was another option. Or I could bike a little further down the Esplanade, to the playground and the gardens, sit on a bench or something and watch the river. I wouldn't be able to see the marina from there, but at least I would be close to it.

I got on my bike and was just turning into the gap in the low wall to the gardens in the shadow of the castle when Dylan's phone buzzed in my pocket. I coasted over to an empty bench, leaned my bike against it, and answered.

"Hello?"

"What the fuck do you think you're doing?"

It was Dylan.

"You told me to get off the boat!"

"I didn't tell you to fart around downtown where anyone can see you. Have you completely lost it?"

He was watching me. I looked around me, as though he would be standing right there. There was no sign of him. "Where are you?"

"Never mind. Where the fuck's Jim?"

"He said he's working. In London. He's going to come and pick me up."

I heard him sigh heavily. There was a pause.

"Dylan! I really need to talk to you."

"Go back to the road. There's a white van. See it?"

I looked back to the Esplanade. There was a huge oak tree between me and the road, and behind it I could see the rear end of a white van. "Yes."

"Fucking hurry up, then!" he said, and disconnected the call.

I jumped on the bike and cycled back to the road. By the time I got there, the van's side door had opened. Dylan was in the driver's seat. He didn't smile, or look at me. His eyes were watching the road, and looking to the mirror to see what was coming up behind us. Through the half-open window, he said, "Put the bike in the back. Get in, shut the door, hold on to something."

I did as I was told, lifting the bike awkwardly over the step and pushing it into the dark space. There was nothing to secure it to, so I laid it down on its side. Shut the door with a slam. Before I could even sit down on the bare wooden floor, the van was moving.

I sat down quickly and held the bike by its saddle as it slid toward the van's rear doors. It was dark in here, a chink of light showing around the door hinges. The van turned sharply to the left and then to the right. I tried to think, my heart thumping. It must be the little traffic circle. We were heading toward the marina. On the straight road I shuffled back against the rear of the cab, found a wooden rail to hold on to. One hand on the bike, the other on the rail, I braced myself for the sharp turn at the end of the road, the steep hill up toward Borstal village, the bike heavy and desperate to throw itself at the back doors.

I'd caught only a glimpse of him. He looked rough, rougher than he used to after several nights of too much vodka and no sleep. I was surprised by the force of excitement I felt at seeing him again.

I heard his voice, raised above the rattle of the engine, through the wooden partition separating the back of the van from the cab. "You all right back there?"

"Yes. Where are we going?"

"Not far. I'll stop in a minute."

At the top of the hill the van slowed. I could hear the click-click of the turn signal. As I'd expected, the van swung to the right. Still heading toward the marina. Slight downhill, and then up again. In the darkness I pictured the same route I'd cycled this morning. Any minute now he'd slow down and turn right.

But the van didn't slow. In fact it accelerated slightly, with a crunch as he shifted up a gear. Where were we going? I tried to think about what was beyond the turn for the marina, but I never went this way—there was a road that led to Wouldham village, a winding road through the fields that snaked under the Medway bridge and followed the curve of the river for miles, heading toward Maidstone.

Then, abruptly, a turn to the right.

It caught me by surprise. I'd relaxed my grip on the wooden rail and I gasped as the bike and I swung around, the tire banging off the side of the van, my foot out to brace against it as I slid across the splintery wooden floor. The van was moving slowly now, bumping over potholes and then over some sort of bump that felt like a mountain and ground against something metallic at the back as we crawled over it.

The van stopped. The engine shuddered and cut out. I heard the driver's door open and slam shut with a hollow clang. Then the side door of the van slid open and I blinked in the sudden light. He filled the doorway, brightness behind him. I let go of the bike and shuffled to the open door, intending to put my arms around him, but by the time I got there he'd turned and sat on the edge, his back to me.

I sat next to him. My legs dangled over the side; his reached the rocky rubble on which we were parked.

"Where are we?"

All around us were bushes, trees; through a gap in them I could see the river. I could hear the traffic on the highway bridge just as I could from the deck of the *Revenge*, but I couldn't see it until I jumped down from the van and picked my way through the uneven ground to the gap in the bushes.

The bridge rose up, mountainous, to my right, one of the pillars just a few yards away. The traffic roared overhead.

"Stay out of sight," Dylan said.

Tearing my eyes away from the soaring height of the bridge, I realized where we were—on the bend in the river past the marina. I could see the back of the *Revenge of the Tide*, the edge of the *Scarisbrick Jean*. If I went a little further, I would be able to see the whole boat, and most of the marina. A few steps out onto the muddy shore, and I might be able to see right up to the parking lot and the office. A thin dock made out of pallets held together with bits of rope stretched out across the mud. I remembered the tracks I'd seen in the mud leading to the porthole. This was where whoever it was had started their walk to my boat. It must have been Dylan, then.

I saw movement out of the corner of my eye. On the deck of the *Scarisbrick Jean*, Malcolm's shorn gray head popped up and then went below again. I moved quickly back into the shelter of the bushes and turned toward the van. He'd driven it through a gap and parked it in a space tucked away in between two trees. From the rocky, unpaved road, the van would have been invisible; from the northern bank of the river, it would have been possible to see the back of it sticking out, but little more than that.

"Is this where you've been all this time?" I asked.

He shook his head. "On and off. I've been here solidly for the last couple of nights. But I had to go back to London, too, last week. And I was over there for a bit," he said, pointing directly across the river to Cuxton. The public waste site was on the opposite bank and I could just about make out the line of cars waiting to dump broken furniture, hedge clippings, and whatever else into the Dumpsters.

I sat next to him again. His shoulders were bowed, and when I looked at his hands, gripping his knees, I realized they were shaking. I put my hand over his, squeezed it. His skin was cold, rough to the touch, the knuckles scarred and dirty. I looked at his face, but he was staring resolutely out across the part of river we could see in the space between the greenery.

"What's going on, Dylan?" I asked quietly.

He made a noise, like a grunt of sheer hopelessness. A *Where do you want me to start?* kind of noise.

"What happened to Caddy?"

"Wrong place. Wrong time."

"What do you mean?"

"Fitz thought he had a leak. He thought Caddy was it—he was having her followed. They followed her all the way to your boat. Apparently they lost her at the marina, then she suddenly popped up in front of them—don't ask me how or why, I don't know. She started yelling. One of the morons punched her and she went down. That's what they said to Fitz when they got back to the club, anyway."

I stared at him, the thoughts spinning and whirling around my head. "You mean it was an accident?"

"No, it was them being complete fucking idiots. It was an accident that it happened near your boat. A coincidence, I guess. Apart from the fact that you invited her to your party."

It was all my fault, was what he meant. I was still processing this when I realized he was saying something else.

". . . thing is, Fitz didn't know where you were. In fact, he'd almost forgotten all about you. And then when the morons went back to the club and told him what had happened—when he'd come down from the ceiling—he started wondering what she was doing in a boatyard. And he found out you were here."

"So what?"

"So, now he thinks you and Caddy were in on some scheme together. He doesn't know what. But sooner or later his paranoia will bring him to bloody invent something. Which is why you're in big trouble."

"I thought it was the package," I said, vaguely.

He gave a short laugh. "The package? You mean the one I gave you? I don't think so. Not unless you've been waving it about."

"Dylan. Someone took it. I don't know when. I'm sure it was there on Thursday, then this morning when I looked it was gone."

He was staring at me with an amused smile on his face.

Whatever reaction I'd expected to the news that his precious package was missing, it certainly wasn't this.

"You never looked in it?" he said.

"No. Of course not. I just hid it, like you told me to."

He rubbed a hand over his scalp and sighed. "Put it this way. Whichever idiot has it will get a big shock when they finally open it."

The clouds were thickening over the bridge, moving so fast it looked as though the bridge was swaying and might fall at any minute. It was dizzying. It was starting to get dark.

"Why are you here, Dylan? If you're not here to pick up the package, what are you doing here?"

He didn't answer at first, looking out across the gray-brown river to the opposite bank, to the trees and the grass and, in the distance, the cars lining up to dump their garbage.

"I'm here because of you, of course," he said, so softly that I wasn't even sure I'd heard him.

"Me?"

"I was watching out for you."

My first reaction was to blurt out that he hadn't been doing a very good job, considering the number of times I'd felt threatened and afraid in the last few days, but I bit my cheek instead. "Does Fitz know you're here?" I asked at last.

"Of course not."

"Where does he think you are, then?" I asked, remembering how Dylan was like Fitz's shadow, the one out of all of them who seemed to be completely trusted, always there.

He shrugged. "Told him I was going to Spain to see Lauren."

"You won't have much of a tan when you go back."

He laughed then, a throaty laugh that ended in a cough. "I'm not much for sunbathing," he said.

"No, I guess you're not. Jim said you'd taken off."

"Did he now?" he said. "That's interesting."

"You weren't answering when he called you, just like you weren't answering me. Why did you do that?"

"I called him when I needed to."

"And why did you call me the night after Caddy died? I answered the phone and you didn't say anything."

"I wanted to check you were okay. Then Fitz turned up and I had to pretend I was listening to voice mail. It's not that easy to make private phone calls in that place, you know that. Always someone watching. Anyway," he said with finality, "I'm not going back."

"What?"

"It's a long story. But I can't carry on doing this forever. I've had enough. Like you."

"What are you going to do?"

"I'm going to go to Spain," he said. "Set up my own club, a bar, something like that."

"Sounds like a really good plan," I said. "I wish I could come with you."

He looked at me properly for the first time. His eyes were dark, and the twinkle behind them I'd always thought made him look cheeky, not dangerous like the others, wasn't there anymore.

"That wouldn't be a good idea," he said.

"Why not?"

"Fitz will come looking for me," he said. "He doesn't take kindly to people who let him down."

"Like Caddy?"

"Yeah, if you like. You need to stay where you're safe."

"I'm not exactly safe here, am I?" I said. "Why should I stay?"

I felt him tense up next to me and for a moment I wondered if I'd said completely the wrong thing. I was almost expecting him to lose his temper, shout at me.

But when he spoke again, his voice was even quieter. A calm, measured response.

"It won't be forever."

"What won't?"

"You're only in danger because of Fitz. Once he's taken care of you'll be fine."

"Taken care of?" I echoed. "What do you mean? Who's going to take care of him?"

"Christ!" he said, raising his voice for the first time. "You and your fucking questions! And to think the reason I liked you so much is that you knew when to keep quiet about shit like this!"

"I'm sick of being the only one who doesn't know what's going on! Why don't you trust me?"

"I do trust you. There's just a lot of stuff you're better off not knowing."

"What's in the package, Dylan?"

When he answered, his reply was so unexpected I thought I'd misheard him and I had to ask him to repeat it. "What?"

"Flour. It's just bags of flour. Self-rising, to be exact."

Chapter Thirty-Eight

It was starting to get dark already, the gray clouds moving overhead getting grayer and darker, until the streetlights on the opposite bank of the river came on. I was standing at the edge of the bushes, looking through the giant concrete bridge supports to the marina, to my beautiful *Revenge of the Tide*, and the smaller shape of the *Scarisbrick Jean* just beyond it.

"Why the hell would you give me bags of flour to look after?" I asked, and when he didn't answer, I stood up and walked away, trying to work it out for myself. None of it made sense. Fifty thousand pounds, to look after a package full of flour?

"I needed you to get out of London," he said.

I looked back at him, still sitting in the open side of the van.

"You wouldn't have gone," he said. "I couldn't trust Fitz to keep Arnold out of your way. You'd gone and gotten yourself implicated in Fitz's deal because you were at his house that night. And as if that wasn't bad enough, they were going to raid the club and I didn't want you to get caught up in all that shit. Without the money you wouldn't have gone. And you wouldn't have just taken the money if I'd offered it to you, would you?"

"Wait. You knew about the raid before it happened?"

He stared at me, not answering. Somewhere, the light was dawning. "You're working for the police," I said.

I remembered what Jim had said. He'd told me he'd known Dylan for years. He was a friend. And as I started to process it, I realized something else. "You're the leak. You're betraying Fitz."

"Yeah," he said.

"My God. He'll kill you."

"Yes, he will. If he finds me."

"He doesn't know yet?"

Dylan shrugged. "Maybe he does, maybe he doesn't. It was easier when he suspected Caddy, to be honest—he wasn't even thinking about me. Then, when those idiots killed her, he started looking at you."

"If you'd stayed in London, he wouldn't have had any reason to suspect you. If he finds out you aren't in Spain after all . . ."

"That's why I've been sleeping in a van for the past few nights."

"Jim told me you'd been friends for years. He said you were at school together."

"Yeah, well, what was he supposed to tell you? It's not something you can just slip into conversation."

I turned my back on him and looked over the rocky ground and the expanse of mud and water to the boats. Everything was so quiet over there, as though nothing could possibly disturb the peace. I went back to the van and sat in the doorway next to him, out of the wind.

"Why did Fitz's men want to search my boat? And why did they kill Oswald?"

"Who the fuck's Oswald?"

"Malcolm and Josie's cat. They killed him and left him on the dock next to my boat."

"No idea," he said. "Maybe one of them was allergic. When did they search your boat?"

"Nearly a week ago. Remember, I told you yesterday when you called Jim's phone? They tied me up and knocked me out. When I came to, the boat had been turned over."

"Hold on," he said. "They knocked you out?"

"Yes."

"They were only on there for a few minutes. That moron next door scared them off."

"What?"

"You mean Nicks and Tony . . . Wednesday night, right? They were supposed to ask you what you'd been talking to Caddy about, give you a gentle warning. That was all. I watched them go on board your boat, and three minutes later that guy with the frizzy hair had seen them off."

"I was out cold. Nicks hit me on the side of the head."

"Fuck's sake. No wonder they keep killing everyone and everything, it's ridiculous. Why can't they just talk to people?" He lifted his hand to my head, stroked my hair. It was the first time he'd touched me.

Three minutes later that guy with the frizzy hair had seen them off . . .

"I've got to get back to the boat," I said.

"What, now?"

"Yes, now. And you're coming with me."

"Don't think so."

"Yes, you are. I've just worked out which idiot took the package. And if we don't hurry up, they'll kill him."

Chapter Thirty-Nine

We were standing by the office, looking down toward the boats. There was no sign of life at all—nobody skulking in the shadows, watching; no one in the office, or the showers, or the laundry room. Nobody around the boats. Silence.

I called Jim again, and this time it went straight to voice mail.

"What should I do?" I asked Dylan. "Should I leave a message?"

He shrugged, all his attention focused on the boats. He started walking toward the dock.

"Jim, it's me. Just to tell you I'm with Dylan. We're going back to the boat. Come and meet us there, okay?"

There was blood on the deck of the *Scarisbrick Jean*. I saw it as Dylan and I made our way down the dock toward the *Revenge of the Tide*.

It was a smear, a long streak of brown and red, along Josie's proudly scrubbed wooden deck, as though something large or heavy had been dragged through it. It went into the cabin through the doorway that was now tightly closed and locked. And a smear, maybe a handprint, on the gunwale, as if someone with bloody hands had steadied himself while leaving the boat.

"Oh, God," I said. "Look—there's more . . ."

There was another handprint on the gunwale of the *Revenge of the Tide* as well, a smear. Spots of blood on the deck.

Dylan went first. He was different now, tense, his body solid and even bigger than it had been just a few minutes before. He was readying himself.

The lock on the door was broken off. I followed him down the steps into the cabin and they were there. The main cabin was crowded with people. It was like some kind of fucked-up Barclay reunion. Fitz, in a pair of jeans and designer sneakers, and Nicks, lounging on the sofa, making themselves at home. In the galley, Leon Arnold, leaning against the cooker, and the one who'd watched the door for him that night he'd attacked me—Markus, sitting on the table at the dinette, swinging his feet and looking cheerful.

I looked away from them.

And on the floor, his wrists tied behind his back and not moving, was Malcolm. His short gray hair was stained red. His eyes were closed.

"What have you done?" I said to Nicks, shaking with rage. "What did Malcolm ever do to you, you bastard?"

Fitz smiled at me. "He thought he had a brain. Didn't you, you little piece of shit?"

He aimed a kick at Malcolm's back and Malcolm arched away from him, groaning, an animal sound.

"Don't do that!" I said. I crouched down, touching his head, trying to see where the blood was coming from.

His eyes opened, panic in them. He whispered, "Sorry . . ."

"It's okay," I said. And added, pointlessly, "Don't worry."

"And Dylan," Fitz said. "Nice to see you. Spain not quite to your liking, was it?"

Dylan didn't answer immediately, just kept his bulk between Nicks and me, his back to the door. "You shouldn't be here, Fitz. Wherever you think your leak is, it's not here."

Fitz laughed, then Nicks, the two of them, like a couple of

school bullies. "I know exactly where my leak is, Dylan, old boy. You think I'm here for her? You seem to think I'm thick or something. Do you?"

He got to his feet, then walked toward Dylan, who stood his ground. He wouldn't try anything, surely? Dylan was at least a foot taller, and twice as wide.

"I'm here for *you*," Fitz said. His voice was almost gentle, but as he said it he dug his index finger into Dylan's ribs.

"What's he doing here?" Dylan asked, his voice still casual, casting a single glance over to the galley.

"I'm looking after my interests, mate, same as you are," said Arnold.

Dylan snorted. "What interests?"

"We had a deal going," Fitz said, "before you went and fucked it all up for us."

Where was Josie? Maybe they didn't know about her. Maybe she was safe, shopping somewhere. On the floor, Malcolm let out another groan, longer this time, louder.

"I *said* . . . shut the fuck up!" Fitz said, kicking Malcolm in the shoulder.

"Dylan's just here to see me, no other reason," I said.

"I know that, love," Fitz said, looking at me directly for the first time. "He's been a bit distracted lately. Haven't you, Dylan? Can't keep his mind on the job. Funny, that. And you disappear off to the wilds of—where are we?—Kent, and, what a surprise, there's Dylan all ready to keep an eye on you. Touching, I call it."

"Must be love," Nicks said. And they laughed.

"Look," I said, my patience wearing thin, "I'm getting sick of all this. Whatever it is you want, just take it and get off my boat. Leave us alone. Leave us all alone."

"We've got things to work out first. Right, Dylan?"

Dylan turned to look at me, and for a second I saw the old Dylan, the guy who used to watch me dance with a face of stone, not giving anything away with his expression but somehow saying much more with his eyes.

"You need to go," he said to me quietly. "Take Malcolm with you and go."

"I don't think so, sunshine," Fitz said.

"Let her go," Dylan said. "You don't need her here. You have what you came for."

"Not yet."

Like a petulant child demanding attention, Malcolm let out another cry.

I don't know what I had been expecting. I was alert, aware that this confrontation was not going to be easy or straightforward, but I wasn't at all ready for what came next.

"Will you fucking *shut up*, you annoying little shit?"

Fitz pulled a gun from the waistband of his jeans and aimed it at Malcolm. I saw the gun a second before he fired it. The noise of it was deafening in the small space, and I jumped back without even realizing it, just as Malcolm's body jerked on the floor. Blood started seeping from a wound in his shoulder. He cried out, just once, and then he was silent and still.

Both my hands clasped over my mouth with the shock of it. Struggling to breathe. And then it all got much, much worse. Fitz was pointing the gun directly at Dylan's head. I screamed, and Markus took me by the arm and pulled me toward the bedroom.

Dylan took a step toward me and for the first time I saw real fear in his eyes. "No!" he said.

And then Leon Arnold stood and blocked my line of vision as both of them took me into my bedroom and shut the door. Markus turned on the light and I wriggled free of his grip and lunged for the door.

"Now, now," Arnold said, putting himself in my way. "You don't want to watch him do it, do you, Viva?"

I tried to push past him to get to the door. And then he hit me, casually, across the face. It hadn't looked as though he'd put much force behind it, but even so, my feet left the floor and I ended up in a heap against the berth. I pulled myself up into a sitting position, my head spinning. From the main cabin I heard a yell—Dylan's voice or Malcolm's? A noise of such pain and accompanied by a crash, as though something heavy had fallen—

"Dylan!" I shouted, as loud and hard as I could, sobbing at the end of the word as Markus came for me and dragged me to my feet before smashing his fist into the side of my head.

I heard Leon Arnold laugh as I fell to the floor, and then a ringing in my ears, and blood in my mouth, and for a moment I passed out.

I was being dragged up off the floor. I gasped and coughed, pulling with weak fingers at the hands that gripped under my arms. Then I was thrown back on to something soft—my bed? I opened my eyes. Everything was a confusing whirl and the emotions behind it all were alien—and then, my pounding heart, and the realization that I was in my bedroom with these two men, and the door was shut. And out there, in the main cabin, noises—shouting...

"Dylan," I said.

"Never mind him," said Markus. "He is a dead man."

I think it was the first time I'd heard him say anything. He had an accent, from somewhere in Eastern Europe. The words and the way he said them chilled me to the core.

"Let me go," I said, "please let me go." My own voice sounded odd, dulled above the ringing and surging in my ears. I touched a hand to my jaw; the side of my face was throbbing.

Leon Arnold was looking through my clothes. He had opened the drawers and was pulling out underwear. I tried to get up off the bed but Markus pushed me back with a single hand.

"What are you doing?" I said, my voice high and panicky. "Leave that alone, it's mine."

At the back of the drawer, he had found something that stopped him. "What about this, Markus? What do you reckon?"

From the tip of his finger, a sequined thong dangled. I'd even forgotten it was there—the last few pieces of skimpy underwear from my dancing days.

I felt sick at the sight of it.

"Put that back," I said, trying to make my voice stronger, more in control.

He seemed to notice me then, and came over to the bed. "Are you going to be difficult, Viva?"

"Get the fuck off my boat, you disgusting little man," I said.

He laughed. "That's a yes, then."

He pushed me back and before I could move or struggle he'd put one forearm across my throat, leaning over so close to my face that I could feel his breath on me. I clawed at his arm, scratching him with my short, practical nails, kicking with my legs. And then, someone holding my legs. While I fought and bucked, I felt someone—it must have been Markus, although all I could see was Arnold—undoing my jeans.

I thought about Jim. I wanted him to come and save us, so badly. I wanted him to be here and take these horrible men away. I thought about him until I could almost hear sirens, too far away, fading, then getting closer, then fading again.

I tried to speak, tried to say no. But I couldn't breathe, or speak. When he relieved the pressure on my throat I heaved in air, coughed, gasped.

Arnold sat companionably next to me on the bed while Markus pulled my jeans down. I kicked him as hard as I could, aiming for where I thought his face would be.

That was a mistake. Arnold pushed me back again, this

time spreading his hand across my throat, squeezing with his fingers.

"Viva," he said, "if you keep fighting, you're going to get hurt. Do you understand?"

Panic was rising inside me. I nodded, my eyes wide. He let go of my throat, and as I gasped and sucked air in, I heard the unmistakable sound of the engine starting. Abruptly Arnold got up off the bed and left the room.

It gave me such a shock that I half sat up. The whole boat rattled and shook. I could hear the water churning at the stern, and the splashing of the water against the hull. The keys were still in the pocket of my jeans. They must have bypassed the ignition somehow. What were they doing?

Markus was sitting on the edge of the bed, looking toward the door.

In that moment I could have tried to fight back—choked him, maybe, hit him with something—but there was nothing within reach. My hands were shaking and there was no fight left in me. No fight. Only fear.

I shrank away from him to the corner of the bed, hugging my knees. Trying to disappear.

There was a shout from the main cabin, something I didn't quite catch. Markus went to the door and looked out down the hall—was he talking to somebody? Then he shut the door behind him and stood facing me with his back to the door. Guarding it.

I moved slowly to the edge of the bed. My jeans were on the floor. I reached down for them, expecting at any minute he would stop me, shout at me, hit me even. I stretched out my arm for them and pulled my jeans toward me slowly, as though he would only notice quick movements, as though he was some kind of wild animal I was trying not to disturb.

But he still wasn't looking at me. It was as though I had ceased to exist for him, as though he was there to guard the room and anything in it.

The sobbing started again when I was dressed. I curled into a ball in the corner, my back to the door, my body shaking with it.

I was still curled up like this when Arnold came back. "Get up," he said.

When I didn't move, he grabbed my arm, digging his fingers in and dragging me backward over the bed. I yelped in pain and fear, gripping the waistband of my jeans, horrified at the thought of being undressed again. But he needed me for something else now.

"Get up on deck. Fitz wants you to drive the boat."

Drive the boat?

I stumbled through to the main cabin. The boat was swaying and rocking in a way I'd never felt before. The tide was rising, but not quickly enough—every few moments I felt a jolt and a scrape when the hull brushed against the riverbed.

There were two bodies on the floor. Malcolm's and Dylan's. Standing over them, Fitz, the gun he was holding aimed at Dylan's head.

I held back a scream. I had no words left.

The whole scene was alien to me. My Dylan, lying on his back, not moving. Oh, God . . .

My boat felt alien to me, a strange place now with these people here, with these events taking place inside it.

Then I realized something. If Fitz was still pointing the gun at Dylan, that meant he was alive. And in that moment I heard him make a noise. His head was covered in blood, as though they'd kicked him repeatedly. He was lying awkwardly, half on his back, his legs sprawled wide. And his foot moved. Very well, then. He was alive. And then I saw Malcolm's hand, lifted and moving in a vague, graceful wave before falling onto his chest.

"Get up there," Fitz said, jerking his head up to the wheelhouse. "Get up there and I might not kill your fucking shit of a boyfriend. Yet."

As I hauled myself up the steps, I could hear the sirens. Nicks was waiting for me at the top of the steps. He had his hands on the wheel but it was jerking out of his grip, as first the tide took it and then the silt, the rudder catching against the bottom. The engine roared and rumbled and I could hardly hear myself think.

"You," he yelled, "steer this thing. Get us to deeper water. Right?"

"You need Malcolm," I shouted back. "I've never done it before."

"Who?"

"Malcolm. The guy he shot. Down there. He knows the river."

The *Revenge* was adrift, maybe fifteen yards from the dock. I could see blue flashing lights coming toward us down the hill. The marina was in darkness.

The boat jolted again, harder this time, enough to make Nicks lose his footing.

"I said you need Malcolm!" I yelled at him.

He stuck his head through the door to the cabin and shouted something to Fitz. And then, a few moments later, Malcolm was being shoved up through the doorway. Battered, bloody, but still it was Malcolm. He looked at me, squinting and frowning as though he had no idea what was going on.

"Are you okay?" I said, trying to get him to focus on me.

"Yeah, yeah . . ." he said.

"You need to steer," I said, putting his hand on the wheel.

He looked blank. Nicks was in the doorway to the cabin, conferring with Fitz. I got close to Malcolm, close enough to smell the sweat and the blood and the fear.

"You need to steer. Right?"

Finally he got it. He gripped the wheel and turned it gently, and the *Revenge* started to move away from the dock again. Blue lights now, flashing outside the gate to the marina. One car pulled into the parking lot, then a second.

The *Revenge of the Tide* eased off the mud and rocked into the flow of the river. Malcolm steered the boat around, back toward the opposite bank. Nicks stepped back as Fitz came up the steps and into the wheelhouse. I moved out of the way. He had blood on his hands, blood down the front of his jeans. The gun was still in his hand. The boat was roaring out into midstream now, away from the bank and the police officers who were gathering on the dock, their powerful flashlights shining over us, beaming into the wheelhouse.

"Where do you want to go?" Malcolm shouted at them.

Fitz was slapping Nicks on the shoulder as though they'd done something smart, outwitted the cops, escaping from under their very noses. "I don't know, mate. Just keep driving for now, okay?"

Malcolm was turning the wheel slowly, bringing his hands back to the two-o'clock position each time. And Fitz and Nicks had to move to the stern to keep watching the dock. I wondered what Malcolm was up to. The *Revenge* was heading straight for the other bank now.

Fitz was laughing, cupping his hand to his ear as the officers on the dock shouted things that none of us could hear. Nicks was next to him, almost leaning over the edge.

"What did you think you were doing, Malcolm?" I asked him, trying to get him to look me in the eye.

He shook his head.

"Malc! Did you call him?"

"I was trying to help, okay? I was trying to get rid of it for you."

"By *selling it to Fitz*?"

"I know, I know," he said. "It wasn't my finest moment, all right?"

I looked over his shoulder at Fitz, who seemed to have given up on taunting the police. He looked joyous, as though he'd just done the best deal of his life. "What are you two gossiping about?" he shouted. "Get on with it, you fuck!"

I turned back to Malcolm and he looked determined, focused, a gleam in his eye that I hadn't seen before. "Get ready," he said, and I didn't understand what he meant until there was a great bang, like an explosion. The boat stopped dead and I was catapulted sideways, down the steps and into the cabin, landing on my back with a crash. I skidded backward along the floorboards and hit my head on something, one of the cabinets in the galley.

My ears were full of the grinding of the engine, louder than ever, vibrations coming through the floor and rattling the cups and plates. A book, papers, a bowl fell off the top of the galley worktop and landed on my head. Above it all, shouting, yelling, noises from the deck.

I struggled to my feet and hauled myself upright. The boat was listing to port and the floor was at a crazy angle. Dylan had rolled over and was lying in a jumble of limbs and broken bits of furniture, cushions from the dinette, against the bottom of the sofa. I scrambled over to him.

"Dylan? Can you hear me?"

His face, his poor face. Even in the darkness I could see so much blood on him. I touched his cheek, crying.

"I'm so sorry," I sobbed. "I should have listened to you, I should have listened."

He made a noise then, not quite a groan. A cough, above the noise of the engine churning. And he said something—I couldn't hear him.

"What?" I put my ear next to his mouth. "What did you say? Say it again."

"I said okay."

I kissed his cheek and tasted blood. He coughed again, raised an arm and pushed me away. I was going to have to leave him here.

A weapon—I needed a weapon. I scrambled back to the galley. All the knives had fallen out of the knife block except for one: a small vegetable knife. It wasn't going to be much good against Fitz's gun, but it was the best I could do.

I pulled myself back up the steps. Malcolm was there, leaning back against the wooden wall of the wheelhouse, holding his head. Blood was pouring from a cut above his eye. Fitz was lying on the ground in a heap, not moving.

"What happened?" I yelled. "Where's Nicks?"

He waved a hand to the deck and I went to look.

Nicks had fallen from the deck into the water below. But we had run aground. In the dim light I could see him, half-swimming, half-wading toward the boat. The water was coming in almost visibly, the tide tugging at his legs and pulling him backward. The more he struggled in the mud, the more it pulled him back. And then he fell forward into the water. Pushing himself upward with his hands in the mud now, his legs stuck up to his knees, he was never going to make it.

I slipped the knife into my pocket and went to the storage locker on the deck, found a lifejacket, pulling it clear. They'd come with the boat. I had no idea if they'd ever been used, or worn.

"Hey!" I shouted.

Nicks was flailing in the water, struggling to remain upright. He tried to turn, but that made him lose balance and he fell again.

I threw the lifejacket at him. It flew through the air and landed in the water a few yards away from him, but it might as well have been a mile. He stretched and tried to reach it, and one of his legs, miraculously, came free of the mud and he fell backward into the water. At that moment the stern of the boat caught a surge of tide and, with nobody at the wheel to guide it, turned in a slow, graceful arc. The momentum of it was powerful and fast, and before I realized what was happening I saw Nicks's face illuminated in flashlight from the dock, saw the fear in his eyes as the hull swung toward him.

There was a thud, a bang, and the boat passed over him. I raced to the port side, hoping to see him come up, but there was nothing. Nothing.

And then there was another sound, a shout from behind me, a crash. Fitz was wrestling with Malcolm on the deck, the two of them rolling over and over on the slope until they ended up in a heap against the port gunwale. Fitz was punching Malcolm's face, his fist coming away bloody, blood spraying in droplets.

"Stop it, stop it!" I yelled, my voice drowned by the churning engine and carried away by the wind.

I pulled at Fitz's back but he was slippery with mud, and cold. I felt for the knife. It was small, just a little kitchen knife, but before I could think about it too hard I jabbed it into his upper shoulder. Not hard, or deep, just enough to make him stop.

Blood started seeping into the fabric, blooming into a wide crimson flower, and he turned, struggling to his feet. Malcolm lay still, his face away from me against the storage locker on the port side.

"What the fuck did you do that for?" Fitz yelled at me, trying to reach behind his shoulder to feel the wound. "Are you fucking crazy?"

I still had the knife in my hand but he swiped at it, grabbed for it. I kept hold of it and as Fitz turned his body toward me there was a bang, a shot, loud above the noise of the engine, echoing across the empty space. I didn't feel any pain. I looked down at my body in shock, expecting to see blood, expecting to see a hole somewhere. Then Fitz let out a scream and crumpled into a ball.

Malcolm was still. Fitz was on his side in the fetal position, making high wailing noises.

Above that, and above the painful grinding noise of the engine, I could hear more sirens. They seemed louder, the vibrations passing through my feet and into my chest with a discordant rhythm. And another sound, distant, a helicopter . . . but too far away?

Dylan. I wanted Dylan.

I ran down the steps. It was dark, the cabin was a mess and the floor was wet, slick with blood. I looked across to the bottom of the sofa. He wasn't there.

The engine finally spluttered and cut out. Then I could hear it, the definite thud-thud of a helicopter, and a spotlight shone down on the deck of the boat and in through the open wheelhouse door. I could see blood on the walls, on the floor. A bloody handprint on the wooden siding near the door to my bedroom. And noise—I could hear movement. And a sudden bang, the noise of wood cracking and splintering.

The door was open. The bedroom was a mess, a tangled, angled mess with bedding and dark blood on the walls. On the floor, against the bed, Leon Arnold lay still, his leg twisted beneath him. He wasn't moving.

The noise again. I looked to my left, to the open doorway of the second bedroom. The two figures inside it fighting, a snarl of bodies, fists; and it took me a moment to realize that it must be Dylan, must be Markus—but which one—and what could I do?

In the corner of the room, tipped on its side, was my crate of tools. I lifted the nearest—a plane, heavy and solid. And at that moment the light shone through the porthole and Dylan was on the floor, and Markus with his knee on Dylan's chest, a piece of wood he'd broken away from the edge of the berth, a two-by-four raised back at shoulder height ready to swing it into Dylan's skull.

I must have hit him with the plane. I had it in my hand and then he was lying on the floor, slipping a little on the smooth floor and sliding to a stop against what was left of the berth.

I dropped the plane. I was on my knees next to Dylan, not knowing where to touch, not knowing how to help him.

Noises from the cabin, shouts and steps, lights shining down the hall. I thought it was Fitz. I lay my body across Dylan's and held him, protecting him.

Chapter Forty

The hospital in the middle of the night: a soul-destroying place to be.

Josie and I had been sitting in the same hard plastic chairs bolted to the floor for the past two hours. Before that, we'd been allowed in to see Malcolm, or at least Josie had. I'd watched through the doorway, a police officer standing next to me in case I did something, or said something, or tried to run—I didn't even know. But they were here in any case. I stopped paying attention after a while and the next time I looked the male officer had gone and a female officer was there in his place. She spoke to me, random words that made sense at the time, and I nodded to her and said, "Yes, okay," and that seemed to satisfy her because she was quiet after that.

The police officer had brought me a cup of brown liquid that might have been coffee. It burned my throat but I scarcely noticed. My head was trying to work through what had happened, but none of it made sense. It churned in my brain and every version that came out was somehow wrong, faulty, failed.

Josie had given up asking me questions. Every time she mentioned Malcolm's name, I cried. She told me that she'd gone into the *Scarisbrick Jean* and found flour, several bags of it, piles of it tipped up on the floor. Flour everywhere. She had no idea what that was all about.

That was the one part that made sense to me. Malcolm had taken the package out of the hatch, expecting it to contain drugs. Then he'd phoned them, had made contact with Fitz, believing the package to be a shipment of drugs belonging to the criminal gang. And Fitz had come down himself to take care of the mess, thinking maybe that he'd finally discovered that someone was skimming a cut from the drugs he was importing, and that the stash was in Malcolm and Josie's boat. And, of course, when they opened the package in front of Malcolm, poor Malcolm, who was as half-assed at being a criminal as he was at everything else and hadn't thought to look inside the package himself first, the kilos of cocaine they'd all been expecting turned out to be six bags of self-rising flour.

"It's that one from before," Josie said, and I looked up.

Jim Carling was striding up the hall toward us.

He was dressed in jeans and a brown jacket, frowning and looking left to right as though he were lost somehow, and cross with himself for not knowing what was going on.

I rose to my feet, wanting to call to him or wave, but not sure what he would say, how he would react. But when he saw me he smiled. He touched my arm gently, as though he wanted to hold me, but I moved away. We stood awkwardly a few feet apart. This was, after all, a professional meeting rather than a social one. "Where were you?" was the first thing I said.

"I tried to get there. As soon as I got your message I sent patrols out to the marina..."

"They nearly killed him, Jim. They nearly killed Dylan. And Fitz shot Malcolm. It was so awful, it was..." I was crying again, the tears that didn't seem to stop for more than a few moments at a time.

He took me in his arms and this time I didn't pull back. I sobbed loudly, out of control, and he held me tighter, and stroked my hair, and made soothing noises that somehow made it all worse, not better.

In the end he said to me, "Come for a walk."

The sobs had subsided to jerky breaths, my hands shaking. He put his arm around my shoulders and steered me down the hall, past the reception desk to the entrance.

Outside it was chilly, the air crisp. I breathed it in deeply. I thought that I would never take breathing fresh air for granted again. We found a wooden bench and sat there for a few moments in the darkness. I wondered if he'd come to tell me Dylan was dead. They'd taken him away in an ambulance. Every time I asked, nobody seemed to have any idea what had happened to him.

"You know they're going to arrest you," he said.

"I think I hit him with a plane."

"Yeah, don't tell me anything, I don't want to know about that. I'm just letting you know."

"You'd think they'd be grateful, wouldn't you? He would have killed Dylan if I hadn't stopped him."

He shot me a look. "That's just the way the criminal justice system works, Genevieve. You know that as well as I do."

"How's Dylan?" I asked. "Have you heard anything? They won't tell me."

Jim's face was grave. "He's going to be fine," he said.

"Have you seen him? Is he really okay? I thought they'd killed him. I thought Fitz had killed him."

"No, he's all right. Fitz is in a room somewhere upstairs. You know, he shot himself in the balls."

"What?"

"Accidentally, of course. Occupational hazard, keeping your pistol tucked in your waistband. He's been arrested. They've got a guard on him."

"And the others?"

"Leon Arnold's just got a concussion, would you believe? The other one is upstairs with head injuries. Not as bad as it looks."

I waited for him to say something about Nicks, but that was all he said.

"What about my boat?"

"The marine unit's getting a tug and they're going to bring it back to the marina at high tide. I think it's all right."

"You know they were after Dylan," I said.

"Yes."

"You need to keep him away from them, Jim."

"Yeah, that's kind of what I spend my whole working life doing, keeping Dylan out of trouble."

"You told me you'd been at school with him. I knew you were lying; I just didn't know why."

He looked at me steadily. "I wouldn't have lied to you without good reason."

The sky was turning gray at the edges, the shapes of the trees standing out now against the clouds and the sky. I was tired, numb, cold. I wanted to go home and sleep forever.

"What's going to happen now?" I asked.

"Fitz will be charged. You'll be interviewed and, with a bit of luck, bailed. And then you and Dylan can do whatever it is you want to do, and I'll quietly disappear and think about what might have been."

I felt my cheeks flush. I'd behaved very badly, toward both of them. "I'm sorry," I said.

He was quiet for a moment, then he gave a short laugh. "Yeah, well, I should have known I'd never be that lucky. Besides, you're one of the most infuriating women I've ever met."

I looked up at him then and saw the hurt behind the smile. "Me, infuriating? You were the one who wasn't around when I really needed you."

That was the wrong thing to say. I saw him almost flinch.

"Look, I didn't mean that. You did your best, didn't you? It wasn't your fault I decided to go back to the boat, when you'd told me not to. I was an idiot."

"No, you're right. I let you down. Both of you."

An ambulance pulled up outside the entrance around the corner, sirens screaming and then abruptly silent. We got up off the bench and walked back toward the doorway.

"Can I see Dylan?" I asked.

That look again. The hurt behind his eyes. "I'll see what I can find out," he said.

Chapter Forty-One

The morning of Caddy's funeral brought bright blue skies across London. I caught the train from Maidstone East and now I was waiting outside Bromley station, wondering if I should have worn lower heels, tugging my skirt down a little. Opaque tights made the outfit more sober.

The black BMW pulled up next to me without a sound and, while Dylan got out of the driver's seat and went around to open the door at the back for me, I opened the passenger's door and jumped in. Despite the occasion, I smiled to myself as I watched him through the side mirror. He stopped, rolled his eyes, shook his head slightly and came back to the driver's side. He got in and shut the door.

"All right?" I asked.

"Yeah."

That was it. The engine started up and we moved off into the traffic.

At first I stole sneaky glances at him out of the corner of my eye, and then I gave up and twisted in my seat so I could look at him properly. His gaze remained resolutely forward, and, while he seemed perfectly relaxed and calm, both hands were gripping the steering wheel. Dark glasses, partly hiding the mess they'd made of his face. He was wearing a suit, the way he always did, even though he wasn't supposed to be going to the funeral. He'd offered to drive me there and wait for me, and, because it was the only time he'd agreed to see me since the night I'd nearly managed to get him killed, I'd readily accepted.

"You should come in with me," I said at last. "They probably won't even notice."

"They'd notice," he said. "I don't exactly blend in."

I wasn't even sure why Caddy's family had extended an invitation to me, since I was possibly the only one who could have saved her, could have gotten to her in time. But it seemed that Caddy had talked about me, and, since I wasn't a dancer anymore, that was it: I got an invitation.

"You, on the other hand," he said, nodding toward my black skirt, "will fit in just fine. You look like a solicitor."

"Do I?"

"Maybe a solicitor who dances in her spare time."

"Why won't you see me?" I asked, out of the blue, since he seemed to be relaxing at last. "Why are you being so distant?"

"I'm here now, aren't I?" he said with a deep breath in, as though I were some tiresome child asking the same question for the hundredth time. The car had stopped at a traffic light, the sound of the turn signal's subtle click on-off-on hypnotic and soothing.

"You heard from Jim?" he asked.

"Not since the hospital," I said. "You know he's been suspended."

"Yeah, I heard. He told me they arrested you."

"Yes. Not going to help me get another job, is it?"

"Did they charge you?"

"They charged me with assault, and then they gave me a warning. Could have been much worse, I guess, but it still goes on my record."

"You should talk to your boyfriend, Jim," he said. "Might be able to make it disappear if you ask him nicely."

"He's not my boyfriend. And in any case, he's not supposed to talk to me."

"Well, I guess it will give his eardrums a chance to recover."

"Why did you offer to give me a lift, Dylan, if you're going to be a rude, grumpy bastard?"

He laughed then, and I thought he might be softening again. "Why do you think? Wanted to see you in a skirt. Been a long time since I saw you in a skirt."

"You're such a tease."

"Yeah, you love it. Anyway, we're here."

We drove slowly up a long, curved driveway between manicured lawns, trees, wooden benches, and flower beds, and over speed bumps. There was a parking lot discreetly tucked behind a large yew hedge, and as we pulled in, other cars were disgorging their occupants.

"I'll wait for you here," he said.

"Please come with me," I asked. For some crazy reason I wanted an excuse to hold his hand.

"I'll wait here," he said again.

So fucking stubborn, the man. I slammed the door as hard as I could, but it only made a reassuring clunk.

There were roughly forty people, maybe a few more, waiting outside the chapel at the crematorium. A woman of about fifty could only have been Caddy's mother—she was exactly like her: petite, curvy, beautiful, with dark hair scraped into a neat bun. She was crying a lot, silently, dabbing her tears away while a girl who might have been Caddy's younger sister stood by with no expression on her pale face. Trying to establish the family relationships passed the time.

I stood awkwardly on my own, wishing I'd worn flatter shoes, wishing I hadn't worn quite so much black.

The car arrived with the coffin, and I recognized Beverley Davies, the officer who'd interviewed me, at the back of the crowd. She looked different today, fashionably dressed in a gray pantsuit, and wearing a gray, grim smile.

The service was over in half an hour. I sat at the back and listened while they talked about Caddy, and for a while I wondered if I was in the wrong chapel after all, because everything they said related to a different woman, a woman I'd never met: she was a loving sister, a talented pianist and singer; she'd gotten a degree in English and had received her teaching certificate. She'd taught for a year and had loved it, and then had taken time off to work in London. They didn't mention that she was also an accomplished dancer. They didn't mention the Barclay.

I stopped listening. When the curtains started to close around the coffin, I shut my eyes.

We all filed out of the back of the chapel while they played Adele, which made me want to cry. And then I found myself stifling a giggle as I had the thought that they should have actually played the Pussycat Dolls' "Buttons"—which had been Caddy's favorite dancing track.

I joined the line of people waiting to speak to Caddy's mother and sister. I tried to run through what I was going to say. What possible things were there, in those circumstances? *I'm sorry I didn't save her? I'm sorry I invited her to the party? I wish things had been different?*

"I'm so sorry," was what I actually said. "Your daughter was a beautiful person."

"Thank you for coming," Caddy's mother said. She was already looking past me to the next person in the line.

Caddy's sister was crying now, a boyfriend, with earrings and a straggly growth of beard, providing a comforting shoulder.

People had started to head back to the parking lot and I followed them.

"Genevieve?"

It was Beverley Davies. She tried for a smile and then gave up, walking alongside me.

"How are you?" she asked.

"I'm all right, thank you. Do you know how Jim is?"

"I can't—sorry."

"He didn't do anything wrong," I said.

"They'll take your statement into account. I just wanted to say thank you for coming. I know the family—they've had a very difficult time of it. Losing their daughter like that . . . then having to wait until the investigation was concluded to bury her. It's been hard on them."

"Yes."

"Are you coming to the pub?" she asked.

"I don't know—I don't think . . ."

"Well—if I don't see you . . . Take care." She went off toward a dark gray Vauxhall that was parked at an angle half on the grass and got into the driver's seat. I watched her drive away.

The BMW's windows were open and I could see Dylan studying me through the gap in the hedge as I walked back toward him.

"They're having drinks in a pub," I said through the open window, "do you want to go?"

"Nah."

"Suit yourself," I said, climbing into the passenger seat. "In that case, you can drive me there and wait for three hours or so while I get pleasantly hammered."

The Bull's Head on Chislehurst High Street was crowded with people, and although most of the people dressed in black seemed to be outside in the garden, in the end I managed to persuade Dylan to come in and mingle. I'd already spent twenty minutes standing on my own, like a lost soul, nursing a vodka. I wanted some company.

"You don't need to talk to anyone," I said as I dragged him in.

"Damn right I don't."

He waited at the bar to get me another drink and I spotted Beverley Davies again. I turned away. Dylan had talked to Jim, I knew he had. Jim had worked with Dylan for years, but their alliance went deeper than that. I'd almost expected there to have been some sort of argument between them, some sort of dispute over me; but it seemed I'd overrated my own importance in that respect. Dylan seemed to be utterly convinced that I should be with Jim now. Since they'd let him out of the hospital he'd avoided me, ignored my calls, refused to talk to me, and above all given me no indication about how he felt. And the cooler he was, the more he pushed me away, the more I wanted him.

We stood awkwardly in the beer garden, my heels sinking into the grass so that I was left perching on my tiptoes.

"So," I said, "when are you going to Spain?"

"Soon."

"What if I need to get hold of you?"

"You won't."

"But what if something happens? What if I need to talk to you?"

He sighed heavily.

"For fuck's sake, woman. Jim knows where I'm going. He's the only one who knows. So if there's any sort of emergency—not that I can imagine there will be—but if there *is*—Jim knows. All right?"

"Can I see you again, before you go?"

"You don't give up, do you?"

"No," I said. "I don't. Unlike you."

He swallowed three big, slow gulps from his pint. "What's that supposed to mean?"

"You've given up on me."

"I never had you in the first place," he said.

"I'm not going to stay here without you, Dylan."

He waited for a few seconds before answering, scanning the faces in the beer garden as though he was expecting to see someone he knew.

"You've got Jim," he said.

"Jim's being investigated for some sort of misconduct because of me," I said.

"That'll all be over with soon enough."

"He doesn't want me anyway, Dylan."

He raised his eyebrows. "That's what he wants you to think. Poor bastard blames himself for what happened."

"Well, it wasn't his fault. It was mine. The whole thing."

"Well, there would have probably been a lot less drama if you hadn't slept with him."

That hurt. I took it in and felt tears stinging my eyes, looking away from him, across the crowded beer garden at the blurred faces.

"Well," I said at last, "since you don't care about me, it doesn't really matter anymore."

"Who said I don't care?"

"Why do you make things so hard? What is wrong with you?" I demanded, trying to angle my face into his line of sight. "Dylan?"

He finished his pint, put the glass down on the top of a plastic garbage can, and headed through the gate and out into the parking lot. I ran behind him, trying to keep up, but he was already in the car with the engine on, the tires sending an arc of gravel flying as he accelerated toward me.

I stood firmly in the middle of the parking lot as the car headed straight for me. Then the brakes slammed on and the car stopped, the bumper about a foot from my knees.

I got in the passenger seat and pulled the door shut with force.

Neither of us spoke.

He was heading for Bromley, back to the station. I was

running out of time. "Look," I said at last, "can you give me a ride back home? I don't want to go on the train."

"Public transportation beneath you now, is it?"

"No. I've had too much to drink. I don't want to be on a train drunk like this."

He let out a short laugh. "You want me to drive you all the way to Kent?"

"It's not that far. Please?"

He let out a heavy sigh that implied I'd just ruined his day, but at the next junction he turned back toward the A2. I leaned my head back against the headrest and closed my eyes, trying to think. The alcohol had filled my brain with a cloud. Everything I thought of saying sounded stupid, or desperate, or selfish. How could I begin to deal with someone so stubborn? What could I possibly say that would make him change his mind?

I had to fight the urge to reach out and put my hand on his knee. If words weren't going to work, then maybe some kind of physical contact would do the trick. But he would have just removed my hand, deliberately placed it back on my side of the hand brake.

I opened my eyes and looked at him.

We were on the highway now, speeding past the suburbs of South London. Another forty minutes or so and I'd be home and my chance would have gone. I'd never see him again, after this.

"I was worried about you," I murmured.

I thought he wasn't listening because he didn't react; staring straight ahead at the traffic, he might as well have been alone in the car.

"I thought you were dead. I thought Fitz had killed you."

He took a deep breath in through his nose. He wasn't going to make this easy for me. "Well, he didn't. I'm still here."

"Do you miss the club?" Oh, so many stupid questions. I couldn't think of the right one.

"No."

"What are you doing?"

"What?"

"I mean, are you working?"

"No."

Silence again. I closed my eyes, half-wishing I hadn't asked him for the ride after all. If he'd dropped me at the station, this torture would have been over with by now.

I must have dozed, because the gentle click of the turn signal woke me. I sat up straight and looked out of the window.

"Oh, don't get off here."

"What?"

"I've moved the boat."

The BMW moved swiftly out of the exit lane for Rochester and Strood, and back on to the main highway. A car behind us beeped. Dylan looked in his rearview mirror at the driver.

"Right," he said. "So where the fuck is your boat?"

"Allington. Near Maidstone. It's the next exit. Sorry, I should have said."

We were on the Medway bridge by this time. Beneath us, the marina where I'd lived for six months in total, where I'd made some good friends, and where it had all fallen apart. I couldn't see it from up here. Just the straight lines of the highway and, in the distance, to the left, Rochester Castle, a flag flying from the battlements.

"When did you move the boat?"

"A few weeks ago. That was an ordeal, I can tell you. I had to pay Cameron to help me."

He didn't say anything. At the next exit he turned off toward Maidstone, down a long, steep hill with a view over the Medway valley. "It was difficult," I said, even though he hadn't asked. "You know, with the people in the marina. They're lovely, all of them, but they've chosen this quiet life, you know? Or at least, that's what they were hoping for, until I turned up and ruined it for them. And Malcolm and Josie . . . We did try. We were talking about it all. But Josie blames me for everything that happened. And I blame myself."

"It wasn't your fault," he said at last. "He was the fucking idiot that brought Fitz to your door."

"No," I said. "I did that. Malcolm just hurried him along a bit."

He fell silent again, concentrating on the short stretch of the M20 that would take us back toward Maidstone. I couldn't bear the quiet. The minutes were flying past, the precious time I had with him was slipping away like sand through my fingers.

"It's a nice place, anyway," I said. "Not a marina. Just a few moorings, and there's a nice pub, too, with a restaurant. There's even a shower room; it's supposed to be for kayakers, I think, but I used it anyway, until I finished the bathroom last weekend. And the river isn't tidal because I'm above the lock. I get ducks and swans now, instead of bloody seagulls. It's a nice place. You'll like it."

"I'll like it?"

I smiled at him, hopeful. "I think you will."

"I like the sound of the pub."

"You have to walk across the lock to get to it. I'm on the wrong bank."

"And it's all right there? Safe?"

"Yes. I feel safe."

"Good."

Maybe it was the fact that we were a long way outside London now, but I could feel him thawing. His shoulders were not as rigid, his grip on the steering wheel more relaxed.

"Your boat's all right?"

"Yes, I think so. I'm still repairing things. But now I'm just getting it straightened out so I can sell it."

"Why?"

We made eye contact for the first time since we'd left Chislehurst.

"I can't live there anymore. I moved the boat because I thought it would help, but it hasn't. So much happened on that boat, Dylan. Everything I look at reminds me of that night. Of Malcolm getting shot, of what Arnold was going to do. Of you nearly dying."

"You can't just give up on your dream. You need to give it time."

I shook my head. "It won't change how I feel. I can't stay there. You need to take the next turn on the left. That one, there, look."

The car turned into Castle Road and slowed as the road narrowed, toward the end. Minutes, that was all I had left. Just a few minutes with him.

"What will you do?" he asked.

I couldn't cry, not now. I forced the tears back. "I don't know what I'll do." I wanted so desperately to hear him say the words *Come to Spain. Come with me.* But he didn't.

At the end of the road was a turnaround, with the entrance to the lock-keeper's cottage and, beyond it, the parking lot that led to the ramp into the river. And we were there. The car's tires crunched on the gravel and we pulled to a stop. The *Revenge of the Tide* was moored against the concrete bank, a few feet from where we were parked. It was sandwiched between two narrowboats and it looked huge and out of place, crouching like a grown-up between two kids, dominating the bank.

I took a deep breath. "Will you come inside?"

He shook his head.

"I can't," he said. He was actually gritting his teeth.

"Can't what?"

He paused, ran a hand over his forehead. "Can't—do this anymore. Why won't you just leave me alone?" And he finally turned to look at me for what felt like the first time.

I reached across to him, put my hand up to stroke his cheek. "Because I love you," I said. "And I know you love me, even though you won't say it. I know you do."

He stared at me for a long moment and I stared right back at him, challenging him to refuse, or make a joke about it, or laugh. When he did none of those things I put my hand up to his cheek, stroked it gently, and then clambered over the central console of the BMW and kissed him, ignoring the wince as my weight fell against his bruised chest, pushing him back against the door as I put my arms around his neck so he couldn't move until I'd made him change his mind.

Author's Note

Readers who are familiar with the Medway may well recognize some of the locations mentioned in this book. However, the marina where the *Revenge of the Tide* is moored is an imaginative blend of several of the boatyards along the river and therefore does not exist as it is described in the story. The Barclay is also entirely fictional.

Acknowledgments

The first draft of *Dark Tide* was written in November 2010 for National Novel Writing Month (NaNoWriMo) and was excitedly presented to my editor, Vicky Blunden, as a 90,000-word draft. The transformation of that tangled mess of ideas, characters, and plot into the final book is thanks to her, and to the brilliant team at Myriad, including Candida Lacey, Corinne Pearlman, Linda McQueen, Anthony Grech-Cumbo, Adrian Weston, Dawn Sackett, and Emma Dowson. Thank you all.

The US edition has given me a chance to develop Genevieve's story further, and for that, and for her insightful and diligent editing, I would like to thank my editor at Harper-Collins, Jennifer Barth. Thank you, too, to the team at HarperCollins who has worked so hard on the book and been incredibly supportive: Jonathan Burnham, Maya Ziv, Heather Drucker, Richard Ljoenes, David Watson, Kathy Schneider, Katie O'Callaghan, Mark Ferguson, Virginia Stanley, Cindy Achar, and Douglas Johnson.

I would also like to thank Vanessa Very and Linda Weeks for reading early drafts and making invaluable suggestions that changed the course of the story completely. Vanessa, who seems to be making a habit of resurrecting characters I try to kill off, saved Dylan from just such a fate.

While I was conducting research for the book, Jill Zago very kindly let me spend some time on her boat, *Tobias*, and helped me with all my questions about living aboard. Thank you very much, Jill!

Two reference books in particular were also invaluable, and I can highly recommend them to any reader: *A Home Afloat* by Paul Cookson, with wonderful photographs of boats that provided inspiration for the interiors of the *Revenge of the Tide*; and *Living Aboard* by Nick Corble and Allan Ford, which helped me with the practical aspects of converting a barge to living accommodation.

I would also like to thank Jane Salida, Louise Payne, and Keli Stephenson of the fabulous Pole Saints, who introduced me to pole fitness, and to the other class members who let me draw stick figures while they did all the hard work. Thank you, too, to Nikki W., who kindly answered my questions about working in London clubs. For a detailed account of a dancer's life, I can highly recommend the excellent book *Girl in High Heels* by Ellouise Moore.

So many people provided support and encouragement while I was writing this book that it would take several pages to list them all. So thank you to all my wonderful friends and colleagues at Kent Police, especially to Lisa James and Mitch Humphrys, who kindly checked my manuscript for procedural accuracy. To the talented Medway Mermaids, and to the inspirational Rochester and Chatham Book Club—thank you, ladies. And for all my online friends, especially the Kent NaNoWriMo participants who went through the madness of November with me—thank you.

The last and best thanks of all to my boys, David and Alex, I love you.

About the Author

Elizabeth Haynes is a police intelligence analyst. *Dark Tide* is her second novel; rights to her first, *Into the Darkest Corner*, have been sold in twenty-five territories. Haynes lives in England in a village near Maidstone, Kent, with her husband and son.